The Uses of Psychoanalysis in Working with Children's Emotional Lives

New Imago: Series in Theoretical, Clinical, and Applied Psychoanalysis
Series Editor: Jon Mills,
Canadian Psychological Association

New Imago: Series in Theoretical, Clinical, and Applied Psychoanalysis is a scholarly and professional publishing imprint devoted to all aspects of psychoanalytic inquiry and research in theoretical, clinical, philosophical, and applied psychoanalysis. It is inclusive in focus, hence fostering a spirit of plurality, respect, and tolerance across the psychoanalytic domain. The series aspires to promote open and thoughtful dialogue across disciplinary and interdisciplinary fields in mental health, the humanities, and the social and behavioral sciences. It furthermore wishes to advance psychoanalytic thought and extend its applications to serve greater society, diverse cultures, and the public at large. The editorial board is comprised of the most noted and celebrated analysts, scholars, and academics in the English speaking world and is representative of every major school in the history of psychoanalytic thought.

The Uses of Psychoanalysis in Working with Children's Emotional Lives

Edited by Michael O'Loughlin, PhD

JASON ARONSON
Lanham • Boulder • New York • Toronto • Plymouth, UK

Published by Jason Aronson
A wholly owned subsidiary of The Rowman & Littlefield Publishing Group, Inc.
4501 Forbes Boulevard, Suite 200, Lanham, Maryland 20706
www.rowman.com

10 Thornbury Road, Plymouth PL6 7PP, United Kingdom

British Library Cataloguing in Publication Information Available

Library of Congress Cataloging-in-Publication Data
The uses of psychoanalysis in working with children's emotional lives / edited by Michael
O'Loughlin.
p. ; cm.—(New Imago)
Includes bibliographical references and index.
ISBN 978-0-7657-0919-6 (cloth : alk. paper)—ISBN 978-0-7657-0920-2 (electronic)
I. O'Loughlin, Michael. II. Series: New Imago.
[DNLM: 1. Psychoanalytic Therapy. 2. Adolescent. 3. Child. 4. Psychology, Educational. 5. Schools.
6. Students--psychology. WS 350.5]
616.89'17—dc23
2012050568

Printed in the United States of America

Contents

Acknowledgments

The work in this book and its companion volume, *Psychodynamic Perspectives on Working with Children, Families and Schools*, represent a collaboration of more than fifty contributors. For each of those writers the work has been driven by a desire to share a vision of professional practice. Since the ideas in these two volumes are intimately tied in with the professional practices of the contributors, the writing is particularly intimate. I wish to thank all of the authors for their contributions and I particularly want to note the passing of Bertram Cohler in May 2012. The book that Bert edited with Kay Field and Glorye Wool in 1989, *Learning and Education: Psychoanalytic Perspectives,* served as inspiration for this book project. Happily, Bert had completed his chapter with his coauthors and it appears in this volume. I wish to thank my friend and colleague Marilyn Charles of Austen Riggs Center for directing me to Jon Mills, and deep thanks to Jon for accepting both books in the New Imago series that he edits for Jason Aronson. My work on these books has been supported particularly by members of the *Schools Committee* of *The American Psychoanalytic Association.* Thanks also to colleagues in the *Association for the Psychoanalysis of Culture and Society* [APCS] and in *Reconceptualizing Research in Early Childhood Education* [RECE] who are tremendous sources of intellectual support and friendship. I wish to particularly thank Nigel Williams, who graciously agreed to write a foreword for this book. Thanks to my editor, Amy King, at Jason Aronson/Rowman & Littlefield for her professionalism and support of the work, and to assistant editor Stephanie Brooks, who ably steered this book through the production process. Special thanks to Raquel Castello, Cheryl Huber, Meredith Musgnug, and Melodie Piciullo who assisted with proofreading and index preparation. Finally, thanks to my wife, Margaret Healy, who has endured my preoccupation with this project with unwavering support.

Foreword

Nigel Williams

The Uses of Psychoanalysis in Working with Children's Emotional Lives, so ably edited by Michael O'Loughlin, is a book for our times. It is a collection of urgent, often harrowing, but deeply creative attempts by various educators, teachers, and therapists to do something different with and for children. It spans situations in schools and clinics in North America, the United Kingdom, and Israel.

The narratives in this book run against the grain of neoliberal cultures of classroom, school, and state management; against the grain of testing and psychological assessment. The urgent and pressing message from this group of practitioner-writers is that children in deep trouble can be reached and helped by psychoanalytic method and insight when informed by open libertarian child centered pedagogy. This book documents ways in which teachers and practitioners can equip themselves to create the relationships and conditions that, however brief or tentative, can make a difference for troubled children failing within current educational practices.

The burden of the message from these case studies is that children are not just failed by poor or unimaginative teaching; they are failed by systems, by politics, and by culture.

This is an ambitious and wide-ranging book, and written by people with a wealth of therapeutic and pedagogical experience. It is not to be read at a single sitting, but to be used as a resource and inspiration over time. The quality of the writing is high and the depth and complexity of the case studies and narratives challenging and compelling. This is a book full of the fruits of learning from experience; it is at once an invitation and support to others to do the same.

The book will be essential reading for trainees of many different kinds: psychologists, teachers, carers, psychotherapists, and counselors but perhaps, most important of all, parents. It has much to say also to managers, policy makers, politicians, and opinion formers about the state and condition of childhood in the twenty-first century. It is a barometer of where we are as a culture with teaching children and the news is worrying!

The narratives in this book show that the pathway that each writer or group of writers chart is not an easy one. We see the journey that the practitioner and educator has to make beyond their initial training, or the strictures of their working situation, and what moves them to step into the unknown with their children subjects and colleagues to make the interventions they make. Many of the stories speak of the courage and determination to right wrongs, to respond to children's distress, to tackle neglect and professional compassion fatigue.

I'm going to quote Michael from his own chapter in this book as he shows us the link between the idea, as promoted by Anna Freud, that teachers and parents should know something about psychoanalysis, and about liberation pedagogy, to address the profound cultural losses and alienations that trouble so many young people.

> In articulating a role for psychoanalysis as an underpinning of pedagogy, I will mention some elements that would not have been out of place in Anna Freud's (1935/1979) *Psychoanalysis for teachers and parents*, written some eighty years ago. However, in keeping with my work on the development of what I called elsewhere (2010) a *psychoanalysis of the social*, I will argue for a broadening of the uses of psychoanalysis in ways that can allow it to serve as one of the underpinnings not only of an emotionally focused, humane, person-centered pedagogy, but also of a pedagogy that has a capacity to address the sociohistorical constitutedness of subjectivity and hence the sociopolitical purposes of schooling and the possibility of what Paulo Freire (1969, 1970) termed "education as the practice of freedom."

This is important; it is a political and cultural manifesto that challenges the split between the psychological, the social, and the political that our professions in western culture have been so effective at (often inadvertently) promoting. This book crosses boundaries, it transgresses, and it questions whether discreet and specialized professions can really do very much, and suggests they may often indeed be part of the problem. In this there is uncomfortable criticism for all of us who perhaps for good and complex reasons have said or say, "my work and responsibility for this person, this child, this situation stops here, I can only do so much." All of these writers in some way speak of experiences where their own sense of what it is to be a professional was altered and challenged by trying to respond to the signs of disturbance and trouble in children's lives.

This is an inspiring compelling collection of writings about what I think of as "psycho-social" interventions. Perhaps these practitioners are part of a new interdisciplinary breed who from whatever their original profession or training find themselves compelled to make psycho-social interventions, against the grain, informed by personal and professional experience in conjunction with psychoanalytical ideas and compelled by a sense of injustice to take action.

The narratives that these practitioners give us convey vital information about our children and the consequences of our failure to understand what troubles them. This book is full of writing for our own and for our children's future; indeed for the future of our culture . . . read on!

Nigel Williams
Senior Lecturer in Psycho-Social Studies
University of the West of England
Bristol, UK

Introduction

Michael O'Loughlin

The impetus for this book and its companion volume, *Psychodynamic Per-spectives on Working with Children, Families and Schools*, arose from two competing impulses. On the one hand, in the fifteen years that I have been a psychoanalyst and a clinician working directly with children I have become increasingly convinced of the power of psychoanalysis both as a very effec-tive means for relieving child suffering (e.g., O'Loughlin. 2006, 2007, 2009a, 2010a, 2012a; O'Loughlin & Johnson, 2010; O'Loughlin & Mer-chant, 2012) and as a powerful analytic tool for understanding the larger institutional and societal contexts in which children must live (e.g., O'Loughlin, 2008, 2009a, 2009b, 2010b, 2012b, in press; O'Loughlin & Charles, 2012). My teaching load at Adelphi University is divided evenly between psychology and education. In psychology I teach courses to candi-dates in clinical and school psychology, and in mental health counseling. In education I teach courses to teacher candidates at the beginning and at the end of their teacher preparation. I am constantly struck by the absence of any emotionally-focused discourse in the preparation of teachers. The reductive-ness of outcomes-based and supposedly evidence-based methodologies has crept up into university preparation in the U.S., primarily through the influ-ence of the accreditation process which has increasingly constricted the space in which either philosophical ideals, imagination, or emotion can be dis-cussed (cf. Biesta, 2007). My discussion with colleagues in other Anglophile countries suggest that similar developments are taking place elsewhere, con-comitant with the neoconservative accountability movement and business models for schooling that were revived during the Thatcher-Reagan era and that continue to frame schooling from within industrial rubrics.

It is comforting to lay the blame at the feet of corporatist bogeymen such as neoconservative politicians and faceless bureaucrats in government and accreditation agencies. However, as Paul Stepansky (2009) noted in *Psycho-analysis at the Margins*, psychoanalysis has contributed to its own lack of influence—and some would say rapid decline—through attitudes of elitism, snobbishness and myopia. Many psychoanalysts are not interested in social issues nor in the sociopolitical or sociohistorical situatedness of the difficulties people face. Many are also disdainful of the "impurity" of working in contexts that require adaptation and modification of orthodox analytic technique, such as working in single rather than multiple sessions weekly. What, after all is real psychoanalysis? Who are the true inheritors of Freud's legacy? That an obscurantist stereotype has become the popular image of psychoanalysis is unfortunate as there has long been a tradition of social activism and of social analysis in the field (O'Loughlin, 2010b, Watkins & Shulman, 2008). Our failure to communicate this history and the important work that psychoanalytically informed teachers and clinicians continue to do is a real disservice to the field, and a major purpose of this book and its companion volume is to address this lacuna. As I noted in the introduction to *Psychodynamic Perspectives on Working with Children, Families and Schools*:

> The specific purpose of these collections is to introduce readers to the power of psychodynamic ways of thinking about children and schools. Professionals who work with children psychodynamically draw on diverse frameworks including the work of Anna Freud, the long tradition of the Tavistock Clinic in London, the writings of Klein, Winnicott and their colleagues, and French analysts in the Lacanian tradition. This work is valuable but often inaccessible to school professionals because the writing is somewhat specialized, and because there is no tradition of teaching such work in professional preparation in those fields. There is also a prejudice that psychoanalysis is neither social nor practical. I believe psychoanalysis is both eminently practical and has powerful things to say about children's social worlds, something these books illustrate persuasively. The purpose of these books, therefore, is to open the door to the possibility of introducing psychodynamic frameworks to education and human service professors and school professionals and professionals working with children so that they may elevate their professional gaze beyond the given to the possible.

While *Psychodynamic Perspectives on Working with Children, Families and Schools* focused at a somewhat more macro level on the uses of psychoanalysis in thinking about children, families, and schools, the purpose of this volume is to offer very specific illustrations of psychoanalytic ways of thinking and working in both clinical and pedagogical contexts with children. This book, then, is designed precisely for professionals who work with infants, children, and adolescents, and who are seeking modes of working that respect emotions, that embrace context, and that privilege imagination and possibility. Hopefully, for professionals who already practice in ways that are sympathetic to these modes of working, the scholarly underpinning of this work will offer a rationale for taking a stand in favor of emotionally-focused, child-centered work and in opposition to systems that negate the lives of children. This book then is for caring professionals who devote their lives to creating spaces for children to find their own paths and is intended to serve as a source of sustenance and support for such work.

In the opening chapter I offer three windows into the uses of psychoanalysis. In the first section, "Being a child," I explore my own childhood to illustrate the ways in which my early history informs my interest in working with children and the preoccupations I have around child welfare. Readers who wonder about my concern for the creation of spaces that value communality, imagination, and creativity in schools, and about my persistent concern about the corrosive role of anxiety and the risks of subjective annihilation in schools will see correlates and antecedents to those concerns in the privations of my own childhood and a palpable feeling of misrecognition at school:

> Why did the teachers not *see* me? Why were they not attuned to my suffering? Why was there no space in the school where other children and I could inscribe our lives and find our paths? Was it the case that the adults who supposedly taught us, just like the teacher in Chamoiseau's *School Days*, were so out of touch with their own inner lives that they could not serve as containers for our anxieties, nor as attuned listeners to our spoken and unspoken—and perhaps even unspeakable—narratives?

In the second part of the chapter, "Being with children existentially and therapeutically," I detail the principles underlying my clinical work with children—work that revolves around receptive listening, attunement to the child's unconscious, and a commitment to reanimating the subjectivity of the child by returning to the child aspects of her or his own unconscious experience. I conclude this section with details from my work with a young child with significant autism and emotional communication difficulties, concluding:

> The animation of subjectivity in persons with autistic disorders, and the reanimation of subjectivity in persons with depression or psychosis is the inverse of so much of what passes for psychotherapy or pedagogy in society. If external demand is intrusive, why offer treatments that privilege externality? Is Boris Cyrulnik (2005) not correct that an invitation to enter the existential space is what is required? This invitation requires the acutely attuned receptivity of an adult who values unconscious expression and receives it in whatever guise it chooses to manifest itself.

In the final section of the chapter, "Being with children pedagogically," using my notion of "a psychoanalysis of the social" I argue for a pedagogy that is not only emotionally validating, but one that acknowledges the sociohistorical constitutedeness of the child's subjectivity and the possibility of a depth pedagogy that very much mirrors what Paulo Freire described as "education as the practice of freedom":

> [A] social-historical psychoanalytic approach calls for subjectivization as a primary goal. Pedagogy ought to provide opportunities for an intensive engagement with spoken and unspoken experience, with history, lore, ancestry, and imagination so that each child can enter into a dynamic relationship with the ruptures and gaps of the past, and with multiple possible futures. A minimal condition of depth pedagogy, therefore, is the reclamation of narrative threads and the location of children as subjects in history—people with genealogical filiations, narrative continuity, and a possibility for becoming that is informed by, but not constrained by, ancestral, historical, and familial legacies.

Enid Elliot (chapter 2) frames caregiving work with very young children in terms of the dialogical possibilities of the narrative that is coconstructed between infant and caregiver, focusing first on the contribution of the infant to that dialog, and then considering the caregiver perspective. Drawing on Louise Kaplan's notion of *human dialogue*, Enid skillfully depicts the infant's active entry into relationship with adults who bring "their own dialogues that carry the ghosts and shadows from past conversations as well as angels of benevolence from past experience." Describing one father, whose approach to caregiving seemed rather defended and brusque, Enid describes the baby's instinctive response:

> Ashley had also heard her father. I watched as she got ready for him to appear. She pulled in her head and pulled in her arms and legs so that she was a compact bundle. She had already learned that was the most comfortable and likely safest way to be picked up by her father. With an energetic swoop, he swung her in the air totally disregarding the need to support her four month old head. She had already done what she could to protect herself against his exuberance. Here was a thread in the human dialogue with which Ashley was already engaged.

Enid goes on to discuss the role of alloparents in care-giving, drawing attention to the important work of Hungarian pediatrician Emma Pikler on baby's rights, and focusing on the existential rewards and demands of intentional caregiving. In the final section of the chapter Enid focuses on barriers to listening, reflecting on Tillie Olsen's terrible regret that the precious baby who was a miracle to her, was no miracle at all to the woman downstairs who was charged with her care. Enid discusses Pikler's notion of primary caregiving and she explores the countertransferential obstacles that prevent allocaregivers from allowing themselves to freely love the children in their care. She concludes:

Finding a path through the powerful emotions elicited by children and their families and sharing narratives that make sense of those emotions can be a comfort and allow caregivers to continue to be present for the children in their care. This path is not easy or untangled, "the intention to understand is already an emotionally wrought experience, for it returns us to times when we cannot understand and when we ourselves feel misunderstood."

In discussing *Chances for Children*, a psychoanalytically informed intervention program for teenage mothers and infants, Hillary Mayers (chapter 3) illustrates the power of a sophisticated integrative approach to emotional intervention work with babies and young mothers. Hillary describes how this program is built around infant developmental considerations; considerations of the adolescent development status of the teenage mothers; theories of motherhood, and most particularly Daniel Stern's notion of *motherhood constellation*; considerations from attachment theory and Fonagy's work on mentalization; and applications of psychoanalysis, particularly through the work of writers such as Selma Fraiberg and her invocation of "ghosts in the nursery" to capture the workings of intergenerational trauma transmission. All of this makes for rich reading, but most compelling of all, however, are the three illustrative case studies that Hillary presents that demonstrate the power of video analysis, and individual and group therapy in promoting mindfulness and reflective function in these young mothers. A key feature of the *Chances for Children* protocol is the use of video analysis, which is conducted from a *strengths-based perspective*, to allow therapist and mother to "forge an alliance as 'baby-watchers'":

> One young mother remarked tearfully after seeing herself on video with her baby, "This is the first time I really felt like I was a mother." Video allows the parent to see the child as separate from herself, setting the stage for thinking about her specific baby's individual self.

In referring to the response of "Melissa," the subject of the first illustrative case study, Hillary illustrates the depth and importance of the work, as well as reiterating the powerful role of the child in the kind of human dialog that Enid described so deftly in chapter 2:

> Melissa and Marcus sat together on a padded mat playing with stacking cups. When Melissa stopped playing and assumed her "still face," Marcus also stopped, confused. He looked at his mother, smiled uncertainly and crawled closer to her. He tapped her knee and waited. Getting no response, he tried again and then looked away. He banged his cup noisily looking directly at his mother. Then he threw the cup and began to protest loudly. Next he stopped, looking confused and anxious and rubbed his eyes. Opening them, he stared at her, crawled as far into her lap as he could get and began to whimper.

> Seeing this in slow motion was a revelation to Melissa who quickly perceived Marcus's distress. "I can't stand seeing him like that . . . it's like I was there but gone . . . he looked so miserable, lost, . . . like my mother I guess . . . she is still there but really she's not." As she continued to talk, she was able to talk about how guilty she felt feeling angry at her mother since "I knew from the beginning what would happen." She spoke of her distress at not only finding herself thrown out of her mother's home, but into a home where going to school was considered tantamount to killing her baby. She felt totally stifled, as unable to breathe as her son. Yet despite this, she could appreciate the effect her mood could have on her baby and began to observe him more closely in her different states of mind. This helped her use his needs to motivate her to change her behavior with him even when she was feeling miserable.

The three case studies provide windows into the exquisite complexity of each of the young mother's lives, and Hillary carefully documents the patient effort of therapists who employ video work, individual therapy, and group therapy to assist these young women in improving their mentalizing capacities and their receptiveness to the emotional communications of their infants. She also explores the complexities of countertransference and the mental strain that such work imposes on therapists and caregivers.

In chapter 4 Nathaniel Donson takes on an aspect of the human dialog that is often neglected and sometimes appears taboo in our professional discussion of child rearing. In addition to exploring the importance of fathering in general, Nathaniel also poses the difficult question of the dynamics of *father-hungry children*, some raised only by women, others with weak or severely disturbed fathers, positing a powerful and continuous existence of a father presence in the lives of all children. Reviewing the history of theories of masculine identity and the development of notions of fatherhood in children of both sexes, Nathaniel notes that it was not until the nineteen fifties that a professional paper acknowledged healthy boys' wishes for babies, or the possibility that a healthy masculine or paternal identity must involve a boy's sustaining of his feminine and nurturing qualities.

Nathaniel's own son Jeremy provides a delightful example:

> Jeremy, age two years: His mother is due in a month with our next child. He is sitting happily on the toilet, smiling, and pointing to his belly. "Jeremy has a baby in his belly." Naively I respond, "No Jeremy; mommy has a baby in her belly." His face falls; but then his pointing finger moves down and he gives me a delighted look. "Jeremy has a penis; mommy doesn't have a penis."

Evoking Fraiberg's "ghosts in the nursery," Nathaniel is well aware of the relational difficulties that can lie in the way of internalizing a loving paternal capacity, and he underlines the importance of love in a boy's formation. Hopefully, the ideal experience of fatherhood will evoke a man's love, resonant with a loving identification with his own mother and father, who had themselves been nurturing figures during his childhood, in support of his masculine and paternal identity. Drawing on the essays of John Munder Ross, he notes that it is during a man's reproductive years that the assumption of a caring father role allows him to come to terms with earlier conflicted and repressed maternal desires.

Turning to the experiences of children who have father issues, Nathaniel discusses their difficulties in terms of Herzog's concept of *father hunger*. While boys and girls can suffer from father hunger, Nathaniel sees this as an additional problem for boys because active engagement with a father serves as a regulator of masculine aggression. He suggests that in single-parent families where children are raised exclusively by women acting as a paternal gatekeeper, the demonization of absent fathers is particularly damaging to the self-regulation and identity of boys. Nancy Boyd Franklin's work further emphasizes that father hunger fueled by absence, prohibition, and denigration is particularly likely to produce deep rage and emotional difficulty that leads to difficulties in the transmission of both masculine identity and of good fathering across the generations.

Nathaniel notes the persistent influence of all fathers—present or absent in this way:

> In loving maternal hands, a lifetime sense of a lost, although psychologically present good father, may become a healthy support for a child growing up; but an absent father, depending on how the loss is handled by present or surviving members of a family, may also become deforming and malignant. Either way such fathers remain a powerful force in the inner lives of surviving parents and their children, and remain a uniquely enlivened presence within every child at each developmental stage.

Nathaniel describes the dire consequences for children whose mothers denigrate absent fathers, and proposes working with such parents to help them create for their children a paternal imago ("virtual father") that is positive, healthful, and loving in order to assist their children in internalizing a good paternal object rather than a conflicted or rage-filled identification. For this to happen the mother's experience as "gatekeeper to a despised father" must be set aside—with the requisite mourning which that entails. If this can be achieved, a new kind of emotional conversation can begin that allows a father hungry child to begin the emotional work of reparation and healthy introjection of paternal identifications even if a physical father is absent.

The authors of chapter 5 are an interdisciplinary team of psychiatrists, social workers, and psychologists from the former Chestnut Lodge Hospital who call themselves the Chestnut Lodge Study Group and who, now that the former Chestnut Lodge Hospital has been forced to close, are attempting to implement its intensive team-based approach to care in a non-residential

setting, the Lodge School. Unfortunately, treatment for children and adolescents in interdisciplinary settings is often beset by rivalries between different
professionals, and the work of the Chestnut Lodge Study Group offers an
exemplary illustration of how interdisciplinary teamwork—in this case united by a shared psychoanalytic vision—can produce extraordinary gains. In
addition, in a time when, in the United States, managed health care has begun
to impose stringent rationing, this chapter offers bold ideas for how children
with complex disorders, who would previously have been treated only in
residential settings, can benefit from carefully coordinated, comprehensive
care in a therapeutic day school.

The chapter is constructed around a single case study of an adolescent girl
"Alexa." She "was a school-avoidant adolescent girl with chronic somatic
problems connected with Lyme disease, significant trauma history, family
conflict, self-injurious behavior, psychotic symptoms and a mood disorder."
The chapter offers a compelling account of the relationship between Alexa's
somatic complaints and her psychological distress, and follows the treatment
team as they pursue a treatment plan from containment of symptoms, through
the vicissitudes of working through, to eventual successful termination. As in
Hillary's work (chapter 3), the emphasis here is on the creation of a supportive milieu and the use of individual and family therapy to support an increasing capacity for mentalization and reflective function in a young woman
who is experiencing considerable emotional difficulty, that, in this case has
emerged in a rather puzzling somatization as Lyme disease. For clinicians or
educators who would wish to find solutions to complex psychosocial problems in simple once-a-week out-patient therapy, or in the dispensation of
psychotropic medication, this work offers a powerful antidote, revealing how
a child whom conventional approaches has failed, and who has become
"treatment resistant" in the jargon of the field, can be helped by a team-based
biopsychosocial approach. The authors wrap up this compelling case study
this way:

> Finally, while it is true that this integrated, intensive approach requires consid-
> erable resources, the gains represented in this case are measured in dramatic
> changes in the trajectory of a young person's life and the lives of those who are
> connected to her. Schools that are organized to provide services for disturbed
> adolescents so that they can be educated can look to this case and this ap-
> proach as example of the power of a psychoanalytically informed, comprehen-
> sive treatment to significantly improve educational and quality of life out-
> comes.

Erika Schmidt, Aileen Schloerb, and the late Bertram Cohler (chapter 6)
offer another illustration of how psychodynamic intervention can be used
therapeutically in school contexts. Erika and her colleagues are concerned
about the pervasiveness of violence in the lives of children in many urban

communities that are poor in the United States. They developed a project whose core idea is the creation of growth groups to assist children who have encountered systemic violence in processing their experiences. Drawing on psychoanalytic understandings of trauma, the authors describe the psychic consequences for children and explain how they developed non-directive small groups in which children were invited to share their experiences and they explore the complex process of gaining entrée to public schools and building trust among administrators and teachers. The work is brought to life by compelling clinical material which reminds me once again of the power of psychoanalytic ideas applied to complex social trauma. Consider, for example, this extract from a kindergarten group:

> When children are invited to share their thoughts and feelings with one another and to connect with these feelings, it often produces an internal crisis that engenders coping behaviors that include the physical release of tension rather than the containment of energy.
>
> For these inhibited kindergartners, the initial anxiety of being together in this new way expresses itself through disconnection and isolated preoccupations. Jayden sits quietly and solemnly and looks blankly at the group leader when asked questions. Antonio is interested in the snack but once he finishes eating his and asking for more, he busies himself with looking around the room or off into space, isolated from the others. Nehemiah fills the group space with a stream of disjointed talk. He begins to talk about his father's car being broken, then of the two mice in his bed. He is interested in the apples they were offered at the end of a story the group leader told about a lonely star in the sky in search of friends. The leader invites the children to make pictures of what they wish for. Tevin draws a picture of himself in colorful shoes. Jayden plays with the colored pencils. Nehemiah's picture of monsters, cars, and fire extends past the edges of his paper and onto his desk. Antonio draws all over the front and back of his sheet of paper and fills it up with dense scribbles.

And for illustration of the mutative power of this non-directive group for these young children consider the story of Antonio and Tevin:

> When the children are invited to make pictures of the significant others in their lives, Antonio begins by drawing one rock and then another. He follows this with faceless bodies representing a mother, three brothers, two sisters (he isn't sure of the count at first) and himself. This is all done in black. Then he picks up a green crayon and begins at the bottom of the page to systematically cover the underlying picture in a layer of green. Someone asks what he is drawing and he reports that it is water. As the water climbs higher and higher over the figures, we wonder and someone asks if he can swim. He says that he can't and adds fish and sharks to the water. Tevin, who has been drawing Jayden and himself as the significant people in his world, becomes quite concerned. He says that he wants to make a net to help Antonio out of the water. We ask

Antonio if Tevin can draw a net into his picture. Antonio agrees and Tevin draws a picture of himself with a net at the top of the water.

Erika, Aileen, and Bertram offer powerful illustrations such as these to show how containment, mentalization, and group process can create healing spaces for very wounded children in the everyday context of their local public schools. This is the antithesis of the *bare life* (cf. Agamben, 1998; Fassin, 2010) that public schools and public housing projects all too often offer vulnerable children as ostensible spaces for growth.

Silvia Silberman and Arie Plat (chapter 7) tackle the issue of violence from another angle. In their chapter, Silvia and Arie interrogate the very nature of the school experience and question whether the illusory yearning for order in schools creates conditions that actually facilitate the possibility of violence. Drawing parallels between the *Towns without violence* movement in Israel and the *Zero tolerance* policies that dominate U.S. public schooling, the authors suggest that these movements are based on a failure to analyze the dynamics of schooling. After clarifying the distinction between aggression and violence, they go on to argue that if violence is rooted in relational and attachment difficulty, then much greater attention needs to be paid to processes of containment and mentalization in creating a climate where the conditions that precipitate violence become speakable. They point out that such an approach can never occur if the school embodies a didactic philosophy and the focus is on transmission of knowledge rather than on critical reflection on school, on society, and on points of conflict between individuals and groups. After some further discussion of the dynamics underlying processes such as school bullying, Silvia and Arie then go on to explore how the very dynamics of the school itself can be a contributor to violence, raising a very troubling problematic that is all too familiar:

> In contrast, violent interpretations (in general and in the schools) that are unidirectional (from adults to youngsters; from power holders to others) carry the color of the unique truth ("What I saw is what there is") and use traditional didactics (those who "know" teach those who "don't know"). They imply an unquestionable truth about the listener and leave no possibility for exploration ("You obviously didn't make an effort"; "It's good, someone surely helped you"). They are truths given to be swallowed ("You need medicines for your attention disorder") without digestion or elaboration, and they fail to promote development and change. Violent interpretations in the school ("Children from this background always have difficulties in learning") contain social stereotypes, reflect social stratification, power structures and confusion between proper use of power and the abuse of it, i.e., between exercising authority and imposing coercion.

The remainder of their chapter is devoted to describing an anti-violence initiative in Israel that is based on the principles of group dynamics discussed here, and which engages teachers, school administrators, and interested community stakeholders in learning how to use techniques of containment and mentalization to promote dialog that can lead to mutual understanding and hence to the implementation of interventions and micro-interventions that have an impact in the community, also by reducing violence.

Burton Seitler reaches back to the early days of his career in chapter 8 to recount the story of his struggle to engage a troubled young person, "Grey," with the possibility of coming to imagine life otherwise. Grey, a rather oppositional defiant young person, confronts Burton with anger and expletives, something that Burton, while still a novice, recognizes as a defense against vulnerability. Burton invites us into the story by sharing his thought process as he tried to build a potential space where Grey could work through the difficulties that had produced such an aggressive defense. As Burton noted, "when Grey was most furious, Grey was also most frightened." Drawing on Bion's notions of alpha and beta elements and Fonagy's writings on mentalization, Burton illustrates the complex cognitive/emotional difficulties this person is experiencing. Early on, when Grey's dreaded secret was revealed, namely profound shame at an inability to read even the simplest written words, Burton's response was explicitly analytic:

> I had spent a great deal of my "free" time thinking about Grey. My thoughts were not organized around a specific plan, structure, any preset ideas or anything solid or tangible. I was interested in and curious about Grey. How did Grey become the person I was seeing? Was there something underneath the persona that was being presented? If so, how was it formed, and how come? Although these ideas are fairly well formed as I write them down for this chapter, when they were first buzzing around in my mind, they seemed to be amorphous, wandering thoughts. In some ways, they bear some resemblance to what Bion referred to as the reverie a mother has when imaging her child (1962b).

The end product of this reverie was a rather unconventional pedagogic solution to Grey's dilemma. Burton managed to engage Grey in putting feelings into words in "an acceptable, even relieving manner," without perpetuating on this wounded young person the violence that had already elicited a violently defensive response. Burton's chapter raises the troubling question as to why institutions such as schools can evoke such violent defenses in some young people, and his insightful receptivity offers guidance as to how to engage such youth in a path toward healing.

Sue Wallace (chapter 9) takes us to Edinburgh, where she works with vulnerable young women, many teetering on the edge of homelessness. Not only have these young women had challenging home lives, but school has also failed them:

. . . despite their evident lively intelligence only rarely have these youngsters achieved any qualifications, and the primary reason for that is that they equally rarely attended school. When they did, they report that rather than a respite from constant trauma of their home lives it was quite likely to be an additional source of miserable shame and humiliation. Their repeated absences meant that they were unable to keep up with their academic studies and perhaps even more significantly they had struggled to secure or maintain a place within established peer groups. Their reaction to this additional pressure would most usually lead to repeated exclusions from school and this combined with domestic circumstances would lead to an entrance into the "care system" or "secure accommodation" frequently experienced by these children as neither caring nor secure.

Interspersed between heart-wrenching vignettes that take us into the room with these wounded and vulnerable young women, Sue offers a sophisticated description of the core psychoanalytic techniques—mentalization, attunement, attachment, containing, mirroring, separation/individuation, and so forth—that she uses to attempt to engage in a human dialogue of trust and possibility with the young women. Here is a brief excerpt from the case of one such person, Miranda:

As usual her intelligence and insight impress me and yet these characteristics are so fundamentally undermined by her vulnerability and the unrelenting sense of her own worthlessness. Miranda speaks of the reduction she has managed in smoking hash which at one level she knows is not good for her, yet at another it seems something impossible to dispense with. The discussion moves to a recent visit to her mother and brother; she had made a special effort and looked forward to the games she planned to play with her young brother. Barely had she arrived, she told me, than her mother's criticisms of her began and the visit she had so eagerly anticipated became more and more difficult until finally, feeling unable to defend herself she left, vowing never to return; until the next time.

I am aware of the endless cycles of attempted separation and eventual rapprochement between this girl and her mother. Aware too of all the efforts that have over the years, gone in to trying to bring them together in a room, efforts that Miranda's mother would always refuse. Her refusal would be that the difficulty was located in her daughter and had nothing to do with her. I am aware too of Miranda's mother's post-natal depression and the way that her child was moved constantly following her father's death. I see clearly that Miranda has been imbued with an ever present expectation that she will be rejected and abandoned because she is unlovable.

Dealing with young women at the edge of despair and often on the precipice of homelessness, Sue is under no illusions that psychoanalytic therapy is a panacea, but her work illustrates the inestimable importance of the existential meeting, the I—Thou relationship, to opening the door to possible healing.

Meditating on the potential reparative role of schooling in vulnerable children's lives, Sue concludes:

> I believe that there are a number of ways in which a difference might be made. A teacher who has the capacity to retain an open mind about a troubled young person and to attempt to continue to think with them even when under pressure may be helpful to them. It is especially important not to retaliate when tested by their actions. If that teacher has the capacity not to experience behaviors as personal attacks even though they may have been designed by the child to feel very personal, this may also be significant. A young person will benefit if, however personal the behaviors feel, the person interacting with them is able to see them as very limited and primitive ways of expressing feelings that cannot be recognized and certainly not put into words.

Marilyn Charles, a clinician at Austen Riggs Center, a psychiatric hospital in Massachusetts, opens chapter 10 with four vignettes of young adults who have experienced psychosis. In the United States the prevalent biological perspective in psychiatry focuses on symptom relief, often by means of psychotropic medications. What Marilyn has learned from years of treating young people who have experienced psychosis in young adulthood is that psychosocial stressors often serve as precipitants of psychosis. In this chapter Marilyn focuses particularly on bullying and social exclusion in schools as potential underlying causes for serious psychiatric disturbances later in life. A key implication of her work is that if school personnel can recognize the kinds of interpersonal difficulties that result in potential adult psychosis, and intervene appropriately, those difficulties may well be attenuated or eliminated. Marilyn notes "the importance of the availability of empathic others who might recognize signs of excessive strain in children and help to moderate distress and allay anxiety. For some children, an empathic teacher can be an important moderating factor, helping to provide support and resources through which the vulnerable child might build greater resilience and adaptive capacity." Marilyn goes on to explore the importance of mirroring and of keeping each child in mind, and she explores in detail the damaging effects of shame on not only a child's emotional regulation but also on their capacities for reflective thought and effective learning. She reviews in detail research that suggests that bullying and social exclusion have "been linked with a higher incidence of psychotic-like experiences, which, in turn, is linked with a higher risk for psychotic illness later in life." Marilyn describes the markers for both emotional vulnerability and cognitive difficulty in children and adolescents that may presage later psychosis. With respect to bullying, in particular, she notes that

> [A]lthough it is difficult to entirely separate cause from effect, it should be noted that the potential toxic effects of bullying are wide-reaching, with impli-

cation for both the victim and the bully. Longitudinal evidence shows a link between bullying in elementary school and later impulsivity, substance use, and violence and criminal behavior (the latter linked particularly to the bully) in early adolescence (Tharp-Taylor, Haviland, & D'Amico, 2009) and in young adulthood (Kim, Catalano, Haggerty, & Abbott, 2011).

Marilyn's chapter concludes by arguing for an intensive multi-modal intervention in schools and a strict no-tolerance policy toward bullying. Underlining the relational bases of bullying and social exclusion, Marilyn argues that teachers need to be sensitized to recognize the symptoms of psychic vulnerability. More important, echoing Silvia and Arie's argument about schools as places that either foment or attenuate violence (chapter 7), Marilyn argues that schools need to make a systemic shift toward becoming expressly prosocial environments. Marilyn concludes her chapter by returning to her four case vignettes. Each of these young people was "at least to some extent 'driven mad' by bullying or social exclusion." Arguing that such a terrible price should not have to be paid, Marilyn concludes with an exhortation to individual teachers and to schools as a whole to engage in attuned listening and to place a much higher priority on the creation of accepting, inclusive, prosocial places for all children in schools.

John Tieman, a teacher for all of his professional life, takes up the topic of shame in schools in chapter 11. John views shaming and ridicule as tools of systemic oppression in school and he courageously details his own participation in these practices early in his career before he trained in child and adolescent development at the St. Louis Psychoanalytic Institute. John offers a psychodynamic explanation of the workings of shame, interspersed with lively dialogues from his teaching life. John begins by noticing the pervasive link between the humiliation of children and the equation of school discipline with compliance and submission. Instead of seeing oppositional or aberrant behavior as a symptom to be eradicated, John, nowadays, adopts a psychoanalytic posture:

> When I discipline, I do not ask, "How do I stop that child from cursing me?" I ask, "What is going on *between us*, such that this child chooses this communication?" To borrow from Martin Buber (1960), I am not concerned with the behavior of the It. I am concerned with the we-*ness* of the I-Thou. The psychodynamic view is of two minds interacting.

Drawing on the writings of Freud and Erikson, John describes the developmental consequences of shame for children and adolescents and he is careful to note that while shaming is often part of the institutional discourse of schooling, it is also intimately linked up with countertransference and with the ghosts of humiliation and shame in the childhood lives of teachers and school administrators. John recalls how shame recapitulated his own childhood experience: "Shaming resonated with me in a manner that, at the time, was not self-apparent. I remembered the times that, as a boy, I had been shamed and how I had complied" and, more generally he notes:

> It is worth repeating that these stages of development provide avenues from which we regress into this earliest shame based template, as well as platforms, in and of themselves, for shame. When teachers and principals shame, they draw upon their personality formation, a template that is formed long before they began their careers. This then becomes the platform for today's shaming of the student. Let me restate it this way. The child acts in a way that the educator deems punishable by humiliation. The educator unconsciously senses his or her own experience with humiliation. The educator's experience with humiliation becomes then the platform for shaming the student.

The outcome of shaming, John notes, is rage, as this vignette from early in his teaching career illustrates:

> . . . one day Christopher just would not shut up. I kept him from going to recess with his 7th grade buddies. "Okay, young man, you want to play around in my class, and blow-off your English lesson. Fine. Drop out of school. But before you go, I have one last English lesson for you, all the English you'll need for the rest of your sorry life. Repeat after me. Would you like fries with that order?" Before he could respond, I had to go to the door, and talk to another teacher. As we chatted, out of the corner of my eye I noticed Christopher pounding his desk with his fist. But he shut-up. Which, for the moment, was good enough for me.

Shaming, of course, "works." If compliance and submission is the goal it is as good a tool as you can find. Teachers, John notes, are encouraged to be passionate, open, and even loving with children. Yet at the same time, schools are saturated in a cognitive-behavioral ethos. "It is as if no one has a mind anymore—all we have is behavior." John concludes that rather than succumb to instrumental and overbearing prescriptions, teachers would be well advised to be open to their own emotional experiences or, as John says: "In three words, to love ourselves."

Gail Boldt and Billie Pivnick open chapter 12 with a concern that in the "era of high-stakes accountability" that has come to dominate U.S. public education, the capacity for some children to find a potential space in which to construct meaning has been eliminated. They focus on entry into literacy and interpret children's resistance to learning to read in terms of the classic understanding of resistance in psychoanalytic theory. Drawing on the work of Hesse and Main (2000), they note that "[t]he expectation that a text cannot be mastered can create disorganized behavioral responses indicative of 'fright without solution.'" Much of their chapter focuses on an intensive case study of a young boy who developed reading resistance early on, most probably after an encounter with a teacher and system that proved incapable of receptivity either toward Nick's natural interests, or his palpable anxiety at his inability to just pick up literate discourse. Gail and Billie argue that the kind of textual engagement required for reading demands "implicit relational knowing" and they analyze Nick's subsequent success in entering literacy with a receptive tutor, using the notion of *moments of meeting* articulated by the Boston Process Study Group as well as Winnicott's notions of play, holding environment, potential space, and intersubjectivity. What emerges from this chapter, therefore, is a psychodynamically-based intersubective theory of pedagogical practice. Discussing Nick's need for a reparative intersubjective experience, the authors note:

> It is critical in working with children who have developed a resistance to reading that we not simply repeat the same kinds of interactions and procedures that caused the child to feel like a failure in the first place. Rather, what is required is a perspective that honors the child's integrity as a person able to make his or her own demands to be recognized and respected, already in possession of many strengths and resources, and capable of choosing to learn, grow, and change for his or her own purposes. Nick needed a reparative relationship to help him reintegrate the creative and supportive, intersubjective approach to reading that had worked for him prior to first grade. It was critical that this relationship would involve pivotal encounters with an instructor that would reshape his experience of reading in the presence of another to more closely resemble the original, playful context that allowed him to succeed and that would also allow him to tolerate the more task-oriented demands of reading skill development. These kinds of relational encounters are precisely the sort of social events that generate the procedural knowledge of how to be with another person, which the Boston Process Study Group (2010) calls intersubjective "*moments of meeting.*"

Echoing many of the authors already discussed above, Gail and Billie point out the importance of teachers developing attunement to underlying causes rather than simply reacting to overt behaviors:

> Nita saw Nick's resistance not as a sign that he would not work, but rather as a sign that he was trying to find a way that would allow him to cooperate without being overwhelmed once again by humiliation. Nita responded to all forms of Nick's resistance and anger with a stance of active and deliberate patience, refusing to become punitive and taking the position that her job was to learn from him how best to work with him. She spoke empathetically with him about how angry she felt on his behalf about how hard reading was for him. She accepted his skateboard drawing, saying that she imagined that sometimes he must feel that way about having to read with her. Importantly, many of the things that Nita might have interpreted as resistance she instead understood as an effort on Nick's part to take what she was offering and make it usable. When, in response to a book they were reading about shapes, Nick

spontaneously lay on the floor to match his body to the illustrations, she praised him for his involvement and initiative, later suggesting that Nick was modifying her ideas for how they might read together in order to make the work his own.

A coda to this chapter, and indeed a key element of many chapters in the companion volume, *Psychodynamic Perspectives on Working with Children, Families and Schools*, is an increasing concern that the shift toward more systematized, accountability-oriented, and test-driven curricula in schools in the United States and elsewhere is steadily shrinking the space in which emotional work might be conducted in schools. The concern is that our schools will produce increasing numbers of children with Nick's difficulties, and further, as Marilyn noted in chapter 10, that some of these children may present as adults at risk for serious psychiatric disturbances later in life.

Colette Granger (chapter 13) notes her use of "psychoanalytic theory as a hermeneutic aims not for 'the *application* of psychoanalysis to pedagogy' but toward 'the *implication* of psychoanalysis in pedagogy and of pedagogy in psychoanalysis'" (Felman, 1982, pp. 26–27; italics in original). Colette discusses both the psychodynamic complexity for the child of taking up a second language and the equally complex dynamics of the language teacher's response. Colette's chapter provides a fine illustration of the power of psychoanalysis to move beyond narrow intrapsychic considerations to include interpersonal dynamics between two people or groups, as well as the situatedness of complex activity, such as teaching, in larger contexts. After some general consideration of factors affecting language learning, Colette explores resistance to language learning among adolescents, suggesting that some of that resistance might be interpreted as part of the adolescent working through of identity and sexuality. Speaking of the time-worn ruse by which adolescents try to maneuver a teacher into saying foreign words that are homophones for taboo English words, she notes:

> Questions about *seal* and *push*, through which a student "makes" the teacher say "bad words," form a linguistic feint that projects onto that teacher—and onto her language—the young adolescent's renewed but unauthorized preoccupation with, and curiosity about, acts and body parts that remain off limits, both in the classroom and for the superego. Simply put, by putting words in the teacher's mouth the learner ostensibly keeps them out of his own. And doing so disrupts both the lesson and the language.

As Colette astutely notes, "a move away from identification with family and toward adult autonomy that makes getting away *with* something a purposeful (albeit unconscious) part of getting away *from* something—is the demand to determine his own values." Turning to resistance to language, and drawing on Adam Phillips, Colette argues that entry into language is, as Phillips calls it, a "loss of the unspoken self" and a demand that a child enter a second language may re-awaken these primal losses: "Thus the second-language learner struggles not only with the echoes of his pre- or first-language self but also with his inability to represent himself fully in the new language, either to the world or to himself." Colette presents a variety of vignettes from different language groups and contexts to tease out further the degree to which evocation of psychic losses may or may not be a major contributing factor to language learning difficulty, and concludes:

> Here, then, is a set of moments that helps illustrate psychoanalytic theory's usefulness in understanding relations between the individual psyche and the social realm (the "inside" and the "outside") in connection with learning. Could it be that growing up in more than one language, or where multilingualism is normalized and even expected, or where the target language is seen as more socially and economically advantageous than the mother tongue, might somehow facilitate the psychical move away from the pleasure urge, expedite the reality principle's arrival and solidify its influence, despite those repressed memory-traces of early difficult separation experiences? We might understand this as an expedited fading of memory-traces over time. Yes, these ghostly echoes of early separations and psychical losses reawaken with each new demand to "translate" the self into a new language, but their influence diminishes so that we "get used to" these self-translations as the reality principle brings to the fore factors that are less worrisome and more reality-focused: success in learning a language, positive experiences to which that learned language has been put, and the cultural and social approval and even privilege attaching to possession of and facility with that language.

In the final section of her chapter, Colette explores countertransferential reactions of hatred by teachers toward students, She notes that "we begin to sense a kind of double counter-resistance on the teacher's part: first to the learner's apparent insistence on changing the terms (metaphorically and literally) of the learning, second to challenges to her vision of herself as one who loves, but who never, ever hates. For that is simply not how things are supposed to go." As Colette's chapter reveals, psychoanalysis lends itself to complexifying and illuminating pedagogical tasks such as language learning that produce resistances that at first glance may seem disproportionate and perplexing.

In chapter 14 Alex Moore takes us into a classroom in a culturally diverse British urban school to study the significance of emotionality in children's and teacher's lives. Alex laments "the ways in which emotionality is routinely pathologized and effectively ostracized" in schools. His chapter explores what he terms "the 'authorization' of affect—that is to say its public acceptance and de-pathologization" in schooling. The project consisted of interviews with teachers and young children about their emotional experiences with schooling. The official rhetoric of the school, corroborated by the apparently sincere views of teachers, was that the school was a caring, inclusive community that privileged student voice, that fostered collaborative learning, and that valued the development of empathy. However, as pressure for improved test performance grew, the research team, drawing on these interviews, supplemented by informal discussion and observations, noticed a subtle shift from an ethic of care to an all-too-familiar ethic of expedience that favored getting work done and meeting academic goals. One teacher described it this way:

> And I do think you should be interested in the children, and have some concern over their well-being and their background and what goes on for them out of school, but basically our job is to teach them when they are here. And if something is impeding that teaching, be it that they are turning up late every day, you can make an effort to deal with that, but really you just have to manage to teach them despite that. If you can change it then that is great.

Alex comments:

> . . . the teacher's insistence on teaching "despite" the absence or presence of well-being in the child seemed to position teaching as something external to the child, which *can* occur without the child's engagement or desire to learn, preferable though such conditions might be. This concurs with the teacher's understanding of emotional impact as occurring essentially and principally as a result of factors *outside the classroom*, or at least outside what is official and sanctioned *within* the classroom (such as problems with parents or home life, or teasing and bullying by peers)—rather than as a result of any *internal dynamics* that structure the children's relationship with their teachers and with one another . . .

Perhaps it is not a surprise that interviews with children revealed that they were perfectly aware of the gap between the official rhetoric and the practice of school:

> whereas the teachers self-perceived as caring, loving practitioners who had their students' best interests at heart, the children's view of their teachers tended to be of a group of adults who did *not* understand their differences or their needs, who did *not* care for or about them, and who did little to make learning the enjoyable experience it was supposed to be.

After offering some poignant examples of children's struggles to stay on task despite the worries in their lives, Alex goes on to raise another troubling issue. Despite the profession of a commitment to student-centered and collaborative learning by teachers, Alex noticed that the children learned early on that love could only be earned in school by (1) getting the right answer; and (2) getting the answer ahead of your classmates. The children wanted to be loved and felt that affect and validation were only authorized for speedy achievement. Drawing on Zizek's discussion of imaginary and symbolic identification, Alex explains the dynamics underlying the child's desire for love and acceptance both on a relational and an achievement level, and he shows how schools easily place children in an impossible position when it comes to getting their needs met. Turning next to the sociopolitical pressures on schools to continually improve measurable outcomes, Alex illustrates how this trickles down into an ethic of competitiveness, and even cruelty among children that further militates against the development of healthy emotional lives. Alex concludes by exploring the many factors that militate against the validation of affect in classrooms, and he leaves us with the troubling thought that for many children a school that values their voices, assuages their anxieties, and frees their imaginations can indeed be a chimera.

Eileen Brennan (chapter 15) offers a psychodynamic understanding of autism, a perspective that is well established in some parts of the world but that is decidedly a minority perspective in the United States. Eileen begins with an exploration of Freud's observations of his baby grandson throwing and retrieving a toy, in what has come to be known as the *fort-da* game. Eileen describes the auto-sensuous self-experiencing involved in the child's flowing motions and accompanying humming and singing. As Eileen notes, "Repeated tactile experiences with the soft flexible string and the hard wooden toy are pleasurable and introduce thinking skills supportive of differentiation." The differentiation referred to here, of course, is separation from the mother and the child's emergent capacity to experience a self independent of the separate self of the mother. This emergent self-regulatory capacity is crucially lacking in children who have characteristics that place them on the autistic spectrum, and Eileen devotes the remainder of her chapter to expounding the theoretical perspectives on autism of two legendary psychoanalysts, Frances Tustin and Hyman Spotnitz, and then illustrating the playing out of a therapeutic relationship she had with a young person with autism over a lengthy period of time.

From a psychoanalytic perspective, fear, terror, catastrophic anxiety, and unmodulated aggression are viewed not as behaviors to be managed and controlled, but symptoms that communicate meaning and thereby require patient receptivity and invitation to dialog. To put it simply, if autism is a defense, a full-tilt assault on autistic behaviors is undoubtedly counter-therapeutic. Eileen explains this in detail, and teases out the nuances of difference between Tustin and Spotnitz, and the somewhat divergent—or perhaps complementary—therapeutic approaches entailed in combating the "stone wall of narcissism" that autism entails. What is special about psychodynamic approaches to autism, as Eileen details, is a recognition of unmodulated anxiety and developmental challenge as key issues in need of therapeutic response. It is astounding how rare this insight is in the United States, with the notable exception of the work of the late Stanley Greenspan and his associates. The emphasis by Spotnitz on contact is described by Eileen:

> Spotnitz seldom interpreted any communication until the ending months of the psychoanalytic relationship. He depended upon the child's level of contact to guide his response. When a high level of withdrawal was present, Spotnitz sat quietly and mirrored the child's low level of recognition of the analyst's presence. Through these initial silent responses the analyst demonstrated to the fear-filled child a depth of self-control, creating a sense of safety within the analytic process. As the child initiated some contact Spotnitz responded in kind. As the child's talking skills developed and as Spotnitz's ability to listen to the non-verbal and verbal language of the child increased, the process of reversing autistic communication advanced slowly. Spotnitz posited that a psychoanalyst's use of contact functioning lessened the child's pathological defensive use of autistic strategies and frequently contra-indicated the analyst's intrusion that would come from offering interpretations.

Following a discussion of key concepts from Tustin including autistic objects, autistic encapsulation, and autistic entanglement, Eileen takes us on a twelve-year journey with a patient, "Gabe," who simultaneously yearns for and flees from contact. I will leave it to the reader to follow this journey, but here is a brief vignette that illustrates its complexity:

> His session remained wall-to-wall empty words. Each week he retold the events of each day since our last session. The words sounded like a grocery list and it felt as if he were piecing together segments of his life. Non-verbally, his body was telling a story of rage and self-hatred. His legs were covered in mosquito bites that he never let heal. When a scab formed he immediately scratched it off and made the bite bleed. He stopped bathing and the body odor, like his many words, defined his presence and filled the space. He developed more than a dozen boils across his back that wept and stuck to his tee shirt. He told me that part of getting ready for bed involved ripping his shirt off and making the boils weep. On occasion he passed gas and by the end of our session my office smelled intensely foul. His skin and orifices communicated the intensity of his self-hatred and anxiety. In his refusal to bathe, to follow the basic rules of hygiene, it seemed as if Gabe were trying painfully to birth himself. In his foul smells I actually felt OK, struggling to survive the unwanted aromas.

Reading Devra Adelstein and Judith Pitlick's discussion of the evolution of conscience in the young child (chapter 16) brought to mind Spike Jonze's (2009) sensitive movie rendition of Maurice Sendak's *Where the Wild Things Are*. Sendak earned the admiration of child analysts and child sympathizers everywhere with his rendition of the tempestuous inner life of the child, chafing against adult restriction and struggling with unbridled rage, regret, and simultaneous desires to be swaddled and set free. Devra and Judith bring us sympathetically into the lives of eight such children, and they offer insight into the complex journey that parents and society demand of the child as she or he is ostensibly set free to discover life, while simultaneously being subject to demands for assimilation to prevailing norms and strictures.

Devra and Judith begin with a review of the developmental tasks involved in acquiring an internalized conscience or superego. As they note, in an ideal situation the conscience evolves to become a trusted friend and advisor. After walking through the milestones of infancy and early childhood, they focus particularly on the latency period, the period during which the movement from external stricture to internal superego is most fraught: "Many children feel distraught, such as Anthony, age six, who told his teacher that there were too many rules in kindergarten. Greg got a stomachache every morning, describing first grade as too hard, saying that he could never finish his work." The authors note that the demands of the conscience can either produce a tendency toward perfectionism and self-punitiveness, or else lead the child to the kind of externalization that elicits punishment from adults that is typically less burdensome than the consequences for the child of facing his or her own harsh superego. Devra and Judith also raise the all important issue of repair. In my own experience with adult patients in therapy, I notice that those that have the most intractable relational difficulties are those who have accumulated large piles of unmended fences—the capacity for repair is lacking. Adults who equip children with a healthy capacity for repair, and a means of attenuating excessive guilt contribute to the development of a healthy conscience, as the authors note. Devra and Judith conclude with eight vignettes that describe the ways in which particular children navigate the internalization of parental and societal prohibition. Included in these examples is the cautionary tale of Sarah, a child the teacher experienced as a pleasure in class:

> At the autumn second grade parent teacher conference, seven-year-old Sarah's teacher exclaimed, "Sarah is a pleasure to have in class. She is attentive, polite, and I never have to ask her to do anything twice. She is a model student." Sarah's parents were thrilled, especially because her older brother Matt was so difficult that they wanted Sarah to be perfect. Sarah was a bright, sensitive girl who could see how disappointed her parents were with her brother's angry outbursts. Sarah's parents were not entirely surprised by the teacher's evaluation. At home too, Sarah did as she was told. The parents felt she was sulky and the zest for life she'd had as a younger child, seemed to be missing. Six months later at the spring parent teacher conference, Sarah's teacher still sang her praises, but now she had become a bit worried about Sarah's perfectionism. Sarah could not tolerate making mistakes, and if she erased one answer she had to start all over again on a fresh piece of paper. If she made a spelling error it would ruin her whole day. It was at this point that Sarah's parents decided to consult a therapist. The therapist helped them understand about Sarah's inner life, and how she had excessively high expectations of herself.

Devra and Judith comment:

> Children who are dutiful often suffer. Under the aura of goodness and obedience the child may develop a conscience that is problematic. When this occurs, the child does not learn to make decisions for him/herself, but rather acts to gain acceptance and admiration through pleasing others. Karen Horney (1950) discusses a concept which she calls "the tyranny of the should" (p. 164), explaining that a person requires him/herself to be an idealized self at all times. She elaborates that such a person feels that s/he "should be able to endure everything, to understand everything, to like everybody, to be always productive." (pp. 64–65)

In the final chapter Almas Merchant and Leon Hoffman invite us into the thinking of experienced child analysts. These analysts discuss the nuances and complexities of working with children through play, and of engaging collaterally with parents whilst simultaneously acknowledging the role parental difficulties can have in the production of a child's difficulties and they also reflect on the aspects of the analytic relationship they believe are influential in producing change. The analysts discuss issues of transference and countertransference, the creation of a play space, the co-construction of the analytic space, and the kinds of interpretations that are warranted in work with children and adolescents. The discussions are honest, as illustrated by one participant who confessed to the kind of countertransferential failure that is familiar to any of us who engage in this kind of work:

> One kid I was seeing, a little kid, he must have been eight or something. . . . And we would play [games] in the play room . . . he would obviously cheat and it must have really gotten to me, in terms of my countertransference, and at some point I made a comment to him . . . "gee I don't understand, how come every time . . . [I win] it doesn't count or it was a mistake" and he went out screaming to his mother who was waiting outside, "Doctor Maura called me a cheater" and that was the end of the case. And I clearly, did not empathize enough with his vulnerability.

Another analyst captures the complexity of analytic work with children in ways that are reminiscent of my own case study, mentioned earlier and discussed in chapter 1:

> I do largely think about the individual and the individual reacting with me, but in the individual reacting with me, I have been very influenced by infant dyadic work and attunement. . . . So, I really try to get attuned to my child patients and follow their lead and help them. So, it's like in ego psychology therapy with adults, where you try to let them keep expanding what they are able to say and talk about, it is trying to help kids explore with action and play, without it becoming disorganized or unraveling or over-stimulated. . . . It's

trying to stay in the sweet zone where their observing ego and planning ego and creative ego is functioning and they are expressing themselves and they are enjoying the experience of expressing themselves with a shared partner, who is not taking it all in the partner's direction but staying with them. It's very consistent with Greenspan's ideas of Floortime. It's a lot like a more grown up version of Floortime.

For readers with an appetite for more after completing this book, I hope you will also consider consulting the companion volume, *Psychodynamic Perspectives on Working with Children, Families and Schools*, also published by Jason Aronson.

REFERENCES

Agamben, G, (2005). *Homo sacer: Sovereign power and bare life*. Stanford, CA: Stanford University Press.

Biesta, G. (2007). Why "what works" won't work: Evidence-based practice and the democratic deficit in educational research. *Educational Theory, 57*, 1, 1–22.

Fassin, D. (2010). Ethics of survival: A democratic approach to the politics of life. *Humanity: An International Journal of Human Rights, Humanitarianism, and Development, 1*, 1, 81–95.

Hesse, E., & Main, M. (2000). Disorganized infant, child, and adult attachment: Collapse in behavioral and attentional strategies. *Journal of the American Psychoanalytic Association, 48*, 1097–1127.

Jonze, S. (2009). *Where the Wild Things Are*. (DVD): Warner Brothers.

O'Loughlin, M. (2013). Reclaiming genealogy, memory and history: The psychodynamic potential for reparative therapy in contemporary South Africa. In C. Smith, G. Lobban, & M. O'Loughlin (Eds.), *Psychodynamic Psychotherapy in Contemporary South Africa: Theory, Practice, and Policy Perspectives*. Johannesburg, SA: Wits University Press.

O'Loughlin, M. (2012a). Countering the rush to medication: Psychodynamic, intergenerational, and cultural considerations in understanding children's distress. In U. S. Nayar (Ed.), *International Handbook on Mental Health of Children and Adolescents: Culture, Policy & Practices*. Delhi, India: Sage.

O'Loughlin, M. (2012b). Trauma trails from Ireland's Great Hunger: A psychoanalytic inquiry. In B. Willock, R. Curtis, & L. Bohm (Eds.), *Loneliness and Longing: Psychoanalytic Reflections*. New York: Routledge

O'Loughlin, M. (2010a). Ghostly presences in children's lives: Toward a psychoanalysis of the social. In M. O'Loughlin & R. Johnson (Eds.), *Imagining children otherwise: Theoretical and critical perspectives on childhood subjectivity*. New York: Peter Lang Publishing.

O'Loughlin, M. (2010b, October). Reclaiming a liberatory vision for psychoanalysis. In symposium *The Psychologies of Liberation: Clinical, Critical and Pedagogical Perspectives* presented at *Annual Meeting of Association of Psychoanalysis, Culture & Society*. New Jersey: Rutgers University.

O'Loughlin, M. (2009a). *The subject of childhood*. New York: Peter Lang Publishing.

O'Loughlin, M. (2009b). An analysis of collective trauma among Indigenous Australians and a suggestion for intervention. *Australasian Psychiatry, 17*, 33–36.

O'Loughlin, M. (2008). Radical hope or death by a thousand cuts? The future for Indigenous Australians. *Arena Journal, 29/30*, 175–202.

O'Loughlin, M. (2007). On losses that are not easily mourned. In L. Bohm, R. Curtis, & B. Willock (Eds.), *Psychoanalysts' Reflections on Deaths and Endings: Finality, Transformations, New Beginnings*. New York: Routledge.

O'Loughlin, M. (2006). On knowing and desiring children: The significance of the unthought known. In G. Boldt & P. Salvio (Eds.), *Love's return: Psychoanalytic essays on childhood teaching and learning*. New York: Routledge.

O'Loughlin, M., & Charles, M. (2012). Psychiatric survivors, psychiatric treatments, and societal prejudice: An inquiry into the experience of an extremely marginal group. In G. Cannella & S. Steinberg (Eds.), *Critical Qualitative Research Reader*. New York: Peter Lang Publishing.

O'Loughlin, M., & Johnson, R. (Eds.). (2010). *Imagining children otherwise: Theoretical and critical perspectives on childhood subjectivity*. New York: Peter Lang Publishing.

O'Loughlin, M., & Merchant, A. (2012, June). Working obliquely with children. *Journal of Infant, Child & Adolescent Psychotherapy, 11*, 149–159.

Stepansky, P. (2009). *Psychoanalysis at the margins*. New York: Other Press Professional.

Watkins, H., & Shulman, H. (2008). *Toward psychologies of liberation*. New York: Palgrave Macmillan.

Chapter One

The Uses of Psychoanalysis

Michael O'Loughlin

BEING A CHILD

I am sitting with my class viewing Eleanor Longden's (n.d.) story of her catastrophic descent into severe psychosis and subsequent recovery. I am struck by her resilience, and struck especially by her acknowledgment that her recovery was in large part a matter of luck. After years of abusive psychiatric treatment she met Pat Bracken, a humane psychiatrist, who assisted her in recognizing the possibility that she had value as a person and, eventually, in recognizing that she had agency in shaping her own path to recovery. Her story is haunting and inspiring. But then a doubting voice creeps into my awareness, questioning the wisdom of starting this chapter autobiographically: surely my story will not measure up. Perhaps I have not suffered enough to impress.

I come home and sit in my consulting room with an adult patient who has returned to treatment after a long absence. As all psychotherapy patients do, she knows me probably at least as well as I do her. Listening to her recap her history of childhood trauma and anguish this week, after telling me last week about the anguish in her professional life because of the sadism and irrationality of some of her colleagues, I am struck by the parallel between past and present. I make the intellectual observation that Freud, attentive to people's tendency to recapitulate painful experiences, labeled this phenomenon the repetition compulsion. I go on listening and finally, sentient to her suffering, I ask if she ever does anything to take special care of herself. "Like what?" she challenges me. "Like a day treatment at a spa," I fumble a reply. She bursts out laughing at my preposterous suggestion: "You'd never treat yourself to a day at a spa. Admit it!" she says. She is all too correct. Another ghost has tapped me on the shoulder.

Although it is rarely addressed in the public record, those of us with an interest in children have reasons for our preoccupations. Mine, I think, are rooted in existential loneliness, gnawing anxiety, and a tentativeness about my place in the world that, while not absolutely preventing me from taking leaps of imagination, can make the psychic cost of such leaps very high. While Eleanor Longden uses the term recovery, she is as acutely aware as I am that recovery does not mean cure, or banishment of pain. Rather, it means taking ownership of our experience, mourning our losses as Alice Miller (1997) would have it, and, in the words of Wilfred Bion (1994), developing a capacity to "learn from experience." How, I wonder, can we sensitize adults to creating emotionally facilitative spaces in which children can grow to, as I put it elsewhere, "imagine themselves otherwise" (O'Loughlin & Johnson, 2010)? How can we sensitize adults to the deep concerns that may preoccupy children's minds? I think for example of the vulnerability of some of the children in Joanna Lipper's (1996) filmed portraits of children and I cannot forget the little girl that Alex Moore brings to us in chapter 14 of this volume:

> Yeah. [And] you can't concentrate, because there's something in your head and it stays there. [. . .] It's a bit like when my dad died and I came back to school. It was really difficult. . . . I kept on thinking what my mum was doing, because I stayed with my mum for a week at home.

Childhood is complicated by the lack of a reference point. As an adult I can measure my progress by life indicators that give me a sense of how well I measure up against various reference groups. However, for the most part children live their lives. Rumination on living is not a feature of the terrain of most children's lives, though the constant press for objective success and comparative evaluation in schools undoubtedly initiates a comparative referential process way too early. Thus, for each child, the boundary of possibility, and indeed normality, is defined by the circumstances of their own childhood . . . unless, of course, they are lucky enough to encounter believing mirrors that enable them to expand their identificatory possibilities and imagine themselves otherwise. Boris Cyrulnik (2005) refers to such mutative existential moments of meeting as "silent but deeply meaningful encounters" (pp. 62–65). Children who engage in excessive rumination—such as the little girl I saw in my office recently who fears falling asleep because she is thinking of death—are brought to therapists because we worry that such premature spectral preoccupations are burdensome and inhibiting.

One of the core strengths of psychoanalysis is the notion that the talking cure is about much more than mere verbalization. Judy Atkinson (2002), for example, speaks of lore, and of a catastrophic condition of lorelessnesss for people who have had the continuity of their genealogical filiations or life stories ruptured. While psychoanalysis is about the recuperation of ruptured or severed narrative, this narrative is not necessarily available to consciousness and hence readily speakable. As Prophecy Coles (2011) aptly noted, we are subject to "uninvited guests from unremembered pasts" who can drop by unannounced and linger for a brief visit or a protracted sojourn. Understanding our pasts, therefore, requires more than merely retelling narrative. It requires attention to the spectral presences and unvoiced aspects of our experience that seek expression. Rumination often begins precisely because we are perplexed by intrusive voices or images, or because we experience somatic reactions that surprise us. Why does my child patient, Joe,[1] open and shut the toilet seat precisely twenty-four times before using the toilet? Why does my adult patient, Janine, have a particular pattern to turning off the apartment lights before sleeping? Why does Carolyn Ramsay have a compelling need to feed people (see O'Loughlin, 2012a)? Why has Glenn, now twenty-two, been hearing voices since age ten, and why has Derek been hearing voices since age four? Why did young Aparna become selectively mute? Why did little Maria stab a chicken to death in her farmyard? Why do I suffer claustrophobia, and why must I accumulate pots of jam in far greater quantities than any "normal" person might need (see O'Loughlin, 2010a)? Analysts view the process of rebuilding narrative capacity as about understanding the messages of particular symptoms as much as it is about listening to verbal accounts of patient lives. As Davoine and Gaudillière (2004) note in the epigraph to the title of their book, *History Beyond Trauma*, "Whereof one cannot speak, thereof one cannot stay silent." We either speak of our symptoms or we are spoken by them in the elegant but disguised communication of the messages from our body; in the eccentricities of our ways of being; and in the preoccupations that constitute neuroses, compulsions, obsessions, and even psychosis.

Clues to my own childhood, and hence to a sensibility toward children that has drawn me to psychoanalysis, can therefore be found in my recollections of my childhood; in my reconstruction of my childhood through fragments such as family lore, photographs, and objects; and through my evolving sensitivity to what Christopher Bollas (1987) calls the "unthought knowns" that are silently but insistently expressed through my body and my demeanor. The work of exhuming shards of my life has been slow and painful (e.g., O'Loughlin, 2007, 2009a, 2010a, 2012a, in press) but it has released me from a silence that had imprisoned me in writer's block and a hesitance to put my ideas forth for many years. The signifiers of my difficulty are unmistakable. I wrote in one paper of unexpectedly receiving some long-forgotten photographs from my childhood as a Christmas gift from my sister, and becoming suddenly enmeshed in a depressive sadness. In the week that I have been incubating the ideas that are becoming the introduction to this chapter I have had dreams every night that either evoke the punitiveness of my family's reaction to my book *The Subject of Childhood* (2009a), or that have activated somatic responses that cause me to experience the kind of anxiety that produces panic. Are such unruly, uninvited guests to be ignored? Ought they be banished through medication? Or should they, perhaps, be embraced as signifiers not only of childhood loss but as potential harbingers of meaningful adult existential purpose? Derek Wolcott, speaking of the fragmentation of the Antilles through colonial conquest, remarked in his Nobel acceptance speech, that sometimes the vase that is shattered and re-built possesses a very special beauty: "Break a vase, and the love that reas-sembles the fragments is stronger than the love which took its symmetry for granted when it was whole. The glue that fits the pieces is the sealing of its original shape . . . and if the pieces are disparate, ill-fitting, they contain more pain than their original sculpture" (1992, unpaged). This metaphor captures both the love and the pain of the journey to self-recovery.

My infancy did not get off to an auspicious start. Born with a severe gastric disorder, I was frequently hospitalized during my first two years and my parents were dissuaded from visiting too often as their visits "were too upsetting for me." Saved emotionally, perhaps, by a nurse who became an object of significance for me, I survived, and, despite having gone into ar-rested development, my life path eventually resumed its course. Just like Colin, the invalid boy in Frances Hodgson Burnett's (1987) *The Secret Gar-den*, I had a delicate disposition throughout my childhood. However, instead of acquiring a tyrannical persona as the aristocratic Colin did, I gained a rather tenuous foothold on life. My brother's oppositionality could easily have arisen from his struggle to survive as a three- and four-year-old in our family during the preoccupying time of my illness. However, living with the difficulty produced by the resulting conflicts and tensions at home exacerbat-ed my anxiety as well as my concern for my parents. This, coupled with family poverty and the sequelae of intergenerationally inherited trauma in my family (see O'Loughlin, 2007, 2009a, 2010a, 2012a), as well as my own sense of the weight of my illness on the family, all conspired to pull me toward a parentified stance. From her research into children of the Holocaust, Louise Kaplan (1995) notes that because of their acute attunement to the suffering of those around them, some children redirect the libidinal invest-ments that should drive their own developmental trajectory, using that libidi-nal energy, instead, to allow them to serve as caretakers to wounded others. Such children seek to take care of depressive parents, and they often become the peacemakers in family conflicts. Andre Green's (Green, 2001; Kohon, 1999) discussion of the introjections of the depressed mother reflects a simi-lar dynamic, as does Edward Emery's (2002) writing on ghostly interjects. Children with such acute sensibilities, therefore, often become symptom bearers—the carriers of their families' difficulties.

I became that child. I became dutiful, concerned, anxious to a fault. In-stead of responding in externalizing ways such as becoming oppositional or enraged, I internalized the experience. Some of it became sublimated in my parentifying preoccupations, and some produced the somatic and psychic symptoms that I used to manage my anxiety. These are the forebears of the ghosts that still tap me on the shoulder today when primal anxiety or early embodied memories are aroused. Like Eleanor Longden, I too got lucky. Perhaps it was because of my intellectual aptitude. More likely, perhaps, my over-identification with my mother allowed me to absorb not only her depressive parts but also her passion for reading—her mode of escape. Either way, a passion for reading became my passport to worlds of possibility, sensibility, and imagination. It began as a literal escape: "Look at Michael. His head is always stuck in a book." Then it became a source of cultural capital and prestige for my parents as I earned a scholarship to secondary school. Eventually it allowed me to pursue a career in the academy. As I noted in earlier writing (O'Loughlin, 2009a), this gift was not an unalloyed blessing. Burdened by my father's painfully limited proficiency in literacy— produced by an appalling lack of access to education during his childhood— my identification with him caused me to have profound ambivalence about my emergent intellectual capacities as I feared that I would overshadow him. This served to underline my tentativeness about claiming my place in the world, and unfortunately, it did so in the area of intellectual achievement, the arena in which I had the greatest potential for success.

And Then I Went to School . . .

As I noted in *The Subject of Childhood*, my early school experience in a rural Irish school was far from idyllic:

> For the most part, my schooling mirrored the kind of experience described by Charles Dickens (1854/1994) in hard times. The teacher was not the subject supposed to know. The teacher did know. The children were ignorant recipients of the teacher's knowledge. As Oliver Goldsmith stated in the village schoolmaster, a poem from my childhood, "And still they gaz'd, and still the wonder grew, that one small head could carry all he knew" (Goldsmith, 1770/ 2003). The environment in which our mastery of skills and facts took place was crafted to maximize anxiety and fear so that we were neurotically focused entirely on the demand of the teacher. At first, avoidance of punishment and the winning of approval were all that mattered. Later, the emphasis deftly shifted to the pursuit of grades and credentials as means of satisfying external demand. Apart from acquiring a high capacity for conformity and a high level of the kind of neurotic personality characteristics described so ably by Karen Horney (1991) and Harry Stack Sullivan (1968), the subjective possibilities were abysmal. Did you get it done? Did you get it right? How many did you get wrong? These were the trembling queries we posed to each other. And as for the catastrophic consequences of failure, these came in the form of the daily ritual of Sín amach do lábh! [Open up the palm of your hand] as we

waited for the delivery of slaps from the teacher's rod, a switch that one of us
had personally been ordered to pluck for him from a nearby ash tree. Anxiety.
Fear. Humiliation. Anxiety. Fear. Humiliation. Anxiety. Fear. Humiliation.
Annihilation . . . (2009a, p.58)

So, here I am, an anxious, nail-biting child, sitting in a small rural school
where teachers meted out brutal corporal punishment on a whim. In my
junior infants (pre-kindergarten) class, I read the entire "Dick and Jane"
reading primer the morning it was issued, and I did not receive another piece
of reading material for the whole year. I recall that I chewed so much of that
book that almost half of each page was gnawed out of existence before the
year was over. Max Van Manen (1986) argues in the tone of teaching, that
not only does every child need to be seen, every child needs to experience
being seen. This was not to be. There was no place for the "silent and deeply
meaningful encounters" that Boris Cyrulnik (2005) so strongly suggests are
critical to our capacity to experience recognition. I lived in a world of misrecognition. We were only seen whenever we were perceived as deviant, and
then the punishment was unequivocal.

This climate of willful emotional annihilation, together with a tolerance
for bullying, took an enormous tool on many children. My suffering was by
no means the most egregious, not least because my academic abilities protected me from the worst excesses of teacher wrath. Nevertheless, just like
the protagonist Little Boy in Patrick Chamoiseau's (1997) *School Days*, for
me the school was an anxiety-provoking and even dangerous place. Lacking
the capacity to convert my hurt into rage or self-destructive oppositionality
the way my brother did, and lacking any kind of receptive listener to receive
my vulnerability, I became susceptible to bullying and I was left with no
place to which I might turn for relief. Why did the teachers not see me? Why
were they not attuned to my suffering? Why was there no space in the school
where other children and I could inscribe our lives and find our paths? Was it
the case that the adults who supposedly taught us, just like the teacher in
Chamoiseau's school days, were so out of touch with their own inner lives
that they could not serve as containers for our anxieties, nor as attuned
listeners to our spoken and unspoken—and perhaps even unspeakable—narratives? As I noted in *The Subject of Childhood*, although I liked to read, my
capacity for questioning and imagining was very tentative, and the foreclosed
pedagogy of the school almost murdered this questioning child and almost
killed his capacity to dream. As it happened, I kept my dreams secret and so
they survived, but putting a foot forward to express my desire, achieve my
dreams, or claim my place, was for too long unthinkable.

And then I became a teacher, a psychologist, and psychoanalyst who, for
forty years, has been seeking reparative opportunities for children and, by
extension, for the unrequited child within.

BEING WITH CHILDREN EXISTENTIALLY
AND THERAPEUTICALLY

In thinking then of what might be curative for the array of childhood difficulties that cause children to show up for therapy, my own life experience suggests that the provision of a facilitiative space with minimal demand is most likely to prove useful in allowing the child the opportunity to articulate desire or, at a minimum, voice the pressures of external parental or teacher demand. If being a certain way produces difficulty for the child, it would seem that a space that values unconstrained being might prove advantageous in promoting the possibility of becoming. A therapeutic encounter, therefore, is an opportunity for existential meeting, unencumbered by the structured obligations and demands that are invariably present in families and schools: "If you decide to come here," I tell every child at our first meeting, "all I ask is that you show up. You can talk if you want to, but you don't have to. You can play if you like, but you don't have to. You can draw if you feel like drawing, but you don't have to. You don't have to do anything at all except be here, and I will be here with you." We live in a world where the culture of therapeutic prescription, just like the culture of prescriptive schooling, is oriented toward instrumental quick fixes—often embodied in acronyms such as ABA, CBT, and so forth. I spend a lot of time with trainee psychologists exhorting them to "do nothing" and to suppress the urge "to do something" when a child presents for therapy. What if what the child needs from us is not a solution or an answer, but rather a place to pose the question and to experience unencumbered thought? Bion's exhortation to the analyst to listen "without memory, desire, or understanding" and to cultivate a state of reverie (Symington, 1996) is highly applicable to the work of a child therapist seeking to cultivate a posture of nonjudgmental receptivity and hence an existential meeting with a child.

Inherent in this approach is an acknowledgment of the importance of an existential encounter in promoting authenticity and wellness. Eleanor Longden's moment of insight came when, after identifying herself to psychiatrist Pat Bracken as "a paranoid schizophrenic," he replied, "I didn't ask you what others say you are. I want to know who you are" or words to that effect. This existential acknowledgment of personhood—Buber's I-Thou relationship—begins the moment a child shows up at my office door and we meet, and it concludes with a parting greeting when we leave. In the worlds of hospitals, schools and clinics, where the impersonal, the instrumental, and the objective too often prevail—what Didier Fassin (2010), following Giorgio Agamben (2005) calls "the bare life"—a therapeutic or pedagogic space can still hold out the possibility of hospitality (Nouwen, 1986), phenomenological validation of personhood (Van Manen, 1986), and the restorative possibility of existential mirroring that comes from being in relation in a meaningful way

(Cyrulnik, 2005). This, in itself, is inherently restorative, and may be a major contributor to recovery.

Psychoanalysis, of course, addresses the unconscious. The cultivation of a state of receptivity or reverie in the therapist and the creation of a zero-demand space that mirrors Freud's original idea of free association combine to create a space where the unconscious of the child can emerge. If a child comes in ventriloquating in the *parole vide* ("empty speech") of external parental or school demand, we seek to engage that child with the possibility of *parole pleine* ("full speech") that comes from the claiming of desire. The "do nothing" imperative alluded to earlier comes from the certain knowledge that given a blank canvas, either the child's desire will emerge, or the limiting conditions of demand will be put on display. The analyst then, animated by the child's unconscious, gives it back to the child in a way that re-animates the child's subjectivity and makes a new conversation possible. Donald Winnicott's clinical work, and particularly his development of the Squiggle game, offers powerful illustrations of the kinds of conversations that are possible in the potential space between a child and an attuned therapist (Winnicott, 1971a, b; 1977; see also Farley, 2011; O'Loughlin, 2006, 2012b; O'Loughlin & Merchant, 2012).

Mai: Animating the Elusive Subject

By way of illustration I will present an excerpt from my clinical work with a child with significant autism. Because of the emotional communication difficulties involved in severe autism it represents a limit case for the possibilities of psychoanalytic therapy—a therapy that is premised on the possibilities of emotional receptivity and communication. Mai is just six. Her parents brought her for therapy because they felt something was missing in the panoply of therapies and programs she received at school. Mai is echolalic, and rarely makes eye contact. She can be affectionate without boundaries: "Hug?" she will utter effusively, hands outstretched. Like so many children with autistic syndromes, eye contact appears frightening for her. However, unlike many of the other similar children I have worked with, Mai is not suffused with evident anxiety. She is impulsive. She laughs a lot. And, of course, she cannot be easily maneuvered into contact.

As I noted recently, and consistent with the work of Michael Balint (1992) on the basic fault, and of French analysts in the Lacanian tradition, following Maud Mannoni (1970, 1999; cf. also Danon-Boileau, 2001, Mathelin, 1999), I work obliquely with children (O'Loughlin & Merchant, 2012). Laurent Danon-Boileau (2001) advances a beautiful image of the analyst as a drowsy nanny, waiting to be aroused by the unconscious of the child. I like to think of the analyst as a limp puppet who can only become animated by the subjectivity of the child, and who, in return, reanimates the child's subjectivity with corresponding animation. Adopting a position of reverie, the child analyst's goal is receptivity, not active interpretation. However, there is a mindful aliveness to every child, no matter how acute their communication difficulties may be. Writing with Ally Merchant, I recently described the rationale for this work as follows:

> In keeping with Mannoni (1999), we see our goal in working with children as "enabling them to survive as subjects" (Brenkman, 1999, p. xxiv). We hope, following Mannoni, to enable each child to "refind the play space of child-hood" (Mannoni, 1999, p. 47)— a space that we imagine as similar to the space so artfully depicted in Joanna Lipper's (1996) filmed portraits of the depth of children's yearnings, losses and longings. Critical to our approach is to create a space as free of demand as possible, a space where the child may, perhaps for the first time, experience the possibility of their own desire, a process that is initiated through the experience of being seen in some deep existential way (Cyrulnik, 2005; Van Manen, 1986).
>
> It is vital that the analyst have access to his or her own unconscious in order to animate vital aspects of the unconscious of the child—an animation that ought to be free from contaminating demand that the child become a certain way. The analyst, therefore, adopts a languid posture, a posture charac-terized by Danon-Boileau (2001) as that of a "drowsy nanny" or limp puppet. Having animated the child's desire the limp analyst then waits for the child's unconscious to reanimate the analyst's interest. This reanimation leads to new aliveness in the analyst which validates the existence and efficacy of the child's unconscious and allows for a new dynamic to emerge. Such animations are to be found in gestures such as a glance, a provocation, a joke, a sharing, or even the simplest expression of desire—all gestures that are signifiers pointing to the animation of an attunement between the subjectivity of the child and the subjectivity of the analyst. (O'Loughlin & Merchant, 2012, p. 154–55)

What then does Mai offer? I have a toy motorcycle which can be made to run by pulling a toothed strip across its gear wheel. Mai squeals in delight, and after a few attempts where I launch the motorcycle and retrieve it, reminis-cent of Freud's fort da game, I say "Get me the bike" in an animated voice, and she retrieves it. Now she can play, and until she tires of the game she retrieves the motorcycle, all the while verbally articulating a demand: "More." Likewise, I have a car launcher that launches Matchbox cars across the floor. After one or two observations, I animate my voice and say "Get the car" and Mai retrieves it. Soon she is pushing the launch button: "Push." We are playing with an assembly of gears, and unable to fit the gears on the spindle, Mai surprises me by taking my hand and pushing it onto the gears, clearly signaling intentionality. She can be tickled, and my threat of tickling invites excited anticipation and uproarious laughter. Wheeling a toy car across her forearm gives her the chills. She asks for more. We are indeed meeting, however fleetingly. The late Stanley Greenspan's Floortime embod-ies many of the same characteristics:

Floortime meets children where they are and builds upon their strengths and abilities through creating a warm relationship and interacting. It challenges them to go further and to develop who they are rather than what their diagnosis says. In Floortime, you use this time with your child to excite her interests, draw her to connect to you, and challenge her to be creative, curious, and spontaneous—all of which move her forward intellectually and emotionally. (As children get older, Floortime essentially morphs into an exciting, back-and-forth time of exploring the child's ideas.)

For any age child, you do three things: Follow your child's lead, that is, enter the child's world and join in their emotional flow; challenge her to be creative and spontaneous; and expand the action and interaction to include all or most of her senses and motor skills as well as different emotions. (http://stanleygreenspan.com/, retrieved 9/22/12)

The animation of subjectivity in persons with autistic disorders, and the reanimation of subjectivity in person with depression or psychosis is the inverse of so much of what passes for psychotherapy or pedagogy in society. If external demand is intrusive, why offer treatments that privilege externality? Is Boris Cyrulnik (2005) not correct that an invitation to enter the existential space is what is required? This invitation requires the acutely attuned receptivity of an adult who values unconscious expression and receives it in whatever guise it chooses to manifest itself. This does not make Mai an easy patient. As anyone familiar with Catherine Mathelin's (1999) work in France, or the work of the Tavistock clinicians in the United Kingdom (e.g., Alvarez, 1992, 2012; Alvarez & Edwards, 2001; Alvarez & Reid, 1999; Briggs, 2002; Mitrani & Mitrani, 1997; Rhode & Klauber, 2004; Rustin et al., 1997; Tustin, 1992) knows, such moments of existential possibility are swathed in impulsivity, flight, disappointment, terror, and despair. However, receptivity—including the metabolization of the experience and the reanimation of the subjectivity of the child—would appear to be the only human antidote to such feelings. Mai is responding tentatively to this invitation, and her family, too, is entering the circle of receptivity and animation, allowing them to experience hope for the possibility of deeper human conversation with Mai.

BEING WITH CHILDREN PEDAGOGICALLY

In articulating a role for psychoanalysis as an underpinning of pedagogy, I will mention some elements that would not have been out of place in Anna Freud's (1933/1979) *Psychoanalysis for Teachers and Parents*, written some eighty years ago. However, in keeping with my work on the development of what I called elsewhere (2010a) a psychoanalysis of the social, I will argue for a broadening of the uses of psychoanalysis in ways that can allow it to serve as one of the underpinnings not only of an emotionally focused, humane, person-centered pedagogy, but also of a pedagogy that has a capacity to address also the sociohistorical constitutedness of subjectivity and hence the sociopolitical purposes of schooling and the possibility of what Paulo Freire (1969, 1970) termed "education as the practice of freedom."

Phenomenology of School Life:
On Transference and Countertransference

"Absolute rubbish Laddie," the contemptuous schoolmaster snarls at Pink, the incongruously named boy, provoking guffaws of uneasy laughter from his fellow sufferers, in Alan Parker's (1980/2005) movie rendition of *Pink Floyd: The Wall*. The only saving grace for his classmates in Pink's humiliation, is that their own moment of reckoning has been postponed, though, all the while, they are vigilantly attending to the constricted emotional contours and severely delimited imaginative boundaries of their classroom world. If the task of growing up is that of becoming a subject, how is a child to engage this task if the only epistemological and emotional possibilities available are ones that require subjection, as opposed to the fleshing out of subjectivity (cf. Butler, 1997)? My college students, ever compliant, come close to the whiteboard at my invitation and squat on the carpet, much as schoolchildren might do at meeting time or story time. I draw a tiny stick figure of a five-year-old-child, with a voluminous backpack attached. We spend most of the next hour fleshing out that backpack, listing all of the possible characteristics that constitute the child's metaphorical baggage on the first day of school. We talk for a while about the emotional, social, and cultural characteristics of particular children, and how easily this particularity can be barred from the discourses of schooling. An important contribution of psychoanalysis, therefore, is posing the possibility of pedagogy as an intersubjective process—one in which children, fully immersed in the elements of their own latent subjectivities, can be invited to a meeting. This meeting does not seek to specify a destination point. Rather it seeks to invite the child to a journey into being, to experiencing the possibility of feeling seen, and of feeling that new forms of becoming are possible.

Continuing the inquiry, I add a second more formidable stick figure, this one representing the teacher. This time the appended backpack is even larger, and it is graphically evident that for whatever baggage of dispositions, feelings, attributes, and prejudices a child may bring to the meeting, the teacher brings a more deeply layered and textured set of experiences based on simply having lived longer. The teacher is freighted with expectations, too, owing to the very fact of having chosen a career that entails being with children. What unrequited needs and unaddressed longings is this teacher seeking to recapitulate or repair? I speak with my students of the inner child of the teacher, and of the desire to be loved so typically exhibited by young teachers, who, as

Rudolf Ekstein (1989) noted, are at an early stage of their own journey—a journey that will entail moving from teaching for love toward a mature love of teaching. In psychoanalytic parlance, the two backpacks represent the transference and countertransference aspects of the pedagogical relationship.

While this is soil that is well tilled in the psychoanalytic literature, relatively little attention has been paid to either the powerful transferences of children toward teachers or the concomitant power of teachers' emotional predispositions toward children.[2] My students and I speak about recognizing behavioral manifestations and visible psychological dispositions such as anxiety, anger, oppositionality, defensiveness, clinginess, withdrawal, and so forth as mere signifiers for what lies beneath. I pose for them the question of what is euphemistically called "classroom management" not as a problem of demanding compliance but rather as an opportunity for the construction of a communal place—a community in Alfie Kohn's (1996) terms—in which individual and group emotional and intellectual work is possible. Anna Freud recognized early on that such work could not happen unless teachers embarked on their own emotional journeys. Sadly, with technocratic, information-oriented teacher education, few teachers are given such an invitation. Too often pedagogy is presented as being about instrumental teachers acting instrumentally on children. No wonder my students are puzzled when I first suggest that whenever we upbraid or sanction a miscreant child it has very little to do with the actual child standing before us either trembling or defiant, and a lot to do with the unaddressed needs of the child within each of us that is evoking our responses. We read Haim Ginott's (2003) *Between Parent and Child* and Marilyn Watson's (2003) *Learning to Trust* to try to develop a counter-imaginary to the prevailing ethos of children as chopped meat in the sausage factory, so ably depicted in the school scene in *The Wall*.

Finally, despite my limited artistic abilities, I add one more element to the drawing on the whiteboard. This time I sketch a brick wall, depicting the institutional forces at work to impede the capacity of well-intentioned teachers to engage in a pedagogy of love and possibility in an age of supposed accountability and external control over teachers and hence over the lives of children. Addressing the teacher's pedagogical stance is difficult because of the widespread recognition that schooling is typically controlled by political authorities and that teachers, irrespective of their individual good intentions, are inserted into larger discursive systems that are typically designed to preserve the status quo, maintain structural inequalities, and perpetuate privilege. Persistent critique of life in schools[3] appears to have yielded little evident effect on pedagogical practices. In fact, with the push toward standardization, accountability, and putatively "evidence-based" approaches to assessing educational outcomes, it often feels like education is losing whatever gains were made during more progressive eras. It is increasingly difficult for teachers to find the space to engage children with the subjective, imaginative, and political possibilities of making meaning and identifying satisfying life paths. Nevertheless, it has always been individual teachers in their classrooms who have shown the courage to teach in children's interests, as Herbert Kohl illustrated in *36 Children* (1967) and in his later works (see http://herbertkohleducator.com). Teachers who yearn for more control over their work must be able to make their case in terms of the evident benefits for students of the alternative pedagogies they advocate. A progressive psychoanalytic vision of pedagogy offers one possible underpinning for a humane, student-centered, imaginative, and sociohistorically located pedagogy.

Reading the Narrative and Social Bases of Lived Experience: Toward a Critical Depth Pedagogy

Earlier I made a fleeting reference to Judy Atkinson's (2002) concepts of lore and lorelessness. As Atkinson's writing, and the writing of French psychoanalysts Françoise Davoine and Jean-Max Gaudillière (2004) illustrates, all humans are born into life narratives and ancestral inheritances that give texture and meaning to daily life. In the case of indigenous Australians, Atkinson argues that severance from ancestral epistemologies and spiritual practices has produced a condition of lorelessness that is quite catastrophic (see also O'Loughlin, 2008, 2009b). Her work complements that of Kai Erikson (1976) who showed how the forced disbanding of the community of Buffalo Creek, Virginia, after a mining disaster, caused a severance of social bonds that led to traumatic rupture in community life and in the cohesion of individual lives. Lacking the kind of continuity that comes from attachment to land, lore, and spirit, people encounter considerable psychic difficulty in simply going on being. Addressing attachment difficulties in families, Selma Fraiberg and colleagues tell us that every child is born into a family and society where the ghosts of the past "take up residence and conduct the rehearsal of the family tragedy from a tattered script" (1975, p. 165). Fraiberg and colleagues estimate that ruptures in child-rearing practices can be traced to family trauma originating as far back as ten generations.

The notion of rupture in narrative continuity or genealogical filiation (cf. Apfelbaum, 2002; O'Loughlin, in press), and an understanding of the role of ghosts, specters, and unvoiced trauma from both familial and historical pasts have been of great interest to psychoanalysts and others.[4] The crux of the matter is that unspeakable or unspoken trauma that cannot be worked through continues to move down the generations, producing "trauma trails" from the original injury that continue to assert themselves in the lives of descendants (Atkinson, 2002). Davoine and Gaudillière (2004) note that the consequences can be severe enough to produce madness in a future generation. Suffering that has not been experienced directly but that has been absorbed through intergenerational inheritance is quite intractable because it has no concrete referents in the life of the current bearer of the trauma and is therefore not amenable to any kind of rational analysis. Reparative work requires assisting an afflicted person in voicing the "unthought knowns" of their own experience, restoring genealogical filiation, and assisting the sufferer in stitching together the frayed or ruptured threads of family lineage and historical process, however painful the genealogical origins of the traumatic rupture may be. Ghosts and spectral shadows that haunt the psyche cannot be willed away. They can, however, be embraced, claimed, and spoken with. From an analytic perspective, drawing on Davoine and Gaudillière, I summed up the process this way:

> The task of analysis is to detect ruptures in social linkages because these are the moments that have produced the unsymbolised material—the unspoken and unspeakable events—that leave us with only the cryptic communication of the symptom as remnant. The process of recreating social linkages, reweaving ancestral and narrative threads of continuity, is one of taking "a piece of history that has escaped History" (Davoine & Gaudillière , p. 11) and assisting the patient in inscribing it into his or her personal history. Davoine and Gaudillière suggest that this is the most vital moment in clinical work, the moment when the therapist can create conditions for the return of the Real, the feeling of "nameless dread," the encounter with the ghost. They propose that the therapist become an "annalist," i.e., a chronicler of the moment when "the thread of speech may be radically cut" (p. 71), leaving the patient with unsymbolised experience. As Bollas (1987) noted, in discussing "the unthought known," our work is to bring patients for the first time to visit familiar places where they have dwelt for a very long time. "Regaining a foothold in history" (Davoine & Gaudillière, p. 47) is the antidote to dissociated or unsymbolised experience. Elsewhere Davoine and Gaudillière refer to the primary influence of the therapist as that of a curious other who reignites a process of "subjectivation," i.e., the possibility of becoming a subject, in the patient (p. 67). (O'Loughlin, 2013, pp. 257–58)

Turning then to pedagogy, a social-historical psychoanalytic approach calls for subjectivization as a primary goal. Pedagogy ought to provide opportunities for an intensive engagement with spoken and unspoken experience, with history, lore, ancestry, and imagination so that each child can enter into a dynamic relationship with the ruptures and gaps of the past, and with multiple possible futures. A minimal condition of depth pedagogy, therefore, is the reclamation of narrative threads and the location of children as subjects in history—people with genealogical filiations, narrative continuity, and a possibility for becoming that is informed by, but not constrained by, ancestral, historical, and familial legacies. Each child possesses a latent culturally constituted unconscious that embodies ancestral history and ways of being, as well as inherited traumas due to displacements, wars, genocides, familial trauma, and other forms of unspoken and unmetabolized suffering. Ought not a teacher be prepared to tap into these resources to help children better understand their locations in history?

From a pedagogical perspective, in addition to creating an inviting inter-subjective and emotionally secure dialogical space, teachers, "should understand how to evoke the unconscious in children through their own evocative presences. A teacher with a passion for myth, storytelling, drama, memory, and the wisdom of elders will draw these evocative knowledges into the classroom, and will elicit evocative responses from students that allow students to experience their own inner knowledges as namable and addressable" (O'Loughlin, 2009a, p. 160). This kind of work has resonance with the Freirean notion of a pedagogy grounded in generative themes (Freire, 1970) and in the idea of a political literacy embodied in the phrase "reading the word, reading the world" (Freire & Macedo, 1987). The radical potential of this kind of work, in keeping with the liberatory leanings of early psycho-analysis (cf. Danto, 2002; Moskowitz, 1996; O'Loughlin, 2010a; Watkins & Shulman, 2008) and of critical psychoanalytic practice today, is that it seeks to assist people in learning to question (Freire & Faundez, 1989), rather than giving them the illusion of understanding.

The notion of annalist implies a receptivity to documenting story in all its cultural forms, spoken and unspoken. The notion of analyst implies a receptivity to the unconscious and a capacity to give back thoughts that pose questions. Together they offer rich possibilities for an imaginative, genera-tive, located enactment of pedagogy.

NOTES

1. All patient names are changed, and any patient details are either disguised or presented as composite portraits to protect patient identity.

2. For some recent writing that addresses these issues see, for example Basch,1989; Britz-man, 1998, 2003, 2006, 2009, 2010; Cozzarelli & Silin, 1989; Littner, 1989; and Taubman, 2011. For a non-psychoanalytic but relevant study of teacher transference issues see Pianta, 1999.

3. For critiques of U.S. schooling see, for example, Kozol, 1985, 1990, 1992; MacLeod, 2008; Paley, 2005; and Polakow, 1992, 2000; in the United States, and for international cri-tiques see, for example, Freire,1970; Giroux, 2001, 2011; Goodman, 1966; Illich 2000; and McLaren, 2006.

4. See for example, Abraham & Torok, 1994; E. Balint, 1992; Coles, 2011; Davoine & Gaudillière, 2004; Derrida, 1994; Faimberg, 2005; Garon, 2004; Gordon, 1997; Pisano, 2012; Lear, 2006; O'Loughlin, 2010a, 2012a, 2013; Rogers, 2006.

REFERENCES

Abraham, N., & Torok, M. (1994). *The shell and the kernel.* [Edited, translated and with an Introduction by N. Rand]. Chicago: University of Chicago Press.

Agamben, G. (2005). *Homo sacer: Sovereign power and bare life.* Stanford, CA: Stanford University Press.

Alvarez, A. (2012). *The thinking heart: Three levels of psychoanalytic therapy with disturbed children*. London: Routledge.

Alvarez, A. (1992). *Live company: Psychoanalytic psychotherapy with autistic, borderline, deprived and abused children*. New York: Routledge.

Alvarez, A., & Edwards, J. (2001). *Being alive: Building on the work of Anne Alvarez*. New York: Routledge.

Alvarez, A., & Reid, S. (1999). *Autism and personality: Findings from the Tavistock Autism Workshop*. New York: Routledge .

Apfelbaum, E. (2002). Uprooted communities, silenced cultures and the need for legacy. In V. Walkerdine (Ed.), *Challenging subjects: Critical psychology for a new millennium*. New York: Palgrave.

Atkinson, J. (2002). *Trauma trails: Recreating song lines: The transgenerational effects of trauma in Indigenous Australia*. North Melbourne, Australia: Spinifex Press.

Balint, E. (1992). *Before I was I: Psychoanalysis and the imagination*. New York: Guilford Press.

Balint, M. (1992). *The basic fault: Therapeutic approaches to regression*. Evanston, IL: Northwestern University Press.

Basch, M. (1989). The teacher, the transference, and development. In K. Field, B. Cohler, & G. Wool (Eds.). *Learning and education: Psychoanalytic perspectives*. Madison, CT: International Universities Press.

Bion, W. (1994). *Learning from experience*. Northvale, NJ: Jason Aronson.

Bollas, C. (1987). *The shadow of the object: Psychoanalysis of the unthought known*. New York: Columbia University Press.

Briggs, A. (Ed.). (2002). *Surviving space: Papers on infant observation*. London: Karnac.

Britzman, D. (2010). *Freud and education*. New York: Routledge.

Britzman, D. (2009). *The very thought of education: Psychoanalysis and the impossible professions*. Albany: SUNY Press.

Britzman, D. (2006). *Novel education: Psychoanalytic studies of learning and not learning*. New York: Peter Lang Publishing.

Britzman, D. (2003). *After-education: Anna Freud, Melanie Klein and psychoanalytic histories of learning*. Albany: SUNY Press.

Britzman, D. (1998). *Lost subjects, contested objects: Toward a psychoanalytic inquiry of learning*. Albany: SUNY Press.

Butler, J. (1977). *The psychic life of power: Theories in subjection*. Paolo Alto: Stanford University Press.

Chamoiseau, P. (1997). *School days*. Lincoln: University of Nebraska Press.

Coles, P. (2011). *The uninvited guest from the unremembered past*. London: Karnac.

Cozarelli, L. & Silin, M. (1989). The effects of narcissistic transferences on the teaching-learning process. In K. Field, B. Cohler, & G. Wool (Eds.), *Learning and education: Psychoanalytic perspectives*. Madison, CT: International Universities Press.

Cyrulnik, B. (2005). *The whispering of ghosts: Trauma and resilience*. New York: Other Press.

Danon-Boileau, L. (2001). *The silent child: Bringing language to children who cannot speak*. London: Oxford University Press.

Danto, E. (2002). *Freud's free clinics: Psychoanalysis and social justice, 1918–1938*. New York: Columbia University Press.

Davoine, F., & Gaudillière, J-M. (2004). *History beyond trauma*. New York: Other Press.

Derrida, J. (1994). *Specters of Marx: The state of the debt, the work of mourning, and the new international*. New York: Routledge.

Ekstein, R. (1989). From the love of learning to the love of teaching. In K. Field, B. Cohler, & G. Wool (Eds.). *Learning and education: Psychoanalytic perspectives*. Madison, CT: International Universities Press.

Emery, E. (2002). The ghost in the mother: Strange attractors and impossible mourning. *Psychoanalytic Review, 89*, 2, 169–194.

Erikson, K. (1976). Loss of communality at Buffalo Creek. *American Journal of Psychiatry, 133*, 302–5.

Faimberg, H. (2005). *The telescoping of generations: Listening to the narcissistic links between generations.* London: Institute of Psychoanalysis.

Farley, L. (2011). Squiggle evidence: The child, the canvas, and the "negative labour" of history. *History and Memory, 23,* 2, 5–39.

Fassin, D. (2010). Ethics of survival: A democratic approach to the politics of life. *Humanity: An International Journal of Human Rights, Humanitarianism, and Development, 1,* 1, 81–95.

Fraiberg, S., Adelson, E., & Shapiro, V. (1975). Ghosts in the nursery. *Journal of the American Academy of Child Psychiatry, 14,* 387–421.

Freire, P. (1970). *Pedagogy of the oppressed.* New York: Continuum.

Freire, P., & Faundez, A. (1989). *Learning to question: A pedagogy of liberation.* New York: Continuum.

Freire, P., & Macedo, D. (1987). *Literacy: Reading the world.* Westport, CT: Bergin & Garvey.

Freire, P. (1969). *Education for critical consciousness.* New York: Continuum.

Freud, A. (1979 [1933]). *Psychoanalysis for teachers and parents.* New York: Norton.

Garon, J. (2004). Skeletons in the closet. *International Forum of Psychoanalysis, 13,* 84–92.

Ginott, H. (2003). *Between parent and child.* New York: Three Rivers Press.

Giroux, H. (2011). *On critical pedagogy (Critical Pedagogy Today).* New York: Continuum.

Giroux, H. (2001). *Stealing innocence: Corporate culture's war on children.* New York: Continuum.

Goodman, P. (1966). *Compulsory mis-education, and the community of scholars.* New York: Random House.

Gordon, A. (1997). *Ghostly matters: haunting and the sociological imagination.* Minneapolis: University of Minnesota Press.

Green, A. (2001). The dead mother. In A. Weller (trans.). *Life narcissism/death narcissism.* London, New York: Free Associations Books.

Hodgson Burnett, F. (1987). *The secret garden.* New York: Random House.

Illich, I. (2000). *Deschooling society.* New York: Marion Boyars Publishers.

Kaplan, L. (1995). *No voice is ever wholly lost: An exploration of the everlasting attachment between parent and child.* New York: Simon & Schuster.

Kohl, H. (1967). *36 children.* New York: Plume.

Kohn, A. (1996). *Beyond discipline: From compliance to community.* Alexandria, VA: ASCD.

Kohon, G. (Ed.). (1999). *The dead mother: The work of André Green.* London, New York: Routledge.

Kozol, J. (1992). *Savage inequalities: Children in America's schools.* New York: Harper Perennial.

Kozol, J. (1990). *The night is dark and I am far from home.* New York: Touchstone Books.

Kozol, J. (1985). *Death at an early age.* New York: Plume.

Lear, J. (2006). *Radical hope: Ethics in the face of cultural devastation.* Cambridge, MA: Harvard University Press.

Lipper, J. [Director]. (1996). *Inside out: Portraits of children.* [DVD]. Available at http://joannalipper.com/films_insideout.html.

Littner, N. (1989). Reflections of early childhood family experiences in the educational situation. In K. Field, B. Cohler, & G. Wool (Eds.), *Learning and education: Psychoanalytic perspectives.* Madison, CT: International Universities Press.

Longden, E. (n.d.). Knowing you, knowing you. [DVD]. Lewis, UK: Working to Recovery Limited. [Also viewable at http://www.youtube.com/watch?v=MB869Pk390Uon 9/26/12].

MacLeod. J. (2008). *Ain't no makin' it: Aspirations and attainment in a low-income neighborhood.* Boulder, CO: Westview.

Mannoni, M. (1999). *Separation and creativity: Refinding the lost language of childhood.* New York: Other Press.

Mannoni, M. (1970). *The child, his "illness," and the others.* London: Karnac.

Mathelin, C. (1999). *The broken piano: Lacanian psychotherapy with children.* New York: Other Press.

McLaren, P. (2006). *Life in schools: An introduction to critical pedagogy in the foundations of education* (5th Edition). New York: Pearson.

Miller, A. (1997). *The drama of the gifted child: The search for the true self.* New York: Basic Books.

Mitrani, T., & Mitrani, J. (1997). *Encounters with autistic states: A memorial tribute to Frances Tustin.* Northvale, NJ: Jason Aronson.

Moskowitz, M. (1996). The social conscience of psychoanalysis. In R. Perez Foster, M. Moskowitz, & R. Javier (Eds.), *Reaching across boundaries of culture and class: Widening the script of psychoanalysis.* Northvale, NJ: Jason Aronson.

Nouwen, H. (1986). *Reaching out: The three movements of the spiritual life.* New York: Doubleday.

O'Loughlin, M. (2013). Reclaiming genealogy, memory and history: The psychodynamic potential for reparative therapy in contemporary South Africa. In C. Smith, G. Lobban, & M. O'Loughlin (Eds.), *Psychodynamic psychotherapy in contemporary South Africa: Theory, practice, and policy perspectives.* Johannesburg, SA: Wits University Press.

O'Loughlin, M. (2012a). Trauma trails from Ireland's Great Hunger: A psychoanalytic inquiry. In B. Willock, R. Curtis, & L. Bohm (Eds.), *Loneliness and longing: Psychoanalytic reflections.* New York: Routledge

O'Loughlin, M. (2012b). Countering the rush to medication: Psychodynamic, intergenerational, and cultural considerations in understanding children's distress. In U. S. Nayar (Ed.), *International handbook on mental health of children and adolescents: Culture, policy & practices.* Delhi, India: Sage.

O'Loughlin, M. (2010a). Ghostly presences in children's lives: Toward a psychoanalysis of the social. In M. O'Loughlin & R. Johnson (Eds.), *Imagining children otherwise: Theoretical and critical perspectives on childhood subjectivity.* New York: Peter Lang Publishing.

O'Loughlin, M. (2010b). Reclaiming a liberatory vision for psychoanalysis. In symposium, *The Psychologies of Liberation: Clinical, Critical and Pedagogical Perspectives.* Presented at *Annual Meeting of Association for the Psychoanalysis of Culture and Society.* New Jersey: Rutgers University.

O'Loughlin, M. (2009a). *The subject of childhood.* New York: Peter Lang Publishing.

O'Loughlin, M. (2009b). An analysis of collective trauma among Indigenous Australians and a suggestion for intervention. *Australasian Psychiatry, 17,* 33–36.

O'Loughlin, M. (2008). Radical hope or death by a thousand cuts? The future for Indigenous Australians. *Arena Journal, 29/30,* 175–202.

O'Loughlin, M. (2007). On losses that are not easily mourned. In L. Bohm, R. Curtis, & B. Willock (Eds.), *Psychoanalysts' reflections on deaths and endings: Finality, transformations, new beginnings.* New York: Routledge

O'Loughlin, M. (2006). On knowing and desiring children: The significance of the unthought known. In G. Boldt & P. Salvio (Eds.), *Love's return: Psychoanalytic essays on childhood teaching and learning.* New York: Routledge.

O'Loughlin, M., & Johnson, R. (Eds.). (2010). *Imagining children otherwise: Theoretical and critical perspectives on childhood subjectivity.* New York: Peter Lang Publishing.

O'Loughlin, M., & Merchant, A. (2012, June). Working obliquely with children. *Journal of Infant, Child & Adolescent Psychotherapy, 11,* 149–59.

Paley, V. (2005). *A child's work: The importance of fantasy play.* Chicago: University of Chicago Press.

Parker, A. [Director]. (1980/2005). Pink Floyd: The Wall [DVD]. Sony Pictures.

Pianta, R. (1999). *Enhancing relationships between children and teachers.* Washington, DC: American Psychological Association.

Pisano, N. G. (2012). *Granddaughters of the Holocaust: Never forgetting what they didn't experience.* New York: Academic Studies Press.

Polakow, V. (2000). *The public assault on America's children: Poverty, violence, and juvenile injustice.* New York: Teachers College Press.

Polakow, V. (1992). *The erosion of childhood.* Chicago: University of Chicago Press.

Rhode, M., & Klauber, T. (2004). *The many faces of Asperger's Syndrome.* London: Karnac.

Rogers, A. (2006). *The unsayable: The hidden language of trauma.* New York: Random House.

Rustin, M., Rhode, M., Dubinsky, A., & Dubinsky, H. (Eds.). (1997). *Psychotic states in children*. London: Routledge.

Symington, N. (1996). *The clinical thinking of Wilfred Bion*. London: Routledge.

Taubnan, P. (2011). *Disavowed knowledge: Psychoanalysis, education, and teaching*. New York: Routledge.

Tustin, F. (1992). *Autistic states in children*. London: Routledge.

Van Manen, M. (1986). *The tone of teaching*. Portsmouth, NH: Heinemann.

Watkins, M., & Shulman, H. (2008). *Toward psychologies of liberation*. New York: Palgrave Macmillan.

Watson, M. (2003). *Learning to trust: Transforming difficult elementary classrooms through developmental discipline*. San Francisco: Jossey-Bass.

Winnicott, D. W. (1977). *The Piggle: An account of the psychoanalytic treatment of a little girl*. Madison, CT: International Universities, Press.

Winnicott, D. W. (1971a). *Playing and reality*. New York: Routledge.

Winnicott, D. W. (1971b). *Therapeutic consultations in child psychiatry*. London: Karnac.

Wolcott, D. (1992). *The Antilles: fragments of epic memory*. New York: Farrar, Straus & Giroux.

Chapter Two

Listening with Two Ears

Caregivers Listening Deeply to Babies and to Self

Enid Elliot

A few years ago, I was facilitating a workshop exploring the losses and grief that infant/toddler educators experience in their work when a group of women burst into tears. An educator/caregiver had shared her story of saying good-bye to a group of toddlers; she continued to find sadness and guilt in the memory. As she said, ". . . the grieving process continues outside of mundane awareness" (Elliot, 2007, p. 153). In telling her story she reminded the other women of their own narratives of grief and loss in their practice of caring for babies and toddlers. Each of them had a story of watching a child leave their care, a story of guilt for not being able to adequately support a child or family in times of need, or despair at witnessing the negligent care of a child.

I shared with them my research concerning the complexity of working with babies and toddlers in a group setting. I had heard and was continuing to hear about the complex emotions that are part of this work of caring for babies in group care. I had myself worked with infants and toddlers in a group setting and understood the tensions and pulls that were part of the job. After many years of working with children and families, creating child care programs and working with early childhood students, I had delved into the research and deeply studied a range of theoretical perspectives in order to widen my own approaches and understanding. Having had the time and permission that a doctorate gives, I had observed, listened and engaged in dialogues with women who worked with babies and toddlers.

My research grew out of my work with infants and toddlers and the knowledge that very young children are increasingly in care outside of their family (Hrdy, 1999; Willms, 2002). While Canadian women who have been part of the workforce can take almost a year of paid maternity leave, most return to work when their children are just a year old or younger, and need either full or part time care for their babies. Without a national comprehensive system of child care, parents scramble to find care for their baby with relatives, neighbors or in a licensed group child care situation. Many of these alternative caregivers, *allomothers* as Hrdy (1999) calls them, develop deep and caring relationships with the children and come to know both children and their families well, but not all of them are able or willing to enter into such deep or caring connections. For caregivers, watching a child grow and acquire skills and experiences can be a privilege; many become attached to the children and it is with sadness that they watch them leave their care only to welcome new children on a regular basis, often filling the place of a known and loved child with a new child the next day.

THE HUMAN DIALOGUE

Babies enter this world ready to enter into relationships with their parents, their families, their communities and their surroundings (S. Fraiberg, 1987). As D. W. Winnicott (1987) said, "There is no such thing as a baby; there is a baby and someone" (p. xx). Babies need someone to care for them; they need human partners "who become for the baby the embodiment of need satisfaction, comfort, and well-being" (S. Fraiberg, 1987, p. 21). They seek out and connect with their parents and families joining in the on-going family dialogue, taking up the family realities, dreams and nightmares. This *human dialogue* "begins with an exchange of gestures between parent and infant" (S. Fraiberg, 1987, p. 9) and a baby quickly learns the communication style and language of the people around her and soon she adds to the *lingua franca* of their surroundings.

Most parents can testify to the intense emotions and enormous pull that their small newborns exert on them. For example, Roiphe wrote, "I had given up my boundary, the wall of self, and in return had received obligation and love, a love mingled with its opposite, a love that grabbed me by the throat and has still not let me go" (1996, p. 6). Relationships with babies and very young children are often filled with powerful emotions. Within these relationships bonds of attachment grow, family narratives become more complex and communications with others, past and present, deepen and spread.

The protective instinct we have toward small children may be grounded deeply in us, but actualizing our protective feelings will have cultural, historical and personal roots (Gottlieb, 2004) influenced by our histories, experiences and family stories. Cultural and familial customs construct many of our beliefs about babies: when and how to respond to cries, whether a baby sleeps alone or with someone, how to speak to an infant. Each family and their community have important rules that govern relationships with babies (Gonzalez-Mena & Eyer, 2003; Rogoff, 1990, 2003) and these rules and responses, which are subtle and may involve smells, touches, sounds, and gazing, are often unacknowledged and unquestioned; yet to transgress them is often unthinkable.

Memories of being loved and loving, as well as memories of disappointment, sadness and anger, provide meanings and models for both childhood and adult relationships. Babies appeal and are appealing to the adults in their world, and their presence triggers memories and feelings of the adults in their environment. Relationships hold both positive and negative experiences. In the "good enough world", like Winnicott's "good enough mother" (Lear, 1990), the baby discovers not a perfect mother but a mother who responds sensitively and carefully *most* of the time. As familial relationships grow and develop meanings, each adult contributes his/her known and unknown memories of past and present attachments.

Often viewed as passive recipients of care and concern, needing to be responded to warmly and sensitively, babies' contribution to relationships can often be overlooked. Babies are not passive; their unique style and energy influences the tone and color of the relationships in which they engage (Cassidy & Shaver, 1999; Degotardi & Pearson, 2009). Joining the *human dialogue* (Kaplan, 1995), babies do not take long before they have actively inserted themselves in existing and evolving conversations, learning to make sense of the dialogue and the important narratives flowing around them, experiencing their parents and caregivers' loving care and thoughtful responses, as well as their own and others' frustration, anger and sadness. Over time these dialogues grow in complexity and depth, with adults bringing their own dialogues that carry the ghosts and shadows from past conversations, as well as angels of benevolence from prior experiences (Lieberman, Padron, Van Horn, & Harris, 2005), all of which influence the relationships which babies experience.

Babies bring their own determination and skills to the dialogue with others. Take for example, Ashley, who had her own dialogue with her father. Ashley[1] was four months old and a beautiful baby. Round and dimpled at knees and elbows, she smiled and responded happily to people. It was a pleasure to be in her company and receive her chortles and attention. One afternoon on a warm autumn day while I was sitting beside her and enjoying the warmth and peace of that moment, I heard Ashley's father come in; he strode into the daycare room with loud boots, despite a policy of removing shoes to keep the area clean and to create a transition space for entry into the baby's area. He was a medium-sized young man with a well-developed set of muscles that he was well aware of, as were all of us; even on chilly days he wore a sleeveless undershirt. There was an air of danger about him and we could sense the potential violence in him.

Ashley had also heard her father. I watched as she got ready for him to appear. She pulled in her head and pulled in her arms and legs so that she was a compact bundle. She had already learned that was the most comfortable and likely safest way to be picked up by her father. With an energetic swoop, he swung her in the air totally disregarding the need to support her four-month-old head. She had already done what she could to protect herself against his exuberance. Here was a thread in the human dialogue with which Ashley was already engaged.

We did not know what beliefs this young father had about babies or what narratives of care and love he brought with him. He had very little engagement with his daughter's caregiver and had shared little of himself. We can only wonder at his approach to his daughter. Fraiberg, Adelson, and Shapiro (1975, p. 3) speak of the ghosts that hover within our dialogues and un/consciousness, those "visitors from the unremembered past of the parents; the uninvited guests at the christening" in the nursery, that influence parental behavior and experience. O'Loughlin suggests, "Suppressed memories are encased in our bodies and transmitted silently across generations, often with catastrophic consequences" (O'Loughlin, 2009, p. 148). Children feel the presence of those "uninvited guests" and often absorb their message into their own bodies and souls. While her father was rough and unpredictable, Ashley engaged as fully as possible with him; she did all within her immense capabilities to accommodate her father's interactions. She had heard some of his narrative through her body and she had learned that in her relationship with him she should protect herself. She had a different quality of relationship with her mother and yet another relationship with her caregiver. In other relationships she would hear different stories. Through other relationships she could learn that the world had possibilities of care and sensitivity and could be loving and responsive (Lear, 1990). Lieberman et al. (2005) speak of the "benevolent presence of angels" that counteract the negative, distraught voices of neglect and abuse in a parent's or caregiver's past. These are alternative relationships and stories that can shift the meaning and impact of ghostly dialogues and whispers.

CHILD CARE EDUCATORS: JOINING THE DIALOGUE CARE/ FULLY

Entering child care, babies and toddlers bring with them their knowledge, understandings, and experiences from home as well as memories of communication with/in their families. Caregivers welcome the infant and her family, starting their own dialogue with the baby, creating a narrative that will be woven into the stories already in progress and meanings already constructed. Into the child care setting come the multiple dialogues of the families they serve. A "chiaroscuro of ghosts and angels" (Lieberman et al., 2005, p. 506) come to peer over the shoulder of participants at the beginning of new dialogues—the ghosts both of infants and caregivers.

Within an infant/toddler program, caregivers are meant to respond sensitively to the children providing a secure and warm environment (Brooks-Gunn, Sidle-Fuligni, & Berlin, 2003). Palacio-Quintin summed up the characteristics of good child care for babies, in general, as "a qualified and stable staff, a good educational program, good teacher-child and parent-day-care relationships, groups that are not too big, a reasonable amount of safe space, and safe hygiene practices" (2000, p. 20). Warm and sensitive care and quality interactions promote relationships of attachment. Howes, Phillips, and Whitebrook (1992) describe an engaged type of caregiving they call "involved teaching", which involves high levels of touching, hugging, talking and engagement between baby and caregiver. Touching is one key to developing intimate relationships, and babies experience touch regularly as their diapers are changed, as they are lifted into their cribs, and as they are fed. Through touch the dialogue begins.

While providing welcoming on-going care, caregivers must respond sensitively to each baby, getting to know that particular baby's signals and cues (Elliot, 1995; Fein, Garibaldi, & Boni, 1993; Howes & Hamilton, 1993; Howes & Smith, 1995). Brazelton and Kagan, among other child psychologists and researchers (e.g., Brazelton & Cramer, 1990; Brazelton, Koslowski, & Main, 1974; Kagan, 1978, 1984) have drawn the public's awareness to the individual differences that can be seen in newborns. Lally (1995) cautioned that infants are developing an identity, and suggests that infant-toddler caregivers will "participate either knowingly or unknowingly in the creation of a sense of self and that attention must be paid to that unique responsibility" (p. 67).

There have always been *alloparents*. Communities and non-maternal individuals across all cultures have looked after children for centuries. Like parents, caregivers will and usually do develop relationships with children and those relationships contribute to children's developing sense of self. Konicheckis (2010) reminds us that "children's creative activity can develop only through the attentive and caring presence of the adults around them. It is important for the child to experience a continuity of being. The baby is autonomous enough so that she or he can modify and transform psychic and emotional experiences that threaten this feeling" (p. 5).

While children create the world into which they arrive, they also arrive at a world not of their making (Britzman, 2009) and they inherit the past dialogues of their parents and grandparents (L. Fraiberg, 1987). When we develop responsive and attentive relationships, the energy and conversations flow in two directions, affecting both participants; so if the baby becomes attached to the caregiver, then it is possible that the caregiver can become attached to the baby. A caregiver holds a baby close and feels the weight of his body against her body, the baby nestles into the neck of the caregiver and they smell each other. The relationship between the two is as complex, multi-layered and unique, as is the relationship the baby has with her parents. While the baby learns through dialogue with the caregiver, the caregiver, in turn, can learn about herself through her connection with the baby, as she recalls her own narratives as a young child.

As we hold a baby close we feel, smell, hear, and see the particular qualities of that baby: her weight, her smell, and her sounds. Each baby is different and evokes different reactions within the adult's holding and caring for them. Working with babies is particularly intimate; the closeness and intimacy creates physiological and psychological responses in both the baby's body and the adult's body. As a caregiver comes to know a baby through the softness of her body, the joy of her laugh, the excitement of her daily discoveries she is engaged intellectually and emotionally. As the dialogue with the baby becomes deeper and more profound the caregiver may become aware of her own narrative as a baby, who was "once a child with frustrated thoughts and fears over loss of love" (Britzman, 2009, p. 17). Babies' bodies hold their stories and experiences, and listening closely to a baby may elicit embodied memories of caregivers. Staying aware of one's own past history and experiences can be uncomfortable and difficult for caregivers as they comfort a child, but naming and understanding these feelings may promote and support a genuine encounter with the baby. Emmi Pikler, a Hungarian pediatrician who ran an orphanage in Budapest after World War II, was convinced that the rights of babies could even be respected in an institution and wrote that "the infant still needs an intimate, stable, adult relationship . . . and a satisfactory relationship between adult and child is formed primarily *during the physical contacts* [italics added], i.e., dressing, bathing, feeding, etc., when the adult and child are in intimate contact" (Tardos, 2010, pp. 90–91).

Eager to join the human dialogue, the baby, as Kaplan suggests, "begins with an exchange of gestures between parent and infant" (1995, p. 9) and starts to develop his or her own vocabulary. Joining and adding to this dialogue, an infant/toddler caregiver must be ready to listen and watch closely. She must be present, which "requires a person to do more than merely see or hear; to be present means to be able to feel and experience what is happening" (Kaplan, 1995, p. 218).

Caring for infants on a daily basis requires thoughtful decisions and emotional connections. In optimal situations caregivers/educators work within caring relationships, juggling their responses and responsibilities to children, parents and colleagues. Each relationship demands a different dialogue and calls on skills of listening, noticing and responding. Being present to the babies and their families requires an attitude of welcome and acknowledgment. As Henri Nouwen says, "listening is an art . . . it needs the full and real presence of people to each other. It is indeed one of the highest forms of hospitality" (Nouwen, 1975, p. 95).

POSSIBILITIES . . .

To develop a meaningful relationship with an infant, a caregiver must welcome the baby, invite a conversation and begin an intentional dialogue. This begins with listening carefully to a baby with all of one's senses—to the pauses and silence, as well as the expressions and exclamations. It includes "interior listening, listening to ourselves, as a pause, a suspension, as an element that generates listening to others but, in turn, is generated by the listening others give us" (Rinaldi, 2006, p. 65). The baby is also "inviting dialogue. And because someone is responding to this invitation, from the beginning the newborn has the impression she is entering a world that understands what it is like to be a baby" (Kaplan, 1995, p. 26). Together a space is created in which meanings and perspectives are shared and new understandings may emerge.

When a baby enters into a child care situation, she hopefully enters into a meaningful dialogue with a caregiver. Interacting with a primary caregiver in a child care situation provides the baby with one particular person with whom the baby can develop a deep conversation, allowing their relationship time to unfold. Caregivers care for infants in intimate routines: being cared for by one particular person most of the time allows for the development of deep relationships. Emmi Pikler advocated listening carefully to the baby during the daily rituals of physical care. "The care situation is the scene of the meeting of two persons. While the mother or the adult caregiver provides the infant's physical needs, she establishes a direct contact with him [*sic*]. The infant can experience how the adult adjusts to his signals" (Tardos, 2010, p. 3). Thus, a dance of care and response begins, while the care situation can be a space for a unique dialogue with each baby and toddler. When deep relationships of listening are established, a child is free to share their emotions. As the dialogue with the caregiver evolves, the child can extend the dialogue and the investigation with the world and the caregiver can have a richer and deeper connection with the child.

LISTENING CLOSELY

In one center in which I worked, we were having a hard time with eighteen-month-old Jim. For weeks, he had arrived each morning and started emptying shelves and throwing toys. Once he had emptied the shelves he turned his attention to the smaller toddlers and began to push them over. As our oldest toddler, he was also the biggest and a push from him could send some of the slighter babies flying.

Jim was a sturdy boy and he had been in our program for over a year. We had seen him grow from a round smiling infant to a big toddler, comfortable with our program. His mother, Danielle, was very shy and we had taken almost a year to establish a relationship with her. For the first few months, she had said almost nothing to any of us; after a while she started hanging around more and chatting with us. She was in a somewhat unsettled and, at times, volatile relationship with Jim's father. These types of relationships and toddlers don't always mix.

We knew that things at home were difficult for Jim as his strivings for independence ran headlong into the young couple's need for his compliance. Their skills to cope with his energy were minimal. They sometimes locked him in a room when they could no longer cope. We tried our usual tactics of engaging Jim in an activity as he arrived in the morning, anticipating his assaults on the younger children, intervening and asking him to be gentle, but we were not making much headway. He talked very little and, of course, a toddler does not have the concepts, let alone the words, needed to explain what is bothering him.

Adults find it useful to have someone present for them when they are trying to understand the confusions and dilemmas that life presents. In his book, *On being a therapist*, Kottler wrote that "This healing relationship between people goes beyond mere catharsis: human beings have an intense craving, often unfulfilled, to be understood by someone else" (Kottler, 1993, p. 8). Toddlers want to be understood, too. We decided to pay close attention to Jim's commentary on his life and so we found the space and time to listen.

Following our plan, when Jim next arrived, his caregiver, Martha, met him at the door and took him to a small room where there were a few toys and pillows. The other caregivers managed the rest of the children as Martha took time to be with Jim and "listen" to what he had to tell her. She described what she saw him doing and wondered how he was feeling. It was a "therapy" session without a great deal of words, but with an attitude of attention on Martha's part. Listening happens on many levels and is felt by both participants. Jim expressed himself to someone he trusted and he felt heard. After half an hour or so, Jim returned to the group ready to join in. This process continued for about two weeks until Jim seemed more relaxed on arrival and no longer needed a container for his anger and frustration.

What Kottler goes on to say is true of work with infants. "Intimacy means being open, unguarded, and close to another. To facilitate trust, the therapist must feel comfortable facing intimacy without fear. This closeness helps the client to feel understood and appreciated; it teaches him [*sic*] that true intimacy is indeed possible, that a relationship based on regard and respect is desirable" (Kottler, 1993, p. 44).

Caregivers can provide children with relationships that not only are rich, but healing as well. Within different relationships a child has different experiences. Lieberman et al. (2005) suggest that the presence of angels in the nursery can "square off against their more famous siblings, the ghosts" (p. 506). Children have experiences of benevolence and pleasure, which can be a counterbalance to ghosts and provide a more "nuanced appreciation of early relationships with primary caregivers and encourage a greater sense of worth" (Fraiberg et al., 1975, pp. 506–507).

BARRIERS TO LISTENING . . .

But not all children have relationships with *allomothers* that can provide a positive and caring perspective on relationships. Not all caregivers will engage deeply in dialogue responding to a child in a manner that acknowledges her emotions and experiences. This deeper and more profound dialogue can be avoided and in its place a monologue can occur. The caregiver objectifies the child into *diapers* and *feedings*; the care routine, rather than the child, becomes the focus (Elliot, 2007). Imagine the effect on the babies and toddlers.

Tillie Olsen, feminist author and activist, tells of her first child who was a "miracle to me" (Olsen, 1961, p. 10). Being young and deserted by the father, she "had to leave her daytimes with the woman downstairs to whom she was no miracle at all, for I worked or looked for work . . ." (p. 10). Returning home her baby "would break into a clogged weeping that could not be comforted, a weeping I can hear yet" (p. 11). Babies have no words to explain their misery or ways to comprehend the unhappiness of others who might not want to care for them. But with what memories and shadows are they left?

Leavitt (Leavitt, 1994, 1995; Leavitt & Power, 1997) shared her experiences and observations in infant/toddler programs, where she found a silencing of children, a disregard of children's emotional experiences, and the lack of nurturing relationships. These relationships, so lacking in compassion and nurturance, are reflections of the fact that the caregivers have little emotional engagement with the babies in their care. Seeing the routines of changing diapers, feeding children and putting them to sleep as chores to be managed rather than opportunities for connection put babies at the mercy of their caregivers, who may end up seeing babies as objects to be serviced, not subjects to be cared for. Thus caregiving becomes the delivery of a set of technical and managerial skills, rather than the possibility of a relationship to be nurtured and sustained. Among Leavitt's caregivers, there is no listening, no responsive dialogue that creates relationship; they are emotionally disengaged and being disengaged, their "abilities to comprehend and respond to the perspectives of the children" are inhibited (Leavitt, 1994, p. 60).

Relationships such as these do not provide children with a sense of being seen or heard. Children form many relationships—with their family, their peers, and their environment—and learn, sometimes for better or worse, from each one, but they depend on the adults to form a safe circle within which they can explore the potentials of each of these relationships. Responsive relationships with adults provide a sense of a good enough world, "a lovable world is a loving, responsive world . . . in tune with the infant's needs and who can satisfy them in a reassuring and caring way" (Lear, 1990, p. 185). The caregivers Leavitt writes about are not attuned to the children in their care.

CAREGIVERS ENGAGING EMOTIONALLY

Caregivers are encouraged to create responsive and sensitive relationships with infants and toddlers as this is considered good practice (e.g., Doherty, 1999; Lally, 1995; Lally et al., 1995; Whitebook, 2003). When entering into responsive and caring relationships with babies, caregivers are necessarily engaged emotionally with them. While there is an increasing trend to establish a primary care model for infants in child care (Raikes & Edwards, 2009), a system in which an infant is attended to by one person rather than several, primary caregiving is not a recent idea. In the 1970s, for example, Provence, mentions primary caregivers in her description of her day care program for children under the age of two at the Yale Child Study Center. She states, "We gave each child a primary caregiver . . . because of the stability of our staff— there was very little turnover—it worked out that the children came to know all of the child care staff very well. Nevertheless, to have the person who knew him best available through most of the day was important for obvious reasons, making him more secure and comfortable" (Provence, 1974, p. 11).

More recently, others have associated primary caregiving with good practice (Lally et al., 1995; Lally & Keith, 1997). An advocate of primary caregiving, Lally et al. wrote ". . . when the separation-individuation process is considered as an important component of the child care experience, it makes great sense to limit the number of caregivers with whom a child must interact each day and to structure his experience so that it is easy for him to form an intimate relationship with a known and trusted adult. This is best done by assigning a primary caregiver to each child" (1995, p. 64).

An early proponent of primary caregiving was the Hungarian pediatrician Emmi Pikler, who began her work in the 1930s. Pikler, aware of the ideas of Bowlby and his colleagues and aware of the psychoanalytical trends of the time (e.g., Bowlby, 1951; Freud & Burlingham, 1974), began to develop her ideas of respecting infants and their innate abilities. In her work with parents and babies, she emphasized the autonomy of the infant. She believed young children to be competent, and believed infancy to be a stage of life with experiences as vital and meaningful as those of adults (Penn, 1999). Pikler (1979a) was also clear that the infants should be active participants in their dialogues and relationships with the world and their caregivers.

In North America, the primary caregiver system has focused on the relationship between caregiver and infant, rather than on that of infant and environment, or infant and peers. In Pikler's institution, caregivers remained with their infants maintaining consistency and continuity of care, but she also felt the physical environment should be constant and predictable in order for babies to have "freedom for activity and adequate space. Their environment must be stable, varied and colorful" (Pikler, 1979b, p. 91). In that sense, she was anticipating later research demonstrating that children become attached not only to their caregiver, but also to the physical surroundings and the other children as well (Whaley & Rubenstein, 1994).

Primary caregiving can be seen as a commitment to developing an in-depth dialogue with a family and their baby, and this commitment can arouse fears in staff who worry there will be a baby they might not like, or that the child will get "too attached" to them, or that it will be too difficult for other staff if a child's primary caregiver at the center is away. To invite someone to join you in a dialogue, to listen and to be heard, is to be vulnerable within that encounter. Becoming vulnerable we open to our own possibilities and growth. We also open to our own ghosts and fears. As Bakhtin suggested, we learn of ourselves through engagement with the other; "the two languages frankly and intensely peered into each other's faces, and each became more aware of itself, of its potentialities and limitations, in the light of the other" (Bakhtin, 1994, p. 465). As the dialogue deepens and each starts to learn the other's language, babies can become attached to caregivers other than their parents and so the caregivers can become attached to them.

Once engaged in caring for and about a child, the caregiver can experience joy in the child's joy and concern for a child's situation and sorrow at the child's departure. Open to experiencing joy in the baby's pleasure and the baby's very physical presence, the caregiver also becomes vulnerable to the feelings of sadness and anger that arise when caring for and about someone. Children come and go from a child care program and caregivers welcome them and send them off. As one caregiver told me, "they are not your family. They are not your children. But in the same sense, you are offering them care. There is no fine line; it's sort of like a weaving" (Elliot, 2007, p. 87)

Learning from Hector ...

I have memories of my first experience as a caregiver in an infant/toddler program, one of the first in New York City. Hector was under a small table hollering and holding onto the table's leg. His mother was screaming that it was time to go home and hauling on one of his legs to pull him out. I was hovering ineffectually between them. I tried to soothe the mother while explaining to Hector it was time to go home.

Two-year-old Hector enjoyed being at day care. Each day, he happily involved himself in a project when he arrived, and he stayed involved in one project or another the entire time he was there. One morning, he worked hard to figure out how to undo the drain to the water table. He succeeded and there was water everywhere.

This particular day, he was deeply involved with the trucks.

His mother was an impatient young woman who liked to move fast. With long legs and dressed in stylish short skirts and big shoes, she was usually in a hurry to get to the next place. This day, she had plans.

I was a young teacher with idealistic notions about the care of children. I tried to keep the atmosphere in the room calm and nurturing. I tried to support parents. I cared about the children whom I cuddled, read to, chatted with, and played with every day.

That afternoon, I was not maintaining a peaceful, nurturing environment.

I cared for Hector, I empathized with his mother, and I managed to help them get out the door. I absorbed the emotional energy of Hector, his mother, and the children in the room. Afterward, away from the children, I burst into tears. At times, the emotional tensions of the job were overwhelming.

Remembering my own vulnerability as a child and my own fear at an adult's anger, I empathized with Hector. I also knew his mother was young and was impatient when he did not move fast enough. I understood impatience from my own need to move fast. I also liked to keep things tranquil as I liked that tempo for the group; I was happy when everyone was playing and engaged in their particular interest. As Hector clung to the table leg while his mother screamed and pulled at him, I remember having a sense of his anxiety, as well as what seemed to be his mother's anxiety, the other children's anxiety, and my own anxiety. The tension of that moment seemed resolved when they left the room, but on a closer look, it remained with me. I had an awareness of the quality of relationship between Hector and his mother, and I needed to maintain relationships with both. I had also been reminded of my own feelings as a child when helpless.

While being in relationship, there is always a risk of losing one's own sense of self, of empathizing so closely that one loses perspective. Caring for another also means being vulnerable to grief at the loss of that person, of that relationship. Psychologist Robert Kegan (1982) wrote, "we can never protect ourselves from the risks of caring. In running these risks we preserve the connections between us. We enhance the life we share, or perhaps better put, we enhance the life that shares us" (p. 20).

The caregivers spoke of a range of griefs that may appear small, but these daily small sorrows come from being attached to children and families. When caring for very small children and becoming attached to them, one does so with an awareness of their future departure. Saying good-bye to children as they move to another situation means the caregivers experience a loss—an anticipated loss—but a loss nevertheless. Caregivers also grieve the circumstances in which some babies live, for example, the poverty, or the chaotic family situations that the babies live within. Were caregivers to ignore these realities of separation and loss, or deny the reality of the lives of some children, they would be in danger of distancing themselves from the children in their care.

When the incident with Hector happened, I was unaware of all the pulls on my emotional equilibrium; I just felt overwhelmed. Fortunately, I worked in a therapeutic nursery so there were colleagues with whom I could debrief and reflect. I had people I could consult--a psychiatrist headed up the project and there were experienced caregivers present (Resch, Lillesov, Schur, & Mihalov, 1977). Most caregivers working in the emotionally fraught world of infant care are not so fortunate.

GRIEF, ANGER, AND CAREGIVERS

Maintaining a sense of self within a web of relationships proved challenging at times for the caregivers with whom I spoke. Maintaining her own values while accepting parents' voices and values could stretch a caregiver's empathy. Being critical of parental approaches could create distance with a family, while staying open to a family's lifestyle required a willingness to be open to compassion and understanding. This can be an uneasy balance, maintaining one's beliefs in the face of parental styles and behaviors.

Caregivers who are not involved in a primary caregiving system, share the responsibility for the entire group of eight to twelve children with other co-workers. A caregiver's patience and skills are spread out over all the children as they try to maintain relationships with all the children in the group and there is limited time and energy left over to respond to parents. In this situation sensitive responses to children and to parents can be difficult and create tensions within a caregiver and within the program. One caregiver expressed her frustration to me when faced with a sick child and parents who kept sending the child into the center, saying, "Something that most of us at work get really frustrated about is when children are sick. You've called and talked to the parents to come pick them up and then the next day they are back again and you are thinking, why? You choose to have your children, you choose to raise your children but sometimes it seems that the work is more important and they can't take that time to nurse their child back to health" (Elliot, 2007, p. 121).

Her frustration was understandable. A sick child needs extra attention, and parents working in jobs with little room for sick time often are caught between the needs of the child and the demands of a job which they need to support their family. Part of the problem is a system that does not give parents sufficient options and does not seem to value the work that caregivers do. Frustration causes the caregiver to find a source on whom to both direct and project her anger.

Another primary caregiver, who was responsible for three babies and their families, found it easier to feel the difficulty of each. Her sympathies were with the child, yet she also understood the parental dilemma: "Sometimes they would send their children in and I don't think they were healthy enough to be here. The child will need one on one and will be upset and you can tell they are obviously not feeling well . . . the tough part is you feel bad for the child and you know the parent is needing to be at work and they have their own pressures" (Elliot, 2007, p. 121).

Caregivers must constantly address the conflicting feelings that arise from the commitment and caring they have for the child. Judgments must be re-framed so that both parent and child are encompassed in understanding. Caregivers spoke to me of learning from these places of uneasiness. Anger and sadness can be triggered by such caregiving situations. A woman I worked with for several years admitted, "I don't like to say good-bye. I would rather not go to work [on a child's last day]. I thought, yes, this is something I need to work on" (Elliot, 2007, p. 121).

Saying good-bye is hard; struggling with the emotions of the job takes active engagement. Becoming conscious of and acknowledging feelings, caregivers learn about their own fears and histories. Turning away from the self-awareness that emotions offer could be a temptation in order to simplify the process of caregiving, but to adequately meet the needs of the babies caregivers cannot turn away. Becoming aware of one's vulnerabilities to doubts, fears and painful memories is challenging. Clinchy (1996) argues that "fully developed connected knowing requires that one 'affirm' or 'con-firm' the subjective reality of the other, and affirmation is not merely the absence of negative evaluation; it is a positive effortful act" (p. 217). Emo-tional difficulties seemed to loom in many caregivers' minds, and perhaps the lack of willingness or ability to engage in "fully connected knowing" was the path chosen by the caregivers described so poignantly in Leavitt's (1994) work.

In a workshop I delivered for infant/toddler caregivers, a strong objection to primary caregiving was raised. There was lively and heated discussion, not necessarily the usual response in a workshop of ninety people who have come together for the afternoon. A group of people with a strong spokeswoman felt that having one primary caregiver was detrimental to the child because the child would be too attached to the caregiver and too sad upon saying good-bye. Eventually, it was revealed that this individual had had a babysitter who had left town after a year of caring for her after school and on holidays. This caregiver had missed her babysitter terribly when she left, and felt that the sorrow was unbearable. How the rupture took place was unknown, but the feelings of abandonment were there and the grief was painful enough for her to want to avoid further feelings of loss. Her emotions of grief and loss colored her approach to her caregiving practice and, as she was an influential member of the community, this had an impact beyond her own decision-making sphere.

Caregivers do experience sadness at the departure of the babies and toddlers they have fed, nurtured, and rocked over weeks and months. About saying good-bye to some of the children in her care, a caregiver told me:

> I'm always bawling. I'm the one in the center who is always crying. That's just the way it is. I think because of the person I am, I really, really care. It's hard. It's really hard. I mean some are harder than others. You know, because, you know . . . you have not your favorites, but you have children whom you are really connected with. And this year I actually have three whom I have been with for two years. It is the first group that I have had all of them—being with them and working with them all the time. It's going to be a hard year, because the moms are already talking about it. So they are feeling it too, which is incredible. (Elliot, 2007, p. 122)

Being aware of parents' loss as they move on and being able to discuss it with parents, a caregiver can understand and appreciate her own, as well as the other's feelings. The child can learn from the adults about ways to negotiate these emotionally difficult times. As one of these caregivers said, it is important to feel the sadness of saying good-bye, because "it actually hurts more to shut it down, because it is incomplete, it is unresolved." To leave the emotions and connections unacknowledged has the potential to do more harm than good. It is painful to turn from saying good-bye to a baby who had been in one's care for a year or more, and to welcome a new baby immediately. I was told, "And then, you know, you may have a new baby the next day and it is like, 'I don't want my new baby yet, I want my old one back.' This one you don't know yet. It's tough, you've got to put them in the old baby's bed and it is very hard. Often the next day it happens."

While it might be important and appropriate to acknowledge the feelings of loss and sadness of the caregivers, there is usually no time for them to grieve given the practical realities of having to fill the empty space. Throughout their training, caregivers do not have the opportunity to talk about the built-in sense of loss that they should feel if they truly attach to and care for babies and infants, and neither do they learn to understand their feelings or how their histories and experiences shape their responses to emotionally difficult places. The injunction to respond sensitively to a baby and to the family, to create relationships, does not acknowledge that to do this one must also be affected and vulnerable emotionally. Caregivers happen on this knowledge of the reciprocity of relationship in different ways. Further education was a door for some. This was shared with me by a woman who went back to finish a BA several years after her early childhood education training:

> I get really attached to the baby and really attached to the parents. And actually it is interesting, because right now in my class we are doing a lot of counseling things and about closure. I never really thought about closure for myself . . . Like how do I say good-bye to infants and how do I separate. . . . But how do I deal with it? It's interesting, I never would have been able to articulate this until I had to [for her class]. I just ignore it is even happening. And I was never even aware that it was even happening. I'm the kind of person who would leave a party without saying good-bye. And I never realized I did that. But that's how I deal with it. So now I think, let's go to a different place with this now. I'm ready to move to a different place with it. Really experience it. For me, I think it was about that loss of relationship. (Elliot, 2007, p. 123)

Allowing herself to experience the loss of her relationship with a child deepened her practice and also connected her to the loss the child was experiencing. Staying emotionally present to the tensions created by the losses kept the caregiver involved in her work and her practice dynamic.

Naming the emotions they struggled with, the losses they were experiencing and by looking at it from all angles, caregivers grew and learned about themselves and their practice, both within and through relationships. Benner and Wrubel (1989) suggested that "the person who learns to 'manage' (ward off, distance) emotions effectively eliminates the guidance and direction provided by those emotions" (p. 60). Wien (1995) said, "At the points of conflict lie the routes to change" (p. 131). Places of sadness, places of discomfort, can encourage reflection and discussion. At these points, if caregivers can stop to look within and find "what works for them," they can bring an understanding to issues of separation. Some centers have made space or time for reflection, for the articulation of and discussion of difficulties. Paying attention to these uncomfortable feelings can teach us, and by bringing this discussion more clearly into our practice we honor the caregiving process.

Telling stories of our own grief at separation, our own helplessness and vulnerability, opens up space for empathy on many levels. Sharing with colleagues allows us to "place our own present in relation to the other's past"

(Britzman, 2009, p. 120) and sharing stories allows for us to have "resources for our conversations" (Gergen, 2006, p. 204).

DEALING WITH GRIEF

These emotions of grief can be shared with colleagues as the caregivers work to understand the deeper meanings of the sadness experienced. When we feel safe, we can begin to uncover our own ghosts in the nursery, delving into our own stories of disappointment, rage and sorrow. Grief, once triggered, can remind us of other griefs and sadnesses that have overwhelmed us in the past and continue to cast shadows into the present. Becoming aware of the connections to our own earlier experiences and memories and their influence on our present reality helps to free us to feel the immediate loss of a child's presence or concern over a child's circumstance.

To avoid visiting our places of sorrow and grief may be tempting, but the energy and defensiveness required to do so creates a rigidity that threatens to negate all feelings and disrupt any possible dialogue. The "magic of intimacy", as Winnicott calls it, contributes to "a sense of feeling real and of being, and of the experiences feeding back into the personal psychical reality, enriching it, and giving it scope" (Winnicott, 1986, p. 31).

Caregivers who form responsive relationships with babies should be able to stay open to the relationship and dialogue in which they are engaged. As Bakhtin suggests "the word in language is half someone else's" (Bakhtin, 1994, p. 77). While we cannot see ourselves as others can, others can give us the gift of their sight of us as well as the context in which we are embedded, and we, in turn, can share what we see of them and their context.

The words we use, as well as the discourses within which they are embedded, structure our vision, understandings, and perspectives. As O'Loughlin (2009) reminds us, "subjectivity is actively constructed at the vortex of ancestral memory, sociohistorical circumstance, local discursive practices, and the mediating influences of language, schooling and other official regulatory processes" (p. 22). Meanings can shift and fracture depending on the context, speaker, and history; any utterance is "overlain with qualifications, open to dispute, charged with value, already enveloped in an obscuring mist" (Bakhtin, 1994, p. 75).

Bakhtin speaks of language and Winnicott speaks of actions and presence. With both actions and language we bring our own fears, ambiguities and narrative fragments to the dialogue with the infants for whom we care. Our life histories are "always full of ruptures, uncertainties, contradictions, and inconsistencies" (Ruti, 2011, p. 367). If we must be in responsive relationships with young children and families to offer them the possibility of dialogue that is rich and nurturing, then we are challenged to become aware of the ghosts that trouble us and the places of discomfort that confound us. Britzman suggests, "if we have the strange work of trying to understand the minds of others and still keep our own mind, if we have the work of welcoming what cannot be understood and the responsibility for a hospitality without reserve" (Britzman, 2009, p. 44) then our education and understanding can begin.

Within safe spaces and trusting environments we can share our stories of loss and create other stories that bring different meanings to our understanding of leave taking, of letting go and of caring for others. Speaking of her experience with babies, one infant/toddler caregiver said that in school she did not learn "any of the stuff I'm learning now . . . the attachment, the caring, the love, the emotional connections, the relationship building. I learned a lot through the moms and the babies I work with. . . . And working with other people. I've gotten a lot from the staff that I've worked with, so much . . . the emotional side of it" (Elliot, 2007, p. 122).

These narratives can hold our emotions and allow us to look at them. Elfer and Dearnley speak of a process of "enabling people to think about and talk through threatening or anxiety-producing ideas with someone who can listen and think about them, returning them reframed in an emotionally more manageable way" (2007, p. 269) to help nursery nurses deal with the emotional demands of their jobs. Finding a path through the powerful emotions elicited by children and their families and sharing narratives that make sense of those emotions can be a comfort and allow caregivers to continue to be present for the children in their care. This path is not easy or untangled, "the intention to understand is already an emotionally wrought experience, for it returns us to times when we cannot understand and when we ourselves feel misunderstood" (Britzman, 2009, p. 95).

Becoming curious about their places of discomfort and uncertainty, combined with a willingness to investigate these spaces, may help caregivers stay present to their dialogues with babies and their families. Acknowledging their emotional connections to the babies in their care may support these investigations and allow for a deeper look at the affects that interrupt and disrupt caring.

NOTE

1. All names are pseudonyms and all identifying information has been disguised to protect the identity of families.

REFERENCES

Bakhtin, M. M. (1994). The dialogic imagination (M. Holquist & C. Emerson, Trans.). In P. Morris (Ed.), *The Bakhtin reader; Selected writings of Bakhtin, Medvedev, Voloshinov* (pp. 74–80). London: Arnold.

Benner, P., & Wrubel, J. (1989). *The primacy of caring, stress and coping in health and illness.* San Francisco: Addison-Wesley.

Bowlby, J. (1951). *Maternal care and mental health* (Vol. 2). Geneva: World Health Organization.

Brazelton, T. B., & Cramer, B. (1990). *The earliest relationship: Parents, infants, and the drama of early attachment.* Reading, MA: Addison-Wesley.

Brazelton, T. B., Koslowski, B., & Main, M. (1974). The origin of reciprocity: The early mother-infant interaction. In M. Lewis & L. A. Rosenblum (Eds.), *The effect of the infant on its caregiver* (pp. 49–76). New York: John Wiley & Sons.

Britzman, D. P. (2009). *The very thought of education: Psychoanalysis and the impossible professions.* Albany: SUNY Press.

Brooks-Gunn, J., Sidle-Fuligni, A., & Berlin, L. (Eds.). (2003). *Early childhood development in the 21st century: Profiles of current research Initiatives.* New York: Teachers College Press.

Cassidy, J., & Shaver, P. (Eds.). (1999). *Handbook of attachment: Theory, research, and clinical applications.* New York: Guilford Press.

Clinchy, B. M. (1996). Connected and separate knowing: Toward a marriage of two minds. In N. Goldberger, J. Tarule, B. M. Clinchy, & M. Belenky (Eds.), *Knowledge, difference, and power: Essays inspired by Women's Ways of Knowing* (pp. 205–247). New York: Basic Books.

Degotardi, S., & Pearson, E. (2009). Relationship theory in the nursery: Attachment and beyond. *Contemporary Issues in Early Childhood, 10, 2,* 144–155.

Doherty, G. (1999). Elements of quality. In S. Sullivan, K. Bose & L. Levesque (Eds.), *Research connections Canada: Supporting children and families* (pp. 5–56). Ottawa: Canadian Child Care Federation.

Elfer, P., & Dearnley, K. (2007). Nurseries and emotional well-being: evaluating an emotionally containing model of professional development. *Early Years, 27, 3,* 267–279.

Elliot, E. (2007). *"We're not robots": The voices of infant/toddler caregivers.* Albany: SUNY Press.

Elliot, E. (Ed.). (1995). *An introduction to attachment theory.* Paper presented at the Attachment Implications for Infant/Toddler Caregivers Conference, Victoria, BC.

Fein, G. G., Garibaldi, A., & Boni, R. (1993). The adjustment of infants and toddlers to group care: the first 6 months. *Early Childhood Research Quarterly, 8,* 1–14.

Fraiberg, L. (Ed.). (1987). *Selected writings of Selma Fraiberg.* Columbus: Ohio State University Press.

Fraiberg, S. (1987). The Origins of Human Bonds. In L. Fraiberg (Ed.), *Selected writings of Selma Fraiberg* (pp. 3–26). Columbus: Ohio State University Press.

Fraiberg, S., Adelson, E., & Shapiro, V. (1975). Ghosts in the nursery: A psychoanalytic approach to the problems of impaired infant-mother relationships. *Journal of the American Academy of Child Psychiatry, 14,* 387–421.

Freud, A., & Burlingham, D. (1974). *Infants without families and reports on the Hampstead Nurseries 1939–1945.* London: Hogarth Press and Institute of Psycho-Analysis.

Gergen, K. (2006). *Therapeutic realities: Collaboration, oppression and relational flow.* Chagrin Falls, OH: Taos Institute.

Gonzalez-Mena, J., & Eyer, D. W. (2003). *Infants, toddlers, and caregivers* (6th ed.). Columbus, OH: McGraw-Hill College.

Gottlieb, A. (2004). *The afterlife is where we come from: The culture of infancy in West Africa* (1st ed.). Chicago: University of Chicago Press.

Howes, C., & Hamilton, C. E. (1993). Child care for young children. In B. Spodek (Ed.), *Handbook of Research on the Education of Young Children* (pp. 322–336). New York: Macmillan.

Howes, C., Phillips, D. A., & Whitebrook, M. (1992). Thresholds of quality: Implications for the social development of children in center-based child care. *Child Development, 63,* 449–460.

Howes, C., & Smith, E. W. (1995). Relations among child care quality, teacher behavior, children's play activities, emotional security, and cognitive activity in child care. *Early Childhood Research Quarterly, 10, 3,* 381–404.

Hrdy, S. B. (1999). *Mother nature: A history of mothers, infants and natural selection.* New York: Pantheon Books.

Kagan, J. (1978). *Infancy: Its place in human development.* Cambridge: Harvard University Press.

Kagan, J. (1984). *The nature of the child.* New York: Basic Books.

Kaplan, L. (1995). *No voice is ever wholly lost.* New York: Simon and Schuster.

Kegan, R. (1982). *The evolving self: Problem and process in human development.* Cambridge: Harvard University Press.

Konicheckis, A. (2010). Being in movement. *The Signal, 18, 3–4,* 5–6.

Kottler, J. A. (1993). *On being a therapist.* San Francisco: Jossey-Bass.

Lally, J. R. (1995). The impact of child care policies and practices on infant toddler identity formation. *Young Children, 51, 1,* 58–66.

Lally, J. R., Griffin, A., Fenichel, E., Segal, M., Szanton, E., & Weissbourd, B. (1995). *Caring for infants and toddlers in groups: Developmentally appropriate practice.* Washington, DC: HREE Press.

Lally, J. R., & Keith, H. (1997). Early head start: The first two years. *Zero to Three, 18, 2,* 3–8.

Lear, J. (1990). *Love and its place in nature: A philosophical interpretation of Freudian psychoanalysis.* New York: Farrar, Straus & Giroux.

Leavitt, R. L. (1994). *Power and emotion in the infant-toddler day care.* Albany: SUNY Press.

Leavitt, R. L. (1995). The emotional culture of infant-toddler day care. In J. A. Hatch (Ed.), *Qualitative research in early childhood settings* (pp. 1–19). Westport, CT: Praeger.

Leavitt, R. L., & Power, M. B. (1997). Civilizing bodies: Children in day care. In J. Tobin (Ed.), *Making a place for pleasure in early childhood education* (pp. 39–75). New Haven: Yale University Press.

Lieberman, A., Padron, E., Van Horn, P., & Harris, W. (2005). Angels in the nursery: The intergenerational transmission of benevolent parental influences. *Infant Mental Health Journal, 26, 6,* 504–520.

Nouwen, H. J. M. (1975). *Reaching out: The three movements of the spiritual life.* New York: Doubleday.

O'Loughlin, M. (2009). *The subject of childhood.* New York: Peter Lang Publishing.

Olsen, T. (1961). I stand here ironing. In T. Olsen (Ed.), *Tell me a riddle* (pp. 9–21). New York: Dell Publishing.

Palacio-Quintin, E. (2000). The impact of day care on child development. *Isuma, 1, 2,* 17–22.

Penn, H. (1999). *How should we care for babies and toddlers? An analysis of practice in out-of-home care for children under three* (pp. 66). Toronto: Childcare Resource and Research Unit, Center for Urban & Community Studies, University of Toronto.

Pikler, E. (1979a). Forms of hospitalism in our days. In M. Gerber (Ed.), *A manual for parents and professionals: Resources for infant educarers* (pp. 95–102). Los Angeles: Resources for Infant Educarers.

Pikler, E. (1979b). A quarter of a century of observing infants in a residential center. In M. Gerber (Ed.), *A manual for parents and professionals: Resources for infant educarers* (pp. 90–92). Los Angeles: Resources for Infant Educarers.

Provence, S. (1974). A program of group day care for young children. *Psychosocial Process Issues in Child Mental Health, 3, 3* (Spring 1974), 7–13.

Raikes, H., & Edwards, C. P. (2009). *Extending the dance in infant toddler care giving: Exploring attachment and relationships.* Baltimore: Paul H. Brookes.

Resch, R. C., Lillesov, R. K., Schur, H. M., & Mihalov, T. (1977). Infant day care as a treatment intervention. *Child Psychiatry and Human Development, 7, 3,* 147–155.

Rinaldi, C. (2006). *In dialogue with Reggio Emilia: Listening, researching and learning.* London and New York: Routledge.

Rogoff, B. (1990). *Apprenticeship in thinking: Cognitive development in social context*. New York and Oxford: Oxford University Press.

Rogoff, B. (2003). *The cultural nature of human development*. Oxford: Oxford University Press.

Roiphe, A. (1996). *Fruitful: Living the contradictions: A memoir of modern motherhood*. New York: Penguin.

Ruti, M. (2011). "Winnicott with Lacan: Living Creatively in a Postmodern World." *American Imago (Assn. for Applied Psychoanalysis)*, *67, 3*, 353–374.

Tardos, A. (2010). Introducing the Piklerian developmental approach: History and principles. *The Signal, 18, 3–4*, 1–4.

Whaley, K., & Rubenstein, T. S. (1994). How toddlers do friendship: A descriptive analysis of naturally occurring friendships in a group child care setting. *Journal of Social and Personal Relationships, 11*, 383–400.

Whitebook, M. (2003). *Early education quality: Higher teacher qualifications for better learning environments: A review of the literature*. Berkeley, CA: Center for the Study of Child Care Employment.

Wien, C. A. (1995). *Developmentally appropriate practice in "real life": Stories of teacher practical knowledge*. New York: Teacher's College Press.

Willms, J. D. (Ed.). (2002). *Vulnerable children*. Edmonton: University of Alberta.

Winnicott, D. W. (1987). *The child, the family, and the outside world*. Reading, MA: Addison-Wesley.

Winnicott, D. W. (Ed.). (1986). *Home is where we start from*. New York: W. W. Norton.

Chapter Three

Teen Parents and Babies in School Together

The Chances for Children Teen Parent-Infant Project

Hillary Mayers

This chapter describes Chances for Children (CFC, chancesforchildren-ny.org), a psychoanalytically informed school intervention that targets the very youngest students, babies of teen parents who are enrolled in nurseries on-site in high schools where their teen parents attend classes. This setting offers a unique opportunity to reach both parent and child at a critical time of development for each, allowing us to apply the newest research findings in early brain development, as well as a rich psychoanalytic understanding of the tasks (and conflicts) of parenthood and adolescence. Combining this information with the tools offered within the burgeoning field of infant mental health, we can hope to prevent the intergenerational transmission of traumatic family relationships, physical and sexual abuse, addiction, and dropout. At the same time we can identify the need for early intervention at the earliest possible moment to prevent destructive mental health conditions from impinging on the parent-child relationship.

The chapter outlines the theory behind the protocol used, the structure of the program, and the strategies used for implementation (in particular video-feedback techniques and mentalization) in different aspects of the program. Three clinical cases illustrate the effectiveness of psychoanalytically-based work with mothers and infants that combines developmental theories of infant mental health, adolescence, and motherhood with theories of mentalization, attachment, and psychoanalysis.

INFANT MENTAL HEALTH

Current theories of infant mental health rest in part on the famous saying by Winnicott, "There is no such thing as a baby. . . ." (Winnicott, 1960, p. 587). By this he implied that a baby cannot survive without a context of "good enough" (Winnicott, 1958) care. In short, babies and their environments need to be considered together. Thus a good-enough caregiving context is essential for infant mental health. It will maximize social-emotional competence and minimize developmental difficulties in the future, and be flexible enough to change with the developmental changes of the child. Within such a context, a child will learn to regulate and express emotion, explore the environment, and learn, while forming solid, positive interpersonal relationships. Without this context, babies can become mentally and emotionally unwell, which is evident in babies who are indiscriminately friendly to strangers, babies who bang their heads and pull out their hair, babies who will not eat and do not gain weight, and babies who flinch and shudder when approached. Despite this evidence, because the idea that an infant can have problems serious enough to be regarded as mental illness is so horrifying, society has difficulty acknowledging it.

Adolescence

Theories of adolescent development address the vast social-emotional, physical, and cognitive changes that occur during this period, when children begin to prepare for adult life without parents. Developmentally, adolescence can be divided into three sub-phases, each with its own tasks (Levy-Warren, 1996). In *early adolescence*, which spans roughly the years from ten to fourteen, the teen must manage dramatic physical changes and the emotional confusion that hormonal changes generate. The sudden sprouting of height, hair, pimples, breasts, bad breath, and stinky armpits makes the adolescent a stranger even to herself. She struggles to define who she is by how she looks. The young adolescent's attention focuses less on family and turns toward peers who are coping with similar challenges.

Middle adolescence, approximately the ages from fifteen to eighteen, is even more peer-focused. Siegler (1997) identifies five core fears of adolescence, one of which is the fear of being alone. The need to have friends and fit in is all-consuming, and being left without friends replaces the childhood fear of being left without parents. "In adolescence, acceptance is all — aloneness equals anxiety" (p.105). The search for social groups into which a teen can fit gives rise to many inconsistencies, such as the vegetarian who smokes, or the track star who guzzles beer. Teens become susceptible to the lure of gangs and cults as they search to define themselves as separate from their parents, defining right and wrong for themselves. Most important, during this period the teen confronts the task of forging and consolidating a sexual identity. Simmering beneath these challenges is the adolescent's underlying anxiety about her capacity to manage this metamorphosis. Can I invent a self in a new image to replace the childhood me who is no longer my familiar me? Can I become an adult? Can I lose my way and find it again?

Finally, in *late adolescence* the teen must find a balanced view of self and family, with internalized ideals and values, and primary responsibility for herself. Completing these tasks successfully generally requires "good enough" earlier parenting, and not all teens manage the challenge successfully.

What happens when, while struggling with these typical developmental tasks, a teen "finds herself pregnant?" The stage of development each teen parent has reached will influence her impending parenthood. Instead of one new body, there are two; instead of one metamorphosis from child into adult, a second metamorphosis of adolescent into parent is now critical.

MOTHERHOOD

A compelling theory of motherhood is set forth by Stern in his extraordinary book, *The Motherhood Constellation*. Stern (1995) suggests that "with the birth of a baby, especially her first one, the mother passes into a new and unique psychic organization that I call the motherhood constellation. As a psychic organizer, this 'constellation' will determine a new set of action tendencies, sensibilities, fantasies, fears, and wishes . . . this new organization is temporary. Its duration is very variable, lasting months or years, but during that time, it becomes the dominant organizing axis for the mother's psychic life and pushes to the side the previous nuclear organizations . . . that have played a central role" (p. 171). A major theme in the motherhood constellation is the "identity reorganization theme" (p. 180), a dominant part of which is the shift from daughter to mother, and in our population of teen mothers, the shift from being the boyfriend's "baby" to the boyfriend's "baby mama." In Stern's schema, this shift also requires a reengagement with supporting maternal figures, a "supportive maternal matrix" who will "accompany, value and instruct" the new mother. In essence, she needs wise elders who can "mother the mother." Here developmental conflicts become all too apparent, and the adolescent mother finds herself challenged by an entirely new set of requirements. Typically developing adolescents are preoccupied with themselves: they are moving away from the family sphere toward that of peers, they are impulsively trying out new roles and behaviors, and their self-regulation is at best unreliable. In contrast, the new parent is preoccupied with the infant and the infant's survival. She needs the encouragement and wisdom of older women, particularly her mother. She needs to provide consistency and reliability for her child, and she needs predictable self-regulation to be able to regulate her baby. These contending pulls are critical areas for intervention with teen parents. In our experience the intervention is most effective when informed by mentalization and attachment theory.

MENTALIZATION

Mentalization (sometimes referred to as "reflective function") is a concept that is both simple and complex. It is defined by Halsam-Hopwood et al. as "interpreting behavior as based on mental states, such as beliefs, wishes, dreams, ambitions, hallucinations . . . and includes attending to mental states in oneself and others" (Allen & Fonagy, 2006, p. 252). Fonagy calls this "holding the mind in mind" (Fonagy, 2001). When this capacity is developed, it results in increased self-regulation, more positive relationships, and the ability to make appropriate choices. In addition, it makes frustration more tolerable and boosts self-esteem (Fonagy et al. 2002; Fonagy & Target, 1997). The increasing number of mentalized-based treatments that address different populations and different diagnoses (Allen & Fonagy, 2006; Bateman and Fonagy, 2004; Fonagy & Target, 1998) have a basic core of strategies: they reflect back affect states, thoughts, and the capacity to reflect; they link behaviors to affects; and they consider multiple perspectives, question certainties, and encourage developmental thinking across time.

ATTACHMENT

Attachment theory derives its origins from the work of John Bowlby (1907–1990) when he tried to understand a group of delinquent boys, and found striking similarities in their early histories and their "affectionless" characters (Bowlby, 1944). The theories of attachment, separation, and loss were consistent with findings from other work being done by Spitz with institutionalized children (Spitz, 1945), ethnologists like Tinbergen, and cognitive researchers like Harry Harlow, who were observing similar behavioral phenomena in animal species as well (Tinbergen, 1953; Harlow & Zimmerman, 1959). Bowlby (1988) postulated that human infants are born programmed to seek proximity to caregivers through behaviors like crying, following, calling, and smiling to maintain their survival. He believed the bonds that the infant forms with a caregiver are necessary to both physical and psychological survival such that prolonged separation from the caregiver leads to predictable patterns of protest, despair, and detachment. When the caregiver is "good enough" (Winnicott, 1949) the infant is able to develop and learn normally. She internalizes a sense that the caregiver can be consistently relied on to protect, soothe, and regulate her. To Bowlby, the bedrock of positive development rested in an unbroken affectionate tie to a specific caregiver, an inborn system of social behavior he called the attachment system, which is particularly activated in the face of fear and threat. Normal development consists of the fluid, back and forth fluctuation of attachment behaviors and exploratory behaviors, which is captured succinctly in a diagram created by the Circle of Security Program (Marvin et al., 2002). Here a pair of hands symbolizes the secure base away from which a child moves to explore his world, the top of the circle, and the bottom of the circle indicates the child's need to return to the secure base of the parent for comfort, rest, and refueling.

Many brilliant minds have expanded and elaborated on Bowlby's work (Ainsworth et al., 1978; Main & Hesse, 1990) and have produced clinical applications (Slade, 2000; Steele & Steele, 2008) and critical research (Grossman, Grossman, & Naters, 2005; Sroufe et al., 2005). This research indicates that the attachment relationships which mothers form early in their own histories will predict their relationships with their own children at one year (George, Kaplan, & Main, 1985; Steele, Steele, & Fonagy, 1996). We will return to discussion and application in case descriptions later in the chapter. (For a discussion of attachment theory in relation to different psychoanalytic models, please see Fonagy, 2001.)

PSYCHOANALYSIS

Though historically there has been serious antagonism between advocates of psychoanalytic and of attachment theories, more recently a number of analysts have fashioned a fruitful détente. Fonagy argues that both attachment and psychoanalytic theories have an important element in common, namely the central symbolic function of mentalization (Fonagy, 2001). Hence mentalization plays a dual role: at the same time that it provides a guiding concept on its own, it also serves as the basis for an important bridge between attachment and psychoanalysis.

The meeting ground of attachment and psychoanalytic theory is graphically illustrated clinically in the work of Selma Fraiberg, particularly in her seminal paper, "Ghosts in the Nursery" (1987b). In this paper Fraiberg describes two cases where unresolved conflicts with caregivers in the parent's past invade the present nursery as ghosts who breed disruption in the parent-child connection. Fraiberg struggled to treat a young mother with a failure-to-thrive infant, a young mother whose own history of abuse and neglect so sabotaged her capacity to "hear her baby's cries" and respond to them, that her baby was slowly wasting away. Only when she felt that her own cries had been heard, and the split-off affects associated with her own memories were reconnected, was this mother able to begin to hear and respond to her child.

From this case and others like it, Fraiberg developed a model of infant-parent psychotherapy where past and the present can be linked, and split-off affects recovered. "In each case," says Fraiberg, "when our therapy has brought the parent to remember and re-experience his childhood anxiety and suffering, the ghosts depart and the afflicted parents become the protectors of their children against the repetition of their own conflicted past" (1987b, p. 136). Fraiberg treated mother and baby together, tangibly linking past and present, creating the opportunity to move back and forth from parent to child, and from present to past. This psychoanalytic model of infant-parent therapy is widely used in infant mental health practices today and continues to be expanded by Alicia Lieberman and her colleagues at San Francisco General Hospital. (Lieberman & Pawl, 1993; Lieberman & Van Horn, 2005.)

DESCRIPTION OF THE "CHANCES FOR CHILDREN PROGRAM"

The directors of Chances for Children (CFC) created the program to address the mental health needs of teen mothers and their babies who were enrolled together in high schools that housed nurseries in their buildings. The program, a result of collaboration among CFC, a psychodynamic training institute, and an urban department of education, was developed to strengthen parent-child relationships and support vulnerable, at-risk families. Having the teen mother and her infant in the same building during the day offers an unusual opportunity to observe and support young families in the most formative time in their relationship. Interactions in these first years of life are critical because the infant brain, particularly the orbitofrontal cortex, is rapidly developing during the perinatal period, between the last trimester of pregnancy through the first two years of life (Schore, 2001a; Siegel 2001). This area of the brain is critical to regulating stress and reading emotion. Its wiring appears to be influenced by early relational interactions, and can be damaged by traumatic interactions (Schore, 2001b). Clearly, intervention during this period can be critical to the well-being of both the teen mother and her child, and can help promote healthy attachments.

The Chances for Children Program is designed to seize the opportunity offered in these first years to pursue its mission to strengthen relationships between at-risk mothers and their infants, provide coping skills for these young parents, and prevent destructive interactions from interfering with the healthy development of both parent and child. Our goals include: strengthening attachment between parent and child; increasing positive interaction and reducing negative interaction; diagnosing and providing early treatment for mental conditions such as depression, post-traumatic stress and anxiety disorder; assessing children for early signs of pathological development; improving parenting skills; and improving coping skills. To operationalize these goals, CFC designed the following protocol, which draws on models of infant-parent treatment for difficult-to-engage populations (Lieberman & Pawl, 1993; McDonough, 1993; Marvin, Cooper, Hoffman, & Powell, 2002).

CFC Recruitment and Protocol

CFC recruited mothers by inviting prospective participants to a pizza lunch during which we presented the program. Interested mothers completed the necessary paperwork, including permission for videotaping, and scheduled appointments for a first meeting. Interestingly, participation rates were very high even though the program was entirely voluntary. This may be due in part to the use of video recording and the promise to provide copies for the parents as a record of their child's development. Video is a powerful tool in treatment, particularly with adolescents. It speaks to the adolescent's focus on herself and, by extension her baby. Video makes the mother-baby relationship tangible, observable, and reality-based. One young mother remarked tearfully after seeing herself on video with her baby, "This is the first time I really felt like I was a mother." Video allows the parent to see the child as separate from herself, setting the stage for thinking about her specific baby's individual self.

During the first session, CFC recorded a ten-minute video of mother and infant who were instructed "to play together as they might at home." The remainder of the session was spent gathering history and hearing the story of the teen's pregnancy and delivery. After the session, clinicians reviewed the recording, began formulating an assessment of the family's needs, and arranged a meeting for video feedback with the mother. In the second session, clinician and mother viewed the video together from a *strength-based perspective* and began the process of thinking about the baby together, forging an alliance as "baby-watchers."

Because different families have different needs, CFC tailored intervention to the needs of each particular parent and child. CFC used three different intervention models: developmental guidance, supportive psychotherapy, and infant-parent psychoanalytically based psychotherapy. Each family was assessed and our protocol was adapted depending on which model, or combination of models, was deemed to be most effective for the particular family. All parent-child dyads received one session weekly, and all parents also attended a weekly parents' group without children. When needed, some parents participated in individual sessions and some children received individual play therapy (see Mayers, 2005; Mayers & Siegler, 2004). In addition, many small, important therapeutic encounters occurred spontaneously in the nursery and the halls.

Regardless of the particular intervention model the family received, CFC worked to emphasize *reflection* instead of *reaction*, seeking to help mothers insert *thought* rather than habitual, dysregulated *response* into mother-child interactions. In all sessions, we worked to help the mother appreciate the extraordinary abilities of her infant and the effect she has on her child, as well as to read the baby's cues and reflect on her desires as a mother both for herself and her baby. All CFC interventions are based on the psychoanalytic assumption that our own histories shape the way we come to understand the world and the ways we act in it. A young parent brings to her parenting not only her current life situation, but her own history of being parented, her own history of separation, and her attachment experience.

The following three cases describe the kinds of interventions CFC offered. They represent the range of clinical issues we encountered, as well as the range of stressors that impinged on the teen parents apart from those usually associated with their stage of development. These cases illustrate how on-going assessment and theory informed our intervention decisions, and how we attended to the dramatic countertransferential challenges inherent in infant-parent work.

DEPRESSION: MELISSA[1]

Melissa is an alert, soft-spoken, sixteen-year-old, "A" student. When she began menstruating at age twelve, her mother laid down the rules: if you get pregnant, you leave my house. Now Melissa lives with her nine-month-old son, Marcus, in the home of her baby's father's family, where she is expected to cook and clean for her room and board. Her child has asthma and Melissa misses school repeatedly to take care of him. The baby's father's family is increasingly pressuring her to leave school to care for the baby at home "where he won't be catching germs from other babies in the nursery." Melissa has dreams of graduation, college, and a career, but the pressure is wearing her down. She misses her mother and is worried about the baby. She cries continually.

In Melissa's first video with Marcus, they are seated together comfortably on a play mat on the floor. Marcus, eight months old, is clapping two blocks together and Melissa is moving her head in time to his "music." At first they are playful and easy together. Melissa follows Marcus's lead and elaborates on his play ideas. Melissa seems more lively than I have seen her since we met, but after only a few minutes, she seems to run out of steam. Marcus, while trying to pull himself to standing, catches her long hair in his fist, and Melissa bursts into tears. Marcus starts to scream. Apologizing profusely Melissa pours out her story, telling me how exhausted she feels. Her dream is to go to college, a "real four-year college," to become an accountant. She has always believed that she could do it, though now it seems hopeless and impossible. It isn't the baby, she says, she can clean and cook and study, but she misses her mother and is haunted by the idea that she is harming the baby by bringing him to the nursery. "I feel I have no one; they [her boyfriend's parents] act like I am killing my baby. I cry at every little thing. All I want to do is sleep. My mind is so messed up, I can't even think."

Melissa was without the "supportive maternal matrix" that Stern described above. Melissa certainly did not feel "surrounded and supported, accompanied, valued, appreciated, instructed and aided" (p. 177). "Learning to parent," Stern writes, "is at best an apprenticeship . . . without this form of support, the maternal function is likely to be compromised" (p. 177). For Melissa, just when she most needed her own mother to lean on and learn from, she was instead thrown into a new household, which criticized and frightened her. From an adolescent standpoint, Melissa lost the opportunity to take the developmental step away from her mother herself, but instead, the separation was imposed on her. Feeling abandoned herself, her anger and grief were expressing themselves in a deepening depression with potentially serious consequences for her *and* for her child.

There is a wealth of research documenting the negative effects of maternal depression on infant development, both physiological and social (Cohen & Beebe, 2002; Field et al., 1988; Murray & Cooper, 1997; Tronick, 2007; Tronick & Field, 1986). For example, moments after birth, infants of depressed mothers exhibit poorer motor tone, lower activity levels, more irritability, and poorer endurance than infants of non-depressed mothers (Abrams et al., (1995). At three months postpartum, both mother and infants showed EEG asymmetries in the right frontal scalp region which predicted inhibited behavior at three years (Field et al., 1995). At six months, babies whose mothers were no longer depressed recovered normally and scored at normal levels at one year; however the infants of mothers who remained depressed after six months had inferior scores at one year on the Bayley Mental and Motor Scale (Bayley, 1969), were at a lower weight percentile, and exhibited more problems in pre-school (Field, 1997). Of the numerous theories about the mechanisms that cause these difficulties (see Murray & Cooper, 1997), Tronick's is particularly apt. He postulates that in healthy interactions, parent and infant co-create meaning about the world, and caregivers regulate the affective state of the infant, a function which the infant internalizes (Beebe, 2005; Beebe & Lachmann, 2002; Tronick & Weinberg, 1997; Tronick, 2007). However, with depressed mothers, sudden breaks in engagement can occur so that the feedback a child gets about his behavior may be confusing or entirely absent. In addition, Tronick (2007) reports finding that boys are more emotionally reactive than girls and focus more on the mother (p. 279) and that boys with depressed mothers are at greater risk than girls because they need greater emotional input from their mothers to maintain self-regulation (p. 286).

In the video described above, we saw the inability of Marcus, who was playing joyfully only seconds before, to maintain himself in the face of his mother's tears. Depressed mothers often have selective responses, responding more to negative affect and distress than to positive affect, so that instead of regulated affective states the infant learns "a depressed style of being" (Field et al., 1988). Further, many depressed mothers have more negative perceptions of themselves as mothers than non-depressed mothers and tend to hold more negative perceptions of their children (Field, 1995). When parents attribute more negative intent to their child's behavior, the child is more likely to internalize a negative representation of self.

It was our task then to mobilize adequate support for this pair so they could return to a healthy developmental path physically, emotionally, and academically. We constructed a supportive treatment that offered Melissa and Marcus a safe, stress-free place to be together and play. Here we could celebrate Melissa's considerable mothering strengths, using video to show her the effect of these behaviors on her son and to encourage hope. We offered a place where Melissa could give voice to her rage at her mother and her boyfriend's family without fear of retribution. Here she could begin to reflect on the abrupt change in her relationship with her own mother that occurred just as she was becoming a mother herself. Along with the nursery staff, we built a network of supportive maternal figures she could rely upon for both physical and emotional sustenance. We also offered her information about how to manage her son's asthma in the school setting. Melissa's social relationships had also been compromised. With all her spare periods in school used to cram in schoolwork, she had little time for friends. In our mothers' group she began to renew friendships, which created a system of support for her. They cooked and babysat for each other, and studied together.

Melissa's depression raised important questions. Research tells us that adolescent mothers are more likely to be depressed than mothers in the general population (Osofsky, Hann, & Peebles, 1993), who already manifest more depression than women who are not mothers (Hart, Field, & Roitifarb, 1999). Depression was particularly high in our population of teen mothers, approximately 37 percent. One of the most important findings from our initial outcome study (Mayers et al., 2008) was that with intervention, it is possible to change maternal behavior in spite of depression. This is particularly critical as maternal depression can take considerable time to treat and babies cannot wait. Early in life babies need to develop representations of caregivers as trustworthy, good, and reliable, as well as a self-representation of themselves as effective. These are built in a context of parent-infant interactions that move between coordinated and disrupted states again and again (Beebe & Lachmann, 2002; Tronick, 2007). In this back and forth, an infant creates strategies to repair what has gone awry, and thus learns that he or she can influence social interaction along the lines of, "*Something has gone wrong; I know how to fix it.*" Melissa and Marcus needed a sanctuary in which to build their relationship.

One of the strategies we used in sessions with Melissa and Marcus was a structured interaction between mother and child introduced as an experiment. For instance with a mother who teased her child mercilessly, we might say, "Let's see what would happen if you imitate what he is doing for a few minutes, and when I give you a signal start to tease him." We would video this interaction and discuss it. In this way the therapist assumes the onus of instigating certain negative behaviors (teasing, ignoring, intruding) so that the parent can maintain self-esteem and see the effect on the child without shame. With Melissa and Marcus we used a version of the classic experiment called the still face (Cohn & Tronick, 1983). Here a mother and child are videoed simultaneously in face to face interaction. The mother is instructed to play with the child for two minutes as she usually would, but during the next two minutes to maintain an unresponsive, poker face, not responding or reacting in any way to her baby. During the last three minutes of the recording, the mother is instructed to return to playing normally with her baby.

In the video made in our playroom, Melissa and Marcus sat together on a padded mat playing with stacking cups. When Melissa stopped playing and assumed her "still face," Marcus also stopped, confused. He looked at his mother, smiled uncertainly and crawled closer to her. He tapped her knee and waited. Getting no response, he tried again and then looked away. He banged his cup noisily looking directly at his mother. Then he threw the cup and began to protest loudly. Next he stopped, looking confused and anxious and rubbed his eyes. Opening them, he stared at her, crawled as far into her lap as he could get and began to whimper.

Seeing this in slow motion was a revelation to Melissa who quickly perceived Marcus's distress. "I can't stand seeing him like that . . . its like I was there but gone . . . he looked so miserable, lost, . . . like my mother I guess . . . she is still there but really she's not." As she continued to talk, she was able to talk about how guilty she felt feeling angry at her mother since "I knew from the beginning what would happen." She spoke of her distress at not only finding herself thrown out of her mother's home, but into a home where going to school was considered tantamount to killing her baby. She felt totally stifled, as unable to breathe as her son. Yet despite this, she could appreciate the effect her mood could have on her baby and began to observe him more closely in her different states of mind. This helped her use his needs to motivate her to change her behavior with him even when she was feeling miserable.

Discussion and Summary

In this supportive environment where we "mothered the mother," Melissa mobilized her strength to resist the pressure to abandon school, and found resources to care for her son in school safely and responsibly. Her depression lifted as her anger was heard, contained, and mobilized in the service of increased productivity. Most importantly, Melissa's own history of good-enough early mothering, her intelligence and capacity to observe and reflect, made it possible for her to resist reacting impulsively toward her baby, her boyfriend's family, her mother, and the school. She managed to graduate and to enter college the following year.

TRAUMATIC IMMIGRATION AND THE BIRTH OF A CHILD WITH DEVELOPMENTAL DELAYS: ELENA

Elena was fifteen when she fled to a crowded city in the United States with her mother to escape familial domestic violence and the political turmoil that gripped her small town in Central America. Leaving behind the rural landscape and familiar sights, sounds, smells, foods, and language of her home, Elena and her mother sought help from friends of friends who helped them find a room in an apartment that they shared with three other families. They also helped Elena enroll in school. Two months later Elena discovered that she was six months pregnant. She had had no prenatal care, was poorly nourished during the long trip to North America, and gave birth subsequently to Paolo, a baby boy with significant developmental delays. When I first met Elena she was just turning seventeen and Paolo was a year old.

In their initial video, it is striking how little Paolo moves around. Though he looks and points at what interests him and Elena is ready with a helping hand, he does not crawl or scoot about on his bottom and when he tries to pull himself to standing using Elena's body for support, he falls. At home there is a general effort to keep the baby off the floor "away from drafts, cold, and bugs" so the only floortime Paolo has is in the nursery where there is concern about his motor development. Elena steadfastly resists these concerns, not wanting to know. It is difficult to watch the initial video interaction. Paolo is working hard to pull himself to standing on every possible surface, pillow, and toy he can find, but before gaining his balance topples backwards and hits his head on the mat. "Come on get up," says Elena, pulling him awkwardly by an arm into her lap. Briefly they are face to face, and Paolo begins fingering her sweatshirt string. Elena kisses him quickly and plops him back on the floor where a similar cycle begins again as Paolo's developmental push to stand collides with his body's incapacity to comply. In the course of their ten minute recording, Elena is chatty and energetic. She creates many inventive games but appears to have no awareness of the physical dysregulation that her quick, dramatic, and abrupt movements have on the baby. Somehow the therapist seems to be the only apparent witness to the falling, startling, and assaults Paolo is enduring. During these interactions, Paolo does not cry, but rather appears somewhat stunned, sometimes rubbing his head. Toward the end of the recording, he and Elena become engaged in a peek-a-boo game; Paolo is giggling and pulling the blanket over his head. Within minutes however, he can no longer manage the escalating pace and maintain his center and balance. Inevitably he falls.

How were we to help Elena and Paolo? How were we to understand Elena's imperviousness to Paolo's needs and reluctance to seek help for him? How were we to help her manage her unspoken grief at losing not only her own developmental trajectory, but also the sense of continuity and coherence that comes from being surrounded with historically familiar surroundings?

We offered Elena a three-pronged intervention: individual sessions where she could begin to share the traumatic events of her flight to America and to grieve for all she had left behind; dyadic sessions with Paolo to increase her capacity to understand life from his perspective, and a teen mothers group to help her find friends for support and connection. I will describe elements of her individual sessions, her group participation, and finally, an interaction with the dyad that illustrates the facilitation of mentalization during a brief encounter in the nursery.

Individual Sessions

It was unexpectedly easy to form an alliance with Elena. In individual sessions she virtually exploded with her need to share her story and the jumble of feelings she could barely manage. She spoke both of the beauty of her country, the air, the smells of her backyard and the village store, the fruit so different from the hard tasteless kind she found here, and she spoke of the terrifying middle-of-the-night kidnappings of suspected political enemies, of the unpredictable shooting and looting at random hours day and night. She spoke of the long, dangerous journey to the United States, the cold, lack of food and crowding, and her constant vomiting. At first her relief at having actually arrived safely in the United States, and the excitement and newness of life here were exhilarating, but then the news and reality of her pregnancy intervened. Her mother, already drained and disoriented, became increasingly withdrawn and depressed. The few moments that she and Elena interacted ended in screaming conflict, and they became like two pressure cookers, exploding at one another before they subsided again into withdrawn silences.

Elena and her mother were governed in particular by three cultural attitudes from home: *no pensar*, not thinking about unpleasant things; *sobreponerese*, controlling oneself; and *aguantar*, bearing pain and suffering in silence (Falicov, 2000). As I learned more about these ways of being, I began to understand Elena's difficulty acknowledging Paolo's delays. She had learned to control herself and not notice, not to think of it if mentioned, and should she fail at either of these, bear what she learned in silence and carry on. Not only were these beliefs deeply ingrained in her culture, but they were necessary for survival in the terrifying environment where she had been living, and in this way had been adaptive. As Elena shared more and more of her daily experience in her home country, she found to her surprise that she did not need now to bear it alone, and discovered that others in the mother's group also had survived overwhelming circumstances. She discovered that there were other mothers who were equally without support and alone with their babies, and began to question her persistent ideas that Paolo's difficulties were her punishment for having had sex, and that her badness had created a monster.

Group Sessions

Elena was an active participant in our discussions about video clips in group. Because the babies were in a nursery on-site, we were able to video them during their daily activities. We used these videos in our groups to think together from a strength-based perspective about the needs and minds of the different babies. This encouraged mentalization as mothers discussed what a baby might be thinking or feeling as he played at bathing a baby doll at the water table, struggled to climb up the baby slide, or stack some blocks. What task was the baby working on? What was his mood? How might he be feeling about himself in this activity? How was mom feeling watching her child at his work? These kinds of discussions helped Elena and the others distinguish themselves from their children as different individuals with their own agendas. This observation of other children helped Elena begin to look more closely and objectively at Paolo. She began to think more about what it might feel like to Paolo to keep falling when he wanted so badly to stand, trying and failing again and again. As she allowed herself to see and feel for him, she realized she would have to seek early intervention services. This brought with it an upsurge of anger at Paolo for not being the baby she had imagined having, the child who was supposed to make up for all that had been left behind, the child who would love her unconditionally and make life in this foreign, lonely place bearable, the child who would keep her company and be a success. This was a complicated and difficult time for Elena; she fought with her mother, with her peers, with the nursery staff, and nearly came to blows with a classmate who made fun of her baby's sneakers.

Over time, Elena's anger dissolved into grief at all she had lost, and during Paolo's evaluation for early intervention she managed to work through her grief over his delays so that when services finally started, they represented hope and faith rather than punishment and despair. Elena's ability to achieve this was due in part to our emphasis on mentalization, a primary assumption that permeates all aspects of the Chances for Children interventions, which is that the young mother has a mind (feelings, thoughts, wishes) that we expect her to use, and we are curious about it. The following dyadic interaction offered an opportunity to put this into practice.

One early morning Elena arrived at school looking tired and more disheveled than usual. She seemed impatient with Paolo, who was cranky and clingy. She changed him into his play clothes and plopped him abruptly into a high chair to give him some breakfast. Paolo began to cry and squirm and bang on the tray. "Seems like a tough morning" I said to Elena. "I couldn't sleep," she replied, "I have a big math test and Paolo is so bad this morning. . . . I, I, um I almost hit him this morning," she said turning big scared eyes to me. "It seems like that feeling scared you," I replied. "It does scare me. The worse I feel, the worse he acts, like he knows or something." "Do you think he does know your moods?" I asked. "Si," she replied softly, "he does." By now Paolo had stopped squirming and was eating the cheerios and banana chunks on the tray. We spoke a bit about how she can tell that Paolo understands her bad moods, and why she imagines he might act cranky in those moments. "I think he wants my attention," she says, "and that makes me angrier." "So your idea is that when you feel stressed, it affects how Paolo feels and acts and then that affects the way you feel . . . like a big circle?" Elena smiled, but just at this moment Paolo started to squeeze the banana bits into a big mush which he examined, licked, and then rubbed on his face and hair. "Ay Dios mio Paolo," she moaned, "I have a math test!" "Mommy," I said, "it feels so squishy and smells so good I want to put it all over me!" I told Elena we would take care of the mess and she could go concentrate on her math test. In a dyadic session the next day, we were able to elaborate on how an idea of why a baby might be doing something affects how we respond. On the one hand, if we think the child is bad, the urge is to punish; on the other hand, if we think he is curious and creative, it gives us patience. This kind of intervention that links affects, beliefs, and mental states to behaviors, and that reflects back to the mother her capacity to reflect, begins to strengthen mentalizing.

Before moving on to the third example of the kinds of issues we encountered, it is important to reflect on the therapist's own capacity to mentalize and the effect of strong countertransference experiences on this capacity.

Maintaining the capacity to mentalize may be the most important function of the therapist working with infants and parents. Parent-infant treatment is a true odyssey during the journey to bring a dyad to a secure home while being lured, and often ensnared, by counterproductive identifications, enactments, and unprocessed countertransference along the way. Wright (1992) writes, "In infant parent psychotherapy, the countertransference experience typically involves identification with the person of the patient's infant self or of the

archaic internalized parent" (p. 130). He describes two varieties of identification: *complementary* and *concordant*. In *complementary identification*, the
therapist's identification with the baby draws him into "wanting to be the
'all-good' parent and rescue the infant." In *concordant identification*, "the
therapist merges with the affective state of the infant. This merger can easily
lead to feeling emotional hunger, rage toward the parent, or detached hopelessness in the face of the 'all-bad' parent" (p. 134). "The therapist," he
cautions, "must be able to sustain the assault of the transference and countertransference experience without retaliation or withdrawal" (p. 137). When
confronted with a depressed mother and an infant who displays the grim,
joyless exploration of a toddler who has learned that no one will be on the
other end of the toy phone he is speaking into, it is all too easy to join his
play and rescue him from feeling so alone. In doing so, however, the therapist both abandons and punishes the mother by exhibiting herself as the
"better" mother. In trying to engage a depressed mother who does not have
the background and mental capacities of Melissa, a clinician can easily be
overcome by identification with the hopelessness of both mother and child
and find herself relieved that they were absent from school all week. In Paolo
and Elena's case, it was important to understand our identification with Paolo's stunned distress when he fell over again and again in order to be able to
contain it until we could hear Elena's story and bring her to see her son's
need.

Because the countertransference experience is so powerful in parent-infant treatment, even highly experienced clinicians need the support of colleagues and supervisors for help understanding the induced affective encounters in order to use them productively in the treatment. The following discussion of aspects of Tamika's case illustrates how complex these scenarios can
be.

TRAUMATIC DISRUPTION AND DISORGANIZED ATTACHMENT: TAMIKA

"If you can raise yourself, you can raise a baby."

Tamika is fifteen and living in her ninth foster home with her daughter,
Ruby. Abused physically in her birth home, she was first placed into kinship
foster care at age six, where she moved among a series of relatives. After
being sexually abused at age eight, she was removed from the family entirely. At eleven she began selling drugs and at thirteen, after two additional
foster care placements was arrested and chose to go to jail rather than to do
community service. She spent eighteen months in jail. "I liked jail," she said
"because I got a lot of attention there." Shortly after her release, however, she

became pregnant with her daughter and found herself living once again with a foster family. Having never had a stable family, she had no idea how to be a daughter; having never been mothered herself, she had no idea how to be a mother. Somehow she miraculously traveled to school each day with bottles, diapers, stroller, and baby. In the nursery she found perhaps the only "secure base" she had ever known, and offered us the opportunity to help her become a mother to Ruby.

Tamika was extremely excited to make a video with Ruby and her excitement overwhelmed both Ruby and the therapist. Within sixty seconds Tamika has thrust two dolls, a phone, a ball, and a cup at Ruby, loudly exclaiming "Look! look!, look! Ruby, look! look!" Both are down on the mat in crawling positions and Tamika intersperses her words with noisy kisses on Ruby's cheeks. "Let's show you!" she exclaims delightedly and drags Ruby around to face the camera. "Okay, okay, okay," she says as Ruby starts to whimper. "Look dolly's coming to play! No? Ok let's read . . . look . . . the book is coming to get you! The book is coming to get you!" She chants chasing the retreating baby with the book. At this point Ruby lies flat on her stomach on the floor totally still and expressionless for eleven seconds while her mother continues banging the book on the mat inches from her face.

Watching this video evoked many complicated and difficult feelings similar to those discussed above in Melissa's case. Nevertheless, we are a strength-based program and worked to find the positive in this dyad. Tamika was enthusiastic and interested in having a relationship with her child; she showed us joyful, if somewhat manic, willingness to play and take chances, and she evidenced a budding ability to notice and respond to her child's interests. Tamika was fascinated by the video and we built an alliance watching and discussing the tape, playing together on the floor with Ruby, and so became "baby watchers" together. I wondered aloud about what Ruby might be thinking or wanting or working on developmentally.

CFC faced a formidable challenge on many levels with Tamika and Ruby. In a paper about negative maternal attributions and the intergenerational transmission of violent relational patterns, Silverman and Lieberman (1999) comment that, "Mothers who have been severely traumatized have a great deal of difficulty using discretion or containing their preoccupations and that the child's exposure to the mother's trauma is an everyday occurrence and as such, a central clinical issue" (p. 168). Tamika's traumatic beginnings infused nearly all her interactions not only with her child, but with her peers, teachers, foster parents, and therapists. She cut classes, smoked on the roof, fought with peers and teachers, and threatened repeatedly to leave her foster home. The pervasive sense of chaotic onslaught made it difficult to think, and yet the capacity to reflect coherently was needed most urgently to help her. I found myself making lists with her to organize the chaos: the pros and cons of staying in school or dropping out; the pros and cons of staying with or leaving a boyfriend, of cutting class, of smoking. I began to have a visceral understanding of why Tamika had liked jail; it provided organization and routine, attention and safety, consistency and predictability, things that had been woefully missing from Tamika's life. In describing certain psychological aspects of juvenile delinquency, Winnicott (1946) writes about the delinquent child's behavior as a strategy for establishing limits and controls that are missing in their physical environments. When the environment of the infant or toddler does not offer structure, firm enough expectations, and/or limits, the child has nothing to internalize and must depend on external forces. "If they do not have this as children," says Winnicott, "they must force us later to provide stability in the shape of . . . in the last resort . . . four walls in the shape of a prison cell" (p. 119).

As Tamika's self-regulation was so inadequate; how was she to help Ruby learn to self-regulate? In optimal circumstances, self-regulation is an outcome of a secure infant-parent attachment. Slade (2000) provides us with a useful distillation of the principles guiding attachment:

1. Infants are motivated to form maintain and preserve primary relationships because their emotional and physical *survival* depend on their doing so; (p. 1149)
2. The infant will do whatever is necessary to maintain a primary attachment relationship even at the expense of him- or herself; this adaptation then will affect his sense of self, of others, and his capacity to *regulate, contain and modulate emotions*; (p. 1150)
3. The infant's adaptation to his caregiver leads to stable *patterns* of defense and affect regulation, which become internalized representations of relationships and are carried through life into other relationships; (p. 1151)
4. Patterns of attachment are transmitted *intergenerationally* (p. 1153).

We can see already in the video described above how Ruby has learned to maintain her relationship with her mother by freezing her out, maintaining her own coherence by dissociation. On a nonverbal level, she has learned something like, "When things become too overwhelming, I can go away until I can regain enough equilibrium to find mommy again." In the meantime, the baby is operating in a heightened state of arousal that is disorganizing and compromises her ability to learn and explore, establishing patterns of behavior that will likely govern relationships to come.

Our task was to help Tamika become a non-threatening, self-contained, and containing source of security for Ruby on many different levels. In their current relationship, Ruby relied on her mother for protection and survival but concurrently was overwhelmed, frightened, and disorganized by her. Such a contradiction is one explanation proposed for the emergence of disorganized attachments in children. Here a child must seek comfort from the very person who is threatening her (Lyons-Ruth & Spielman, 2004; Lyons-Ruth, Bronfman & Atwood, 1999; Main & Hesse, 1990; Solomon & George, 1999).

Ruby was showing explicit signs of a disorganized attachment in the ways she both avoided and sought her mother. As we thought about the process of intervention with Ruby and Tamika, we were informed by current neuroscience studies of infants and parents. Researchers believe that something equivalent to a right hemisphere dialogue occurs between mother and infant that mediates attachment (Panksepp, 2001; Schore, 2001a; Siegel, 2001; Trevarthen, 2001), and that one outcome of a flexible dialogue between the respective right brains of a caregiver and her infant is a secure attachment. Besides biological and physiological regulation, the mother-infant dyad also shares the regulation of moment-to-moment stimulus-response interactions that Stern calls "affect attunements" (Stern, 1985). This is consistent with Schore's hypothesis (2001a) that the formation of attachment bonds derives from a recurrent experience of affective rhythms that are appropriately and sensitively regulated, bringing about homeostasis. For this reason he characterizes attachment theory as essentially a regulatory theory, and views the regulation of affect as the central organizing principle of development, motivation, and resilience.

Affect regulation was seriously compromised in Tamika, whose moods fluctuated dramatically. She alternately overwhelmed Ruby with manic behaviors and retreated into irritable withdrawal, leaving Ruby terrifyingly on her own. We needed to find ways to help Tamika with her own self-regulation so that she could help Ruby. We needed to find a way to promote interactions between Tamika and Ruby that were more flexible, more modulated, and more affectively attuned.

Fortunately, Tamika was hooked on video, as were most of the teen mothers in the program. As we isolated different interactions in our videos, we reflected together about past and present, and child and mother, and began to take baby steps toward a more mentalizing stance. Aspects of mentalization are indicated explicitly in the parentheses in the following vignette.

Tamika and I were watching a clip from her first video.

Therapist: So what kind of a mood were you in then? [We are labeling affects.]

Tamika: Excited.

Th: How about Ruby? [We are highlighting different perspectives.]

T: Quiet.

Th: Do you ever feel like that, quiet? [Clarification]

T: No . . . I mean . . . I guess . . . sometimes . . . but I really want to be left alone then. [She links a mood and a wish.]

Th: Tell me more about wanting to be left alone. [Elaboration]

[We explore this idea for some time.]

Th: So you said when "people mess with you too much" you want some space, and that helps you calm down. I wonder if she might be like you in that way?

We talk about different ways babies have of "getting space" or "getting away." We wonder what might happen if we tried an experiment where Ruby is the leader of play during the video, and Tamika is available but "gives her space." (This discussion sets the stage for a video we will make in a subsequent session and will discuss.) Now we return to talking about the video which is running in slow motion. I begin by describing what I am seeing:

Th: So right here Ruby is pulling on the string of the telephone . . .

T: and I give her the doll.

Th: Then what happens?

T: She doesn't want it.

Th: How can you tell? [Helping her link feeling with behavior.]

T: Cause she pushes it away!

Th: Why do you think that might be? [Thinking about what the baby might be thinking.]

T: She doesn't want to play with me.

Th: That's one way to explain it . . . or? [Expanding alternatives.]

T: Um . . . she wants to keep playing with the phone?

Th: You mean maybe she isn't finished yet?

T: Yes.

Th: So you're thinking that she had something in mind about the phone, but you had a different idea in mind. [Implies two people with different minds, thoughts, desires.]

T: Yea—I was bored so I grabbed the dolly. [Links her affect to her behavior.]

Th: To Ruby everything is a new puzzle to figure out, but to us it can be boring after a while . . . what is it like when you and Ruby have different ideas about something?

Tamika was learning slowly to observe and think about her child. Fonagy et al. (2002), after Winnicott (1967), suggest that a baby learns about his own mind by being held in the mind of his caregivers who reflect the baby back to himself. Tamika had never had the experience as a child of being held in another's mind. It was as though she felt that if she wasn't loud and provocative not only would *we* not know she was there, but indeed even *she* wouldn't know she was there. Her noise assured her attention, albeit negative, which was an external confirmation of her being.

Because Tamika needed to feel more grounded, and because her self-regulation was so tenuous, we began to work on becoming aware of body signals. "What does it feel like in your body when you are mad? I asked. Interestingly, what she described was a kind of dissociation: "My heart feels weaker. I'm like a loose feather . . . everything in my body then shuts down, like it goes black and I can't remember anything." She described her experience of anger as though it did indeed annihilate a part of her. It annihilated her mind just as her rageful behavior could annihilate my capacity to think clearly. This kind of dissociation protected Tamika and enforced a limit on her behavior. (Similarly this kind of dissociation was evident in Ruby in the video described above.)

Another way Tamika tried to regulate her intense mood swings was through the use of chocolate and candy which she ate by the boxful when she could get her hands on it. She liked the high, feeling her wild, manic side that covered her grief and despair with provocative behaviors that tested the patience of everyone in the school and in her life. "I never had a childhood so now I am having one," she announced. Though she did not like the lows, she steadfastly resisted all suggestions of a medication evaluation. In these periods she could hardly manage to stay in the room with me and when she was there, she was doing "homework." She placed a large book between us and assured me she could do several things at once. Other times she brought a friend, another mom from the nursery. When I remarked that it seemed difficult for her to stay in the room alone with me, she replied, "I know it is. Why do you think that it is hard for me to stay in class?"

As we talked about her moods, behaviors and feelings, trying to insert thought into her actions wherever possible, we also continued trying to build her ability to know what she was feeling, and to think about it before she acted. She began to notice her mood swings more and feared her inability to control herself. Finally Tamika decided she would go for a medication consult when a death in the community threw her into a serious depression filled with all the memories of her own earlier losses. She started to fantasize about killing herself, walking in front of a car, but saying she'd never do it because of Ruby. Ruby, as we might expect, was also suffering. She was doing poorly in the nursery and seemed depressed. Still Tamika and I made and missed one psychiatric appointment after another.

Tamika continued to lurch between moods, she did no work in school, and play with Ruby was difficult. Ruby began to swat her mother and scurry off to play by herself when she felt intruded on while Tamika complained like a toddler that Ruby was taking toys from her.

Finally in early March just as the school's patience was reaching its limit, I was able to accompany Tamika to a psychiatrist. Increased outbursts of intense anger, confrontational interactions, and loud sobbing in class were becoming untenable. She was given medication which helped her, and we all were able to think more clearly. We identified three triggers that set off her anger: physical threats, the inability to get away (out of a room), and feeling unnecessary. These situations set off an unbearable kind of annihilation anxiety in her. She either blew up in a rage or became louder and louder, more and more provocative. "I like it when people tease me," she announced, "because you know you are a celebrity and you know they got you in their mind."

Tamika needed the kind of external validation inherent in her comment above. She needed to feel she was, indeed, on someone's mind. However, this made her feel unacceptably dependent. In all her relationships, including with Ruby, Tamika fought her feelings of dependency and her need for external validation. Throughout life she had learned that you had to do it alone, depending on anyone simply resulted in their leaving you (as her parents, grandfather, and boyfriend had), and so it was necessary to leave first. This was particularly problematic in her relationship with Ruby as she alternately insisted on the child's attention and ignored her. What would happen, I wondered, if Ruby was angry at her mother and rejected or ignored her, evoking in Tamika the intolerable feelings of being unnecessary and abandoned.

One way Tamika protected herself against these feelings was by using self-destructive acts to destroy hope in those around her whom she depended on. I was thankful for a frame put forth by Davies and Frawley (1994) in their book on the treatment of adult survivors of childhood sexual abuse. They offer a structure of eight relational positions frequently enacted by a therapist and survivor of childhood sexual abuse. They are as follows: sadistic abuser/helpless victim; non-protecting parent/neglected child; seducer/seduced; and omnipotent rescuer/entitled child. I would like to examine the following example in light of this structure.

Just before we parted for the summer, I gave Tamika my private office number in case she wanted to contact me. (This was another advantage to working in the schools where we had the opportunity to work with some families for multiple years.) In typical fashion she phoned saying she really needed to talk to me, but left no phone number where I could call her. All my efforts to reach her failed, and I had to live with the fact that the consistency and reliability that I prided myself on had been undermined, proving to her once again that no one was to be trusted.

As I tried to understand the dilemma I found myself in, I realized how many of these positions we were enacting in this brief episode. Unable to reach her, I was thrust into the position of the non-protecting parent of Tamika, the neglected child. But it also felt truly abusive on my part not to call her back as she had asked; yet her leaving no number made me feel helpless . . . a victim to her omission. On first hearing Tamika's voice on my answering machine I was briefly seduced into believing I might be able to respond, even to help; and finally, in her call she played out the entitled child who could call and expect miracles from an omnipotent rescuer who needed no number to phone her back. Having this narrative helped me not give up in frustration, but instead to send a letter to her foster home. I was then able to wait with more patience, not knowing what had happened, but knowing that it would be fodder for the fall when we reconnected. (I was grateful not to have learned until fall that the letter was never received as the family had moved.)

Two other things helped me stay hopeful during this period, a comment by Selma Fraiberg, mother of infant-parent treatment, who worked with equally troubled young mothers, and the memory of Tamika's final video that we made in June as the semester was ending. Fraiberg (1987a) writes: "We learn that long before the clinical picture of a mother's disorder can change, there are large possibilities for change in the capacity to mother which can be brought about through supportive treatment and guidance" (p. 178). This was critically important for Ruby as she could not wait for Tamika to heal.

In our final video for the year, the frantic quality in the interaction between Tamika and Ruby was gone; Tamika could wait, follow the baby's lead, and not overwhelm Ruby with toys. Importantly, she demonstrated an ability to tolerate rejection when Ruby said "no" to her. Ruby, in turn, stopped pushing Tamika away and looked to her mother for assistance, encouragement, and assurance in increasingly reciprocal interactions. She no longer struggled to stay organized in overwhelming circumstances, but could use her energy and natural curiosity to explore at her own pace with her mother close by, but not "in her space." In Ford's words (2009), the "thinking brains" of both mother and child were no longer overwhelmed by their "survival brains," allowing relationship and exploration to flourish.

WORK IN THE SCHOOL SETTING

Before concluding, I would like to say a word about working in schools. There are special challenges working in a school setting that require a flexibility of technique uncomfortable to many clinicians. Anyone who has offered their services in school knows only too well the boundary and role confusions that can occur as soon as one crosses the threshold between office and hallway. As familiar adults around the school, we are frequently called on for help in real-life situations that reflect the many, often conflicting, needs and expectations of the various cohorts in the school community. We may be asked to step in as mediators or disciplinarians, to proctor an exam, or give homework help. We may be asked to a wake or a christening outside of school, or to visit a prospective nursery school with a teen mother. We may visit a hospital where a mother sits by her child's crib, hungry and exhausted, her family already too overwhelmed to be with her. We are continually required to assess and reevaluate our roles and make our clinical decisions in unfamiliar territory.

These challenges are balanced, however, by many advantages. The opportunities for small, recurrent, reinforcing interventions in salient moments are many and can be the most effective tool we have for strengthening relationships. There is often the question of how well change generalizes from the office to the real world. In school, we have windows into relationships throughout the day that include separations and reunions, meals, naps, exams, celebrations, studying, and socializing. These windows let us monitor the progress of our work in different settings and times. Lastly, we have the reliable presence of teen mothers and their babies already on-site and accessible on a routine basis.

CONCLUSION

The young mothers described above all needed to make sense of their tumultuous circumstances and find the inner resources to mother their babies. To address their needs, we used an approach based on best practices in the infant mental health field. Psychoanalytic theory, both old and new, informed the treatment we offered to these young parents so that they might finish high school and nurture infants who could, in turn, enter school themselves "ready to learn." Such an intervention on-site in schools offers an extraordinary opportunity to support the mental health of parent and child together.

NOTE

1. All names are pseudonyms and all identifying information has been changed to protect the identities of the families.

REFERENCES

Abrams, S. M., Field, T., Scafidi, F., & Prodromidis, M. (1995). Newborns of depressed mothers. *Infant Mental Health Journal, 16*, 233–239.

Ainsworth, M. S., Blehar, M. C., Waters, E., & Wall, S. (1978). *Patterns of attachment: A psychological study of the strange situation.* Hillsdale, NJ: Erlbaum

Allen, J. & Fonagy, P. (Eds.). (2006). *Handbook of mentalization-based treatments.* Chichester, UK: John Wiley & Sons.

Bateman, A., & Fonagy, P. (2004). *Psychotherapy for borderline personality disorder.* New York: Oxford University Press.

Bayley, N. (1969). *Bayley scales of infant development.* New York: Psychological Corporation.

Beebe, B. (2005). Mother-infant-research informs mother-infant treatment. *The Psychoanalytic Study of the Child, 60*, 7–46.

Beebe, B., & Lachmann, F. (2002). *Infant research and adult treatment: Co-constructing interactions.* Hillsdale, NJ: Analytic Press.

Bowlby, J. (1988). *A secure base: Parent child attachment and healthy human development.* London: Routledge.

Bowlby, J. (1944). Forty-four juvenile thieves: Their characters and home lives. *International Journal of Psycho-Analysis, 25*, 19–52.

Cohen, P., & Beebe, B. (2002). Videofeedback with a depressed mother and her infant: A collaborative individual psychoanalytic and mother-infant treatment. *Journal of Infant Child, Adolescent Psychotherapy, 2*, 3.

Cohn, J. F., & Tronick, E. Z. (1983). Three month old infants' reaction to simulated maternal depression. *Child Development, 54*, 334–335.

Davies, J. M., & Frawley, M. G. (1994). *Treating the adult survivor of childhood sexual abuse.* New York: Basic Books.

Falicov, C. J. (2000). *Latino families in therapy.* New York: Guilford Press, 52, 63.

Field, T. (1997). Depressed mothers and their infants. In L. Murray and P. Cooper (Eds.), *Postpartum depression and child development.* New York: Guilford Press.

Field, T., Fox, N., Pickens, J., & Nawrocki, T., (1995). Relative right frontal EEG activation in 3- to 6-month-old infants of "depressed" mothers. *Developmental Psychology, 31*, 3, 358–363.

Field, T. (1995). Infants of depressed mothers. *Infant Behavior & Development, 18*, 1, 1–13.

Field, T., Healy, B., Goldstein, S., Perry, D., Bendell, D., Schanberg, S., et al. (1988). Infants of depressed mothers show "depressed" behavior even with nondepressed adults. *Child Development, 59*, 1560–1579.

Fonagy, P. (2001). *Attachment theory and psychoanalysis.* New York: The Other Press.

Fonagy, P., Gergely, G., Jurist, E., & Target, M. (2002). *Affect regulation, mentalization, and the development of self.* New York: Other Press.

Fonagy, P., & Target, M. (1997). Attachment and reflective function: Their role in self organization. *Development and Psychopathology, 9*, 670–700.

Fonagy, P., & Target, M. (1998). Mentalization and the changing aims of child psychoanalysis. *Psychoanalytic Dialogues, 8*, 1, 87–114.

Ford, J. (2009). Neurobiological and developmental research: Clinical implications. In C. Cortois and J. Ford, (Eds.), *Treating Complex Stress Disorders* (p. 31–58). New York: Guildford Press.

Fraiberg, S. (1987a). Adolescent mothers and their babies. In L. Fraiberg (Ed.) *Selected Writings of Selma Fraiberg* (p. 166–182). Columbus: Ohio State University Press.

Fraiberg, S. (1987b). Ghosts in the nursery. In L. Fraiberg (Ed.) *Selected Writings of Selma Fraiberg* (p. 100–136). Columbus: Ohio State University Press.

George, C., Kaplan, N., & Main, M. (1985). Adult attachment interview (2nd ed.). Unpublished manuscript, University of California at Berkeley.

Grossman, K., Grossman, K. E., & Waters, E. (Eds.). (2005). *Attachment from infancy to adulthood: The major longitudinal studies*. New York: Guilford Press.

Harlow, H. & Zimmerman, R. (1959). Affectional responses in the infant monkey. *Science 130*, 421–432.

Hart, S., Field, T., & Roitifarb, M. (1999). Depressed mother's assessments of their neonates' behaviors. *Infant Mental Health Journal, 2*, 2, 200–210.

Levy-Warren, M. (1996). *The adolescent journey*. Northvale, NJ: Jason Aronson.

Lieberman, A., & Pawl, J. (1993). Infant-parent psychotherapy. In C. H. Zeanah (Ed.), *Handbook of infant mental health* (pp. 427–442). New York: Guilford Press.

Lieberman, A., & Van Horn, P. (2005). *Don't hit my mommy!: A manual for child-parent psychotherapy for young witnesses of family violence*. Washington, DC: ZERO TO THREE Press.

Lyons-Ruth, K., Bronfman, E., & Atwood, G. (1999). A relational diathesis model of hostile-helpless states of mind: Expressions in mother-infant interaction. In J. Solomon and C. George (Eds.), *Attachment disorganization* (pp. 33–70). New York: Guilford Press.

Lyons-Ruth, K., & Spielman, E. (2004). Disorganized infant attachment strategies and helpless-fearful profiles of parenting: integrating attachment research with clinical intervention. *Infant Mental Health Journal, 25*, 4, 318–335.

Main, M., & Hesse, E. (1990). Parents' unresolved traumatic experiences are related to infant disorganized attachment status: Is frightened and/or frightening parental behavior the linking mechanism? In M. Greenberg, D. Cicchetti, & E. M. Cummings. *Attachment in the preschool years: Theory, research and intervention* (pp. 161–182). Chicago: University of Chicago Press.

Marvin, R., Cooper, G., Hoffman, K., & Powell, B. (2002). The Circle of Security Project: Attachment-based intervention with caregiver-pre-school dyads. *Attachment & Human Development, 4*, 1, 107–124.

Mayers, H. (2005). Treatment of a traumatized adolescent mother and her two-year old son. *Clinical Social Work Journal, 33*, 4, 419–431.

Mayers, H., Hager-Budny, M., & Buckner, E. (2008). Chances for Children teen parent-infant project: Results of a pilot intervention for teen mothers and their infants in inner-city high schools. *Infant Mental Health Journal, 29*, 4, 320–342.

Mayers, H., & Siegler, A. (2004). Finding each other: Using a psychoanalytic-developmental perspective to build understanding and strengthen attachment between teenaged mothers and their babies. *Journal of Infant, Child, and Adolescent Psychotherapy, 3*, 4, 444–465.

McDonough, S. (1993). Interaction guidance: Understanding and treating early infant-caregiver relationship disturbances. In C. H. Zeanah (Ed.), *Handbook of infant mental health* (pp. 414–426). New York: Guilford Press.

Murray, L., & Cooper, P. (1997). *Postpartum depression and child development*. New York: Guilford Press.

Osofsky, J., Hann, D., & Peebles, C. (1993). Adolescent parenthood: Risks and opportunities for mothers and infants. In C. L. Zeanah (Ed.), *Handbook of infant mental health* (pp. 106–119). New York: Guilford Press.

Panksepp, J. (2001). The long-term psychobiological consequences of infant emotions: Prescriptions for the twenty-first century. *Infant Mental Health Journal, 22*, 132–174.

Schore, A. (2001a). Effects of a secure attachment relationship on right brain development, affect regulation, and infant mental health. *Infant Mental Health Journal, 22*, 7–66.

Schore, A. (2001b). The effects of early relational trauma on right brain development, affect regulation, and infant mental health. *Infant Mental Health Journal, 22,* 201–269.

Siegel, D. (2001). Toward an interpersonal neurobiology of the developing mind: attachment relationships, "mindsight," and neural integration. *Infant Mental Health Journal, 22,* 64–94.

Siegler, A. (1997). *The essential guide to the new adolescence.* New York: Dutton.

Silverman, R., & Lieberman, A. (1999). Negative maternal attributions: Projective identification, and the intergenerational transmission of violent relational patterns. *Psychoanalytic Dialogues, 9,* 161–186.

Slade, A. (2000). The development and organization of attachment: Implications for psychoanalysis. *Journal of the American Psychoanalytic Association, 48,* 1147–1174.

Solomon, J., & George, C. (1999). The place of disorganization in attachment theory: Linking classic observations with contemporary findings. In J. Solomon & C. George, *Attachment disorganization,* pp. 3–32. New York: Guilford Press.

Spitz, R. (1945). Hospitalism: An inquiry into the genesis of psychiatric conditions in early childhood. *Psychological Study of the Child, 1,* 53–73.

Sroufe, L. A., Egland, B., Carlson, E., & Collins, W. A. (2005). *The development of the person: The Minnesota study of risk and adaptation from birth to adulthood.* New York: Guilford Press.

Steele, H., Steele, M., & Fonagy, P. (1996). Associations among attachment classifications of mothers, fathers, and infants: Evidence for a relationship-specific perspective. *Child Development, 2,* 541–55.

Steele, H., & Steele, M. (2008). *Clinical applications of the adult attachment interview.* New York: Guilford Press.

Stern, D. (1985). *The interpersonal world of the infant.* New York: Basic Books.

Stern, D. (1995). *The motherhood constellation.* New York: Basic Books.

Tinbergen, N. (1953). *The herring gull's world.* London: Collins.

Trevarthen, C. (2001). Intrinsic motives for companionship in understanding: Their origin, development, and significance for infant mental health. *Infant Mental Health Journal, 22,* 95–131.

Tronick, E. (2007). *The neurobehavioral and social-emotional development of infants and children.* New York: W. W. Norton.

Tronick, E. Z., & Field, T. (1986). *Maternal depression and infant disturbance.* San Francisco, CA: Jossey-Bass.

Tronick, E. Z., & Weinberg, K. (1997). Depressed mothers and infants: Failure to form dyadic states of consciousness. In Murray & Cooper (Eds.), *Postpartum depression and child development* (pp. 54–84). New York: Guilford Press.

Winnicott, D. W. (1946). Some psychological aspects of juvenile delinquency. In Winnicott, Shepherd, and Davis (Eds.), *Deprivation and Delinquency* (pp. 113–120). London: Routledge.

Winnicott, D. W. (1958). Mind and its relation to the psyche-soma. In *Collected papers, through paediatrics to psychoanalysis* (pp. 243–254). New York: Basic Books, 1975.

Winnicott, D. W. (1960). The theory of the parent-infant relationship. *International Journal of Psychoanalysis, 41,* 585–595.

Winnicott, D. W. (1967). Mirror-role of mother and family in child development. In: *Playing and Reality* (pp. 111–118). London: Tavistock, 1971.

Wright, B. M. (1992). Treatment of infants and their families. In J. Brandell (Ed.), *Countertransference in psychotherapy with children and adolescents* (pp. 127–139). Northvale, NJ: Jason Aronson.

Chapter Four

Becoming and Being a Father

Some Developmental and Psychoanalytic Perspectives

Nathaniel Donson

I won't lie to you. Fatherhood isn't easy like motherhood. —Homer Simpson

We consider here several tasks: To follow a boy's development in his consolidation of a masculine identity and healthy assimilation of a future paternal role, with the caveat that the early precursors of a developmental line for fathering have a complex relationship to, and are related to but *not the same as*, a masculine identity. To follow the course of a growing child's fathering—from his or her point of view—what happens when it goes well, and also what may happen with disturbed paternal parenting.

This essay will include (1) some stories illustrating children's views of fathers and fathering; (2) the tasks of good-enough fathering; (3) comments about the healthy development of a masculine identity and paternal identity; and some of their developmental differences; (4) the problem of father hungry boys and what they miss and long for without good fathers in their lives; (5) the absolute rule that a father is always psychologically present in the life of a child and family, whether he lives with a family or not; and (6) some suggestions for working with father-hungry children and their families, including a proposal to help such a family create a virtual good father.

CHILDREN'S VIEWS OF FATHERS AND FATHERING: ANECDOTES

Jeremy, age two years: His mother is due in a month with our next child. He is sitting happily on the toilet, smiling, and pointing to his belly. "Jeremy has a baby in his belly." Naively I respond, "No Jeremy; mommy has a baby in her belly." His face falls; but then his pointing finger moves down and he gives me a delighted look. "Jeremy has a penis; mommy doesn't have a penis. Mommy has hair!" We often see pregnancy fantasies in adult men. After the birth of my first child, I realized that during "our" pregnancy I took nine months to write a paper which I then *delivered*. In many primitive cultures a child's father goes through a period of pretend birth ("couvade") which may include an enacted labor and postnatal lying in. In a recent cartoon, a pregnant man says to his surprised friend, "She told me she was the one using contraceptives!" An advertisement for condoms pictures a pregnant man commenting: "You'd be more careful if you were the one to get pregnant."

Ben, age two and one-half: I arrive in the bedroom and Ben's mother is reading to him. "Hi dad! Are you going to sleep downstairs tonight or in bed with mom and me?"

Jeremy again, age four. Without thinking much about it, I give him a sort of sentence completion test: "Mommy . . . ?" He says, "Loves." I ask, "Daddy?" "Takes care of." Years ago a woman I knew mimed her thoughts about father-mother-infant relationships . . . with a fist in the middle as the baby; one hand arched over as mother; and the other arched over the two of them as father.

Speaking of his own fathering, John Munder Ross once told me of playing "kill the giant" with his four-year-old son. His son strikes out with his sword, screaming with delight. The father crashes to the floor, closes his eyes, plays dead, but then feels something funny on his face, opens his eyes, to find his son pretending to eat him with a plastic knife and fork!! A playful attempt by a young boy to orally incorporate his father's strength and power; and that urge becomes especially intense in father hungry children.

In my office, seven-year-old Manny playfully points a toy gun at his father. His dad screams at him, "Don't you ever point a gun at me!!" When his father leaves the room, Manny looks at me. "Doesn't he know it's only a toy?"

DEVELOPMENTAL THEORIES OF FATHERHOOD AS THEY EVOLVED OVER THE LAST CENTURY

The early analytic pioneers had no developmental theories about the healthy formation of a child's paternal identity. They focused rather on a little boy's anxieties in relationship to his father and considered that a boy's wishes to bear and rear babies were primarily defensive attempts to ward off castration anxiety, and thereby left us not only with a view of men who are nurturing as weak, but also with a degraded view of women as passive opposites to men's macho assertiveness.

Freud's (1955 [1909]) signature child patient was four-year-old "Little Hans," whom he treated through conversations with his father. Hans had developed a cluster of phobic symptoms after his mother threatened him with castration for masturbating. She told him that he would be castrated by the same doctor who had delivered his mother's second child—witnessed by Little Hans—amidst her bleeding and screaming. Freud did comment that Hans in fantasy "was a mother, and wanted children with whom he could repeat the endearments that he had experienced" with his mother. However his subsequent writings left us with the view that a boy's identification with his mother resulted primarily from his *envy* of her maternal power, or— during the separation-individuation phase—as a defensive identification to repair the lost maternal relationship. Freud's views of a boy's masculine and paternal development persisted well through the early twentieth century.

In the 1930s and 1940s the child analysts who worked directly with children developed more accurate theories of early masculine and paternal identity. They regarded as healthy a boy's early identifications with his mother—her nurturance and womanliness—including his wishes to be pregnant and to carry and deliver and care for a baby. Certainly, most of the time, through middle childhood, a boy's fragile sense of his masculine identity will lead him to suppress his femininity. And since fathers in our macho American culture don't like feminine qualities in their sons, boys soon learn to deride women as the weaker sex, and especially later in life if they feel insecure about their own masculinity. Not until the 1950s was an essay that acknowledged the healthy development of a boy's wish for a child (Jacobson, 1950) finally published in a respected psychoanalytic journal.

In a series of papers in the 1970s and 1980s, John Munder Ross (1975, 1982) proposed a developmental line for male gender identity, with a particular emphasis on childbearing and child rearing fantasies which then propel later impulses toward generativity and nurturance in boys and men. Ross (1975) wrote of men's identifications with their first caregiver, their mother, emphasizing that:

> their bedrock femininity will always be in conflict with their "equally innate aggressivity." "First of all," he said, "men wish to be women sometimes . . . to be charmed by children, to be passive, sexy, sensuous, feminine." He continued, "A boy starts out being nurtured by his mother; then [acts] to extract nurturance from his mother, and then to partially parent himself by means of transitional zone [transitional object] phenomena. In an identification with his mother during the rapprochement phase, the young boy begins to generate specific wishes to bear and nurse babies. But then something happens. . . . With the ascendancy of an intrusive male identity, with his disappointment in being unable to share his mother's bed, and with the threat of competition by

his father hanging over his head, his best possible solution becomes a compensatory urge to be and to be like his father, productive, caring, giving, and someday to become a father himself. (p. 785)

Judith Trowell and Alicia Etchegoyen (2002) in their book, *The Importance of Fathers* suggested a number of good-father requirements:

> When a man becomes a father it is not only biologic issues that are involved. Becoming a father involves psychological and emotional changes; the child's interests have to take precedence over his own. In order to be mentally and emotionally ready for this, a man needs to have had reasonably satisfactory childhood experiences. He needs to have in his internal world internalized carers who were able to meet his emotional [psychological, physical, and social] needs well enough, most of the time. This is developed [early on] when [he] has had the experience of another who is reliably and consistently available, who can contain and process their own and their child's thoughts and feelings. They must also have been able to manage his and their own anger and envy appropriately. If not, then he needs to have subsequent relationships [for example, with his wife or with close male father-friends] that ameliorate these early adverse experiences. The individual man needs to have a [secure] sense of his [masculine] identity, and also a sense of self—"this is what I'm good at; these are my faults or weaknesses"—so that he feels confident and worthwhile as a person. This sense of a secure base is important if he is to withstand the emotional highs and lows that are an inevitable part of parenthood. Fathers then [may] have the capacity to sustain commitment; caring for a child depends more on commitment and containment than on having glowing feelings. A screaming, vomiting, soiling child in the middle of the night needs commitment. (p. 4)

Trowell and Etchegoyen also added:

> Many men find this transition from carefree young man to fatherhood—becoming one of the parental generation—particularly painful and difficult, and some try hard to avoid it. Another linked developmental step is the capacity to make and sustain satisfying intimate relationships. Whether the parents' relationship has been externally confirmed by society in "marriage" may [or may not] be important, but what certainly is important is that the father has attained the capacity to manage the emotional demands of an intense relationship. (2002, p. 5)

A father may then assist a young boy toward a "father identity," by encouraging his son to feel with him the comfort, joy, and accomplishment which he experiences in caring for a child. And conversely a father may deform a young boy's masculine and paternal identity.

Additional tasks of good-enough fathering may then include: (1) Inviting a son or daughter to separate psychologically from, *but not to dis-identify* from his/her mother; (2) helping a securely attached child emerge into the difficult world of reality outside of the maternal cocoon; (3) in the process helping his child to discover his or her separateness, autonomy, and individuality; (4) additionally, he will provide a model within the culture of origin, for his son to assume, with pleasure, a male gender role identity; and for his daughter to enjoy her emerging femininity. And finally, (5) to help children of both sexes control and become comfortable with the derivatives of their aggressive impulses and fantasies.

Ross wrote that, "Although it is largely the father who is the agent of a boy's masculine development, one of the major characteristics associated with fathers . . . *is their propensity to display aggression and invite identification in kind with their ability to do harm*" (1975, p. 786). Hopefully however, the ideal experience of fatherhood will evoke a man's love, which will resonate with a loving identification with his own mother and father who had themselves been nurturing figures during his childhood, especially in support of his masculine and paternal identity. It is during a man's reproductive years that the assumption of a caring father role allows him to come to terms with his earlier conflicted and repressed maternal desires.

The first paragraph of Selma Fraiberg and colleagues' (1975) classic essay, "Ghosts in the Nursery" begins with the following statement:

> In every nursery there are ghosts. They are the visitors from the unremembered past of the parents: the uninvited guests at the christening. Under all favorable circumstances the unfriendly and unbidden spirits [that is the parent's memories of their own parenting] are banished from the nursery and return to their subterranean dwelling place. The baby makes his own imperative claim upon parental love and, . . . the bonds of love protect the child and his parents against the intruders, the malevolent ghosts. (p. 387)

Although Fraiberg wrote primarily about mothers, a well adapted father's love and appropriate inhibition of his own natural aggression allows him to confine his expressions of hostility and sadism to teasing and playful but safe, risk taking. Such fathers will overpower their children only when they must, when reasonable demands for discipline call for restraint.

MALEVOLENT GHOSTS

Unfortunately, many fathers have their own unconscious "ghosts" so that memories of neglectful, sadistic, or belittling early parenting may explode into action and be replayed in response to a newborn son or daughter. The old saying that, "The child is the father of the man" certainly suggests that fathers may learn to be fathers from their own children; but it may also mean that a father's memories of his childhood parental care will reappear in his behaviors throughout his child's life cycle. In many such fathers malevolent "ghosts' may become dominant in caring for their own children.

Ross (1982), in his paper, "Oedipus Revisited—Lais and the Lais Complex," began with a quote from James Joyce's *Ulysses*: "The son unborn mars beauty; born he brings pain, divides attention, increases care. . . . (His) growth is his father's decline; his youth his father's envy" (p. 169). Ross then commented that all fathers have to contend with destructive impulses, which at best may serve a child's development by moving their fathers to excite and then constrain sons and daughters in the service of socialization.

After all it is usually the father who throws his infant child into the air, as mom gasps in the background! Here is another view of the Oedipus complex which is worth considering—from a Jed Rubenfeld (2006) novel called *The Interpretation of Murder*, a fictionalized potboiler about Freud's 1909 visit to the United States:

> When a little boy enters the scene, one party in this trio tends to suffer a profound jealousy—the father. He may feel that the boy intrudes on his special, exclusive relationship with his wife. He may well want to be rid of the suckling, puling intruder, whom the mother proclaims to be so perfect. He might even wish him dead. But what parent will acknowledge a wish to kill his own issue. What father will admit to being [so] jealous? The more [such] jealousies attack the [father], the more destructively will [he] behave against [his] own children, and if this occurs [he will] turn [his] own children against [him]—bringing about the very situation [he] feared—which a long time ago Freud called the "Oedipus complex." Certainly, when high risk fathers become caught up in their own unrestrained violence, and are not protected by love from their aggression toward their sons, they unwittingly will energize the worst "Oedipal" outcomes, [particularly] their son's retaliatory wish to eliminate his father. (p. 325–336)

In a number of papers by James Herzog, well summarized in his book entitled *Father Hunger* (2001), he explores a child's mental representations of his father in the modulation of his aggressive drives. In a paper on sleep disturbances in young boys, Herzog comments that the sleep disturbed boys he observed had a specific need for their fathers. The loss of their fathers felt to them as though their own aggressive impulses were out of control and were projected and experienced as nightmares, attacking them in the guise of monsters. In boys who have suffered the loss of their father, their unrestrained aggressions, often mobilized and energized by that loss, often give them plenty of trouble. Herzog also offers a similar case of a sleep disturbed young girl, making clear that his ideas apply to the fathering of girls as well as boys. The common element in all of their dreams appeared to be the child's inability to ward off a state of heightened aggression during sleep. Herzog (1980) comments, "A boy [not only] needs his father for the formation of a sense of self, for completion of separation-individuation, and for consolidation of [a] core gender identity, [but particularly for the] modulation of his aggressive [drives]" (p. 229). Herzog calls the affective state which exists when these needs are not being met *father hunger*.

FATHER HUNGRY BOYS

Several years ago at the agency where I work, I was asked to see a five-year-old boy whom I felt was "father hungry." My notes read as follows: "Mother sleeps with him . . . she does not acknowledge the realities of his father's life . . . but simply condemns him and acts as the 'gatekeeper' to her son's relationship to his father. . . . Although his father is demonized, this boy identifies strongly with his father . . . therefore his fantasy life has become frightening because he experiences himself as a scary monster . . . so he is afraid to let himself go to sleep at night." His therapist, who had not yet understood this boy's "father hunger," felt that the ambiance of the therapy was chaotic.

In reading Ross's and Herzog's papers, I realized that almost every one of the most disturbed children I have seen in my office practice and elsewhere, have had either weak, unreliable, absent, or sadistic fathers. I also realized that whenever the therapeutic work with these children was successful, it always included a reworking of their paternal mental representations, and often enough by positive and caring responses from the fathers themselves.

I was asked to consult with his therapist about a wild, angry, oppositional, five-year-old who had spent two years in a therapeutic nursery because of violent behaviors as a toddler. He now acted tough and defiant toward his parents and teachers. When restrained, he screamed and cried. In response to his back talk his mother became anxious, depressed, and withdrawn: "No one can make him behave for long!" He often awoke at night worrying about monsters. He constantly interrupted us, talking about tigers and wolves, about getting beaten up, and played on the floor at violent assaults with King Kong and dinosaur puppets.

I felt however that he would respond to restraint. With his mother's permission, I took him for a walk, sat him in a chair, and held him down. He screamed at me, "Let go!!" I told him to fold his hands; I would release him as soon as he sat quietly and counted slowly from one to ten. He yelled at me that I was hurting him, screamed and struggled, then tried to joke his way out with giggles and pratfalls. But I held him even more firmly and told him harshly, "This is not a game!" It took about five minutes until he knew I meant to hold him until he did what I said. Finally he counted slowly to ten. "Are you gonna keep me here all day?" I released him, and a few minutes later we repeated the whole process. At first he sat on the floor, but when I pointed, he climbed back into the chair; crossing his hands behind him, he told me to "Put on the handcuffs." Back in the consulting room, he was much calmer, happily told his mother about the game we played, and later asked me, "When are we going to play that game again?"

A year later I saw him again after an ineffective treatment in which his father refused to participate, and his mother was never able to physically restrain him. He looked at me and said, "Hey aren't you the guy who played that game with me when I was here before?" . . . and asked to play it again. Later I helped his father hold him when he had a meltdown. After a few minutes, held tightly in his father's arms, he became quieter, calmly turned to his father and asked him to read him a story.

But later, during another melt down, his father was unwilling and apparently unable to hold him firmly, but instead shouted at him to calm down. His screaming just continued. In effect, I felt that this child's treatment would fail, and it did once again. Despite his therapist's attempts to help, his father was never able to provide the sort of calm, strong, intense *physical* restraint which this boy needed to internalize as self-restraint for his own safety and protection. This father was too frightened of his own aggression and therefore unable to be aggressive enough in restraining his son—another variation on the theme of father absence and father hunger.

Some Social and Behavioral Derivatives of Father Hunger

So what eventually happens to father hungry boys? Nancy Boyd Franklin (2001) in her book, *Boys to Men*, vividly takes up the problem of unavailable physically and emotionally absent fathers. In the African American community that she writes about, 50 percent of fathers are unavailable to their sons; and 70 percent of jailed black men had fathers who were chronically unavailable. It would seem that many of these men, in their own childhood father hunger, have, without being aware of it, identified with and relentlessly carried out their own father's criminal life styles—a tragic example of a paternal "trans-generational transmission of trauma."

Franklin tells us that the sons of single mothers often become, by default, her man child, friend, confidant, partner, often the target of her passion, long before a boy is ready for any such roles, let alone with his mother. In addition, many bitter single mothers demonize, devalue, and denigrate their children's fathers; and in doing so become the psychological gatekeepers to their child's fantasied as well as actual relationship to the father. With an absent father, powered by chronic father hunger, these sons (and daughters) will, in middle childhood and early adolescence, inevitably identify with their devalued and criminalized fathers; and in apparently unexplainable acts of rage and spite, will often become angry and defiant toward all of their mother's former rules for good behavior. Certainly some of this may be offset if there is a strong stepfather or grandfather in the picture. Although she writes particularly about the African-American community, Franklin's statistics suggest the very powerful father forces at play in the mind of every father hungry child and adolescent.

It is therefore to be taken as an absolute clinical rule: *The father is never absent; he is always a live and vital presence in the consulting room, whether we can see him or not!!*

THE FATHER IS ALWAYS IN THE ROOM

One of my first patients in practice, a boy who had been reared by a loving mother and adoptive stepfather, suddenly at the age of fourteen began to take dangerous risks, steal from his family and friends, and become truant from school. His mother had become pregnant by a man who promptly abandoned her, and whom she told her son was a worthless criminal and drug addict; his name was never to be spoken at home.

As we explored this adolescent boy's sudden change toward delinquency, we figured out together that he was trying to find out who his "real" father was. In the excitement of his misbehaviors, he was "trying out" some of his father's alleged criminal behaviors. In a family meeting, after a very careful preparation with his mother and stepfather, I suggested that he ask his mother about all the details she knew about his father's life. Very quickly, and for the first time together, they wept, mourning their mutual loss. His delinquent behaviors subsequently disappeared, and to the best of my knowledge the cure was complete. This adolescent's case taught me for the rest of my career that when an absent, damaged, or delinquent father has entered a child's unconscious mind—in the compelling urgency of his paternal need and father hunger—often enough his child may for a time become like him: violent, impulsive, delinquent, sadistic, drug addicted. How often we have heard from a confused despairing single mother who has raised her son in the most loving manner that, "He is becoming just like his father!!"

All studies of families and children whose father's have perished in war (from World War II to the fathers killed in the Israeli wars) show the ever-lasting impact of a beloved father's memory in the lives of his children—growing up and grown up. If a dead father can be such a powerful force inside a child, would not a living father—albeit absent, drug addicted, incarcerated, abandoning, or domestically abusive—persist as a powerful force in a child's development? A lifetime sense of a lost, although psychologically present good father, may become a healthy support for a child growing up; but an absent father, depending on how the loss is handled by present or surviving members of a family, may also become deforming and malignant. Either way such fathers remain a powerful force in the inner lives of surviving parents and their children, and remain a uniquely enlivened presence within every child at each developmental stage.

A colleague of mine, whose father died when he was fourteen, once told me, "I talk to my father every day." Another friend began a poem about his childhood father loss with, "I've borne a loss for fifty years, And in a hidden silent space, With room for only me, And for my long dead shadow . . ." He spoke of his "Need for goodness (in his father's eyes), camouflaged as work," and ended his poem, "The hardest part is debt unpaid, Love's ledger closed too soon for balance. And I forever in the red" (Milano, 2010).

CLINICAL WORK WITH FATHER HUNGRY FAMILIES

Whether you can see him or not, whether demonized or remembered well, whether alive or dead, we must assume that during our therapeutic work *the father is always in the room.*

With father hungry families, we need to find ways to bring the child's family-of-origin father into our therapeutic work—particularly the more elusive father imageries which are kept out of sight—the family's paternal ghosts. This is always the most difficult part of working with single parent families. How will it be possible to evoke a therapeutic alliance with a family in whom the condemning narratives about a violent, abandoning, drug addicted, jailed, or even dead father have been so entrenched for so long? How to help a mother in such a fix to accept our therapeutic advice? That is to *focus on her child's father needs and* begin to tell her children some even-handed truths about their dad, certainly including that something good had once happened between them.

The first task must be to help an angry single mother understand that what she says about the father of her children will have a profound influence on how they turn out; to help her to recognize that her son's and daughter's paternal imageries, memories, fantasies, and inner narratives play an important part in whomever he or she is now and will become some day. And to show her as well that no matter how monolithic her story of a father's evils may be, her experience of the man will in all likelihood be very different from her child's. Their father may not have been so bad or brutal in his child's eyes. Despite a mother's reasonable attempts to protect her child as a paternal gatekeeper, many fathers have tried to give something of themselves during their new pride in fatherhood. My own experience has been that even some of the worst fathers once-upon-a-time wanted very much to be good dads to their children. With that in mind, I have often pursued fathers to come in and work with me, despite a mother's insistence that he is unavailable or not interested.

After hearing a mother's string of terribly condemning stories about a six-year-old girl's incarcerated father, I asked her daughter what she remembered about him; she drew for me a picture of him buying her and her brother ice cream cones; then another of him kneeling next to her to say prayers at bedtime. Is the mother's memory of the man in fact dead wrong? Certainly this mother may not have wanted to recall her own painful memories of disappointment and loss. Is her daughter simply idealizing her father's lost presence? Or is she in fact remembering something about her father—which secretly buoys her up every day so as to feel good and loved within herself? We know that there has been some illuminating work looking at resilient young children who have survived experiences of severe abuse or neglect, apparently without damaging emotional sequelae. Children who did well after such experiences were found to have had strong imagery and an accompanying inner narrative with a virtual parent who was protective, loving, and caring.

If a father is present, you can always wonder out loud, "How did you learn to become the father you are?" searching especially for the father's fathering, embedded in his responses. "How did your mother speak of your father?" "What about your mother's father? Your father's father?" If the father is not present, a clinician may ask a mother similar questions about the child's father, as well as asking about her experiences with paternal relationships throughout her life.

A corollary to my insistence about the presence of fathers in the home is that, in every child's mind, every family is a two-parent family. No mother can take a father's place; she cannot be both mother and father to her son or daughter. It is important too for a mother to understand that the organization of both masculine and paternal identification begins long before adolescence, long before middle childhood, and is in fact well under way during infancy and toddlerhood.

It is often helpful and may come as a relief, for a single mother to know that her child's unruly behaviors did not just come out of the blue, nor should she blame herself for an assumed deficient care, but may represent her son's or daughter's unconscious identifications with an absent father. She can then begin to make sense of what her child is doing! One could tell her that, "Way in the back of his/her mind, every child has a wish to be just like his father. Perhaps you could try to tell him not only what you feel was bad or disappointing about his dad, but also say too what you knew about him that was once good. Such balanced statements will give your child an ability to think more clearly about the kind of grown up he or she would like to be someday."

PERHAPS A VIRTUAL FATHER

A mother could say what she might have wished her child's father could have been for her as well as for everyone else in the family. So here's a proposal, hardly evidence based, but to me very appealing: How might it serve a father hungry family to create a fantasy of a father who is present, who is no longer regarded as missing, a father whose caring image might live within the family from day to day as a virtual good father, stimulating, restraining, loving, and protective? Perhaps members of that family might suggest to each other from time to time that, "If he were here, if he were caring, if he could have been strong and healthy enough" to be all of those things to his children and his family. "Lets just suppose . . ." Could such an invented fantasy of a good enough father become a daily presence, a powerful household myth, and a moral, ethical, and emotional support to an otherwise fatherless family?

Such a father imago for a family could eventually be made up of a combination of wish fulfillment, idealization, reality (even though the uglier truths may be hard to bear), and perhaps narratives of a mother's remembered or wished-for fathers or other good partners.

I am not speaking here of doing this in a magical or religious sense, although I have known families who have preserved an unavailable parent in that fashion. I did not think this up, but have known a number of families with abandoning, dead, or jailed fathers, and one with a dead mother, who have done just that. Certainly the virtual presence in the home of missing or killed wartime fathers has accomplished similar goals. I believe, therefore, that such an operational father-myth may be co-created in active dyadic therapeutic work with a family, and that his virtual presence could contribute to changing a family somehow for the better. In addition to providing an object for identification, a family father-myth would foster the construction of a healthy, restraining, and approving conscience formation in a father hungry child, as well as the consolidation of an encouraging and restraining ego ideal.

A personal experience: Years ago, when I began to play squash and racquetball, my partners would sometime say, "Good shot!" But I never felt really happy about their compliments or had a sense of having done well within myself. I remembered that my own father had never used such encouraging phrases when I did well at something. So I felt the need of, and then invented, an inner "encourager" whose virtual "Good shot!" buoyed me up when I had played well, and whose affectionate urging could sometimes keep me playing or working at a task when it seemed I would not ever succeed at it. And of course I began to realize that my professional mentors, beloved teachers, close friends, grateful students, and particularly one of my several analysts, had all become for me virtual good fathers, by projection of a "good father" imago onto these real persons in my life.

The goals and means of this sort of therapeutic work are not hard to conceptualize. Since each family's tale is unique; each family's creation of a virtual dad would need to be specific to that family's story. But it can only be put in place once the resistance of "mother-as-gatekeeper to a despised father" has been put aside. It will require first the very painful *work of mourning*— illustrated in the above case—that is, a family centered mourning for the husband and father who could have been and is terribly missed. As with any adequate mourning process which frees us to enjoy new relationships in our lives, this will free a family to move on. Working with a mother and child in dyadic treatment—or if necessary through the treatment of the child alone—one could pose questions and suggest answers in order to begin the construction of a virtual "good father" in the family and in the child's mind—the therapist asking repeatedly, "How would it be . . . ? If he were here . . . ? If he could love you the way you might want . . . ? If he could be good to you in the way a father would be good to his wife; to his child . . . ? If he could have seen you at play . . . ? If he could see the good work you did today in school . . .? If he were here to stop you from doing the things that get you into trouble . . . ? If he were, if he could, if . . ."

The perspectives in this essay have emerged from my professional life as an adult, child, and adolescent psychoanalyst and psychiatrist, with a particular interest in infant and preschool mental health. For more than ten years, I have worked with maternally-led single parent families at a New Jersey agency, the Institute for Infant and Preschool Mental Health. Many of the suggestions in this essay came from those families and I am grateful for what they have taught me.

REFERENCES

Fraiberg, S., Adelson, E., & Shapiro, V. (1975). Ghosts in the nursery. *Journal of the American Academy of Child Psychiatry, 14,* 387–421.

Franklin, N. B. (2001). *Boys to men: Raising our African American teenage sons.* New York: Plume Books.

Freud, S. (1955 [1909]). Analysis of a phobia in a four-year-old boy. *Standard Edition,* London: Hogarth Press, 3–149.

Herzog, J. (2001). *Father hunger.* New York: Routledge.

Herzog, J. (1980). Sleep disturbance and father hunger in 18 to 28 month-old boys: The Erlkonig Syndrome. *The Psychoanalytic Study of the Child, 35,* 219–233.

Jacobson, E. (1950). Development of the wish for a child in boys. *Psychoanalytic Study of the Child, 5,* 139–152.

Milano, M. (2010). Loss. *Conversations & Poetry.* Galloway, NJ: Full Court Press.

Ross, J. M. (1982). Oedipus revisited: Lais and the "Lais Complex." *The Psychoanalytic Study of the Child, 37,* 169–200.

Ross, J. M. (1975). Paternal identity: A critical review of the literature on nurturance and generativity in boys and men. *Journal of the American Psychoanalytic Association, 23*, 4, 783–813.

Rubenfeld, J. (2006). *The interpretation of murder*. New York: Henry Holt & Co.

Trowell, J., & Etchegoyen, A. (2002). *The importance of fathers*. New York: Routledge.

Chapter Five

Untangling Psyche and Soma

A Traumatized Adolescent with Lyme Disease[1]

Ann E. Alaoglu, Richard C. Fritsch, Paul M. Gedo, E. James Anthony, Andrew C. Carroll, Vincent Del Balzo, Richard Imirowicz, Karol Kullberg, Lauren Mazow, and Rebecca E. Rieger (The Chestnut Lodge Study Group)

Can severely disturbed adolescents be educated and treated in a therapeutic day school? The purpose of this paper is to suggest that, under the right conditions, they can. We discuss an adolescent, whom we call Alexa Z., who presented with a severe, persistent complex disorder. She was a school-avoidant adolescent girl with chronic somatic problems connected with Lyme disease,[2] significant trauma history, family conflict, self-injurious behavior, psychotic symptoms, and a mood disorder. Outpatient psychotherapy, aggressive psychopharmacological treatment, and short-term hospitalizations yielded no change. Yet, she made considerable progress through her treatment at a therapeutic day school.

We believe this case study illustrates the power of a multi-modal treatment approach, derived from long-term psychodynamically-oriented hospital treatment, adapted to a therapeutic day school. Below we outline the essential elements that anchored this specialized long-term residential treatment, now ostensibly extinguished by managed care organizations, and demonstrate how this model can be retained in less restrictive, school-based programs.

Long-Term Treatment Model

Rinsley (1980), Masterson (1972), and Goodrich (1987) developed similar models for treating severely disturbed adolescents that involved three phases: containment, working through, and termination. Containing the symptoms was considered merely a prerequisite for treating the underlying psychopathology, which included working through problematic intrapsychic and family dynamics in individual and family therapies. The aim was to provide containment through a locked setting and through treatment that often lasted most of the patient's adolescence. Adolescent patients were separated from their families, and sometimes contact was controlled under prescribed circumstances. The model builders believed that this separation from families was necessary to combat the mistrust, denial of illness, and use of impulsive action and somatization that are the principal common features of disturbed adolescents. The twenty-four-hour therapeutic milieu provided active nurturance, protection, and predictability, all of which facilitated the development of trust, the forming of positive attachment, and identification with new models of relating (Fritsch and Goodrich, 1990). Novel attachments allowed the adolescent to engage the world differently and offered hope that new solutions were possible.

These achievements led to a working-through phase, mostly focused on individual and family therapy, and then to a separation and termination phase. The therapeutic elements that supported this treatment mode included the following:

1. A collaborative, multi-disciplinary treatment team that communicated frequently in order to address the inevitable rifts that working with these troubled teens seemed to engender.
2. An active, containing, and interpretive milieu.
3. Separation from the putatively pathological family system, followed by active family work to help this system support the adolescent's new capabilities.
4. Therapeutically supported peer interactions, including group therapy, community meetings, and unit meetings, to improve the patient's ability to relate to peers.
5. Medication to increase the adolescent's capacity for regulating moods and cognitive processes and to reduce impulsivity.
6. Intensive individual psychotherapy to rework pathological identifications, resolve intrapsychic conflict, and promote more mature ego capabilities.
7. A therapist/administrator split which allowed the therapist to attend to the patient's inner world without the complication of managing his or

her daily life in the hospital or being responsible for prescribing medication.

8. A separate family therapist, who also acted as a liaison between family and treatment team.
9. A school to provide elements of ordinary adolescent life and to restore or help develop an interest in learning.

This long-term model shaped the inpatient treatment of adolescents at many psychodynamic hospitals, including Chestnut Lodge Hospital, where many of us worked (Anthony, 1990). Chestnut Lodge was forced to close in 2001, but its school program, now called the Lodge School, has continued operating as a day treatment program under new ownership. This school, where our patient Alexa came for treatment, has adapted the long-term inpatient model to a less restrictive, non-residential format.[3]

Many writers have documented the marked change in delivery of care to patients with treatment-resistant psychiatric disturbance over the past decade (Sharfstein, 2009; Kestenbaum, 2000). The old model of long-term inpatient treatment gave way to short-term hospitalization, which addresses issues of imminent dangerousness, followed by a continuum of care that might include residential treatment, day treatment, outpatient therapy, and special education in schools for students with emotional disturbance. In an effort to maintain patients in lower levels of care, so-called "wraparound services" (Chenven, 2010) or other community-based interventions were designed. An intervention program called Multisystemic Therapy, which includes aggressive case management, comprehensive psychiatric services, and targeted family interventions, was initially designed for conduct disorder and has shown efficacy in that population as well as some utility in treatment of substance abusers and those in psychiatric crisis (Henggeler, 2003).

Increasingly, school-based treatments have been advocated, as all children must attend school (Cooper, 2008). A community-based program called Reaching Educators Children and Parents (RECAP) that includes individual, group, classroom, teacher, and parent interventions, has shown efficacy in both internalizing and externalizing problems in 4th grade students (McClellan, 2003). Other school-based treatments have been used for social anxiety (Masia, 2001) and in the context of the trauma of war (Layne, 2008). However, from our review, while there is a discussion of the application of psychodynamically-informed consultation to schools (Solomon and Nashat, 2010), there has been no report on the application of the biopsychosocial interventions of the long-term model in the school setting.

The efficacy of school-based programs depends on school attendance and can therefore be difficult to achieve with adolescents whose prominent somatic complaints lead to frequent school absences. There are many sources of somatic symptoms similar to chronic Lyme disease in the case to be presented. Somatic symptoms are often seen in the context of a history of sexual abuse (Putnum, 2003) and in association with anxiety disorders (Ginsburg, 2006). School refusal, which is often associated with multiple somatic complaints, also has a significant association with anxiety, especially separation anxiety (King, 2001; Layne, 2003). In the context of recurrent abdominal pain, a somatic complaint frequently associated with anxiety, the long-term outcome in terms of symptom severity and impairment is correlated with anxiety, depression, low self-worth, and negative life events rather than actual severity of pain. This suggests that the treatment of the comorbid psychiatric/psychological symptomatology may improve outcome (Mulvaney, 2006). It is this kind of comprehensive approach that will be illustrated by the following case study.

Applying the Long-Term Model to the Therapeutic Day School

The most glaring losses from closing hospital programs included the containment provided by a locked setting and the new experiences provided by peer and staff interactions within a twenty-four-hour therapeutic milieu. Maintaining the adolescent within the family and the community, while it provides a more normative setting that can reinforce developmental strivings, complicates the task of helping the family and the adolescent develop new patterns of relating. It leaves treatment programs without many of the traditional means of stabilizing, calming, and protecting patients whose internal controls are compromised. Unlike hospitals, schools have no psychiatric nurses or technicians to provide active restraint or seclusion rooms for uncontrolled or dangerous behavior in a crisis. Schools must therefore find other systemic means of providing some of the containing and milieu functions previously available in inpatient programs. Some make use of behavioral techniques, such as level or point systems, while others focus on group interventions and the natural consequences of problematic patterns of behavior. Most programs also make use of psychotropic medications to help provide symptom containment.

The Lodge School program applies a model in which the development of relationships among students, teachers, and clinical staff is expected to provide much of the containment. There is a quiet room staffed by support counselors, who use relationship-based verbal interventions to help agitated students become calmer. Because the containment provided by the school is primarily interpersonal, the admission decision is based in large part on evaluation of the adolescent's potential to form attachments and achieve some degree of internal control. For those adolescents who have the nascent ego capacities for self-control, a relationship-based program in a therapeutic school can employ many of the strategies learned from long-term hospital-based treatment.

Treatment is principally aimed at activating the adolescent's healthy drive to complete development and cope with deficits. Group therapy and an active milieu that includes support counselors for interventions when a time out is needed provide an analog to the active hospital milieu. Psychodynamically-informed individual psychotherapy attends to the patient's conscious and unconscious conflicts and supports active engagement in academic and social skills learning. Family therapy attends to maladaptive family system patterns. A clinical administrator and a principal manage the transactions around admission, transitions, school functions, disciplinary action, parent contact, and funding, thus providing partial insulation for the idiosyncratic courses of the therapies. Furthermore, treatment is measured in multiple school years, which preserves a long-range perspective. Without the pressure to get better fast, the adolescent can do the hard incremental work of clearing out interferences to development and building mature, age-appropriate identities (Gedo, 2010).

Admission procedures involve a review of records from previous educational and therapeutic placements, including psychological and educational testing, and an interview with the young person and parents. Some adolescents are too risky to treat without greater physical containment. Others either lack the capacity to form attachments or have this capacity grossly compromised, and would benefit more from a behavioral rather than a relationship-based approach. Since the Lodge program follows the regular county school curriculum, the student must also have sufficient intellectual ability to participate effectively in classes. The Lodge program requires weekly family therapy sessions. Therefore, the family's ability to commit to treatment is also a determining factor. These four criteria—symptom manageability, accessibility to form attachments, ability to achieve in a regular curriculum, and a cooperative family—serve as the guideposts to the selection.

THE CASE OF ALEXA Z.

We present the treatment of Alexa to demonstrate the effectiveness of this school-based model for difficult cases. Alexa's journey from an adolescent who seemed untreatable to a functioning young adult will help illustrate the model's organizing principles. We discuss Alexa's history, considerations for her admission, her initial presentation, and the therapeutic elements that helped her.

History

According to her mother, Ms. Z., Alexa had no psychiatric difficulties prior to age nine, although Ms. Z. recalled a long history of separation difficulties.

Alexa's father left the family when she was two, and her mother remarried. That relationship ended when she was eight, and this second divorce was difficult for Alexa. Ms. Z. reported that at age nine Alexa became shy, isolated, and depressed. She also developed a variety of physical symptoms including low-grade fevers, headache, sore throat, and fatigue. Around that time she tested positive for Lyme disease and began medical treatment. Her social isolation, shyness, and tendency to depression and somatic complaints continued. Alexa, like many youngsters, was able to manage herself and learn in the comparative safety of the grade school environment with its modest social demands. In middle school, however, the developmental push of adolescence demanded a move away from the family toward greater involvement in the peer group. For Alexa, this transition was too much to manage.

At age twelve, Alexa began psychotherapy and antidepressant medication, which provided little benefit. Around her thirteenth birthday, she was psychiatrically hospitalized for six weeks following a thirty-pound weight loss over three months, worsening depression, anorexia, and insomnia. During that first hospitalization she reported that at age nine, roughly coincident with her purported tick bite and Lyme disease onset, her then fifteen-year-old brother had sexually abused her. Child Protective Services intervened and ultimately decided that her brother had to move out of the house, although he never admitted to the abuse. Alexa was placed on an eating disorder protocol and responded with weight gain. Antipsychotic and sleep medications were added. The hospital recommended day-treatment, but her mother felt that Alexa did not need this intervention. She went home and essentially never returned to school until the Lodge School admission.

Her mother had raised the possibility of continuing effects of Lyme disease while Alexa was a psychiatric inpatient. An infectious disease consultant found that the titers were negative and that no further Lyme treatment was needed at that time. Her mother was not convinced and subsequently took Alexa to an out-of-town Lyme disease specialist, who felt that her symptoms were indeed consistent with chronic Lyme disease and initiated medical treatment at the end of her sixth grade year. This treatment ultimately required placement of an indwelling venous catheter (PIC line) and a long-term course of multiple antibiotics. The temporal coincidence of the tick bite and onset of Lyme symptoms, the onset of psychiatric symptoms, and the putative sexual abuse became a conundrum that complicated treatment enormously.

Alexa attended little school in seventh grade; she was hospitalized again later that year with hopelessness, depression, suicidality, paranoia, and complaints of command hallucinations to hurt herself. Over the two-month stay at the hospital, her symptom picture changed little. The school system referred Alexa to the Lodge School, based on its reputation for helping persistently and seriously disturbed school-avoidant adolescents.

Admission Considerations

Alexa would have been a good candidate for long-term residential treatment. Her clinical presentation was complex, persistent, and severe, and her family situation seemed to be unwittingly exacerbating her difficulties. Since puberty, she had not progressed, either developmentally or educationally, and competent office-based treatment and hospitalizations had failed to alter the trajectory of her decline. Her history certainly gave the school administrators pause. However, the interview process provided some hope that Alexa and her family were ready for a new beginning. Alexa said little in the interviews, but she did focus on the other person and reacted to certain comments with lively facial expressions and an enigmatic smile. Ms. Z. wanted Alexa to resume her education and was open and related in interactions with the principal and clinical director. Though clearly a risky admission, the school decided to take a chance on her. Administrators based their decision as much on the countertransference-derived hunches as on the formal criteria. There was something very plaintive about Alexa's presentation; although silent, she was clearly engaged. She had average intelligence and had achieved success in school prior to her breakdown. Furthermore, the fact that there was a trauma history paradoxically provided a hope that the somatic preoccupations and the psychotic symptoms might represent something other than the prodromal phase of a schizophrenic illness.

Containment: Relational

The first step in Alexa's treatment was to help her attend school on a daily basis. As expected, when Alexa entered the Lodge School, she was often absent because she was not feeling well. The teachers, who recognized her academic potential, were particularly frustrated by her absences. Although she managed to keep up with assignments from home, staff felt uncomfortable teaching Alexa in what they called a "correspondence school" format.

A particularly salient symptom occurred when Alexa was distressed at school. She would jerk her arm vigorously, banging her elbow loudly against the back of the chair. In the classroom, teachers often interpreted this behavior as attention-seeking, but they also saw it as a way Alexa chose to relieve anxiety. When staff inquired whether she needed a time out, she smiled slyly and left to go to the quiet room, which was staffed by the two young female support counselors to whom she had rapidly attached. This symptom therefore appeared both to communicate distress and also to express a wish for contact.

Alexa, like many of the students, was profoundly conflicted about her longings for dependency and relatedness, and the support counselors afforded her an indirect way to seek the comforts of connection that she both wanted and feared. When she came to the quiet room following a flailing episode, the support counselors showed an interest in getting to know her and tried to find ways to help her. This kind of relational intervention helped her quiet down and see the school as a place to be understood rather than controlled.

The school environment affords a child any number of people to whom he or she can try to connect: teachers, peers, individual therapists, family therapists, group therapists, support counselors, the principal, the clinical director, administrative staff. This array of potential relationships offers the child flexibility in finding connections that meet his or her idiosyncratic needs, diminish anxiety, motivate attendance and success, and help him or her engage in the work of the program.

Family therapy is another critical aspect of the containment phase of treatment. This was particularly true in Alexa's case, because initially her individual therapy and psychiatric care were outside the school program. Alexa's family therapist, Ms. Kullberg, began their work by allying with Alexa and her mother, and establishing their therapy as a place where potentially threatening feelings could be tolerated and kept in check. She also helped establish appropriate boundaries between the family and the rest of Alexa's treatment and school functioning, in order to give Alexa the psychological space she needed to engage.

Ms. Z. and Alexa were highly suspicious of family therapy and reported that in the past it had made things worse. The therapeutic strategy of joining the system rather than challenging it was warranted. Accordingly, Ms. Kullberg followed Ms. Z.'s lead initially, giving her a sense of control. They met without Alexa to give Ms. Z. time to share her story, give some history, and develop treatment goals. After several weeks, when Alexa joined in the sessions she remained silent, looked away, and answered questions by shrugging her shoulders. She made eye contact exclusively with her mother, to whom she often looked plaintively and at times coyly, excluding the therapist.

Periodically, Alexa's flailing movements occurred during the family sessions. Alexa's kicks were often directed toward her mother and appeared to intensify with emotionally charged topics and to dissipate with calm. Although Ms. Kullberg understood these actions as expressions of underlying conflict, she did not verbally interpret them as such. Instead, she positioned Alexa's chair away from the wall and furniture and wound a long pillow through the back and arms of her chair in order to cushion her blows, explaining that family therapy needed to be a safe place. Recognizing the family's vulnerability at this early stage of treatment, she met the gestural level expression with an environmental intervention that demonstrated the capacity of the therapist and the family therapy frame to provide containment (Greenspan, 1997).

Ms. Kullberg's ability to respond to Alexa's bizarre movements in an effective but non-judgmental and non-confrontational manner is an example of the relationship-based containment offered by the program. Tolerance for what might otherwise be viewed as threatening behavior at worst and disrespectful means of excluding the therapist at best allowed Ms. Z to trust the benevolence of the family therapist, and by extension, the school. As she and her mother came to see the school staff as allies, Alexa found it easier to come to school, where she could demonstrate growing academic competence and confidence, move partially out of the maternal orbit, and make some use of the ordinary reinforcing pleasures that come from learning, having social contact with peers, and feeling like less of an outsider.

Containment: Psychiatric

Psychiatric treatment is also integral in stabilizing and containing severely disturbed students so that they can engage in the school-based program. With Alexa, targeting symptoms for medication intervention was complex because of her age, trauma history, histrionic attitude toward her body, and ongoing Lyme disease treatment. The relationship between Lyme disease and neuropsychiatric symptoms is controversial. There have now been at least three large scale clinical trials yielding no evidence that extended antibiotic treatment for Lyme disease is beneficial (Klempner et al., 2001; Krupp et al., 2003; Fallon et al., 2008). Also, because of the confusion in how the term chronic Lyme disease is used, experts in the field do not support its use (Feder et al., 2007). Managing this issue was one of the most complex and daunting problems that the treatment team faced. Ms. Z. was convinced that the ongoing effects of Lyme disease accounted for many of Alexa's psychiatric symptoms. Experts in infectious diseases at renowned teaching hospitals disagreed with her, to no avail. The management of psychotropic medication was particularly complicated by the aggressive antibiotic treatment of the Lyme disease. What does the psychiatrist do when she is aware that a medical illness may in some ways serve as a somatic expression of resistance to development, yet the patient and mother are convinced it is the explanation for all of the trouble?

When medication management is fairly straightforward, an outside psychiatrist can effectively work with the student. For more complicated cases, in which medication has psychodynamic implications for the student and the family, this work is often better delivered by a member of the school team. During her first two years at the Lodge School, an outside psychiatrist treated Alexa. While he collaborated with Lodge School staff, eventually his treatment alliance with the family ruptured. Dr. Alaoglu, who was connected to the school, took over her psychiatric care. For Alexa, this change proved pivotal to her improvement. Dr. Alaoglu had several advantages over the outpatient psychiatrist. Her work was integrated with the work of the school and treatment team. She also benefited from having seen the failure of previous attempts to confront the mother on the role of Lyme disease in Alexa's mental health.

When Dr. Alaoglu began to treat Alexa, she was on steroid medication, three IV antibiotics, a bronchodilator, aspirin, and a host of psychiatric medications, including a benzodiazepine, a mood stabilizer, and several antipsychotics. She appeared overmedicated, sleepy, depressed, and anxious, with constantly shaking legs. Surprisingly, however, she told Dr. Alaoglu that she had tapered her benzodiazepine on her own. Perhaps, Dr. Alaoglu thought, the rapid taper explained Alexa's increase in anxiety, but it also indicated her desire to reduce her medications. Dr. Alaoglu suggested that it would be possible to decrease Alexa's neuroleptic, thinking that this affirmation of Alexa's potential for being less ill and more alert was a step toward reclaiming her autonomy and a healthy body. Alexa responded with surprise and delight. In retrospect, this intervention seemed to be a turning point in her treatment. Focusing on her potential for health rather than on her pathology seemed to give her hope.

Dr. Alaoglu was convinced that it would not be possible to attack the family's Lyme disease resistance head-on. This stance yielded interesting results. When her Lyme disease "acted up," Alexa would leave for an extended period to get IV antibiotics. Of great interest to Dr. Alaoglu, Alexa's mother now seemed to see Alexa as functioning better than Alexa herself did. Ms. Z. seemed to feel that Alexa overdramatized her physical symptoms, and she was becoming frustrated with the secondary gain Alexa seemed to derive from the sick role. This development suggested that Alexa's attachment to the Lyme disease as an explanation for her difficulties represented an entrenched style of somatization as a defense. Dr. Alaoglu simply commented to Alexa and her mother that it was regrettable that her frequent absences for IV antibiotics were interfering with her being a teenager. This intervention served to support mother's growing interest in her child's view of herself as capable, rather than ill.

The mutual respect among team members minimized the family's tendency to identify "bad" caretakers and supported management of Alexa's labile moods, psychotic thinking, somatic symptoms, cutting, and allusions to suicide. The team could keep close tabs on Alexa and was available to see her in a crisis. The collaborative team approach allowed Dr. Alaoglu to reduce Alexa's medications without undue anxiety about liability or unchecked regressions, because some of the containment of symptoms expected from medication could be provided interpersonally. A slow and persistent taper of medications resulted in increased alertness and availability for instruction.

Seemingly paradoxically, with the tapering of medications, Alexa's most troublesome symptoms, hallucinations, suicidal ideation, and the ballistic arm movements faded away. By the time she graduated, her medications were substantially decreased.

Working-Through: Family Therapy

The long-term model suggests that as the patient begins to feel stable and contained within the milieu, treatment moves into the working-through phase. The focus of treatment shifts to intrapsychic and family dynamics, which are addressed though individual and family therapy.

The family therapy focus moved toward reorganizing the family dynamics that had encumbered her development. Ms. Kullberg perceived Alexa's extended family as a highly enmeshed system, in which venturing into the outside world and individuating were not easily tolerated. Ms. Z. worked in the family business and was supported financially by her parents. Her father was the patriarch of the family and controlled all decision-making. Turmoil constantly swirled around personal and business issues, which were intertwined. The extended family vacationed, worked, and socialized together. They also kept many secrets from Grandpa, for fear of negatively impacting his health. While critical and controlling, Ms. Z.'s father was also gratifying, rewarding his daughter with cars and a new house. Ms. Z. felt highly dependent on him.

This phase of family therapy focused on Ms. Z's conception of her daughter's difficulties, and how it fit within the larger family dynamic. In sessions, Ms. Z. was extremely anxious and labile, talking, giggling, and crying without pause. She volunteered that she had been coached by other therapists not to speak for Alexa but clearly was unable to restrain herself, though she complained bitterly that Alexa would not speak for herself. Ms. Z described her long struggle to convince doctors of her daughter's Lyme disease. Seeking treatment had become a full-time job, and no one seemed to appreciate her sacrifice. She readily volunteered that she had not been a very good mother early in Alexa's life, since she, too, suffered from anger and mood lability and had been preoccupied with conflictual and abusive relationships with men. In addition to the Lyme disease, a second source of Alexa's problems, according to Ms. Z, was sexual abuse by her older brother, Jack, who was fifteen at the time. Alexa and her mother had many conflicts over Ms. Z's requirement that Alexa attend family gatherings, bringing her into contact with the allegedly abusive brother. Ms. Z. felt compelled to do this, since the grandparents would not tolerate family dissension. The family essentially demanded that Alexa ignore her feelings, which, in her mind, invalidated her experience of victimization. Ms. Z. feared disapproval and expulsion by her father, who financially supported her, if Alexa were to act on her wish to avoid contact with her brother or express her anger openly.

After careful consideration, with Ms. Kullberg's support, Alexa decided it would be helpful for her brother Jack to join some family sessions to address her pain regarding the abuse and to find ways to tolerate his presence, since she simply could not avoid him. While such sessions had the potential to scapegoat the brother further or inflame tensions, the family system seemed to put all the negative feelings and attributes into Jack but failed to deal with the underlying conflict. This dynamic prevented Alexa from claiming responsibility for her own actions and gave her the sense that her own aggression, and therefore her ability to be an agent on her own behalf, were out of bounds. So Ms. Kullberg felt the benefit of reclaiming projections was worth the risk of further alienating sister and brother.

Ms. Kullberg began a series of sessions with Ms. Z., Alexa, and Jack to discuss these old wounds. They realized that after the children's father left, when Alexa was two and Jack was eight, Jack (who resembled his father) had become a constant painful reminder of Ms. Z's loss. He had been expected to be the man of the house and had been left in charge of his younger siblings when Ms. Z was out with men. He became depressed and had difficulty in school academically and behaviorally, but never received treatment or academic remediation. Ms. Z was forthright and unremorseful about her verbal devaluing and demeaning of her son, apparently oblivious to its crippling impact. They all agreed that Alexa had been treated as the "princess," partly due to her position as the youngest child and only girl. As Alexa became symptomatic, Ms. Z. found herself pulled to indulge her, salvaging her sense of herself as a giving mother. Jack was able to relate his abuse of his sister to his own victimization and to his resentment of his sister's special status. He had been, in effect, abandoned by both parents, his father physically and his mother emotionally. This reworking of the past helped Jack rejoin the family system and reduced the need for Alexa to be the special child.

Subsequent sessions addressed Alexa's need to advocate for herself, decreasing her mother's role as her interpreter. She worked to express anger directly and to separate herself from her mother. Ms. Z. commented that "Alexa is just like me . . . she just needs a boyfriend to make herself feel better." Alexa visibly recoiled at this projection and with encouragement was able to tell her mother that she saw herself differently. She gingerly pointed out that although she wanted a boyfriend, she did not "need" one and was not like her mother, who repeatedly returned to abusive relationships in the vain hope that they might change. Ms. Z. was able to hear her observation and confirm its accuracy. Nonetheless, Alexa became anxious that she had angered her mother and needed support seeing that she could be different from her mother and that her mother could tolerate it. Eventually, Alexa defined herself as different from her family by expressing college aspirations. Ms. Z expressed tentative support for this goal, explaining that Alexa would be the first in the extended family to attend college, both a source of pride and also a clear threat to the family system since it might lead to employment outside the family.

Family therapy also addressed how the battle to get treatment for Alexa's Lyme disease had become this family's organizing umbrella. The diagnosis and treatment-seeking maintained Alexa's status quo as dependent on the family. Conflict between Ms. Z. and medical establishments also satisfied some of Alexa's own sadistic wishes, because in criticizing and blaming Ms. Z. for Alexa's difficulties, professionals were acting out some of Alexa's own anger at her. And yet competing with doctors to get treatment for Alexa buoyed Ms. Z.'s sense of self-worth and deepened her sense of attachment to her daughter.

Working-Through: Individual Psychotherapy

Psychodynamically-oriented individual psychotherapy has as its task the re-organization of the student's intrapsychic dynamics, using clarification, interpretation, ego support, and empathy to lessen conflict and create space for new solutions, both within the family and in the mind of the adolescent. Initially, Alexa continued in treatment with her outside therapist. After about a year, however, the family decided to stop that treatment when the therapist tried to pursue the sibling conflicts related to the abuse and mother's belief that Lyme disease was the sole source of Alexa's problems. Her clinical team recommended that she begin to work with a therapist at the school, so that her various treatment modalities could be well integrated and coordinated. Alexa and her family agreed, and she began working with Dr. Mazow in twice-weekly individual psychotherapy.

Alexa filled the early sessions with a heavy, sluggish silence, punctuating the dullness occasionally with coy smiles that seemed intended to provoke Dr. Mazow into asking questions that Alexa would then resist answering. Though largely non-verbal, Alexa was engaging in the way she knew best, maneuvering in the unclear boundaries of a relationship, trying to elicit intrusion by teasing and then stopping short, hinting that something big was going on that she was not telling. Dr. Mazow tried to resist the strong pull which Alexa evoked to ask these questions.

Alexa became increasingly withdrawn and depressed. While she spent the better part of many therapy hours in silence, she tended to spread her thera-peutic material throughout the milieu instead of keeping it in the therapy framework. She actively tried to mobilize the staff's concern about her, re-porting varied forms of physical and emotional distress to the support coun-selors, but not to her therapist. The counselors then felt compelled to tell Dr.

Mazow, who in turn felt compelled to find Alexa outside the hour and check in with her. Alexa would then hint at feeling severe distress, but responded to Dr. Mazow's efforts to assess the severity of these feelings with shrugs.

Alexa intensified her pressure on Dr. Mazow and the team to take initiative over her internal distress by alluding to suicide. She refused to talk to her mother directly about these feelings, and she warned Dr. Mazow not to inform the family therapist, psychiatrist, or clinical director because they would go straight to her mother. If her mother knew about her suicidal ideation she would be more likely to act on it, because her mother would be angry at her.

Dr. Mazow avoided such enactments by refusing to keep Alexa's suicidality secret and by involving the team. These episodes seemed to be enactments of Alexa's internal object world, suggested by the fact that the energy in revealing her suicidality seemed to be mostly in the boundaries of telling—or compelling others to tell for her—and once this happened, the intensity of the threat subsided. Having the clinical director and the team decide safety concerns allowed Dr. Mazow to feel less coerced and gave her the psychic space for reflection. She and Alexa could then examine what transpired between them and the ways they affected each other.

Unlike the typical adolescent, Alexa was most engaged, open, and spontaneous when talking about what was happening in the therapy relationship. Dr. Mazow used her countertransference experiences to guide her interventions, and these interpersonal, self-revealing comments, based on how their interactions made the therapist feel, became the mainstay of the therapeutic work. For example, after bearing stifling silence for a time, Dr. Mazow started to get irritated, impatient, and anxious. So she told Alexa, playfully, that she thought Alexa liked torturing her with silence to see when she would crack. Alexa laughed and agreed. She seemed relieved that her own hostility had been recognized—that it was not unspeakable—and they expressed the idea playfully together by watching the clock and timing how long Dr. Mazow could go without breaking the silence. Another example was Alexa's frequent complaints about being ignored and dismissed by everyone in her family. Then, when she refused to talk or got other people to talk for her, Dr. Mazow told her that she too felt invited to dismiss her. Alexa complained about her intrusive mother, who bombarded Alexa with questions and assumptions about what was on her mind. Then, when she hinted at something she would not reveal, Dr. Mazow said she could feel herself about to become intrusive too, and that Alexa seemed to be a master at driving people nuts trying to figure out what was on her mind.

Dr. Mazow often articulated her dilemmas aloud. If Alexa looked depressed but would not talk about it, she told Alexa she was not sure whether to keep asking and run the risk of being intrusive, or to leave her alone and run the risk of being neglectful. Alexa often responded that she was not sure what she wanted either, allowing the two to reflect on Alexa's conflicts over dependency. In these self-revealing remarks, Dr. Mazow also hoped to show Alexa that she had a mind, with its own workings, separate from Alexa's. Sometimes Alexa seemed to assume Dr. Mazow already knew her thoughts, suggesting both the wish and the fear expressed in her silence—that the other could magically know her mind without her having to say or do anything.

Alexa acknowledged her satisfaction in knowing the therapist's reactions and became increasingly open about how she evoked others' responses. She talked about the period of her abuse and her initial decline into depression, recalling how she had made faces to show she was troubled, but would refuse to explain and would then feel satisfied when people got mad at her. Clearly she too had been furious that those she relied on to protect her had not known what was happening to her. She also talked about her relationship to pets, how her dogs came to her for protection and how she often provoked her cat into scratching her when she felt urges to hurt herself. With the animals, she enacted ways she both longed for others to protect her yet provoked them into either hurting her or failing her. Later, with her constant somatic disturbances, she seemed to express the same conflicted wishes, soliciting care that was either intrusive or at least ineffective.

Toward the end of Alexa's second year at the school, Dr. Mazow announced that she would be going on maternity leave the following October. A resurgence in Alexa's medical treatment and follow-up then kept her away for most of the summer. When Alexa returned for the new school year, she seemed surprisingly bright, alert, and talkative. She had succeeded in getting her driver's license and was getting out of the house more. Dr. Alaoglu had begun reducing her medications, which not only lifted the pharmacological dullness, but also gave her a sense of pride and control over her own functioning. She also seemed enlivened by the growing boundaries on the therapy relationship—the rupture in therapy and the impending maternity leave. She now let herself connect, knowing that the connection would not become too intense.

Alexa started talking about herself in a more balanced and reflective way. She could allow others to acknowledge her successes, whereas in the past she would have felt pressed to undo them, for fear that her pain would be dismissed. She talked about changes in herself, how much more talkative she was now, and wondered whether that made her like her chatty mother. She considered ways she was like and unlike her mother, and started to allow representations of her mother to include vulnerabilities, such as neediness, rather than just cruelty. She discussed times she had felt so lonely that she too had turned toward relationships she knew were not good for her. She described her potential to become physically aggressive, her worries about snapping and punching holes in the wall.

Accompanying this vitalization came renewed periods of intense unhappiness, including panic attacks, suicidality, and the tactile hallucinations of being touched, all of which intensified as Dr. Mazow's maternity leave approached. Everything was coming back to her, she said; she was flooded with things and needed help. Dr. Mazow was both worried and hopeful, because Alexa was feeling tremendous turmoil, but she was letting herself actually feel, even talk about it. Alexa also began to speak for herself, calling Dr. Alaoglu on her own, for instance, when she started to experience floods of panic and psychotic symptoms. Her deepening involvement occurred as Dr. Mazow was about to leave, and she and Dr. Mazow talked about how limits on their connection seemed to free her up to feel it. Alexa resisted this idea but nevertheless spoke quite openly about feeling attached. She talked with impressive self-reflection about how frightening attachment was for her, because of her fears of loss, the terrible pain and guilt of her ambivalences, and her sense that her anger eventually led her to spoil any relationship.

In spite of continuing somatic preoccupations, Alexa was increasingly able to encode her experience in words, thoughts, and affective engagement rather than physical manifestations, leading with her mind instead of her body. In the course of this transformation, she became more invested in her physical appearance and started looking more attractive. She began to assert things she wanted for herself, including a place where she could feel that she belonged. She became very invested in her new job at a pet store and in many ways let herself belong comfortably there. She was admirably dedicated and reliable at work, and she developed some important friendships in the workplace. She began to shift her energy to relationships outside her family, a crucial and long-delayed developmental step. Though still deeply ambivalent about separation in ways she did not recognize, she used her work and her friendships to begin to separate from her mother. She spent the night at her friend's house, the first time she had ever willingly spent the night away from home.

As she began to separate, Alexa was willing to look more directly at the profound confusions and ambivalences she felt about her mother. How could she feel so neglected by a mother who was often so overprotective? Why did she herself feel both protective and dismissive of her mother? How could she feel both guilty and entitled to more, abandoned and intruded upon? This confusion was particularly salient in the long history of Alexa's somatic illness, during which her mother had gone to great lengths, made considerable sacrifice, and taken on the authorities, but during which Alexa still also felt a painful lack of attunement to her needs. Alexa was beginning to untangle confusions about whose needs had been met, about which of her needs her mother could recognize and respond to, and in which ways she felt abandoned and unprotected. In the process, she seemed to be finding access to gratitude and affection she also felt for her mother.

During Dr. Mazow's maternity leave, Alexa met with an interim therapist, who tried to help her maintain her progress through supportive work. Alexa regressed, but not as much as the team had feared. However, following Dr. Mazow's return in the spring, there was a serious setback.

In the spring of her senior year, Alexa was diagnosed with a recurrence of acute Lyme disease stemming from a second purported tick bite. With graduation, termination of therapies, and the prospect of her leaving home all on the horizon at the end of the school year, Alexa's chronic illness rose again to acute prominence. In the therapy relationship, Alexa and Dr. Mazow had a new chance to explore how psychological crises related to her somatic ones: how her body might distract her from her mind, how her physical illness drew her mother back in as caregiver and served to elicit, as though against her will, the nurturing she craved but simultaneously protested. This type of work allowed the therapy dyad to develop Alexa's mental space into something more robust, textured, and distinct than she had known before. By drawing Dr. Mazow into these confusing places, she was asking her for help in sorting through them.

When Dr. Mazow revealed to Alexa what ran through her own mind in the sessions, they could explore the impact Alexa's mind exerted on another's. In this way, they examined how Alexa externalized her internal object world and how it might become manifest in others. When Dr. Mazow found herself resisting an urge to become intrusive, to infantilize Alexa, to shake her in frustration and fury, she considered the possibility that Alexa was evoking this urge in her, so that she might express it for her or toward her. As Dr. Mazow talked through some of this internal experience, Alexa began to see how she steered others to treat her certain ways. The therapist tried to model resisting and reflecting about urges, as well as sorting through the confusing emotions that come with being in close relationships, especially enmeshed relationships like Alexa's maternal one. Alexa began to reclaim some of her own urges, recognizing her own agency, power, and initiative rather than remaining typecast in her own mind as the powerless victim of others' cruelty and neglect. This gave both Alexa and Dr. Mazow the hope that the gains made in the school-based treatment could continue after graduation.

Termination and Outcome

In the setting of a therapeutic school, termination takes on a unique characteristic, because it occurs within the context of high school graduation. Successful completion of high school was an accomplishment that Alexa would not have taken for granted when her treatment began. From the team's point of view, however, the date of the eventual termination is fixed the moment the student arrives. Supported by the therapy team, the family, and the staff, the student prepares to face the challenges of life after high school, whether that means college or work. This is a time of great change, and the events and ceremonies that mark the end of high school everywhere are also part of the Lodge School tradition. These preparations occur alongside senior class trips, dinners, and a prom, and all lead up to a moving graduation ceremony. Alexa actively took part in these senior activities, including the prom. Her family took great pleasure in her ability to bring a date and participate in this adolescent rite of passage. Multiple generations of her family attended her graduation, expressing their pride and gratitude at her considerable academic and social achievements.

Her treatment team still had concerns about how Alexa would do away from the structure and support of the school. She would continue to be followed by her internist for weight and medical issues and see Dr. Alaoglu for medication. However, she did not continue in outpatient psychotherapy or family therapy despite recommendations to do so. So it was with trepidation that the school said goodbye to Alexa and her family.

Over the next few years, Alexa occasionally contacted the school, providing details of her life that allowed for an assessment of her treatment outcome. In this assessment, we followed the Chestnut Lodge outcome studies approach. Poor, fair, or good outcome is a composite of three factors: the number of re-hospitalizations, work functioning, and social functioning. These three domains reflect whether a severely disturbed adolescent whose development has been derailed is able to rejoin a more normal developmental trajectory. According to her report, Alexa was never re-hospitalized psychiatrically and remained in good physical health. Following graduation, she maintained her employment outside the family business and earned positive evaluations and appropriate promotions in the retail business. In terms of social functioning, she moved out of her home, developed and maintained an intimate relationship, and married. She has peer relationships and maintains a positive connection to her family after she and her husband moved out of state. She continues to have affectionate feelings for several teachers whom she contacts via occasional email. In all three domains, Alexa appears to have achieved a good outcome.

Conclusion

How do we understand this positive outcome? Such a complex case warrants a complex perspective on the interaction of treatment, development, and good fortune. A psychopathology model would conceptualize Alexa through her several coexisting psychiatric disorders, including possible schizophrenia, a psychotic level mood disorder, a post-traumatic stress disorder, a somatization disorder, and an obsessive compulsive disorder. This lens provided a view of Alexa that, while descriptively accurate, led to short-term hospitalization, use of increasing kinds and doses of psychotropic medication, and a dismal prognosis. A biopsychosocial perspective, which underlies the treatment model used in the school, provides, from our perspective, a much more nuanced view. Alexa's presenting picture represented her best attempt to adapt to complex trauma, family patterns, and developmental challenges. Her symptoms can be understood as noisy protests over the experience of trauma, the expression of developmental delays and deficits, and the expression of unconscious fantasies. The symptoms represented a form of communication, using an action mode and repetitive enactments (Gedo, 2010), which treatment helped her to understand and encode verbally so that her development could proceed. Treatment within the biopsychosocial model operates from the perspective of removing obstacles to development by analyzing conflict and providing temporary support for the compromised ego functions, so that the normal developmental thrust that has been derailed can return to a more ordinary developmental trajectory. This takes time, requires a sturdy alliance and a coordinated staff and an appreciation for unconscious as well as conscious determinants to thinking, feeling, and behavior.

The first task of our treatment model is to contain the symptoms, which is achieved through medication, development of relationships, behavioral interventions, limit setting, family therapy, and classroom involvement. Different adolescents prosper from different admixtures of these interventions. However, the long-term model sees all of these interventions as means of facilitating the adolescent's availability for treatment, not as treatment per se. We viewed Alexa's, and her family's, behaviors as ways of unconsciously testing (Weiss & Sampson, 1986) the school's ability to provide consistent containment and to facilitate attachment despite their ambivalence, confusion, intense anger, and disillusionment with previous caretaking. Part of the "test" involves trying to evoke familiar responses from others (Sandler, 1976), such as attempts to control Alexa or intrusive insistence that she reveal her thoughts. "Passing" the test involves recognizing this pull and addressing it verbally, rather than engaging in a behavioral repetition.

The first intervention was to admit Alexa to the program, which validated her potential for change. We often find that adolescents who have been out of school for a significant period are hungry for another chance to be part of a regular school experience, and such hunger motivates them to take a chance on something new. This phenomenon is analogous to Freud's view that the patient will be willing to change—that is, to overcome *resistance* to change—because of his or her attachment to the therapist (Freud, 1912). This activated an initial positive transference to the school and its leaders. Alexa began to attend school regularly, allowing her to engage in the therapeutic resources available to her.

Forming attachments and containing symptoms are not linear processes in treatment, however. With each move forward, familiar defenses are unseated and anxieties unleashed, and a powerful counterforce surges to reinstate the status quo ante. When Alexa took steps toward individuating, she often suffered physical symptoms—a "flare-up" of the Lyme disease, with attendant loss of time at the school and therapy. And her success forming new attachments threatened to disrupt the family's fragile homeostasis and expose family secrets, including sexual abuse. Alexa found change to be terrifying; yet, with the continuing support of her teachers and therapists, and a newfound space with her mother, she activated normal developmental urges, took chances on new attachments, and got herself back on track when anxieties threatened to derail her progress.

Having a psychoanalytic perspective helped the team remain hopeful in the face of resistance. The structure of a therapist-administrator split helped diffuse the staff anxiety about this very symptomatic girl. The closely collaborating staff helped surround the patient, family, and team members with a holding environment that minimized splits and enactments. Team meetings and treatment conferences allowed teachers and therapists the opportunity to process their feelings, learn from the various countertransference reactions, and recognize the source and function of any crises that threatened progress.

The psychiatrist's willingness to reduce Alexa's medication was a pivotal point in her treatment. For this to happen, Dr. Alaoglu had to have confidence that the treatment team could help Alexa contain her anxiety, her mother's anxiety, and, significantly, their own anxiety. The school team's ability to sit with uncertainty, to tolerate archaic anger and despair expressed via enactments (Chused, 1991, 2003; Gedo, 2011), and to accept their own angry and helpless feelings evoked by Alexa's suicidality and implicit threats, required close intrastaff trust and communication. This aspect of the model, an integrated team of treaters who are familiar with each other's work, is essential in allowing the team flexibility, even in the face of some risk. With the reduction of medication, Alexa became livelier, and her latent capacities for interpersonal engagement and forming new attachments became available to her.

These changes ushered in the working through phase, where the individual therapy became more of the locus for therapeutic action, accompanied by the reorganizing work of the family therapy. Developing a therapeutic relationship and working to establish healthy boundaries within it were keys to Alexa's treatment. Alexa's work with Dr. Mazow focused on intrapsychic change, the reworking of pathological identifications and the freeing of energy for new identifications based on using her talents to meet stage-related needs. In the process, she began moving from soma to psyche, that is, from body to mind.

Dr. Mazow's demonstrating her own mind within the material was an enormously important aspect of Alexa's treatment. She told Alexa very little personal information. Instead, she revealed some of what emerged in her mind as she related to Alexa. This kind of disclosure served many purposes. It modeled the workings of a relatively intact mind—and all the dilemmas, doubts, reasoning, confusion, affects, and instincts that such a mind, for the most part, contained and expressed as mentation rather than transformed into bodily experience or denied and projected outward. Disclosing mental processes also offered an opportunity for differentiation, as Alexa saw that Dr. Mazow considered her thoughts to be separate, and that she had to work to understand them. Dr. Mazow recognized Alexa's right to privacy and considered her self-disclosure to be both her choice and her responsibility.

As Dr. Mazow described her own responses to being with Alexa, she provided an example of how she "mentalized" her own experience (Bateman and Fonagy, 2004). She elucidated her experience of Alexa's apparent hostility, seductiveness, and other feeling states. When her interpretations were correct, Alexa's delight at having the contents of her mind recognized and given voice was palpable. When she was wrong, this usefully addressed Alexa's developmentally early fantasy that others magically understood her thoughts. Alexa was then motivated to voice her disagreement. In this context the idea of two separate minds with similar but different perspectives was fleshed out, and Alexa became increasingly able to speak her own mind.

The team came to understand Alexa's coy provocative stance in the therapy as a reenactment of the traumas of neglect and incest that she had previously deemed unspeakable. In this way she invited her therapist and others to invade her mind as her body had been invaded. As she was able to delineate the boundaries of her mind, she felt more able to talk about her body, including the traumatic effects of past abuse.

And what of the Lyme disease diagnosis? The Lyme disease symptoms recurred with each regression, but the school's attitude toward it was essentially permissive. The team noted how these symptoms seemed to interfere with her life and slow her development, but were not deterred from their expectation that she would continue to progress. The team essentially thought that Alexa used her Lyme disease as a way of disowning and disconnecting from her strong feelings. Early on during her treatment at the Lodge School, often when Alexa felt strong emotions related to persistent conflict, she would go out of state for her chronic Lyme disease treatments. Most infectious disease specialists would rate these "chronic Lyme treatments" as no better than placebo (Burgdorfer et al., 1982; Tager et al., 2001; Klempner et al., 2001), doubting even the term "chronic Lyme disease" (Krupp et al., 2003). Alexa's Lodge treatment team made a conscious decision not to interfere directly and allowed Alexa to use her Lyme disease as a needed defense against strong negative emotions and unbearable family conflict. However, as Alexa and her family were increasingly able to express complex understandings in words, the physical symptoms no longer needed to serve this function and diminished in their intensity. While such a reorganization of personality and family functioning does not inoculate the adolescent against future life problems, it does, as Freud (1937) stated, put the ego in the best possible position to negotiate new challenges. Alexa and her family had an opportunity for a new way of living and, with the help of the therapeutic village, they seized it.

We draw several important conclusions from this case study. First and most importantly, integrated school-based treatment, utilizing a variation of the biopsychosocial model derived from long-term treatment settings, can be effective for adolescents with apparent treatment-resistant presentations. That is, for some adolescents, who previously only benefited from residential treatment, a school-based program can yield positive results. Second, for the intervention to have the greatest chance of success, there needs to be a team of providers that share the same theory of change and intervention. Consultation and collaboration among treaters and educators are essential for the team to stay on task and make therapeutic use of episodes of regression. Third, the interventions in this case were based on psychoanalytic theory, which attended to the unconscious processes in both Alexa and the family. It is our contention that for severely disturbed adolescents, attending to these powerful forces allows for the maximal opportunities to rework conflict, undo the residue of trauma, and support the development of inhibited or compromised ego functions. Finally, while it is true that this integrated, intensive approach requires considerable resources, the gains represented in this case are measured in dramatic changes in the trajectory of a young person's life and the lives of those who are connected to her. Schools that are organized to provide services for disturbed adolescents so that they can be educated can look to this case and this approach as an example of the power of a psychoanalytically informed, comprehensive treatment to significantly improve educational and quality of life outcomes.

NOTES

1. A version of this chapter received the 2012 Charlotte and Norbert Rieger Psychotherapy Award from the American Academy of Child and Adolescent Psychiatry in October 2012.

2. Lyme's disease is caused by a spirochete (spiral-shaped bacteria) following an infected deer tick bite (Burgdorfer et al., 1982). If left untreated, symptoms can progress from primary to secondary and tertiary (Tager et al., 2001). Most commonly these symptoms are musculoskeletal, but neurological symptoms can occur in 15 to 40 percent of patients (Klempner et al., 2001).

3. The authors would like to thank the clinical director and the faculty of the Lodge School for their invaluable assistance with the research and writing of this chapter.

REFERENCES

Anthony, E. (1990). The long-term setting. *Adolescent Psychiatry, 17*, 99–108.

Bateman, A. & Fonagy, P. (2004) *Psychotherapy for borderline personality disorder*. New York: Oxford University Press.

Burgdorfer, W., Barbour, A., Hayes, S., Benach, J., Grunwaldt, E., & Davis, J. (1982). Lyme disease—a tick born spirochetosis? *Science, 216*(4552), 1317–1319.

Chenven, M. (2010). Community systems of care for children's mental health. *Child and Adolescent Psychiatric Clinics of North America, 19*(1), 163–174.

Chused, J. (1991). The evocative power of enactments. *Journal of the American Psychoanalytic Association, 39*(3), 615–639.

Chused, J. (2003). The role of enactments. *Psychoanalytic Dialogues, 13*(5), 677–687.

Cooper, J. (2008). The federal case for school-based mental health services and supports. *Journal of the American Academy of Child and Adolescent Psychiatry, 47*(1), 4–6.

Fallon, B., Keilp, J., Corbera, K., Petkova, E., Britton, C., Dwyer, E., Slavov, I., Cheng, J., Dobkin, J., Nelson, D., & Sackeim, H. (2008). A randomized, placebo-controlled trial of repeated IV antibiotic therapy for Lyme encephalopathy. *Neurology, 70*(13), 992–1003.

Feder, H., Johnson, B., O'Connell, S., Shapiro, E., Steere, A., Wormser, G., et al. (2007). A critical appraisal of "chronic Lyme disease." *New England Journal of Medicine, 357*(14), 1422–1430.

Fonagy, P., Gergely, G., Jurist, E, & Target, M. (2002). *Affect regulation, mentalization, and the development of the self*. New York: Other Press.

Freud, S. (1912). The future prospects of psycho-analytic therapy. In J. Strachey (Ed. and trans.), *The Standard Edition of the Complete Psychological Works of Sigmund Freud*, 24 vols. London: Hogarth Press, 1953–1974, *12*, 97–108.

Freud, S. (1937). Analysis terminable and interminable. *International Journal of Psychoanalysis, 18*, 373–405.

Fritsch, R., & Goodrich W. (1990). Adolescent inpatient attachment as treatment process. *Adolescent Psychiatry, 17*, 246–263.

Gedo, P. M. (2010). Meanings of self-defeating behaviors in a school setting. *Schools: Studies in Education, 7*, 276–286.

Gedo, P. M. (2011). An island in a sea of madness: The uses of theory for in-patient adolescent treatment. *Clinical Social Work Journal, 39*(2), 132–138.

Ginsburg, G. (2006). Somatic symptoms in children and adolescents with anxiety disorders. *Journal of the American Academy of Child and Adolescent Psychiatry, 45*(10), 1179–87.

Goodrich, W. (1987). Long-term psychoanalytic treatment of adolescents. *Psychiatric Clinics of North America, 10*(2), 273–287.

Greenspan, S. (1997). *Developmentally-based psychotherapy*. Madison, CT: International Universities Press.

Hengegeler, S. (2003). One year follow-up of multisystemic therapy as an alternative to hospitalization of youths in crisis. *Journal of the American Academy of Child and Adolescent Psychiatry, 42*(5), 543–551.

Kestenbaum, C. (2000). How shall we treat the children in the 21st century? *Journal of the American Academy of Child and Adolescent Psychiatry, 39*(1), 1–10.

King, N. (2001). School refusal in children and adolescents: A review of the past ten years. *Journal of the American Academy of Child and Adolescent Psychiatry, 40*(2), 197–205.

Klempner, M., Hu, L., Evans, J., Schmid, C., Johnson, G., Trevino, R., Norton D., Levy L., Wall, D., McCall, J., Kosinski M., & Weinstein, A. (2001). Two controlled trials of antibiotic treatment in patients with persistent symptoms and a history of Lyme disease. *New England Journal of Medicine, 345*(2), 85–92.

Krupp, L., Hyman, L., Grimson, R., Coyle, P., Melville, P., Ahnn, S., Dattwyler R., & Chandler, B. (2003). Study and treatment of post Lyme disease (STOP-LD): A randomized double masked clinical trial. *Neurology, 60*(12), 1923–30.

Layne, A. (2003). Predictors of treatment response in anxious-depressed adolescents with school refusal. *Journal of the American Academy of Child and Adolescent Psychiatry, 42*(3), 319–26.

Layne, C. (2008). Effectiveness of a school-based group psychotherapy program for war-exposed adolescents: a randomized controlled trial. *Journal of the American Academy of Child and Adolescent Psychiatry, 47*(3), 1048–62.

Masia, C. (2001). School-based behavioral treatment for social anxiety disorder in adolescents: Results of a pilot study. *Journal of the American Academy of Child and Adolescent Psychiatry, 40*(7), 780–86.

Masterson, J. F. (1972). *Treatment of the borderline adolescent.* New York: John Wiley & Sons.

McClellan, J. (2003). Evidence-based treatments in child and adolescent psychiatry: An inventory. *Journal of the American Academy of Child and Adolescent Psychiatry, 42*(12), 1388–1400.

McGlashan, T. (1984). The Chestnut Lodge follow-up study. I. Follow-up methodology and study sample. *Archives of General Psychiatry, 41*(6), 573–85.

Mulvaney, S. (2006). Trajectories of symptoms and impairment for pediatric patients with functional abdominal pain: A five-year longitudinal study. *Journal of the American Academy of Child and Adolescent Psychiatry, 45*(6), 737–44.

Putnum, F. (2003). Ten year research update review: Child sexual abuse. *Journal of the American Academy of Child and Adolescent Psychiatry, 42*(3), 269–78.

Rinsley, D. B. (1980). *Treatment of the severely disturbed adolescent.* Lanham, MD: Jason Aronson.

Sandler, J. (1976). Countertransference and role responsiveness. *International Review of Psycho-Analysis, 3*, 43–47.

Sharfstein, S. (2009). Goals of inpatient treatment for psychiatric disorders. *Annual Review of Medicine, 60*, 393–403.

Solomon, M., & Nashat, S. (2010). Offering a "therapeutic presence" in schools and education settings. *Psychodynamic Practice: Individuals, Groups and Organizations, 16*(3), 289–304.

Tager, F., Fallon, B., Keilp, J., Rissenberg, M., Jones, C., & Liebowitz, M. (2001). A controlled study of cognitive deficits in children with chronic Lyme disease. *The Journal of Neuropsychiatry and Clinical Neurosciences, 13*(4), 500–507.

Weiss, J., & Sampson, H. (1986). *The psychoanalytic process.* New York: Guilford Press.

Chapter Six

Growth Groups for Kids

A School-Based Psychoanalytic Group Intervention
Project for Children Exposed to Community Violence

Erika Schmidt, Aileen Schloerb, and Bertram Cohler

THE MISSION

Violence is ubiquitous in contemporary culture, but it has particular characteristics in different communities. Children growing up in socially disadvantaged urban neighborhoods witness violence against family members, neighbors, and friends on the street and in homes. This violence often forms the backdrop of daily life and can take the form of physical fights, assaults with guns or other weapons, abusive assaults, or gang-related activity, and it is also pervasive in the media. The violence may be directed at family or friends or strangers and the child may be a witness, a victim, or an accidental bystander. By virtue of living in urban communities that are poor, no child is immune from exposure to violence.

Findings from a variety of studies of children living in the midst of urban poverty show that between 75 percent and 93 percent of school-aged children have either witnessed or themselves been the victims of violence (Overstreet and Braun 2000). Osofsky and Osofsky (2004) echo this finding: "Community violence exposure, whether isolated, frequent, or, at times, almost continuous, includes frequent and continual exposure to the use of guns, knives, drugs, and random violence. It is now unusual in urban elementary schools *not* to find children who have been exposed to such negative events" (p. 238). A principal of a school in an urban impoverished area described her reaction to the episodes of gunfire outside the school. When she first arrived at the school, she became very anxious at the sounds, immediately dropped what she was doing to call the police, and watched what happened from the window. After three years at the school, she still registers the sound of gunshots but calls the police automatically, barely looking up from her work (Sanders, 2011).

This exposure to violence can take many forms, ranging from temporary interferences in functioning; to depression, anxiety, or behavior disorders; to post-traumatic stress disorder. Whatever form it takes, children often display symptoms of interpersonal or academic problems. Bearing in mind that any individual child's reaction to violence is interpreted subjectively, the response will reflect the child's developmental level, the quality of family relationships and support, the context of the violent episode(s) and the child's position in the violent encounter, and the child's capacity to use personal and social resources to process the experience. In the aftermath of these traumatic experiences, children may complain of frightening dreams, sleep disturbances, intrusive thoughts, flashbacks, fears of recurrence, poor concentration, hyper-vigilance and hyper-arousal, numbness or avoidance, decreased interest in usual activities, and anxiety about safety. They feel helpless and unprotected, often so intolerably that these feelings are transformed into aggression and a sense of omnipotence. In a school setting this typically takes the form of behavior management problems. Children may lose interest in learning, assuming an attitude of disinterest that also serves a defensive purpose to avoid painful feeling states. Often these problems lead to emotional states that make academic achievement and classroom participation very difficult so that children exhibit behavior management problems or disinterest in learning that challenges their teachers' efforts to engage them and can disrupt the classroom process.

Exposure to violence can derail a child's forward development, particularly the emotional resources necessary for learning, such as a willingness to explore, the capacity to focus and concentrate, a sense of curiosity, the freedom to make mistakes or not know, and a sense of the future that makes learning a worthwhile activity. Critical protective factors include the stability of the child's psychological development, opportunities to process and integrate distressing experiences, and social support systems that provide a safe, growth-promoting environment. Intervention programs have been designed to help children deal with the aftermath of witnessing violence. All such programs include helping children explore the traumatic event, develop means for managing the accompanying stress, make sense of the child's understanding of what happened, and include family and others in the child's social network to support the struggle to overcome traumatic experiences (Nader, 2001).

Many children do not have adequate access to the kind of resources and intervention needed to deal with the impact of chronic exposure to violence and its unpredictable eruption in their lives. More significantly, many of the intervention programs available do not account for the chronic nature of the urban child's experience of violence. The violence may occur within the home, it may be directed toward the child or other family members, but inevitably violence will occur in the neighborhood, perhaps to people the child knows and perhaps even within a school. It is an ever-present feature of city life, sometimes in the background, sometimes in the foreground.

THE PROJECT

With generous grant funding, the City Project was designed to provide mental health services that could address the impact of this kind of trauma and its effects on children's ongoing development. To implement this mission, the City Project provides group therapy to elementary school students (grades K through 8) who have been exposed to violence and loss within the community in order to ameliorate the impact on each child's subsequent emotional development. Three features are central to the way the City Project works: (1) it is based on psychoanalytic principles of understanding development and of intervention; (2) it is offered to children in the context of the school they attend; and (3) the intervention modality is groupwork.

The psychoanalytic foundation of the project means that the behavior, thoughts, feelings, and styles of relatedness are understood in terms of the child's developmental status, the impact of trauma and loss to the ongoing stability and integrity of the child's developing self, and the underlying meaning of experiences. Much attention is paid to expressions of transferential meaning and the defensive purpose of behavior and feelings as efforts to cope with overwhelming states of mind. In discussing the value of a psychoanalytic orientation to work with community violence, Osofsky and Osofsky (2004) observe, "For children born into poverty and living under circumstances of chronic violence exposure, their view of themselves and the world around them may be marked by fragmentation, insecurity, inconsistencies, and, at times, chaos" (p. 244). It is this absence of a cohesive experience of the self and the environment that a psychoanalytic mindset can comprehend and the understanding itself can begin to contain the fragmentation. The marker of fragmented experience of the self is the absence of sense or meaning. In the act of understanding, some order can be imposed through the beginning of a narrative sense of what has occurred. It may be as rudimentary as, "You are feeling fragmented because something overwhelming happened to you and those emotional states make sense as a response." In this way, a child can begin to feel contained as meaning and continuity with experience is recognized. Built into the project are fundamental notions of structure, reliability, predictability, and continuity. Equally important are the psychoanalytic principles of listening, observing, nondefensive reactions to troubling interpersonal situations, and awareness of countertransference as a source of information.

Schools have increasingly become sites for the delivery of mental health services. There are pragmatic reasons for this, since children are a captive audience and parental commitment can, to some extent, be bypassed if children are seen in a school setting. But more importantly, schools, at their best, represent the hope for a child's potential and can become the place in which goals and ambitions for the future can be realized. This is never an unambivalently held ideal, as for many students and their parents, schools can also be a place that represents the shame of failure or unrealized hopes. The principal of one of the project schools described the school as an oasis from the continual violence of the neighborhood, so that it became for the students a "refuge and safe haven." Working within the school community, the Project has enhanced the efforts of the schools to support the students' growth and development. In an endorsement of school-based intervention, Pynoos et al. (2004) recommend that "such mental health efforts must be part of a national educational strategy to break the cycle of violence and to promote a school environment in which school personnel and students can offer their best to one another, their own futures, and society" (p. 20).

The modality for intervention in this Project is the group, building on a small psychoanalytic tradition of groupwork with troubled youth (for example, Konopka, 1954/1970; Redl & Wineman, 1952; Sklarew et al., 2004). Pragmatically, groups can serve a larger number of students, though in fact these groups are small, typically with four or five members and, if larger, with two leaders. Another rationale is the value of sharing experiences with peers and the tacit permission of the presence of others to deal with difficult topics. Unlike most group intervention models, particularly in the schools, these groups are not time-limited, nor are they problem-focused, nor are they aimed at "anger management" or psycho-educational in nature. They are structured by the leaders in accord with the needs of the group members. They are open-ended groups that meet through the school year, and that meet year after year. A student may participate for as long as he or she chooses, and most students are eager to continue from one year to the next. An important advantage of the group process is that students can gain reassurance from shared experience and can recognize a variety of ways of coping with adversity. Perhaps most importantly, the groups help create a network of support among the members, a network based on the kind of knowing that grows out of a history of deeply shared experience and the mutual respect that grows from that.

THE CONTEXT

The City Project works well to the extent that the school community can support its goals and as it can find a place within the school community. This process of developing and maintaining working alliances is never uncomplicated and requires ongoing attention. Project personnel are mindful that they are essentially guests within a host institution that operates with very different professional roles and sometimes very different assumptions about the meaning of children's problems and approaches to remediation. Yet, what becomes most important is the joining of the goal of supporting a child's development so that he or she can learn, grow, and achieve his or her full potential. To this end, educators and mental health clinicians are natural partners and it is in this spirit that Project therapists enter these schools.

Schools are identified as potential partners through community agencies to whom a principal expresses interest in the Project. Initially, Project personnel meet with the principal and other administrators to describe the project, discuss how it will fit within this school's culture and how it might respond to the needs of students that school personnel are concerned about. This often means a series of meetings in which we negotiate the terms of our partnership. These conversations contribute to a needs assessment: How does the school community perceive its needs and what kinds of problems do they want help with? How do they understand the identified problems and how do they imagine the Project can be of service to them? And perhaps most significantly, what do they think about the Project and what it can provide? We aim to provide information about what we do and how we do it, and we gather information about the school culture and the most pressing concerns of the school's principal. In this way, we demonstrate a commitment to collaboration as a basis for an ongoing working relationship.

One problem we encounter in establishing this relationship has to do with the differing professional identities and roles of educators and mental health clinicians. Educators are trained to help children acquire cognitive skills and knowledge and their professional education rarely addresses emotional aspects of learning or the psychological development of children. Yet, for the children referred to the Project, these are salient factors. The concepts of empathy, process, emotional responsivity, and the value of expressing a range of feelings are often not part of the educational agenda and some school personnel consider it antithetical to their goals. So, we have to establish some common goals, language, and markers of progress.

We explain the purpose of the groups in terms of the psychological skills children need to acquire to manage their own behavior and feelings, and to help them create the emotional motivation for learning. We explain that a goal is to help children understand themselves better, to figure out how they make sense of experience, so that they can connect their reactions to feelings evoked in them and develop a vocabulary to talk about them. We can then help them develop alternative strategies when they are angry or hurt or upset or overexcited. We focus on developing a reflective capacity so children can examine their experiences, consider their feelings, and acquire a sense of cause and effect. For example, one child concluded through many discussions, "When someone teases me about my father, I miss him and feel hurt that he was killed and taken away from me. That hurts turns into anger, so I lash out and fight." Many teachers and administrators can easily see this connection, though they may not be considering it in the maelstrom of classroom interaction. With some empathy for the child's reaction, the creation of understanding allows everyone to respond with a less punitive reaction to misbehavior, but to help a child institute better controls. We explain that this kind of self-awareness can improve a child's behavior and interest in learning.

The working relationship with the host school is always a work in progress. School personnel initially welcome the support and help we can offer. At a first meeting, one principal greeted us by saying, "You are the answer to our prayers." Because some of the students present such intransigent problems and the demands on the schools for solving society's problems are so great, school personnel frequently feel overwhelmed and underequipped to deal with troubled students. This may lead to an idealization and unrealistic hopes for what can be quickly accomplished. Such expectations are often accompanied by resentment for having to look to outside help or due to fear that any help will be critical or judgmental. Awareness of the transferences and projections that occur in such situations can be very helpful. Additionally, a lot of healthy respect for the hard work and accomplishments of overworked and under-valued educators provides a good foundation for an ongoing working relationship.

Each school has its own way of integrating the Project into its community. In some schools, we are quickly ushered in, and then kept on the margins. In others, we are kept at bay for a while and put through multiple tests of trustworthiness, dependability, and effectiveness. For example, we request a private space for the groups to meet. Since space is at a premium in many schools, this can be a difficult request to meet, yet it is essential for the group process. Confidentiality is also a concept that does not easily translate to a school setting. Around such issues, we have the opportunity to help school personnel understand the work of the project. We are also able to respond to their concerns. For example, teachers often want feedback about a student's progress or advice about how to handle a student, so we create ways to do this. Most importantly, week after week, we have shown up and worked to meet a school's needs, worked with their hopes and expectations, and worked through with them the reactions stirred up by our presence and the nature of the work we do. Year after year, we have stayed true to our commitment to respond as best we can to the needs the school has defined and the needs we come to know. We have admired and respected the work of the schools, while also preserving our commitment to working in the ways we know to be most beneficial to the children and the community.

The Growth Groups

We have named the groups "Growth Groups" to refer to the multiple ways they are designed to promote growth on different levels for the group members. Referrals to the groups come from the principal, assistant principal, school social worker, teachers, and sometimes parents. Typically, children are referred because they pose behavior problems, are disruptive in the classroom, aggressive or quick to lash out, or destructive. With some students, the problems with aggression may lead to some gang involvement, or interest, or bullying behaviors. Other students are referred because of a history of significant deprivation or loss such as abandonment by a parent, loss of a parent through violence or incarceration, or children who are severely neglected. Many students are low performing, lack focus, attention, and motivation in the classroom, and are difficult to engage in learning. As project therapists get to know these students, they discover histories of loss, violence, and complex family situations. Students are organized into groups according to gender, age, and level of interpersonal skill.

The groups begin, as all groups do, prior to the first meetings. When a student is referred, a therapist meets with that student to talk about the group, invite them to participate, and start the process of obtaining parental consent. The therapist tells them that the group is a place they can come each week to get to know themselves better and to know each other better through a combination of conversation, activities, and games. Further, we indicate it is a place where they can talk about things that matter to them and to learn from each other about such important subjects. Most of them want to participate, so they take a letter and consent form for parental consent. They are promised a candy bar when they return the consent form. The therapist also contacts the parents or other caregiver to explain the groups, deal with any concerns the parent may have, and answer questions. They are also invited to talk with the therapist and to participate in a concurrent parent group. This initial process requires a great deal of persistence, reminders to students, repeated calls to parents, and reissued letters, but in the end there is a high rate of return. Some families are very challenging to contact, and the unreturned phone calls or other obstacles to contact only reflect a deep suspicion and lack of trust about the possibility of help. Thus, recruitment can be a frustrating process, but it is critical to the success of the Project, not just because of the high percentage of consents obtained, but because it creates a foundation for a working relationship between the group therapist, the child, and the family.

Once we have consent, we speak more fully with teachers about the reasons for referral and the teachers' perceptions of the students in the classroom, gaining anecdotal information that helps us know the ways in which individual children express their concerns. We also do some pre- and post-intervention screenings that measure levels of academic, behavioral, social, and emotional functioning. These scores, along with a child's progress in school, provide measures of the efficacy of intervention. On occasion, crises arise or a child referred to a group is not able to work in a group setting. There is a small fund within the project for individual work with these children. The groups take place on a weekly basis during the school day. Scheduling groups is always a challenge, working around the demands of the school day. Most groups have three to five members, though groups with two therapists are somewhat larger. Once the group composition is set, the therapists assigned, a time in the school day scheduled, and teachers and parents informed, the groups can begin.

The Group Beginning

As the groups begin, the first task is establishing relationships with the other group members, with the group leader, and with the group itself. During the referral and intake process, groups are framed for children as "a place where you can come to talk about things that matter to you," and "a place where you can learn about yourself and where we can learn about each other." We begin to create the conditions to facilitate such knowing. Though these children all know one another, they come to know each other and themselves differently in the groups through the sharing of their stories and the sharing of the group experience. Taylor,[1] a third grader, tells stories that illustrate something of what the children in our groups carry around inside of them on an ongoing basis. She introduces herself by explaining that her last name belongs to her momma but not her daddy. Her momma knew when she was born that her daddy would not stick around and so she didn't give Taylor his name. Just as her mother predicted, her daddy is now on his fourth set of children. She doesn't see him much.

Taylor's talk about her daddy drifts to a description of spending her birthday with her grown sister. Her mother had had "things to do" and had to go away. Taylor describes how her precious treats had been taken by the boys and thrown at cars on the street. She then shifts to the idea of how much she cares for her sister's little three-year-old son. All of her little nephews and nieces come to her when they can't find their own mommas or other adults around. They need help with this or that or they are hungry and want something to eat. Taylor describes how her three-year-old nephew is afraid to wash his face for fear that the water will be too hot. Taylor gently sprinkles the water on his arm and asks if that feels okay. Her cousin thinks it does and proceeds to wash his face. As Taylor hopes to be cared for and brings these hopes to the group, she recounts the tender care she gives her cousin.

Taylor goes on to recount how upset her nephew was when his daddy got put into a police car with handcuffs. Taylor had heard that before her sister had called her and her mother to "come quick," the police had busted down the door of their home. The time line of events becomes confused as Taylor's narrative shifts back and forth between the present and the past. She tells how her nephew sits on the couch and feels afraid. He cries. The story is confusing, to Taylor who is overwhelmed, and to her listeners who are trying to understand. By listening attentively and asking some questions, the group tries to help Taylor piece together what had happened. The police had busted down the door and searched their apartment. They had put her sister's boyfriend in handcuffs and made him sit in their car. They were out on the street. That's when her sister had called her mother and they ran to the scene. Taylor had run as fast as she could. She was hot from running but it was a cold night and her little nephew had no coat on. She asked if she could go inside and get him some warm clothes but the police said no. She asked if she could wrap him up in her own coat. They wouldn't let her. They had found something in the apartment. She didn't want to say what it was but made a sign with her hands – guns. Her sister's boyfriend is in jail now. Her sister had gone with their son to visit him but their son wasn't allowed in because they lacked the proper paperwork. His father is still there. Taylor misses him. Her mother and sister were in that jail before. Taylor is scared to go there. She does want to see her sister's boyfriend but she feels scared of police. She puts her head down on the table and says she is afraid she is going to cry.

As Taylor's fragmented story indicates, in response to trauma, a child's symbolic and relational connections to themselves and to others are severed. Unprocessed traumatic experience disrupts a child's sense of herself, her ability to relate to others, and cognitive frameworks with which to perceive and interpret the world. In the piecing together of Taylor's story, these connections can begin to be reorganized in the context of support and understanding and tolerance for the intense affect. The group allows Taylor to begin to make sense of her experience, helps her contain the strong emotions involved, and supports her efforts to think about her situation. In this way, the group helps her begin to repair the impact of this traumatic experience.

THE STORY OF ONE GROUP

A kindergarten teacher referred four boys to the Growth Groups program, because she was concerned that these children were not integrated into the life of the classroom and did not interact much with others. One of the boys, Tevin, was identified as having good potential but was scared all the time and would not talk. Another boy, Jayden, had speech problems and was in foster care. He was extremely shy, rarely communicating with others. Nehemiah was described as "living in another world." He was chronically distracted in the classroom and "couldn't get the material from point A to point B." His teacher recounted that he easily became upset and felt lost, often bursting into tears. The fourth member of the group, Antonio, was described as even more withdrawn than the others. He did not respond to anyone, nor did he cry or speak up when he needed to use the washroom and consequently he had accidents in the middle of class. His personal needs were not cared for and he came to school unwashed and unfed.

The work began, as all the groups do, with defining the group as a place where group members will meet at the same time, on the same day of the week, in the same room, with the same group therapist and the same members. We anticipate with the children that they will get to know each other and themselves in new ways. Initially, the groups work to develop a sense of continuity, predictability, and expectation around group meetings as well as a sense of cohesion as a group. While the children are hungry for this experience of being together, it can also be challenging for children who have experienced violence and trauma insofar as they often experience themselves and their world as fragmented, incoherent, and oftentimes chaotic.

One of the first manifestations of trauma exposure comes up when we gather together and sit in a circle to begin our work. This is often a moment when the collective anxiety emerges in the form of chaos. The younger boys cannot stay in their seats and seek out objects to fiddle with or pace around the room. Other children pour out streams of talk, interruptions, and speak over each other. They show us through the immediacy of their actions and chaotic behavior how difficult it is to articulate what they think and feel and how overwhelmed they feel by any awareness of affect. Many of these children can't tolerate being with all that they struggle with inside and often retreat into their most familiar chaotic and defensive behavior style (Ward-Wimmer et al., 2002). When children are invited to share their thoughts and feelings with one another and to connect with these feelings, it often produces an internal crisis that engenders coping behaviors that include the physical release of tension rather than the containment of energy.

For these inhibited kindergartners, the initial anxiety of being together in this new way expresses itself through disconnection and isolated preoccupations. Jayden sits quietly and solemnly and looks blankly at the group leader when asked questions. Antonio is interested in the snack but once he finishes eating his and asking for more, he busies himself with looking around the room or off into space, isolated from the others. Nehemiah fills the group space with a stream of disjointed talk. He begins to talk about his father's car being broken, then of the two mice in his bed. He is interested in the apples they were offered at the end of a story the group leader told about a lonely star in the sky in search of friends. The leader invites the children to make pictures of what they wish for. Tevin draws a picture of himself in colorful shoes. Jayden plays with the colored pencils. Nehemiah's picture of monsters, cars, and fire extends past the edges of his paper and onto his desk. Antonio draws all over the front and back of his sheet of paper and fills it up with dense scribbles.

As the predictability and structure of the group meetings develop, all the children make more eye contact with the group leader, but Antonio remains in his own world and Nehemiah's disorganized streams of talk persist. There is a story within the tangle of Nehemiah's discourse but it needs to be sorted out. He says that he hasn't seen his father because he is in jail. He says that his dad had banged his mother's head. He reports this with flat affect. We talk about how it can be scary for a child to see his parents fight. Nehemiah draws himself, a baby "who has two legs." He draws his dad with teeth that had fallen out like his own missing front teeth. He draws his mother and says that she is pretty. He says that his dad gets mad. When we ask him what makes him mad, Nehemiah says that it's his brother. He begins to answer a question in a logical way then goes off on illogical tangents. The other children are in their own worlds.

Nehemiah cannot yet talk about his experience in a way that is meaningful to him, so within the context of the group, the task becomes one of helping him organize a story out of the fragments. We begin to ask him questions about the details, including the other children in thinking about the story and to help him create a narrative about what happened. We ask, "What was your daddy so mad about?" "What did you do?" We try to get some clarity about what happened and help him get clear in his own mind about what he experienced. The leader comments, "Gee, your dad gets so mad. He has a hard time controlling himself. On the one hand you miss him. On the other hand you may feel relieved that he is not around." She tries to put into words what she thinks Nehemiah is communicating in his fragmented story with the disavowed affect. This recognition of Nehemiah's struggle and the effort to understand it is what creates a basis for growth and learning. This group contributes to this central developmental process.

For many weeks, Antonio remains on the margins of the group, dutifully attending each week. Aside from his interest in the snack, he expresses no real interest in participating in activities or connecting with the group leader or group members in anything other than a superficial way. Antonio's responses to questions always sound hollow, like caricatures of what he thinks one wants to hear. One day we discuss the different kinds of feelings that people can have. We share a story about a child who feels sad and is trying to figure out what makes people feel happy. We talk about the overt signs of sadness and happiness: what do people look like when they experience such feelings, what does it feel like inside, and what experiences evoke such feelings. Suddenly Antonio is hooked. His wandering eyes rivet on the storybook page and he has thoughts about what we are discussing that he wants to share. He says he never has happy feelings, only sad ones or none at all. He talks about there not being anyone in his life to share any feelings with. Antonio begins to stir with life. Having been recognized as a person with feelings that matter, he becomes animated with the possibility of being known by others and being known to himself. When Antonio arrives the next week, he requests the job of passing out treats to the group. Having been helped to be recognized, he can join the community of the group as a helper.

A few weeks later, the group topic is the important people in the children's lives. Antonio had always drawn blobs and suns when asked to make a picture of people in the family, which he then scribbled over so the final image was a page full of dense scribbles that obscured any other representations he had made. On this day, we read a story about a little girl whose mother has just had a new baby and wanting to care for something herself, she adopts a smooth large stone and names and swaddles it. When the children are invited to make pictures of the significant others in their lives, Antonio begins by drawing one rock and then another. He follows this with faceless bodies representing a mother, three brothers, two sisters (he isn't sure of the count at first) and himself. This is all done in black. Then he picks up a green crayon and begins at the bottom of the page to systematically cover the underlying picture in a layer of green. Someone asks what he is drawing and he reports that it is water. As the water climbs higher and higher over the figures, we wonder and someone asks if he can swim. He says that he can't and adds fish and sharks to the water. Tevin, who has been drawing Jayden and himself as the significant people in his world, becames quite concerned. He says that he wants to make a net to help Antonio out of the water. We ask Antonio if Tevin can draw a net into his picture. Antonio agrees and Tevin draws a picture of himself with a net at the top of the water. The therapist acknowledges how much he wants to be a friend to Antonio to help him out of the scary water. When the children present their pictures to the others and talk about them, Antonio points first to Tevin and his net in the picture.

This example points to the ways in which the children can be attuned to one another and critical to the construction of responsive and meaningful environments in which to come to know themselves, each other, and the possibilities of human relationships. By working with groups of children who are also classmates, or at least members of the same school community, the knowledge, skills, and experiences gained in group sessions can also be generalized to their ongoing school experiences outside of group and work in the groups can continue to unfold during the week between group meetings.

The ongoing nature of our group meetings allows group members to expect and depend on the holding environment of the group to be there for them each week. This is significant for children who do not trust that relationships can be depended upon or that someone else is holding them in mind even when they are not together. In a recent meeting of 5th grade boys, Lionel came in looking desperate. The cohesion of this group was punctuated by conflict and competition as old group members teamed up to display bravado and gain privileged status over newer group members. Those conflicts fell to the side as Lionel put his head down on the table. He needed more than anything on this day to use the group to hold his pain and fear and he began to cry. He reported that he had accidentally kicked his teacher and now he was going to be suspended and "get it" at home. When the other boys realized how upset he was, they responded with kindness and understanding. Jalal put a hand on his shoulder and the other boys talked about how unfair that teacher was and how they had gotten in trouble too. From that platform of support, Lionel was able to think about what happened and feel sad about what he had done. The group became a place where trustworthiness was re-established and thinking and feeling could begin to emerge and become understood together. Over time the children internalize the ways in which the group therapist listens and talks with them. Jalal said to Lionel, "You sound real scared, man. What do you think is going to happen?"

The continuity of the child's experience of group serves as an important counterpoint to the multiple sources of discontinuity in the lives of many of these students. The children in groups come to rely on our regular meetings and develop sensitivity to time. Two 7th grade boys argue after we meet again following the school's two-week spring break. One says that we haven't met for two weeks and the other says three. The regularity of group meetings matters to them and they notice the absence of regularity. This is one of the groups among many that have requested the opportunity to meet more than one day of the week. At the end of the last school year, two 6th grade boys made a point of going to the principal to enlist her help in ensuring that the program would continue in their school the following year. A 5th grade boy's teacher reports that he watches the clock on the day of our sessions. The day and time we have been meeting now for two years has become a point of reference in his life at school. If the group leader is a minute late to pick him up, he brings this to her attention. This is his time and he makes a claim on it. The continuity provided by the regular and dependable meetings of the Growth Groups becomes an organizing experience in the school week that the children come to depend on.

In the kindergarten group, the use of repetition, an opening name game in which naming the names of each group member and recognizing their presence, also contributes to a sense of expectancy, familiarity, and continuity in which they have a place to belong. In a recent meeting of the kindergarten group, all members eagerly participated in distributing the elements of our snack. We engaged in a memory game in which each member's names and favorite animals were given voice in the collective space. Jayden spoke frequently and fluidly. It is still not easy to understand his indistinct articulations but he is undaunted in his attempts to communicate. The group itself took on its own life as it organized itself spontaneously around the topic of birthdays and what each child wished for. Antonio turned his drawing of wishes into a collection of "eyes." As we tried to identify what he was creating he laughed uproariously and decided that what he was making was an "eye/I creature." Jayden took his lead and created his own collection of eyes that he turned into twelve faces with mouths. Nehemiah drew a dog and a gun. Antonio took an interest in Nehemiah's picture and drew his own dog and gun. Antonio's vivid imagination has begun to take flight. He drew a tree with seeds in it that turn into boys and whereas he had never formed any letters before, saying that he couldn't write his name, he proudly wrote out an A, a B, and a C and delightedly put legs and feet on them, laughingly telling us they could walk. His teacher reports that he has begun to do his work and engage in the life of the classroom. She made a point of stopping the group leader in the hallway to tell her about his progress. "He's learning!" she said. "He's starting to get it."

The Growth in the Groups

What happened in the group so that Antonio began to "get it"? At first, Antonio is barely recognizable and he eradicates any trace of self-expression, scribbling over anything he dares to draw, demonstrating the way in which he feels his sense of self has been attacked by beginning to represent an emerging self that then must be aggressively hidden, if not destroyed. Week after week, Antonio expressed this about himself, eating the snack and apparently silently taking in the interest, responsiveness, and continuity of the group, its leader, and its members. He was given the time he needed, without any implication that he wasn't meeting expectations or standards. One day, he surprises everyone by talking clearly and directly about the barren emotional environment he has lived in, where no one expresses any interest in him or how he feels or what matters to him. Everyone listens to this and his story touches them, as Tevin so poignantly demonstrates a few weeks later. Antonio draws his world: he is in deep water, he cannot swim, and there are dangerous sharks in the water. Tevin sees that he needs help and represents the group as a net that can capture and hold him, protecting him from deep water and other dangers until he can learn to swim. Antonio joins the community of the group and together they spontaneously express their own needs and wishes. Antonio now draws himself as an "eye/I creature," expressing an emerging sense of self. Having been seen and recognized in the group, Antonio can now begin to see and recognize himself.

The City Project therapists follow the fundamental rules of psychodynamic group psychotherapy. They are trustworthy; they listen carefully and attentively; they provide a model for empathic understanding and responsiveness; they articulate the often inchoate feelings and behavior observed in the room; they support group members in their efforts to work out interpersonal relationships; and they guide the groups members' slowly growing ability to express themselves. Certain features of the group experience are especially important to the growth and development of the children who participate in the City Project. First is the way in which the therapists continually help these children make sense of their own affective and behavioral responses. They help them deconstruct events, so that they can see that these affects and behaviors are connected to their sense of self and to the experiences they have. So often these children are made to feel that they are "wrong" or "bad" to respond in the ways they do, and their anger or outbursts are punished and criticized. In the groups, the therapists offer a different way to understand such behaviors, recognizing that angry outbursts are typically a reaction to shame or humiliation. The therapist can say, "When you didn't know the answer to your teacher's question, your feelings were hurt and you started a fight to get your mind off of those bad feelings." In this way, emotional experiences can be thought about and decoded, which then makes it possible to discover alternative ways of reacting. Though limits are set on destructive behavior, there is much tolerance of a wide range of affect, so that kids can talk about their fear, anger, hatred, excitement, envy, and pleasures. And, with the support of the therapists, they can consider alternative ways of responding.

Second, the groups are structured, but not too structured. The rituals of beginning, sharing, participating in activities together, and ending also open up the opportunity to share experiences, concerns, and fun. As the kindergarten group came to know each other, they generated their own agenda of thinking about the meaning of birthdays. This attention to birthdays, so important to young children, is a reflection of the importance the groups convey to the children of their own feelings and experience, and the acknowledgment of each child's "eye/I creature." There is no curriculum or manual for the groups because each group needs to develop its own modus operandi. All the groups challenge the therapists and there is often a layer of tragedy and despair in bearing witness to the very real violence and deprivation of many of these children's lives. Over and over, the therapists convey to the children their conviction that talking and knowing and thinking are the ways they can help repair the impact of traumatic experiences.

Finally, these groups continue week after week, school year after school year. The children can participate as long as they attend the school. An enormous amount of work goes into creating and maintaining a meeting schedule. The school day, week, and year is full of disruptions for field trips, holidays, illness, student suspensions, teacher training, vacation breaks, and summer. Through all of the changes, the groups continue. The children come to know, through experience and repetition, that the group leader can hold the group in mind through the breaks and disruptions and that the group leader, with the group, will come back together to continue the work. The groups are an ongoing experience in the lives of the children. The reliability, predictability, dependability, and "ongoingness" create structure for the participants and help them build a sense of organization and trust. As the therapists and the group framework do this for the children, they can begin to do it for each other, as they listen to each other, offer encouragement and empathy, and an interpersonal network. Tevin's net is an excellent metaphor for the way the groups hold, contain, and support the growth and development of each child as they navigate treacherous waters while learning to swim.

NOTE

1. All information and details about the children in the groups are disguised to protect their identities.

REFERENCES

Konopka, G. (1970 [1954]). *Group work in the institution: A modern challenge*. New York: Association Press.

Nader, L. O. (2001). Treatment methods for childhood trauma. In J. P. Wilson and T. M. Keane (Eds.), *Assessing psychological trauma and PTSD*. New York: Guilford Press, 291–348.

Osofsky, H. J., & Osofsky, J. D. (2004). Children's exposure to community violence: Psychoanalytic perspectives on evaluation and treatment. In B. Sklarew, S. W. Twemlow, and S. M. Wilkinson (Eds.), *Analysts in the trenches: Streets, schools, war zones*. Hillsdale, NJ: Analytic Press, 237–256.

Overstreet, S., & Braun, S. (2000). Exposure to community violence and post-traumatic stress symptoms: Mediating factors. *American Journal of Orthopsychiatry, 70*, 263–271.

Pynoos, R. S., Steinberg, A. M., Dyb, G., Goenjian, A. K., Chen, S., & Brymer, M. J. (2004). Reverberations of danger, trauma, and PTSD on group dynamics. In B. Sklarew, S. W. Twemlow, and S. M. Wilkinson (Eds.), *Analysts in the trenches: Streets, schools, war zones*. Hillsdale, NJ: Analytic Press, 1–22.

Redl, F. & Wineman, D. (1952). *Controls from within: Techniques for the treatment of the aggressive child*. New York: Free Press.

Sanders, P. (2011). Personal communication.

Sklarew, B., Krupnick, J., Ward-Wimmer, D., & Napoli, C. B. (2004). The school-based mourning project: A preventive intervention in the cycle of inner-city violence. In B. Sklarew, S. W. Twemlow, and S. M. Wilkinson (Eds.), *Analysts in the trenches: Streets, schools, war zones*. Hillsdale, NJ: Analytic Press, 195–210.

Ward-Wimmer, D., Napoli, C., Brophy, S. O., & Zager, L. (2002). *Three-dimensional grief*. Washington, DC: Wendt Center for Loss and Healing.

Chapter Seven

Anxiety and Violence in the Schools

Coping and Not Coping

Silvia Silberman and Arie Plat[1]

Violent incidents that take place in the schools are particularly stressful for all school-connected people and for the surrounding society (Silberman, 1996). We all hope that schools will help our children learn not to get caught up in violent transactions, either as victims or as perpetrators. Most institutions and schools in particular, function under the illusion that organizational order is possible (Silberman & Plat, 2002). The idea of order is related to an unconscious narcissistic fantasy that conceives organizations as perfect, and their managers as loving parental figures (Schwartz, 1990). Often, organizations' goals express the narcissistic fantasy more than their members' experiences and an accurate "reading" of the social conditions. In this way, explicit aims may fade away, and latent unconscious motivations come to the fore and influence decision-making processes more and more.

Schools, too, function as if children are loved unconditionally and organizational order and hierarchy serve members' well-being. Moreover, teachers, parents and most of the social environment (as expressed in the media and writings on education) cultivate the notion that for it to be successful, and for children to reach their highest ideals, education needs an orderly setting. Violent incidents in the schools are thus, not only a threat to the people involved but also undermine the very belief that order is necessary and possible in educational institutions. In the field of education, "order" denotes discipline in school life. It also signals a need to respect the prevalent social order in the surrounding society.

The notions of violence and of aggression, especially in school settings, are as controversial (Parsons, 2006) on the conceptual and theoretical levels as on the pragmatic level. They have generated much thinking, writing and research (Harding, 2006). Unfortunately, theoretical insights and efforts to implement them do not always go hand in hand. Therefore, very often, teachers and other professionals feel isolated in their actual confrontations with violent events and sense they are not helped by the available clinical and theoretical thinking.

Although psychoanalytic thinking has become an integral part of western culture, its implementation with regards to schools falls short. In the quest for orderly lives and explicit hierarchies, conceptualizing about schools has put too little emphasis on unconscious motivations, unpredictable social dynamics (Silberman & Plat, 2011), the discourse of the teacher, and many other controversial aspects. This is unfortunate because there exists a wealth of psychoanalytic thinking that can contribute to a better understanding of organizational and personal dynamics in schools (Gould et al., 2001; Miller & Rice, 1967; Pichon Riviere, 1984). There seems to be a reluctance to apply psychoanalytic thinking to school phenomena out of anxiety about the chance to meet unconscious motivations and disorderly processes. A striking example of this can be seen in those programs called in the United States, "Zero Tolerance" (for violence, but also even for racism and discrimination).[2, 3]

Psychoanalysis perceives human development as an on-going dynamic complexity, in constant change, and at the same time as a repetitive expression of the difficult struggle with drives (such as aggression) and anxiety. If anything, schools, even more than other organizations, need great amounts of tolerance to cope with the unconscious, chaotic and sometimes paradoxical experience of children and their teachers. We have seen in Israel attempts to implement a similar line of thought to the "Zero Tolerance" in the programs called "Towns without Violence," that also call, coercively, for little tolerance for aggression and for violence. For example, the head of the Education Department in a small town in Israel, whose mayor signed an agreement with the Ministry of Education, actively participated in one of our workshops. Her personal aim was to learn how to cope with the coercive spirit that unintentionally, was an inherent part of the program called "Towns without Violence."

In our understanding psychoanalytic insights can make an important contribution in coping with school violence, since they widen our knowledge of overt and latent individual, group and institutional dynamics, and the emotions involved in them. In this chapter we will propose a psychoanalytic conceptualization of aggression and of violence and a methodology which enables school personnel to translate understandings and insights into interventions that can help diminish violence in communities and in schools.

CONCEPTUAL FRAME OF REFERENCE

We believe that it is useful to make a distinction between aggression and violence (Silberman & Plat, 2002). Aggression is a basic drive that has appeared during the evolutionary scale (Panksepp, 1998). It is a drive that strengthens survival behaviors across evolution.

Some writers distinguish between constructive or healthy aggression and destructive aggression (Harding, 2006; Royston, 2006). Others refer to aggression, or constructive aggression, as primary violence and distinguish it from destructive aggression, which is seen as secondary violence (Aulagnier, 2001). Aggression is a part of survival behavior: animals kill to get food, or to defend territory; a child breaks a toy to find out how it works. And too, a student will aggressively challenge a teacher's conceptualization, and try to digest thoughts and so gain a greater understanding in a way similar to how he/she uses energy to digest food.

While aggression is best conceptualized as a drive or as a flow of survival energy, violence is a quality of behaviors whose purpose is to inflict pain or anxiety on the other (Lacan, 2004). The violent person threatens the integrity of the other's body and sense of self. Violence may be physical or psychological, directed toward the actual other or toward the internalized other in the self. We find the distinction between aggression and violence useful as it helps explain why we often need to tolerate aggression as a creative force, while at the same time trying to deal with violence. When the distinction isn't kept, individuals and institutions find themselves punishing aggressive behaviors that are in fact constructive, and also inadvertently causing an increase in violence (Parsons, 2006). Emotions like anger and rage, usually expressions of a deep experience of frustration, may be expressed in forceful aggressive behaviors which are not necessarily intended to produce destructive consequences. When emotions like anger and rage are denied expression, an increase in violent behaviors may follow, as the lack of containment is experienced as a threat to the self, which defends itself by inflicting violence.

The idea that aggression is necessary for the preservation of life was clear to Freud. The need to conceptualize resistance to treatment as one of many ways in which humans attack themselves and compulsively repeat harmful behaviors, led him to the idea of a basic death drive. Aggression was included as one component of this death drive (Freud, 1920). Destructive and constructive behaviors and fantasies have since been understood as expressing a particular combination of life and death drives: aggression (coming from the death drive) tempered by life drive (Eros, libido) and love. The distinction between life and death drives was adopted and developed very creatively by Melanie Klein, but it proved confusing for understanding the life quality of aggression, and progressively lost some of its practical value for the development of social interventions meant to cope with violence.

Many writers on the subject, especially those that focus on behavior, do not make a clear distinction between aggression and violence. Instead, they use these terms to indicate a difference of degree, especially in relation to the consequences (Campbell & Gibbs, 1986). In our work on implementing programs to reduce violence in schools, we found it helpful to follow Lacan (2004) and maintain the distinction between aggression and violence (Silberman & Plat, 2002). While animal aggression is mostly instrumental—it exists in the service of survival—in the case of humans, violent behaviors heighten anxiety in the other as it threatens the others' sense of self. That kind of violence is very rare in the animal world. The threat to the self and arousal of anxiety are at the core of human violent behaviors (whether physical, verbal, or psychological), and as such, are universal. No animals other than higher apes were observed attacking a young member of another tribe when no threat to them was identifiable. The joy they took in the attack resembles the way some humans sadistically enjoy humiliating and causing others to suffer, whether to regain some sense of self and control, or to put a distance between them and the threat, thereby avoiding getting in touch with their own vulnerability or rage.

One hypothesis about human violence is to see the matrix of violence in the introduction of a new born *infans* into the culture (and family saga) by giving it a name (Aulagnier, 2001; Tesone, 2011). The ritual of name-giving makes the newcomer a subject in the culture, and at the same time imposes on him or her a specific meaning within the family saga; naming creates a subject and thereby, forcefully, attributes to him/her a meaning. The importance of this development lies in its human universality. The concept of a matrix of violence (or primary violence) can help explain why all human beings have the potential to behave violently, under "appropriate" personal and social circumstances. If so, it seems clear that violence cannot be eradicated or prevented. At best it can be understood and reduced through the development of awareness of one's emotions and of appropriate coping abilities.

Two different conceptual developments are relevant to our thinking about this subject. From the neuropsychoanalytic point of view (especially Panksepp, 1998) violence is seen as an evolutionary outgrowth of primary animal aggression. Studying the neurobiology of emotions and patterns of behavior led him to believe in the continuity of emotions in evolutionary change, and thus to see aggression and violence as universal. The distinction between them lies in the quality of behavior in relation to the circumstances, following the degree of development of brain mechanisms of the species involved.

On the other hand, relational, interactive and attachment thinking do not accept the notion that in the beginning there were drives. Rather, their basic assumption is that in the beginning there is a dyad (cf., "There is no such thing as a baby" [Winnicott, 1965]) that provides such developmental needs as mirroring, feedback, emotional regulation, soothing and containment from which motivations evolve.

We prefer to think of the aggressive drive as basic. We see it as providing the necessary energy for the baby and the mother to maintain their connection through mutual (but not identical) mirroring, feedback, and regulation that characterize the containment processes. Mutual regulation promotes adaptive development of brain functioning (Panksepp, 1998; Schore, 1994; Siegel, 1999) that furthers emotional regulation and also cognitive development (Bion, 1967, 1970; Main, 1991).

Violence, on the other hand, develops out of attachment (relational) failure (De Zulueta, 1993; Fonagy et al., 2004). This failure damages emotional as well as cognitive functioning. Attachment failure and the ensuing cultivation of violence may start with impregnation and fetal development (Gerhardt, 2004) and continue throughout life, if no interventions are available.

Whether aggression is seen as a primary drive, or as the result of attachment failure (insecure, disorganized, or both), there is wide agreement today that the quality of the early relationships between the baby (fetus, infant, toddler) and caregivers has a strong impact on development. Genetic factors may account for differences in temperament and abilities and for the more or less effective use of caregivers' help. Still, the quality of the attachment relationship is a crucial factor in the development of the individual and his or her emotional, cognitive and social skills. When the relational aspect of development is given a rightful place, we can see more clearly the importance of schooling and psychotherapy. Both can be very effective in offering new, healthy attachment experiences that furnish awareness, understanding and alternative coping strategies (Green, 2008). This is true not less for insecurely attached individual students than for more securely attached ones.

In a way not entirely different from some forms of psychotherapy, schools may further healthy development and also afford insecurely attached children a totally different experience of life and of relationships. School experiences can make a difference for the children and psychoanalytically informed teachers and school programs may contribute widely to their healthier development, and healing of their working models. Daily school events and the content of what is learned, afford opportunities for developing reflective abilities and increased awareness in the students. These will have a notable useful impact on their emotional and cognitive development.

We believe that psychoanalytically informed thinking, while widening their ability to contain and cope, enables teachers to suspend judgment and bear uncertainty. Psychoanalytically informed thinking can also help teachers deal with the complexity of human phenomena, which includes conscious and unconscious emotions, thoughts, fantasies and actions. As the teacher's ability to suspend judgment widens, he/she may also develop a more reflective attitude, which in turn will be a model for the students. In this way, reflection fosters learning from experience by opening a space that is tolerant of action (doing) first and reflection afterward: all incorrect doing (task) can be reflected upon and corrected afterward, as learning takes its rightful place *a posteriori*.

It is possible to look at behaviors and doing, as one form of acting-out. In the psychodramatic tradition (Holmes, 1992; Martinez Bouquet, Moccio, & Pavlovsky, 1975; Martinez Bouquet, 1978) to act is to throw oneself into the scene. In this way the presence of conscious and unconscious elements in every action, and the nature of behavior as emergent are stressed. Only post-factum reflection can clarify whether violent fantasies and intentions filtered into the action (behavior) and to what extent. Reflection and taking a distance afford the insight to growup.

Mentalization processes at the basis of reflective thinking and cognitive as well as meta-cognitive functions require a sense of mutual trust. Confidence that emotions will be contained by the adult (teacher) enables youngsters to experiment. Out of this experience of trust, grows the youngsters' confidence that he/her may contain his/her emotions. The ability to contain feelings, fantasies and ideas will strengthen his/her ability to think thoughts (Bion, 1967, 1970; Fonagy et al., 2004).

While schools often see the transmission of knowledge as their primary task, they tend to insist on undisrupted order in the classroom. Such order helps make for a good lecture but doesn't help students develop appropriate abilities to participate in complex social reality. Usually the explicit primary task covers up latent associated tasks, and the result is that efficient implementation of the primary task may be hindered (Gould, Stapley, & Stein, 2001; Miller, 1989; Pichon Riviere, 1984). Knowledge of psychoanalytic thinking and personal experience may enable teachers to create an atmosphere where complexity is bearable and the teacher becomes more sensitive to unconscious group dynamics and the roles taken by each member of the group in the context of those dynamics (Bion, 1961), and their individual learning. For example, students may disrupt a class as a way of expressing their anxiety toward a difficult task and the fear of having to assume a role of "not-knowing" vis-à-vis the role of "knowing very well." A personalized reaction that overlooks the dynamic function of the disruption for the whole group ("you are hyperactive") hinders learning for the individual and for the whole group. Alternatively, the threat to order is sometimes felt as a personal attack on the teacher and not as a group dynamic event, a situation that prompts attack and at the same time the feeling of burning out (Last & Silberman, 1989).

Unplanned school events afford many opportunities for observation, for reflection and for working through critical incidents, conflicts as well as violent events. A reflective attitude helps elaborate the emotional experiences and builds a buffer between emotions and behavior. It helps contain affects without acting upon them and thus enhances abilities to cope with violence. A child urinates in the class, someone hits a peer—every incident becomes a trigger for reflection when containment is possible and anxiety is bearable.

A pivotal notion in the study of violent events is that of violent transactions (Campbell & Gibbs, 1986). While an understanding of the development of violent processes requires theoretical notions of drive, discourse, behavior, social culture and setting, observations and field work focus on actual events and behaviors. Violent events are the result of interactive transactions between two actors (or groups) that fight or attack each other, or assume the roles of victim and perpetrator in the presence of a bystander. Violent events may also take place within the individual between self and an internalized object, as in self-harm and suicide. In this sense, attacks on the self are also violent transactions that involve more than one actor. Transactions are the result of negotiations that might take place within the self or between individuals or groups and be partially or fully unconscious.

Violent transactions develop in the presence of a concrete (or fantasized) other, a third, a bystander. The need for a bystander in order for a violent transaction to develop does not necessarily mean the encounter has an oedipal or symbolic structure. The development of an interaction into a violent transaction implies a regression to a schizoid paranoid position (Klein, 1952), in which fantasies translate directly into actions and mechanisms of split and demonization prevail. The bystander may interrupt the development that leads to a violent transaction and contribute containment and thus, reflection, balance and integration. This in turn may open the transition to a depressive position (Klein, 1952) and with it enable the development of symbolic thinking. When the bystander does not function as an oedipal third, and does not enable symbolic thinking, as is the case in violent transactions, his or her very presence colludes with the forces that lead the interaction to become a violent transaction.

Cultural norms may promote violent acts, as, for example in sacrificial punishment, family retaliation and exclusion practices. In discrimination policies, cultural norms may function as bystanders as well, by giving them appropriate legitimacy. This may be the case in streaming and special education classes that reflect social class and social background. Whether as cultural norms, as internalized objects or as actual persons, bystanders may unconsciously collude with violent intentions and promote them actively. Collusion may also result from the bystander simply letting the event occur and develop with no interruptions or questions. As a teacher once said to the parents of a bullied student "he is such a good student, what can others do?"

The presence of a bystander is evident in events of bullying in the school, and in violent events within the family. Less evident and more surprising is the case of a teacher unaware of a student in his/her class being the victim of boycott or abuse or the case of parents unaware that their child is being abused by his/her peers. The presence of the bystander legitimates the violence inflicted, whether by "not knowing" what is happening, or more actively by acknowledging that "those things happen" and not intervening appropriately. The question why bystanders don't see violent events is an intriguing one that leads to the study of collusion and the fascination with violence (Guggenbuhl, 1993), two issues we will not explore in this chapter.

Anxiety provoked by violent incidents makes behavior modification techniques attractive: they bring back a sense of order (certain behaviors elicit "appropriate" reinforcement, following an accepted menu), good results are quickly visible, the intervention takes place within the accepted prevalent didactics (grown-ups teach and evaluate youngsters that by and large respond to adult stimuli). Many programs aimed at diminishing violence and bullying in the schools, have been developed within the conceptual field of behavior modification and CBT. Most of them show positive results in the short term, but few long-term results as they promote little independent, autonomous learning. In our experience in Israeli schools these programs foster a dependency on the presence of the responsible team to keep the program working, and fade away when and if the team leader leaves (for example for a sabbatical). In a parallel process children's behavior remains dependent on adult reinforcement. Unfortunately, this dynamic hinders sensitivity to unconscious processes and the development of a tolerant attitude to oneself and the other and therefore contributes little to the development of a reflective attitude and autonomous judgment.

The Intrinsic Contribution of the School to Violence Within It

The quality and quantity of violent incidents in the schools reflect the violent or non-violent dynamics of the community and wider social environment, of which schools are dynamic sub-systems (Miller & Rice, 1967). At the same time, each school develops its own characteristic social climate, related to the environment but also distinct from it. Schools in the same neighborhood differ from one another as to the climate each of them weaves inside it. Each school functions as a different context for the variety of peaceful and violent events that take place within it, and offers a distinct contribution to the surrounding social environment.

In the last part of this chapter we will present a methodology to work with violence in the community and in the schools. We hope to show that limited, helpful interventions (micro-interventions) are feasible and that they have a destabilizing effect that opens the way for experiencing different possibilities of behaving and ways to study their peaceful or violent impact.

The general tendency of those approaching the subject of violence is to stress the impact that violence in the surrounding society has upon the schools. In this chapter we focus on the intrinsic contribution of the schools to the dynamics of violence or peace within them. These dynamics may be carried back into society, through the quality of the relationships of the schools with other institutions (community centers, families) and by the individual students as they grow up.

The contribution of the school, through its endogenous dynamics, lies in its central position as a bystander in students' activities. The typical discourse of the teacher also contributes to the dynamics of violence or tolerance, as well as how he/she interprets the behavior of the students and the social events of which they are a part. Teachers, like most adults in the community, are unaware of the quality of the interpretations (supportive or violent) they convey to their students and their children. In a way not very different from the original process of giving a name (Aulagnier, 2001; Tesone, 2011), they may be unaware of the projections these interpretations have on the development of the subjective experience of the youngsters (O'Loughlin, 2009).

Adult interpretations of the experiences of youngsters are beneficial: the interpretation given is experienced as feedback that enhances their awareness and understanding of themselves. They can be used for further learning. But, if the interpretations are coercive, given in such a way that stresses evaluation and leaves little place to think, learn and widen the experience, then they are not helpful.

Moreover the intrinsic contribution of the school to the peace or the violence that develops within it includes the didactics characteristic of the school, as well as politically overt and implicit messages. It also contains the policy of inclusion or exclusion (persons, themes), the practices of evaluation and classification of individual students, the relationships with the different groups (ethnics, or otherwise) of parents and the interactions with other institutions across well (or not so well) functioning boundaries.

Schools in which violent acts happen are often perceived by the students and the adults as threatening environments. Threat elicits defensive maneuvers such as reactive violence, usually more evident on the part of the students (bullying, and bringing stones and "weapons") and more subtle on the part of the teachers (shaming, using violent interpretations and psychological violence). Threat, defensive shielding and acting out establish a vicious circle, where violence breeds more violence. The perceived inability of the adults to provide a secure learning environment for all, within containing boundaries, breeds further violence (Silberman & Levy, 1996) in the youngsters.

The typical discourse of the teacher has received very little attention in the relevant literature (Silberman, 1996), and it seems to be the least conspicuous of the intrinsic factors and more endogenous to the school as an organization. By asking in which ways the discourse of the teacher contributes to violence, we hope we are opening the way to promote a more benign discourse.

The practice of responding to most of the pupils products with grades (whether with a number, a letter or a word), makes the learning process static. Effective communication (Silberman, 1996) takes place when two loops flow: sender to receiver, feedback from receiver to sender, added feedback from sender to receiver about the feedback received, and back to the sender. Students commonly carry out tasks and tests that receive a grade and little feedback. Grades bring to focus evaluations that interfere with the learning process. Two difficulties grow from this practice: one, by giving grades, attention switches from the individual to his/her distribution point within the class or the school. Most students remain in the same position on the distribution curve throughout school years and feel they never move from the same place ("I was always an average student"). Within this practice, where each task or test receives a grade, the individual students' achievements and gradual incremental improvement in skills and knowledge are overlooked. Thus, grades are violent due to the limitation they impose on the perception of the student and the teacher. A benign alternative includes detailed feedback (about the strengths and deficiencies in the work), and moreover gives the student the opportunity to use that feedback in an improved version of the same task, thereby learning that products are improvable, and that learning is always après coup (a posteriori).

Dynamically speaking the feedback process is an emotional and cognitive outgrowth of the mirroring processes that engage both the child and the caregiver in a continuous and flowing loop. Learning, teaching and enjoying (or crying) all interweave in the interaction. The process of teaching-doing-evaluating without the feedback benefits doesn't allow the student a personal learning opportunity. Things may reach a point at which teaching is confused with learning. On many occasions, at least in Hebrew, teachers use the term *learning* when they mean *teaching*. While teaching may be thought of as the presentation of contents to students, true learning will occur only when each student can go through his/her own elaboration, influenced by his/her past knowledge and emotional experience.

The introduction of effective (inherent) feedback practices has a wide impact on the quality of learning, motivation and communication between teacher and students (Butler, 1987). It is indirectly related to a decrease in violence. Where feedback practices abound, they have a remedial impact on individual learning processes. They also cultivate readiness to be helped by remedial professionals.

Readers' response to (literary) criticism (Suleiman & Crosman, 1980; Tompkins, 1980) and the implementation of psychoanalytic understandings brought to the reading process are unique contributions of interpretation. While the text remains constant, each reading by a new reader is a new and creative experience. Its importance for schooling processes is that it gives a legitimate space for all possible readings (interpretations) by the students and the teachers of texts and of "texts" (everyday events). A similar psychotherapeutic process (Priel, 1994) examines the therapist's reading (interpretation) of the patient's discourse and encourages the patient to read and interpret the therapist's intervention for his or her own benefit, thus enhancing the impact on the patient's subjectivity.

In contrast, violent interpretations (in general and in the schools) that are unidirectional (from adults to youngsters; from power holders to others) carry the color of the unique truth ("What I saw is what there is") and use traditional didactics (those who "know" teach those who "don't know"). They imply an unquestionable truth about the listener and leave no possibility for exploration ("You obviously didn't make an effort"; "It's good, someone surely helped you"). They are truths given to be swallowed ("You need medicines for your attention disorder") without digestion or elaboration, and they fail to promote development and change. Violent interpretations in the school ("Children from this background always have difficulties in learning") contain social stereotypes, reflect social stratification, power structures and confusion between proper use of power and the abuse of it, that is, between exercising authority and imposing coercion.

Another realm in which the teachers' discourse undermines itself is by allowing very little discussion and reflection concerning everyday life experiences, both in school and in social life in general. The unplanned experiences that "just happen" and questions raised by the students are given almost no attention in comparison to the place given planned teaching contents, which are usually chosen by the teachers or the authorities.

Interpretations, like other parts of the discourse, may have the intention of influencing the listener/reader. Paradoxically, some words and expressions ("Invest more!") that are intended to bring about a change, and leave little space for reflection and dialogue, become coercive and rob the same words of their power. The emphasis on formal learning and the use of unidirectional didactics tend to blur the informal group dynamics which emerge from the students' unconscious group processes and promote informal learning. All learning processes, conscious and unconscious, generate anxiety, whether about what is not known, the ability (or inability) to cope with the tasks at hand, and the status one will be able to reach in the class.

French (1997) sees regulation of the students' anxiety as one of the most important roles of the teacher. One can view the multiplicity of tasks in the schools as a form of splitting, the purpose of which is to guard against the prevalent anxiety generated by the learning process. When the teacher fails to assume the role of container to regulate the anxiety, no place is left for the student to assume his/her role as learner. Roles are then relinquished, split into limited tasks that assume the center of the scene (Wilkes, 2002).

METHODOLOGIES FOR INTERVENTIONS IN THE FIELD THAT HELP DIMINISH VIOLENCE IN SCHOOLS AND COMMUNITIES

A methodology we have *found effective* (more in the long run, less in the short) is that of study groups (Miller, 1989) and *Reflection Groups* (Dellarosa, 1979). The goal of these groups is to promote learning from experience (Charles, 2004) and action research by the members. We believe that this methodology enhances the role of the teacher as learner and as container, by furnishing an adequate container. To describe the methodology we shall focus on one of the many exercises we carried out, this one in a small town in Israel.

The primary task of reflection groups is to enable members to study the development of violent transactions in the field. We used a conceptual frame of reference brought by the consultants and elaborated further within the group. An effort is made to try and translate the understandings to pragmatic community interventions, whether through micro-interventions or institutional and community interventions.

A reflection group functions as a container for thinking (Bion, 1970) and experimentation. It also helps contain the anxiety implied in any learning process and thus helps the members while they revise their conceptions and preconceptions. The group enables members to suspend judgment and contain a vagueness that learning, and especially learning from experience, requires. The experience provides teachers with the support and the modeling they need if they wish to help their students question assumptions, hypotheses and behaviors. One major change might be that members move from judging "good" and "bad" student behavior to questioning themselves and asking why they themselves and others behaved the way they did.

Reflection groups may be offered to organic school teams (as an in-service team development); to teachers from different schools, who register voluntarily and to other professionals; and role holders in a community. Groups whom we consulted, and the one referred to here, included some of the following: officials from the local educational and welfare departments, social workers, psychologists from the school psychological service, school teachers, NGOs (dealing with different forms of violence), parent groups, local officials, citizens committees and interested civil society activists.

There are no clear criteria for including or excluding candidates in reflection groups, although most of the members are role holders in the community, and this includes interested citizens. A problematic question about the membership is whether or not to include members of for-profit organizations, who are also interested parties, such as parents who also own a business in the community. Representatives of for-profit organizations may have difficulty distinguishing between the promotion of the community well-being and the promotion of their business. Similarly, a teacher or a parent may be an active member of a political party, in which case a clear distinction must be made between membership in the party and his or her role as parent or as teacher.

A reflection group that includes representatives of different sectors of the community, including parents, NGOs, municipality officials, and so forth, functions as a *community network*, bringing together the different sectors represented and opening spaces for dialogue.

In our experience the working of a community network is especially helpful when the schools in that community have a very high level of violence and the adults in the school collude, usually unconsciously, to maintain that level of violence. Role holders in the schools that participate in the reflection groups may initiate a very slow and indirect process of change, using micro-interventions, when it is impossible to implement more direct initiatives in the school.

The community network may also function as a trigger, stimulating initiatives that will help deal with violence in different community frameworks: community centers, health services, sport institutions, and so forth. Initiatives may focus in one institution or in wider community circles. Usually, they will involve professional consultants, who train participants in group processes and in the understanding of the development of violent events.

Participation in the reflection groups has a definite impact on the relationships of members toward one another and toward issues relevant to the given community. The impact outside the group is circumscribed and small, but it slowly destabilizes the system and leads to changed interactions between sub-groups of the community.

The destabilization of violent patterns through changed interactions translates gradually into less violent transactions of diminished severity. As noted above members of the reflection group are encouraged to translate understandings and field observations into interventions, that in due time help build new patterns and more benign transactions.

Typically, a reflection group will pass through three phases. *The first phase* (four to five group meetings), will usually include:

1. In the first two sessions lectures about notions of aggression and violence, the concept of micro-violence and observation methodology. During the third and fourth session the concepts of bystander and participant observation (that help clarify the function of the bystander)

are introduced. Near the end of this phase the notion of micro-projects and micro-interventions are emphasized. Members are encouraged to carry on their observations outside their work space. The encounter with violent events and the growing awareness of latent violence is anxiety provoking and the group functions as a container.

Micro-interventions, including field observations, sometimes affect norms of behavior on city streets, within families and at playgrounds. Members are encouraged to choose a focus for observations and follow the development of violent transactions (in this phase, with less attention to the context). Gradually, awareness of the frequency of the violent transactions increases and with it thoughts of intervention strategies. Slowly, micro-interventions move more and more toward the schools themselves. For example, the math teacher tells a student to open a window. The student doesn't succeed, and the math teacher says to him "You can't even open a window." The sensitive home room teacher, casually present at that moment in the class takes the student to her office and gives him a task, and allows him catharsis and elaboration. After much hesitation the home room teacher decides to talk to the math teacher about her part in the violent event.

Throughout the group life (twenty to forty meetings, one—two years) the concepts presented in the first part of this chapter find their way to the attention and elaboration of the group members.

2. The discussion that follows enables participants to make connections between issues raised in the lecture and their personal life experience. Later they may make connections between their observations in the field and micro-violence transactions in their everyday life encounters. In the beginning, passive observation is encouraged, with a focus on the transactions and less on the context.

   This poses two difficulties for the inexperienced observer: the first is the anxiety generated by the proximity to violent events. The second relates to the possibility of punishment following the transgression of a cultural norm that prescribes not seeing (bystander), certain violent everyday events that allude to power differences and coercive maneuvers. An observer is a bystander that plans not to collude with the transaction taking place.

3. A group activity that enhances development of required observation skills. Role playing, dramatic work and micro-teaching are some of the techniques used for enabling the members to experiment with their skills and develop them further. Group consultants assume the role of regulating emotional arousal, especially anxiety.

4. Review time is allotted at the end of each session to allow members and consultants to share their experience of the group learning, personal insights, the role they think that they took in the meeting and

their feedback about the group development and the consultancy quality.

In the second phase (five or six sessions) a typical group session may include:

1. Members and consultants talk about issues brought from field observations, and group discussion.
2. The consultant makes a conceptual contribution regarding the observations presented and the discussion that took place in the group. Issues dealt with in the second phase will be chosen by the consultant and then attempts will be made to relate to both emerging messages voiced by the members and his/her own judgment of the group needs and dynamics (Osterweil et al., 1989; Pichon Riviere, 1984). In his analysis of group processes Pichon Riviere chose the word "emerging" (in Spanish: emergente) (Pichon Riviere, 1984), to refer to the group behavior in Bion terms (Bion, 1961). Group behavior emerges as a result of all the forces and all the levels at play in the chosen frame of reference (Bion, 1961).

   In this phase field work has a wider role. Members are encouraged to make observations both at their work setting and outside of it. There may be an increase in individual, situational and social contributions regarding violent transactions. These may refer to "on the spot" use of reflective opportunities, conflicts and the need to live with differences, power structures and their relevance; benign and violent political processes, micro-violence (Debarbieux, 2006; Foucault, 1992) and *micromachismo* (Bonino Menendez, 1998). Discussion may move from an unidirectional didactics to dialogic didactics. It may focus on the notion of role, including its conscious and unconscious components, and on action research and its relationship to participant observation.

   Participant observation enables members of the workshop to come in contact with parts of the organizational culture (Hinshelwood et al., 2000), that regular members of the organization perceive as the only thinkable "reality." Participant observation allows a dynamic view of the routines and their interrelationships, as they lead to an on-going re-creation of that culture. At the same time he/she does this, the participant observer searches inside him- or herself to find subjective (counter-transferential) sensations, feelings and thoughts. These offer clues that may reflect the individual's experience of other people and groups within that culture (Lazar, 2008). There is an important opportunity for learning here, as the observers become familiar with the relativity of local norms and the regularities that characterize the local discourse, the use of resources (space, time, knowledge, abilities), and the defensive and creative ways with which they meet their challenges.

3. Group activities focus on interactions observed and on the development of specific skills and concepts necessary to further the learning and the field work. For example, a violent transaction for which there seems to be no way out allows all the workshop members to check their different styles of coping.

4. Review.

In the third phase (ten to twenty sessions) the focus moves gradually to actual interventions. Each session is devoted to one or two cases of participants' interventions. A typical group session may include:

1. A detailed description of a case, methods of observation and intervention, and discussion of the case.

2. The consultant brings a conceptual contribution relevant to the understanding of the cases presented and to the discussion that took place in the group. Typical issues include the idea of systemic psychodynamic thinking (Gould et al., 2001), the relationship between micro-interventions and the systemic nature of the social environment, distribution of authority and roles.

3. Group activities focus on obstacles to interventions and experimentation with alternative interventions using dramatic group work and auxiliary egos.

4. Review.

AN EPILOGUE: SPACES FOR REFLECTION IN THE SCHOOLS

Participants in reflection groups usually develop spaces for reflection in the institutions at which they work. Reflection groups are suitable for adults, children and adolescents. Teachers in the reflection groups are expected to open reflection spaces as needed, following crises, violent events, conflicts, and so forth. They are expected to use the reflection groups to support their work even in difficult situations. Conflicts, fights, and attacks afford opportunities for reflection and for conflict management. This includes the possibility of working together. This is so even when disagreements are severe. It is nonetheless possible to maintain mutual respect.

The goal here is to learn to be able to identify inevitable violent transactions and open the possibility of dealing with them through reflection. A further goal is the development of communication skills which minimize punishment and other coercive measures that merely lead to more violence.

Effective reflection spaces opened near the time and place of the event offer a different role for the bystander who is ready to take on an active role. It makes it possible to cope with difficult emotions (rage, frustration) and threatening partners. It is important to delegate to the students tasks and roles necessary in the classroom. For example, students will profit by helping the teacher lead and manage a group discussion and finding ways to enable all to participate. The custom of holding a review at the end of the school day opens a great number of possibilities for developing reflection, insight, awareness and consideration of the other.

During the Intifada[4] in Jerusalem we opened a crises intervention service as a section of the School Psychological Service of the Municipality of Jerusalem. With time, the focus on traumatic experiences moved to crises unrelated to the ongoing war. Later still, the focus moved to issues related to the politics of the conflict. Other value-laden and ideological themes became "talkable." In due time, many teachers carried on discussions with the students, without the presence and the help of the professional team of psychologists (Levy & Silberman, 1996).

NOTES

1. We thank Professor Michael O'Loughlin very much for his personal help in making this chapter better. The responsibility for the present version remains with us.

2. There is an Israeli version of the American program, usually called "Towns without Violence."

3. Our reference to "school" is based on our wide experience in Israel and in Argentina, as well as the knowledge of similar issues in Europe and the United States. It is difficult to make overall generalizations to these various countries, but still a certain amount of universality exists.

4. An Arabic word which literally means "shaking off," though it is popularly translated into English as "uprising," "resistance," or "rebellion."

REFERENCES

Aulagnier, P. (2001 [1975]). *The violence of interpretation: From pictogram to statement.* London: Brunner-Routledge.

Bion, W. R. (1961). *Experiences in groups and other papers.* London: Routledge.

Bion, W. R. (1967). *Second thoughts.* Northvale, NJ: Jason Aronson.

Bion, W. R. (1970). *Attention and interpretation.* London: Heinemann.

Bonino Menendez, L. (1998). Micromachismos: La violencia invisible en la pareja. (Online), January 5, 2012. www.joaquimmontaner.net/Saco/dipity_mens/micromachismos_0.pdf.

Butler, R. (1987). Task-involving and ego-involving properties of evaluation: Effects of different feedback conditions on motivational perceptions, interest and performance. *Journal of Personality and Social Psychology, 53*, 866–879.

Campbell, A., & Gibbs, J. J. (Eds.). (1986). *Violent transactions: The limits of personality.* New York: Basil Blackwell.

Charles, M. (2004). *Learning from experience: A guide for clinicians.* London: Analytic Press.

Debarbieux, E. (2006). Violence in school: A few orientations for a worldwide scientific debate. *International Journal on Violence and Schools*, May 1, 2006.

Dellarosa, A. (1979). *Grupos de reflexión*. Buenos Aires: Paidós.

De Zulueta, F. (1993). *From pain to violence: The traumatic roots of destructiveness*. London: Whurr.

Fonagy, P., Gergely, G., Jurist, E. L., & Target, M. (2004). *Affect regulation, mentalization, and the development of the self*. London: Karnac.

Foucault, M. (1979). *Discipline and punish: The birth of the prison*. New York: Vintage.

Foucault, M. (1992). Microfísica del poder. Madrid: Las Ediciones de la Piqueta.

French, R. B. (1997). The teacher as container of anxiety: Psychoanalysis and the role of the teacher. *Journal of Management Education, 21*, 4, 483–95.

Freud, S. (1920). *Beyond the pleasure principle*. Standard edition 18. London: Hogarth Press.

Gerhardt, S. (2004). *Why love matters: How affection shapes a baby's brain*. London: Routledge.

Gould, L., Stapley, L. F., & Stein M. (2001). *The systems psychodynamics of organizations: Integrating the group relations approach, psychoanalytic and open systems perspectives*. London: Karnac.

Green, M. (Ed.). (2008). *Risking human security*. London: Karnac.

Guggenbuhl, A. (1993). *The incredible fascination of violence: Dealing with aggression and brutality among children*. Woodstock, CT: Spring Publications.

Harding, C. (Ed.). (2006). *Aggression and destructiveness: psychoanalytic perspectives*. London: Routledge.

Hinshelwood, R. D., Obholzer, A., & Skogstad, W. (Eds.). (2000). *Observing organisations: Anxiety, defence and culture in health care*. London: Routledge.

Holmes, P. (1992) *The inner world outside*. London: Tavistock/Routledge.

Klein, M. (1952). The emotional life of the infant. *On envy and gratitude and other works 1946–1963*. London: Hogarth Press 1975.

Lacan, J. (2004). *Le seminaire 1962–63, livre X: L' angoisse*. Paris: Editions du Seuil.

Last, U. & Silberman S. (1989). Burning out and drifting away amongst school psychologists: Are there antidotes? *School Psychology International, 10*, 37–46.

Lazar, R. (2008). *From baby to boardroom: The Tavistock-Bick method of observation and its application to infants and institutions*. Presented in a conference held at the Tavistock Centre, October 17–18, 2008.

Levy, R., & Silberman, S. (1996). The development of an in-service training program for school psychologists on emergency interventions. In U. Last & S. Silberman (Eds.), *Issues in School Psychology*. Jerusalem: Magnes (in Hebrew).

Main, M. (1991). Metacognitive knowledge, metacognitive monitoring and singular (coherent) vs. multiple (incoherent) model of attachment: Findings and directions for future research. In C. M. Parkes, J. Stevenson-Hinde, & P. Marris (Eds.), *Attachment across the Life Cycle*. London: Karnac/Routledge.

Martinez Bouquet, C. M. (1982). Teoría de la escena. Historia. In M. Tusquets & L. Satne (Eds.), *Desarrollos en Psicoterapia de Grupo y Psicodrama*. Barcelona: Gedisa.

Martinez Bouquet, C. M., Moccio, F., & Pavlovsky, E. (1975). *Psicodrama Psicoanalítico en Grupos*. Buenos Aires: Kargieman.

Miller, E. J. (1989). *The "Leicester" model: Experiential study of group and organizational processes*. Occasional Paper No. 10. London: Tavistock Institute of Human Relations.

Miller, E. J., & Rice, A. K. (1967). *Systems of Organization*. London: Tavistock.

O'Loughlin, M. (2009). *The subject of childhood*. New York: Peter Lang Publishing.

Osterweil, Z., & Cohen, E., in cooperation with Windzberg, D., Silberman, S., Tamir, M., Leiser, P., & Rubinstein, G. (1989). *Mental health consultation with groups of teachers*. Jerusalem: Magnes (in Hebrew).

Panksepp, J. (1998). *Affective neuroscience: The foundations of human and animal emotions*. New York: Oxford University Press.

Parsons, M. (2006). From biting teeth to biting wit: The normative development of aggression. In C. Harding (Ed.), *Aggression and destructiveness: Psychoanalytic perspectives*. London: Routledge.

Pichon Riviere, E. (1984). *El proceso grupal: Del psicoanálisis a la psicología social*. Buenos Aires: Nueva Vision.

Priel, B. (1994). *The interpretation of the patient*. Paper presented at the Clinical Colloquium, Department of Psychology, Ben Gurion University (in Hebrew).

Royston, R. (2006). Destructiveness: Revenge, dysfunction or constitutional evil? In C. Harding (Ed.), *Aggression and destructiveness: Psychoanalytic perspectives*. London: Routledge.

Schore, A. A. (1994). *Affect regulation and the origin of the self: The neurobiology of emotional development*. New York: Erlbaum.

Schwartz, H. S. (1990). *Narcissistic process and corporate decay: The theory of the organization ideal*. New York: University Press.

Siegel, D. J. (1999). *The developing mind: How relationship and the brain interact to shape who we are*. New York: Guilford Press.

Silberman, S. (1996). *Some reflections on the discourse of the teachers and its relations to violence in the schools*. Paper presented at the Colloquium with Foreign Authors, New York Psychoanalytic Institute.

Silberman, S., & Levy, R. (1996). The use of organizational theory for understanding violence in the schools. In U. Last & S. Silberman (Eds.), *Issues in School Psychology*. Jerusalem: Magnes (in Hebrew).

Silberman, S., & Plat, A. (2002). Coping with hidden institutional violence. Paper presented at the Opus annual meeting, London.

Silberman, S., & Plat, A. (2011). The quest for social change. Paper presented at the Opus annual meeting, London.

Suleiman, S. R., & Crosman, I. (Eds.). (1980). *The reader in the text*. Princeton: Princeton University Press.

Tesone, J. E. (2011). *In the traces of our name: The influence of given names in life*. London: Karnac.

Tompkins, J. P. (Ed.). (1980). *Readers response criticism*. Baltimore: Johns Hopkins University Press.

Wilkes, J. (2002). Personal Communication.

Winnicott, D.W. (1965). *The maturational processes and the facilitating environment*. New York: International Universities Press.

Chapter Eight

A Most Unusual Technique for Helping an Incarcerated Youth Who Was Labeled "Learning Disabled" and "Anti-Social," Learn to Read

A Retrospective Commentary

Burton Norman Seitler

> The human brain's extraordinary ability to make new connections among its existing structures [is] a process made possible by the brain's ability to be shaped by experience. This plasticity at the heart of the brain's design forms the basis for much of who we are, and who we might become. (M. Wolf, 2007, p. 3)

Many moons ago, while I was still in my twenties, in what now seems like another lifetime, I was hired as an assistant clinical psychologist to work in a state-run training school. The term "training school" was an updated, socially accepted way of saying *reform school*. It was located in a rural area of upstate New York. Fortunately, Tom Tunney, its superintendent, was a gentleman who had been trained as a psychologist and who possessed a sound humanistic vision of the kind of services that might be helpful to troubled youths who, for a variety of reasons, had been involved in anti-social activities and had been remanded to our facility.

I was to be in charge of a cottage of thirteen adolescents who had been sent to our campus facility after having been adjudicated by the courts as *persons in need of supervision*, or as *juvenile delinquents*. These are legal, yet at the same time euphemistic designations which politely describe some really tough kids, most of whom that had been involved, to one degree or another, in various kinds of assaults, thefts, sexual acting out, muggings, drug trafficking and/or abuse, intimidation, or other *less-than-noble* enterprises. My main job was to provide them with group psychotherapy. I was also responsible for supervising a staff of seven adults, all of whom were almost, or more than twice my age.

I was awed by what felt like the enormity of the task. Yet, at the same time, armed with the bravado that often accompanies being young, idealistic, and brash, and also very filled with myself, I was more than merely confident in my ability to find effective ways to relate to the staff and to the residents, I was downright cocky. To be sure, as fate would have it, I did not have to wait too long for my mettle to be tested.

TRIAL BY FIRE

Within a few weeks of my arrival at the facility, I received word "through the grapevine" that my youthful, exuberant residents were planning to accost the staff, steal their car keys, and abscond from the campus. I quickly assembled my staff and we developed a plan to face this potentially critical situation head-on. Since my duties centered on developing and conducting a group therapy milieu, five days a week, and providing individual psychotherapy, as needed, it seemed as though the natural place to address this potential threat ought to be in the group therapy setting itself. Although it was no simple matter, I am happy to say the crisis was handled successfully.

How did my staff and I pull this off? Even though I had only been in charge of this cottage for a short amount of time, I managed to discern who some of the leaders were, and which individuals had the potential to become positive influences on the group, if the opportunity arose for them. I shared my impressions with my staff. Their own street smarts, combined with the fact that they had worked at this facility for quite some time, allowed them to get a pretty accurate feel for this group.

Grey[1] was one of the leaders that they and I independently identified. However, because Grey's past behavioral history and current deportment were sometimes so unpredictable, so extreme, and potentially explosive, the staff felt that Grey was incorrigible. They explained that they tried to "get through" to Grey on numerous occasions without success. They argued that it would be wiser to try to develop an alternate leader to Grey, one who could influence the group to use its collective passion and energy for constructive ends, rather than for the purpose of "busting out of the joint," a goal that would eventually end up badly for them—even if their attempt to leave campus was successful.

I told my staff that I understood their position and that it made logical and practical sense for me to consider someone other than Grey. Nonetheless, something in "my gut" (or the right side of my brain, or wherever intuition is stored) tugged on me to give Grey another chance to develop into a growth-producing force in the group. Although it was unlikely that I would fare any better with Grey than they, I had noticed something about Grey that nobody either observed or had mentioned. What I had noted was so faint, so indistinct, and so subtle, that I was not fully certain that I had really seen it or interpreted it accurately; but if I was correct, all might not be not lost with Grey.

The "Not So Co-incidental" Incident

Something occurred one time in the cottage supply room, where Grey had been assigned, that left me with a vague feeling that I simply could not even formulate. It was the kind of feeling that you sometimes have when you know something, but cannot quite put into words, but which feels like it is on the *tip of your tongue* just waiting for you to *spit it out*. What had happened was that I had casually handed Grey a typed invoice slip, because one of the items on the slip was a little bit blurry. I asked Grey for help. "Hey, Grey," I said, "Can you give me a hand with something here?"

I should point out that Grey was very agreeable when it came to helping out with any *physical* activity or chore. It almost did not matter if it was onerous or not, Grey could be counted on to lend a hand. This contrasted dramatically with reports that came from school, where Grey was described as disruptive, typically refusing to participate in most *scholastic* activities, or worse, causing verbal or physical commotions in class. I wondered why there was such a vast difference in behaviors between what was noted in the classroom, and what was observed outside of the formal school setting?

Little did I know—at least consciously—that I was about to happen upon an answer, one that would change everything. I looked at the blurry invoice and asked Grey, "What does this letter look like to you? I can't tell if it's an "E" or a "B." Grey's mood instantaneously changed, turning from helpful and cooperative to highly irritable and irate. "What do you think I am? This is bullshit! You figure it out" came Grey's thundering and resounding reply. Naively, I pressed on, saying, "This looks like more of a 'B,' to me, don't you think?" Grey rapidly repeated, "I don't give a shit!" But just as quickly added, "Yeah, yeah, it's a 'B,' that's right!" I could not tell if this was a dismissive nod to get this conversation over with, a gesture indicating a softening, or a genuine answer to my question.

I reasoned that nothing would be gained at that moment if I were to ask Grey "what did I say just then that made you so angry?" I doubted that Grey would interpret such a question as an innocent observational inquiry merely intended to produce insight, but rather would see it as confrontational and as my (counter-) attack. I felt the timing for making such a "confrontation" would simply have been premature. Moreover, it was important to *hold* Grey's aggression, that is, neither to attack, nor recoil from it. Instead, I took the pragmatic position, which maintains that it was sufficient that Grey was ultimately responsive to my initial question about the "B" or "E" (albeit with some irritability). Accordingly, I decided to thank Grey for helping clear up my confusion about the "B" or "E," and we continued with our task without any further uproar.

Later on, in a private moment, I puzzled over the previous interaction. At first, my thoughts exclusively focused on what I considered to be Grey's tendency towards over-reactivity and possible dismissiveness. It would have taken little or no effort to conclude that this is typical of so-called "socio-paths," who have been said to bully, intimidate, or bluff their way through situations. However, I think that if I had drawn that conclusion, it would have been the equivalent of a counter-transferential match for Grey's earlier dis-missiveness. And, if I had done so, I believe that it would have: (1) kept things at the manifest level; (2) served the superficial purpose of blaming Grey; and (3) would have prevented me from understanding Grey at a deep-er, latent level.

I resisted the use of diagnostic categorical pronouncements, which, de-spite conventional wisdom, really offer nothing useful. Besides applying simplistic, convenient labels to highly complex human beings, they are tanta-mount to name-calling, offering little else in the way of pragmatic *what to do's* for the individual. Instead, I struggled for quite some time to make sense of that incident and to hear—beyond Grey's defenses—what Grey really may have been trying to say.

Eventually, I got it. Much like moments when we misplace something after having looked "everywhere" for it, when we finally sit down, relax, and allow our minds to wander—not terribly different from what Bion refers to as "reverie" (1962a), the location of the missing item suddenly becomes clear. Even before we actually go to where it is located, we know it will be there. We go for two reasons: (1) to find the item; and (2) to confirm what we were certain we already knew. The same thing occurred here.

Something happened in the interpersonal or intersubjective space between Grey and me. Two unconsciouses had a brief, but profound meeting of the minds so to speak, and Grey's long-held "secret" was momentarily and un-wittingly transmitted and uncovered. Invoking the psychodynamic notion of psychic determinism, this event would not be considered to be random, by any means. So, perhaps it was not such an innocent event at all. It certainly was a meaningful one.

The problem, however, was figuring out how to move this process from an unconscious to a conscious mode so that Grey and I could overtly con-front, communicate, and begin to resolve "the secret." In order to do that, I needed to understand that Grey's blatant "in your face," belligerent attitude and behavior were undoubtedly designed to save face, as well as to keep people at a distance.

Resistance Is Often Based on Pain

Harsh as Grey's overt behavior was—I viewed it as a façade of toughness and wondered if it was a cover-up for other emotions, maybe even delicate, tender feelings. Psychodynamically, it would not be incorrect to infer that the defensive façade which Grey exhibited also represented a form of resistance to change. Change, by its very nature, disrupts homeostasis or psychic equilibrium. Accordingly, it is initially regarded with suspicion, and often vigorously opposed by the individual in question. In this regard, it is important to be mindful that most resistance is based on pain, real, imagined, or anticipated. For that reason, I needed to appreciate Grey's presumed pain, respect it, be sensitive to Grey's feelings, and to guide myself—my approach, my words, my pace, and my timing, accordingly.

Listening for the Sound of the Unsaid to Hear the Unheard

Psychotherapists, no matter what school of thought they embrace, need to listen for the sound of the unsaid. Psychoanalytic listening, in particular, tries to help the patient put into words that which had previously been unsymbolized, unformulated, and thus, unacknowledged. Sometimes, when the patient is unable to tell us what hurts, much less what has produced the painful feeling—the analyst attempts to speak on behalf of the patient's unconscious. This is a very delicate operation. We wish to be able to help the patient articulate what was previously unspeakable, or sometimes even unthinkable. At the same time, we need to be particularly careful not to put words into the patient's mouth that do not belong to the patient, either because our assumptions about what the patient is feeling might be incorrect, or even if our assumptions are accurate, if they are offered prematurely they are rendered ineffective, in fact, may possibly be damaging (by virtue of being intrusive). But, should we be so fortunate for our interpretations to be in tune with the patient's unconscious, well-timed, and well delivered, in order for others to begin to listen to us, we must have first—and foremost—be seen as having paid attention and have closely listened to them. But listening by itself, is not enough. We must create a safety zone where what is said; in addition to what is not said (but often felt) all are permitted entry into the room. Thus, "holding the patient" not only means we must listen to the patient, but also that we do so without introducing panic, horror, or judgment that we might feel in reaction to the aura that the patient emits, or to our own reactive feelings.

So I asked Grey to come into my office, where I tried to tactfully and delicately broach the subject of the secret that had previously been hidden behind what I regarded as Grey's fierce façade of ferocity. It is often a difficult task to confront someone tactfully. Nevertheless, it is an inevitable one. What if my words were mischosen? What if my intervention was mistimed? What if Grey was more fragile than I had imagined? The answer is clear; I would have exposed Grey to retraumatization of old, as yet unhealed wounds. With regard to discussing potentially traumatic material with patients, Bromberg (1999) offers the following relevant observations:

> It is that thin line between the unanticipated but containable shock and the unanticipated but uncontainable shock that separates what is perceived as potentially traumatic from what is perceived as safe but "on the edge." The goal is for the patient and analyst to 'stand, together, in the spaces between the realities' and move safely, but not *completely* safely, back and forth across the line. (pp. 65–66)

DISCREETLY DISCLOSING AND DISCUSSING "THE SECRET"

Not surprisingly, when I ultimately raised the issue with Grey, the usual expletives came fast and furious, but when we were done, the secret that had been kept in for so long was now acknowledged between Grey and me. I knew the secret. Grey could not read. This knowledge now could no longer go unacknowledged, even though Grey had strenuously avoided it up to this point. Of even greater importance, Grey no longer had to "go it alone."

Despite an initial angry flurry, Grey eventually calmed down. I think it must have been clear somehow that my intention was to accept Grey as a whole person, despite "the secret;" and it was also understood between the two of us, that it was not my objective to cause any further humiliation for Grey. I was quite certain that Grey had suffered enough in life. There was no need for more.

What now remained was to see how Grey and I would handle the fact that I knew the secret. For me, Grey's difficulty reading was no different than any other symptom of underlying conflicts, and I was prepared to treat it as such. As with any symptom, there was, and would be no moral, or for that matter, *any* judgment attached to it on my part. On the other hand, Grey's feelings about not being able to read undoubtedly were filled with shame, guilt, a sense of inadequacy, and other self-denigrating attitudes.

Reading, a skill that is so fundamental, so quintessential, and which is acquired so early that most of us take it for granted, was a significant source of disquietude for Grey, one which created so much anguish that it needed to be avoided at any price. Any attempt to place Grey in a position where reading was to be required, would run the risk of producing painful feelings of humiliation. In an understandable effort to avoid, if not eliminate even the most remote possibility of experiencing mortification, Grey learned early to adopt the position that *a good offense is the best defense*. This would explain the almost reflexively irate reaction when I asked Grey to clarify a couple of blurry letters for me, in the "not so coincidental incident" described above.

It also now became clear to me why Grey seemed to be reconciled, or perhaps preferred to be diagnosed as a thug or a sociopath, rather than be thought of as illiterate and have to endure the stigma—so often associated with reading difficulties—of being treated as stupid. Horsman (1990) talks about this very issue, namely, the negative manner in which people are treated if they cannot read, for one reason or another.

Horsman insightfully observes that people labeled as 'illiterate' "are stigmatized and manipulated," simply because the label carries with it "an implicit assumption that a set of tasks that are functional for all . . . can be agreed upon. . . . There is rarely reference to the value judgment involved in the selection of tasks included" (p. 132). Going further, Horsman raises a number of excellent questions about some of our assumptions regarding people who have difficulty reading. For example, what is generally assumed when the terms "illiterate," "functional illiterate," or "drop-out" are used? Do these terms become reified and begin to define (and demean) the people to whom they are applied? Do the people who are so-labeled take on pejorative definitions of themselves? Horsman goes so far as to question the very nature of social discourse and social policy with respect to these terms and the people subsumed under them and advances the following practical admonition not to judge those that cannot read as "lazy." Sadly, many of such individuals judge themselves quite harshly for having dropped out of school, even though, as Horsman points out in her close examination of the respective childhoods of the subjects in her studies, they had no other choice available to them. For some, being unable to read (although it has its own set of consequences) was "a way out." This is very similar to what Putnam (1992) has properly referred to as "an escape when there is no escape" (p. 104). Horsman sounds a proper note of caution:

> Rather than judging . . . as unmotivated when they enroll in or drop out of a program because they were sent by a social worker, because their friend is going, or because of the ways in which their lives are disorganized by others, programs should respond to the material circumstances in [their] lives. (p. 224)

Although Grey was concerned about being stigmatized and treated poorly in connection with being unable to read, and while it does account for a substantial portion of Grey's aggressive, defiant behavior, it is not the whole story. More will be said about this later on in the section entitled: "Early Trauma and the Need to Avoid Image-Stimulating Material." However, before going into the connection between trauma, images, and written or ver-

balized words, a few comments may be in order about reading and its corollary—difficulty reading—or so-called *functional illiteracy*.

READING, WRITING, AND FUNCTIONAL ILLITERACY

Humans are the only species on this planet that can read and write. Archeo-
logically speaking, reading and writing are relatively new. According to
Wolf (2007), we taught our brains to read barely a few thousand years ago. In
that miraculous process, the evolution of the brain was altered in a certain
direction and the fate of the human species was changed forever. For most of
us, reading is second nature. And yet surprisingly, it is extremely complex.
To a large extent, we are what we read. Each time we read, the brain changes.
The more we read, the more our brain circuitry is modified.

Bion (in Lutenberg, 2009) says that there are patients who have difficulty
communicating with themselves. He claimed we possess an inner world
which has the potential for producing, as well as blocking, what he referred
to as "alpha-transmissions." He further contended that when alpha-transfor-
mations are inhibited beta-elements are formed, which themselves, are unable to generate thought. In short, our capacity to think, and our ability to
think about ourselves (that is, our individual senses of self) are completely
contingent on our alpha-elements. Accordingly, individuals who experience
difficulties involving problems arising out of a compensated "structural mental void" of the type mentioned above are unable to think. It is the production
of beta-elements, which Bion claims produce the condition of mental functional illiteracy. The following are manifestations of various beta elements
that Bion posits: 1-repetition, 2-embryonic thoughts, 3-the non-edited, 4-
structural mental void, 5-functional illiterate, and 6-mental abortions.

Some of this is similar to Donnell Stern's (1997) notion of "unformulated
experience." In terms of psychotherapy practice, says Bion (1962b), it is the
analyst whose own mind—serving as the external ego for the patient—which
often acts as the primary link in a patient's chain of unthinkable thoughts,
that ultimately allows some of those unremembered, unspoken, and acted out
memories, as Freud (1914) conceptualized the repressed, to eventually come
to the fore.

The actual conversation that took place between us was a lengthy one,
filled with intense emotional material. In brief, Grey became irate when I
indicated that I had discovered the secret. But, as I had inwardly surmised,
when Grey was most furious, Grey was also most frightened. Ultimately, we
hit on a working solution, whereby Grey had a face-saving compromise that
would allow us to work together. We struck an agreement that I would not
tell anyone that Grey could not read. Since I was already duty-bound to
maintain Grey's confidentiality, this was not a burdensome promise for me to

make or keep. To "sweeten the pot," I invited Grey to participate in a rather unconventional, but potentially promising solution that I had concocted. If Grey wanted to opt out at any point, I still would be bound to maintain the secret. Grey ultimately agreed to my proposal, although with some under- standable wariness and hesitancy.

Before going into the unusual approach that I proposed to Grey, let me say that it would have been rejected out of hand, if there had not been an understanding—some of which was without words—that had been estab- lished beforehand between Grey and me. I had spent a great deal of my "free" time thinking about Grey. My thoughts were not organized around a specific plan, structure, any preset ideas, or anything solid or tangible. I was interested in and curious about Grey. How did Grey become the person I was seeing? Was there something underneath the persona that was being present- ed? If so, how was it formed, and how come? Although these ideas are fairly well formed as I write them down for this chapter, when they were first buzzing around in my mind, they seemed to be amorphous, wandering thoughts. In some ways, they bear some resemblance to what Bion referred to as the reverie a mother has when imaging her child (1962b). For Bion, reverie is much more than "day-dreaming." It is the use of one's intuitive faculties to understand in some fashion what is going on *inside* of another. In essence, it is the act of having faith in one's unconscious, which is a prereq- uisite for the alpha function to operate. Fonagy and Target (1997), refer to this as "mindfulness," or carrying the other individual in one's mind.

Apparently, as much as I had been trying to form a picture so I could understand what Grey was like, Grey must have been just as busy making an assessment of me. Only later on in our relationship did it become clear to me that Grey was trying to discern who was safe from who was not, who was to be trusted and who was duplicitous, who might possibly understand Grey and thus be different from all of the others who wanted to, but could not, or those that did not even care to make an attempt to get past that "tough" exterior that Grey displayed in order to know what was behind it.

For some reason, Grey had correctly deduced that I was safe. Perhaps it was the fact that earlier I too was unable to read—at least momentarily. That is, I was unable to discern the letter "E" from another, "B." In addition, on that occasion, I turned to Grey as my "expert" to help me out when I was unable to read. Also, when Grey verbally exploded at me, I was not only able to tolerate it, but I responded kindly, but not in kind. Whatever Grey was keeping pent up inside—which by accretion over time, now felt homicidal in proportion after having being unleashed at me—did not kill me. If Grey previously regarded me as an opponent, I could now at least be seen as a worthy one. In any event, by not over-reacting and retaliating, I quietly became a role model for restraint, for the acceptance and normalization of angry feelings, and served as a safe holding environment for their expression.

As Bromberg (2003) explains, something serendipitous and emotionally helpful occurs when the following conditions are experienced and felt in an atmosphere of safety:

> . . . this necessary synthesis of affective security and relational risk depends on what a given patient and analyst do in an unanticipated way that is safe but not *too* safe—an enactment of the relational failures of a patient's past while allowing "safe surprise" in the here-and-now to occur. (p. 558)

It took a little while for Grey to even begin to believe that reading was possible. After all, there had been many years of successful avoidance, which protected Grey from the humiliation of failure, but which, at the same time (if this defensive maneuver were to continue), would eliminate the prospect of ever achieving success. I knew that one of the last neurological functions to disappear; even after massive brain damage has occurred, is the recognition and expression of curse words. The case of Phineas P. Gage, who suffered extensive neurological destruction of critical parts of his cortex (in Damasio, 2005), is the quintessential illustration of this fact. I was similarly aware that, when working with individuals, it is usually a good idea to make use of their strengths. Grey openly and proudly boasted of being an inveterate *foul-mouth*. Therefore, it required little stretch of the imagination to conclude that Grey's cursing—that had so often put people off or which had intimidated them—might possibly be harnessed and put to good service.

Although Grey could not read most things, the propensity to recognize, understand, and use curse words was still intact and flourished. So we started with the basics and moved on from there. In order to demonstrate to Grey that reading some things was possible, I selected one of the most universal and most powerful curse words as our starting point. Another reason for starting with curse words has to do with their emotional power, which derives from their primal nature. It is not an accident that "rap" music became the voice of the underclass and of the angry renegade, whose protests could only be expressed through the common vernacular of outrage. In this regard, it is not sufficiently relieving to an individual to merely say, "*that troubles me,*" when what is really felt is fury. Thus, anything short of "*that pisses me off!*" entirely misses the individual's experience-near feelings. As Di Benedetto (2001) says:

> The crucial point of every experience of mental growth is the broadening of the quality, extension and depth of the relationships that each of us can establish with our own internal world. When this internal world is insubstantial and full of gaps, a good relationship with someone else contributes to reconstruct it, reintegrate the missing parts and create the conditions for a richer inner dialectic. The "word" is the essential means for this relationship/reconstruction. (p. 48)

The first word we took up was F-U-C-K.

Of course, it would later require demonstrations to show Grey the relevance and generalizability of this word to other forms of reading. From F-U-C-K, we derived SUCK, than LUCK, BUCK, PUCK, MUCK, and so on. Eventually, this led to blends, such as STUCK, STICK, SLICK, PRICK, PLUCK, and on and on. Certainly, this approach would not be prominently featured in the curriculum of any respectable mainstream educational setting. Special education classes would be loath to attempt such measures. And, any teacher who would promote such an approach could expect to be summarily dismissed. But in this venue, comprised of a population of hard-core youths, in the privacy of the consultation room and armed with the patient privilege afforded by confidentiality, it was perfect. This is not meant as a laissez-faire, "anything goes" license. Rather, it is provided here as an illustration of a particular means of joining in with the patient's own language and utilizing it as a rung on a ladder by which fears could be faced and avoidance (of reading) could be surmounted one step at a time.

But this begs the question, *Why was this method utilized as opposed to "whole learning," "phonetic," "the Orton-Gillingham Method,"* or other approaches? There are four central reasons why this procedure was devised:

1. For one thing, there was a strong likelihood that many well-trained, caring, highly motivated teachers had previously utilized a number of such techniques with Grey. Consequently, it made no sense to try to redo, or undo what had been unsuccessful before.
2. Presumably, Grey's aggressive defenses did not let others in and did not allow for the reading problems to be acknowledged, much less overcome.
3. For another, the approach that I advanced flew under Grey's defensive radar.
4. Finally, it appealed to Grey, less because of its originality than for its flouting of authority, all the while, in a socially acceptable manner.

Aside from the initial benefit of releasing anger in our collaboratively developed, non-judgmental forum, we were also able to laugh a great deal together and take great pleasure in irreverently flouting all the prevailing moral strictures and conventions that govern most verbal expressions. In short, we were able to play together and relate to one another. The importance of play cannot be underestimated. Winnicott (1971) was one of the first to establish the connection between play and the holding environment. Adding a more contemporary note to this, Ogden, Minton, and Pain (2006) commenting on the conditions that allow for play to take place, stated:

"Play occurs when safety and energy regulation needs are met; caregiving occurs in the context of attachment and in social relationships where another person requires care" (p. 122).

More recently, others have commented on some possible neurological benefits of play. Panskepp (1998) for one observed that as the cortex develops, play becomes more multifaceted, more versatile, and less reliant on physical outlets. Jokes, puns, and comedic relief now take on a higher order, in which action is now expressed through humor. He regards laughter, emanating from mental humor, as the hallmark of play, claiming that it strengthens attachments and social bonds. Schore (2003) suggests that play actually increases the production of endorphins, producing a feeling of general well being and better physical and emotional health.

EARLY TRAUMA AND NEED TO AVOID IMAGE:
STIMULATING MATERIAL

In the course of Grey's individual treatment, four times per week, many things emerged. One thing, in particular, may shed some light on factors that could differentially contribute to many kinds of reading difficulties. Early in life, Grey was a helpless witness to, as well as a victim of several physical and sexual assaults. The memory of these horrible events was haunting and needed to be stricken from conscious awareness. Van der Kolk's and Van der Hart's (1989, 1991) position regarding memories involving trauma is that such memories often become split off from coming into consciousness, are frequently stockpiled as sensory perceptions or obsessive thoughts, and make their existence known in the form of behavioral reenactments.

Yet, as we know psychoanalytically, nothing is ever *completely* forgotten. There are always residues that are somehow stored, sometimes deep within the somatic warehouse of the body. In Grey's case, the images were never terribly far below consciousness as to be totally inaccessible.

On one hand, this represents a positive note insofar as Grey's upset state can be accessed to some degree. On the other hand, because it is an ever-present source of anguish—much like a raw wound, even the slightest, gentlest, most loving, well-meaning touch can produce agony. When Grey is somehow touched, the immediate reaction is unbridled rage. But this is not limited exclusively to physical touch. Grey was highly reactive to material that stimulates a particular category of thoughts, images, and feelings, any or all of which had the potential to act as reminders of Grey's traumatic experiences. Accordingly, Grey's traumatic experiences could not be easily accessed verbally. And, when verbal recall is impeded, these experiences, memories, images, and symbolic representations often remain unintegrated or unaltered over time. For such individuals, time has stood still. The events of the past are still very much alive and waiting in the wings to be triggered. Although the formation of a narrative between patient and therapist is necessary, by itself it is often insufficient. Van der Kolk (2002) suggests that it is important to help patients "overcome the traumatic imprints that dominate their lives, which are the sensations, emotions, and actions that are not relevant to the demands of the present, but are triggered by current events that keep reactivating old, trauma-based states of mind" (p. 59).

Moreover, Grey's reactivity, in the form of explosive anger, served to back people off. While this "tactic" kept people away and kept Grey relatively safe, it also kept Grey from achieving genuine closeness in a mutual give-and-take relationship. Closeness was dangerous. Being on the defensive worked for many reasons. For one thing, it protected Grey from ever again being hurt physically. Certainly, because nobody was allowed to get close, it kept Grey's secret under wraps and prevented prying eyes from unraveling it. But it also kept the presumed shame associated with all of Grey's secrets from being experienced, acknowledged, and worked through.

WORDS, THOUGHTS, AND IMAGES

Thus, words, those seemingly innocent little sound or letter combinations that we use to communicate either orally or in writing have considerable power to create images. It is these very images that stir up thoughts, memories, and feelings, including ones associated with past traumas. In this light, we can clearly recognize how many instances of reading difficulties may be related to the mind's attempt to avoid retraumatization, or at least associations with toxic images or material. And that is precisely what seems to have happened to Grey.

Regrettably, most educational approaches to reading are unaware of, or do not take into consideration the immense and sometimes negative power of words—written or spoken. Education, as it is presently constituted, attempts to "inculcate," which strays far from its original meaning, which comes from the Latin, "educare," meaning to lead out. With this in mind, I used whatever tools Grey already possessed in order to build upon them. Cursing, therefore, became our means of communication and interpersonal interaction, and served as Grey's eventual, although ironic, means of redemption.

The "cursing" approach allowed Grey and I to be furious together about an external abstraction, namely, "society," and to express our combined ire in an almost mischievous, irreverent manner, all without imposing further harm on or trauma to Grey. It allowed Grey to be "anti" social, so to speak, in an acceptable manner. For the first time, disagreeable elements could now be transformed into tolerable and even enjoyable ones. Even images representing experiences filled with "ugliness" could be redeemed as they go through an almost miraculous metamorphosis process in which reality undergoes a transformation from being a monstrosity—too ugly for Grey to bear, and too horrendous to look at—to being an admirable exhibit.

Words became the medium, not only for the expression of experiences that were once too painful to witness, but also for ones which could not even be uttered. What is more, instead of acting out, Grey could now put feelings into words. Not only did this most unconventional looking at and making use of "curse" words become a vehicle that permitted Grey to deal with images that were upsetting, but it also served to allow the expression of profound hurt. Simultaneously, this provided an outlet for Grey's anger over the rotten hand that life had dealt. All this was accomplished in an acceptable, even relieving manner. As it happened, it turned out to be the perfect instrument for educational, as well as emotional growth.

As a result of Grey's progress in individual psychotherapy, greater involvement, and positive leadership in the group therapy milieu was seen. Grey, who once resisted being influenced by the group process, was now just as formidable an influence on the other members as before, but this time on behalf of non-destructive aims. All this occurred, and more, simply because the vaunted "secret" that Grey had kept hidden behind a facade of aggressive behavior, no longer needed to be kept under wraps. And the shame that was associated with Grey's defense against upsetting images potentially aroused by reading could be broached and worked through. After all, Grey could now read. Simultaneously, the shame that Grey felt about having been desecrated as a child, which underlay the reading symptom, became the focus of our mutual attention in therapy.

As an aside, Grey eventually finished high school, went on to college, got married, had two children, one of whom now teaches English; the other teaches English as a second language.

This case study illustrates how trauma was expressed in the symptom of being unable to read. Inasmuch as this depiction was successful in establishing the possibility of a link between specific traumatic life experiences and an individual's need to dissociate or split off the traumatic images associated with being physically and emotionally violated, it still falls short of getting at a far more important underlying factor, that of how we, as a society, view and treat our children.

In her petition opposing prejudice against children, and her plea for seeing children as human beings with all the rights and proper treatment that adults should have, Elizabeth Young-Bruehl, esteemed colleague and dear friend who recently left us shortly after authoring "Childism," (2012), wrote that children:

> . . . are not lumps of clay to be shaped or blank slates to be written on or helpless beings to be trained into robotic conformity. Not property, not ser-

vants, they are also not empty, bad, wild, or originally sinful beings that childist projections and stereotypes have made them out to be (pp. 291–92).

NOTE

1. "Grey" is a pseudonym and all identifying material has been disguised to protect "Grey's" privacy.

REFERENCES

Bion, W. R. (1962a). A theory of thinking. In *Second Thoughts*. London: Maresfield Library.

Bion, W .R. (1962b). *Learning From Experience*. New York: Basic Books.

Bromberg, P. (2003). Something wicked this way comes: Trauma, dissociation, and conflict. *Psychoanalytic Psychology, 20*, 558–74.

Bromberg, P. (1999). Playing with boundaries. *Contemporary Psychoanalysis, 35*, 54–66.

Damasio, A. (2005). *Descartes' error: Emotion, reason, and the human brain*. New York: Penguin Press.

Di Benedetto, A. (2001). *Before words: Psychoanalytic listening through the medium of art*. London: Free Association Books.

Fonagy, P., & Target, M. (1997). Attachment and reflective function: Their role in self-organization. *Developmental and Psychopathology, 9*, 679–700.

Freud, S. (1914). Remembering, repeating, and working through. *Standard Edition, vol. 12*, London: Hogarth Press, 145–56.

Horsman, J. (1990). *Something in my mind besides the everyday: Women and literacy*. Toronto: Women's Press.

Lutenberg, J. M. (2009). Alpha-transformation, mental void, and edition. *International Forum of Psychoanalysis, 18*, 2, 86–89.

Ogden, P., Minton, K., & Pain, C. (2006). *Trauma and the body*. New York: Norton.

Panskepp, J. (1998). *Affective neuroscience: The foundations of human and animal emotions*. New York: Oxford University Press.

Putnam, F. W. (1992). Discussion: Are alter personalities fragments or figments? *Psychoanalytic Inquiry, 12*, 95–111.

Schore, A. (2003). *Affect dysregulation and disorders of the self*. New York: Norton.

Stern, D. (1997). *Unformulated experience: From dissociation to imagination in psychoanalysis*. Hillsdale, NJ: Analytic Press.

Van der Kolk, B. A. (2002). *Beyond the talking cure: Somatic experience and subcortical imprints in the treatment of trauma in Francine Shapiro's EMDR: Promises for a paradigm shift*. Washington, DC: American Psychological Association.

Van der Kolk, B. A., & Van der Hart, O. (1991). The intrusive past: The flexibility of memory and the engraving of trauma. *American Imago, 48*, 425–445.

Van der Kolk, B. A., & Van der Hart, O. (1989). Pierre Janet and the breakdown of adaptation in psychological trauma. *American Journal of Psychiatry, 146*, 1530–40.

Winnicott, D. W. (1971). *Playing and reality*. London: Tavistock.

Wolf, M. (2007). *Proust and the squid: The story and science of the reading brain*. New York: HarperCollins.

Young-Bruehl, E. (2012). *Childism: Confronting prejudice against children*. New Haven: Yale University Press.

Chapter Nine

Which Of You As Teachers Has Not At Some Point Experienced The Following?

Sue Wallace

A considerable sense of relief when a swift glance around the classroom establishes for you that the child is absent. The sharp intake of breath that may be slowly exhaled following that assurance. The possibility that today your carefully planned lesson might not deteriorate into a battle ground; that on this occasion you might not have to experience a combination of emotions, none of them pleasant, that are always prompted by that impossible child. Excluded repeatedly, he is defiant and aggressive. There are rumors that he struck a colleague in another department, that or he has reduced another to tears. But today, he is absent and in his absence the group will be more cooperative; perhaps even enthusiastic. It is a good day today.

As a student teacher for me the child might have been Anthony. A loud, stoutly built, potentially aggressive boy who specialized in distraction techniques, Anthony was particularly fond of making bull-frog noises. A talent deployed with a monotonous regularity to the despair of students on teaching practice and the apparent delight of his classmates. One of my fellow students had fled the classroom sobbing in the face in his defiance; defiance that meant the successful recruitment of other kids to join him in his scorn for her. It seemed clear to me that taking him on was not the answer.

In my class I complimented him on his bull-frog impersonation and asked the other children to be quiet so that we could properly appreciate it. He enjoyed a couple of attempts and then stopped whereupon gently, I invited him to continue as we were enjoying this. Anthony declined with a grin and I thanked him, he never made the noises again and we struck up an alliance that lasted throughout my time in the school.

I was lucky, Anthony was not a hard nut to crack and the other pupils at this school in a relatively privileged area, were generally easygoing and compliant. I was left with an interest nonetheless at that earliest point in my teaching career, in the way that my interaction with Anthony had evoked such a different attitude from him to what he demonstrated in response to the defensive anger of my fellow student.

Years later, invited to run a group for children in a child and adolescent unit, I worked with two boys, both of whom had been excluded from school for violent behavior. One of them in particular stays with me. Andrew attended the meetings without fail and used the space to talk about how difficult things had been for him. His parents had had a troubled relationship and he had regularly witnessed domestic violence. One day he arrived home from school to discover his mother had left the family home without a word. Always something of a drinker, his father began drinking even more heavily and had no time for his son and this continued until he met a new woman. Once in the new relationship Andrew's father spent most of his time with this woman who was mostly indifferent but sometimes actively hostile to her new partner's child.

This meant that Andrew spent most of his time alone struggling to continue to attend school. During an especially difficult science class, a teacher made a disparaging, personal comment about him and Andrew told us he "saw red." He threw a chair at the teacher and wreaked havoc on the science lab. His behavior was deemed unacceptable and with what appears to have been very little reflection or thought he was swiftly excluded from the school.

Andrew has stayed with me because his capacity for insight and his empathy toward the other children in the group was exceptional. My work with them ended after six months because I had run the group voluntarily and there were no resources to pay me to continue with it subsequently. Andrew presented the nurse who co-facilitated the group and me with a card thanking us. I felt then and still feel many years later, an acute sense of sad helplessness that I was not able to continue to provide a space for him to try to make sense of his experiences. He had used up the "available resource" allocated to him. It seemed meager in comparison to the level of desperation he had at that point. I could only hope that he learned something about himself that in some small way could offer some sustenance in what seemed then to be the lonely, unpromising future that he was expected to forge alone.

Currently I work as a psychotherapist with homeless and potentially homeless people with personality disorders in a Scottish city where levels of deprivation in certain areas have rendered me shocked and disbelieving. My past work in education imbued in me a strong interest in young people and I regularly meet those whose stories reflect similar issues to the ones that I heard from Andrew. These young folk have many differences but there are consistent themes. One of them is that despite their evident lively intelligence only rarely have these youngsters achieved any qualifications, and the primary reason for that is that they equally rarely attended school. When they did, they report that rather than a respite from constant trauma of their home lives it was quite likely to be an additional source of miserable shame and humiliation. Their repeated absences meant that they were unable to keep up with their academic studies and perhaps even more significantly they had struggled to secure or maintain a place within established peer groups. Their reaction to this additional pressure would most usually lead to repeated exclusions from school and this combined with domestic circumstances would lead to an entrance into the "care system" or "secure accommodation" frequently experienced by these children as neither caring nor secure.

The young people I work with mostly have ages that span a similar range to that of a high school from entrance to exit, but a little older from seventeen to twenty-five years. World-weary, they have seen and heard things that their growing minds could not manage. The behaviors that they display often seem out of synch with their chronological age in ways that overwhelm, bewilder, and frustrate those who try to work with them. Most of all, it can feel impossible to continue to think under the pressure imposed by attempts at communication with them. Almost invariably they express a loneliness and isolation that precipitates them into relationships that perpetuate the abuse they have experienced throughout their lives.

ELLIE

I see Ellie coming toward me from the end of the bleak, hospital corridor; this young woman who is little more than child behind the double-locked doors of the intensive psychiatric care unit. I try to gauge whether she looks pleased to see me but she wears the joyless smile I am used to seeing, at once managing to combine resignation and skepticism. The nurse unlocks a side room "to give you more privacy." I am not sure how seriously to take this as the room is walled with glass. We slide onto the uncomfortably utilitarian, wipe-clean plastic seats. I notice a constant parade of pacing that goes on outside of this room clearly visible through the glass walls designed to ensure this visibility at all times.

Ellie is constantly distracted. I note as she turns her head that the attempts to cut her throat are fading to pink streaks under her chin. She peers across to another glassed 'office' similar to the one we inhabit and laughingly sums up the occupants, a young man and an older one in an overcoat.

"He's a lawyer, blatantly."

Whipping round again she continues "That's the lad that fancies me."

I ask her how she has been.

"Ok."

"Really?" I ask her, "because I've heard that pretty heavy things have been happening."

Ellie shrugs, so I tell her the accounts that I have heard of her attempts to harm herself and her violence toward ward staff that caused her to be shipped out of the open ward to another hospital. I tell her of my attempted visit when I learned these things but that I was not allowed to see her. I try to explore with her what triggered such extreme behavior. She grins again like a much younger child then her energy fades and she slumps again on the plastic chair.

"I can't remember."

I gently try to prompt her, explaining that she had visited with an external assessor at the hospital and that the conversation with him seems to have distressed her.

"Did I hit him?" she asks with a spurt of renewed enthusiasm.

Her mood seems stable but bland—it is as if she is completely discon- nected; I doubt I can reach her and she tells me she is tired. I ask her what she has been doing and how she has been passing the time and she replies that she has been "just sitting about." There is nothing to do, she continues, and tells me that she is hungry.

I try to say something about her father whose death precipitated this recent deterioration in her mental health. She tells me that she feels "noth- ing." She jokes instead that she wants to "get out" and the first thing that she will do when that happens is drink. She watches my expression. I repeat my question regarding how she is feeling about things and she repeats "just the same." I tell her I don't know what to say to her because it seems to me that it has been a terrible year for her. Ellie says "You can say that again."

I say, anticipating her, "but shit happens." Ellie laughs and picks up the phone in the office to make a call to her sister. Finally she gets through.

"Are you coming up to see me?"

I cannot make out the other end of the conversation but the tone sounds defensive

"Well I'm here with Sue Wallace," she says, "so I'm going to have to go."

She has been watching me throughout this brief conversation.

"She's not coming," she explains. "She'll be back when she wants mon- ey."

Ellie is just nineteen years old and both her parents died within a short space of time. During the same time frame, her five-year-old child's adoption was finalized.

One of the most moving scenes in Mark Romanek's (2010) film adaptation of Kushiro Ishiguro's (2006) novel *Never Let Me Go* occurs when the young heroine who is very much in love, appeals to the former headmistress of her old "school" for a "deferral" of the process of "donating" organs on behalf of her lover. This process of "donation" is the inevitable fate of the "pupils" of the institution who we have learned were clones bred for precisely such a purpose.

Naively the couple central to the drama believe that an exception to the process may be granted if the exceptional artwork produced by the hero subsequent to his schooldays will provide the missing "evidence" of the quality of his "soul" that he feared he had been unable to show when a pupil. A "school" which the audience knows was designed to attend to the "ethic" of rearing children solely to provide the function of supplying vital body organs for "original" members of the society they live in.

In their innocence the young people believe that an adequate demonstration of their genuine and long-standing love for one another will win them further time before society extracts the price to be paid for their existence. They are horribly wrong and are instead informed by the headmistress that the artwork collected at routine intervals throughout their childhood was not to establish the quality of their souls but merely an attempt to determine whether as "clones" they had souls at all.

We are told that the children had heard rumors that their "originals" were taken from a population that included "down and outs" and "junkies." The film's heroine is caught by her friend in another scene, poring over a pornographic magazine she has found. This we learn later was not out of prurience but because she had interpreted her normal adolescent sexual feelings as an indication that she must have been derived from an "original" involved in outrageous sexual activities and as a consequence her search of the magazine is in the vain hope that she might find her.

Ironically, the way the film plays out, whatever the origins of these young people, it appears that the fine school they attended, the structure and affection offered by their carers, combined with good diet and expert medical care has ensured that they have become model citizens. Indeed, so model are these citizens, that they are prepared to make the ultimate sacrifice of each of their vital organs in turn, as they have been carefully 'programmed' to do before reaching the final point of so-called "completion" that we are very aware is a euphemism for their consequent death.

Among the many questions posed by *Never Let Me Go* is that of the relative importance of nature and nurture in the development of the individual; what we might conceive of as their personality or sense of identity. These questions have vexed child rearing and educational practices for generations, the "spare the rod and spoil the child" attitudes originating from various established religions. Perspectives, such as those confirmed in Christian traditions and informed by notions of the innate "sinfulness" that a child has "inherited" from their "fathers." The "sinfulness" ascribed for example, to the children who featured in Victorian novels where we read of attempts to beat it out of them.

In the same way that there is an apparently legitimized dismissal of humanity toward the clones of *Never Let Me Go*, perhaps too there is a similar orientation toward the least fortunate members of our western societies where accidents of birth determine life potentialities. To what extent are the children of excluded members of society born into conditions which are likely to dictate their future lives? To what extent is there still an unspoken belief that individuals are born bad as opposed to the counter-arguments suggesting that they may have badness thrust upon them.

Recent thinking from the field of epigenetics reveals that this debate is infinitely more complicated than previously believed. Indeed contemporary perspectives would appear to confirm sociologist Norbert Elias's (1991) argument that nature and nurture are not only inextricable but begin the process of that inextricability from conception onward.

Essentially these approaches have determined that genes have multiple potentials and that the expression of genetic material will be determined by a complex admixture of factors including the impact of maternal hormones upon the foetal environment. In its simplest form this means that the conditions impacting upon a mother and in particular, her experiences of acute levels of stress will have a significant impact on the potential development of her unborn child.

Once the child is born the critical integration of nature and nurture continues and this happens most pertinently in regard to the brain. At birth the infant's brain is very different from how it will become in adulthood. Development occurs through the initial prolific creation of neural connections known as "arborization." In the first few years of life these occur at a rate of about seven hundred per second (Harvard Center on the Developing Child). Subsequent to this is a process of "pruning" as connections die off unless they "fire" frequently enough to establish them in a more permanent structure (Schore, 2003). The pruning process is intended to make those connections used regularly more efficient.

This means that the first years of life in turn will be determined by the quality of the attachment that the child has with their primary caregiver because of the physiological responses that the nature of this attachment are impacting on the very structure of their developing brain

JOHNNY

I hear Johnny before I see him, his low gruff voice so at odds with his boyish appearance. His conversation, peppered with heavy duty expletives, gradual-

ly becomes recognizable as the lift approaches the thirteenth floor of the grim grey building.

He arrives with a member of staff from his support project still cursing and steals a look at me from the corner of his eyes, checking my reaction to his stream of invective. I smile at him.

"It's your fault, it's not my fuckin' fault we're late."

His concern with whose fault it is continues in a tirade against the worker. Inside the staff flat that is the venue for our meeting he pulls a thick pile of paper from his pocket—his song lyrics that he has brought for me to see. He says it will take me some time to read them . . . and would I like him to read one to me.

"Please do," I invite. Again the sideways look at his worker.

"She's heard some of these before—they're quite . . . ," he grins again gesturing toward the pages, "aren't they?" He asks proudly but also with a degree, perhaps just a trace of, anxiety.

He reads one to me; raw and graphic in its violent imagery and explicit in its sexual detail, it nonetheless has a strong rhyme scheme and an assertive articulacy. It also conveys something of the chaos in his mind. He is eighteen years old, just, it is overwhelmingly bleak. It blocks the pathway to his future life, this endless preoccupation with the grim detail of his past life; unrelieved, joyless.

We talk about his anger; something he has asked for help with. He describes the incident that led to his recent court case. Another young man put his arm around Johnny's girlfriend. He tells me that he rescued this young woman from the streets and looked after her; he thought he had a relationship with her.

He had not noticed the activity between the two of them at first but it is when his "pal" punches Johnny's girlfriend that the interaction comes to his attention. He drags his rival out of the flat and beats him until his face is "like an exploded tomato." Johnny recites the nature of the charge against him using accurate legal terminology; he seems part proud part worried, I reflect, about what my reaction will be.

He tells me that as he struck the young man he knows he shouted something repeatedly and together we struggle to help him identify what it was he shouted as he continued to hit him even after he had rendered him unconscious.

"Why didn't you stop when he was unconscious?" I ask.

"I didn't notice . . ." It is a bald statement of fact. Then he utters the familiar refrain:

"He asked for it," and "any man who hits a woman should be able to hit a man."

Johnny speaks of a "mate" who tried to stop his violence and who had told him to "leave it be." He is clear that this simply angered him further and more deeply.

We think about what might have stopped him and Johnny tells me about his grandfather who could take him for a walk and show him a view. He would talk to him and calm him down. Now he has died there appears to be no one who can replicate that soothing.

Johnny grew up in a community steeped in violence and tells of the gang culture that shaped his world view. I learn that in parts of this city a young-ster would not dare stray beyond the few streets of their immediate environ-ment for fear of attack from a rival gang. He recounts an incident when he was six years old when he picked up a brick and hit another child with it. I note his explanation and that it involved his concern for his sister. Protection looms large in Johnny's descriptions of his violence.

"I don't start it," he insists, "but I'm not gonna just take it from any bastard."

The Harvard Center on the Developing Child has argued that the critical importance of the impact of adequate attunement upon child development needs to be integrated in policy decisions. In the United Kingdom we seem some distance from achieving that end. A preoccupation with audit friendly "evidence-based" practice, coinciding with a Western trend toward neoliber-alism seems significant in this, For as long as the major determinant of success is seen as an independent ambition (Layton 2009) there seems con-siderable ground to cover before such policies are actioned or even written and the consequences of poor attachment transmitted across several genera-tions need attention now.

It is well over half a century since John Bowlby's pioneering observations of the tragic circumstances of children orphaned following World War II and following on from this his increasing curiosity about children who, though they still had parents with them, behaved in ways that demonstrated similar levels of disturbed behaviors to those that he had observed in the orphaned ones. Such disturbance Bowlby came to describe as "attachment" difficulties.

Bowlby described a number of ways in which these attachment problems were manifested as "style" by the children he worked with. They ranged from withdrawal, detachment, and avoidance to preoccupation and "cling-ing." Most seriously of all Bowlby noted a style of attachment that was neither "avoidant" or "preoccupied" but a confused oscillation between dif-ferent states indicating an inconsistency in the way that the child responded to his or her caregiver. Mary Ainsworth, a student of Bowlby, devised a procedure known as "The Strange Situation" that would help researchers identify the quality of attachment shown by the children assessed. This pro-cedure involved children as young as one year old and was based on their behavior when their mother left them for a brief period and they were introduced to a stranger who would attempt to interact with and soothe them.

As one might predict the infant in this situation sometimes became very distressed and Ainsworth was particularly concerned with how quickly the child would be comforted and would settle at the point of "reunion" with his or her caregiver. She noticed that those children who had a "good enough" or *secure* attachment would quickly respond to the comfort of their caregiver. This she understood as indicating that for these children there was some internal process which enabled them to expect that their distress would be met with an appropriate response from them. A process arising from their expressed needs having been interpreted and appropriately met often enough for them to be confident that this could be relied upon to happen. Their protests following the abandonment of their mother were made in the expectation that these would bring about a response from her and that her swift response would remedy their distress.

In significant contrast to this, Ainsworth and her associates watched as other children were reunited with their caregiver who did not exhibit the same responses as those with *secure* attachment and the alternatives seemed to take a number of forms. She noted that although one group of children showed clear physiological and non-verbal signs of distress, on their caregiver's return they did not protest or seek the comfort of renewed closeness with them. Nor did these children show a preference for their mother over the stranger. They were considered to be *anxious/avoidant* in their attachment style.

Then there were the children whose behavior at reunion indicated that they had considerable difficulty in settling even after being reunited with their mother. Rather than being comforted they might struggle, continue crying, or show distress in a passive way. They were described as *anxious/resistant*. Though manifesting different behavior these insecurely attached children seemed to be just as unsure as the *avoidant* ones of the response that they might get from their mother and to be attempting to manage feelings themselves in another way.

A further category of response noted in a group of children was the most disturbing in that these children would demonstrate bizarre behaviors such as head-banging, hand clapping, or trying to escape from the situation even when their mother was present with them in the room. This group was categorized as *disorganized/disoriented*. Their bizarre and contradictory responses on reunion were thought to come about because they had experienced their caregiver as a source of reassurance but also of fear, and as a result had developed an ambivalent orientation toward them and equally confused motivations in regard to their attachment with them (Main & Hesse, 1990).

From these varying behaviors it was clear that children, even at this very young age had built up a set of expectations in this "strange" situation. For some it was that their protest would be met with an appropriately attuned and soothing response from their caregiver. For the less fortunate it seemed that they were required to somehow manage and minimize their own distress; this seeming to indicate that they did not have a body of experience that would allow them to expect the comfort that their physiological indicators suggested they needed. For the least fortunate, however, it seemed from their behaviors that there was neither the expectation that their distress would be adequately met nor that in the absence of this, their primitive attempts at self-management would bring better consequences for them. It was the erratic aspects of their patterns of response that gave greatest cause for concern; the clear disturbance revealed when these children were reunited with their caregiver.

Work by Alan Schore (2003) suggests explanations for the behavioral manifestations of these disordered patterns of attachment. He describes how these behaviors reveal the impact on the brain structure that infants concerned are likely to develop as a result of their subjection to poor attachments. It is not simply that learned behaviors of children with inadequate early attachments are likely to be detrimental in terms of their subsequent emotional and social development; it is more fundamentally that the hard wiring of their brains is being laid down in ways that are likely to involve them in difficult, dysfunctional interaction with the outside world. For some of these children the patterns of inter-relating that they are exposed to and the attributions that they make about themselves and others as a consequence put them at considerable risk of what may later be identified as personality disorder.

In Scotland the most recent Mental Health Act of 2003 ranked personality disorders alongside learning disabilities and mental illnesses as conditions that need attention. Change, however, happens slowly and attitudes toward individuals exhibiting signs of such disorders remain in place, very negative. In particular this applies to the emotionally unstable/borderline personality disorder that is most associated with disorganized attachment.

It could be argued that the indices of symptoms such those listed by the widely used *Diagnostic and Statistical Manual of Mental Disorders*, Fourth Edition (DSM-IV) have compounded difficulties by attempts to "medicalize" difficulties that might more properly and usefully be seen as having roots equally in societal problems, such as poverty, addiction, and mental illness in parents that may limit their capacity to provide the conditions children need in order that adequate attachments can be forged.

Sociologist Norbert Elias (1991) suggested that individuals were best viewed as "nodal points" within systems of relationships which act to "constrain" them. Adopting this framework requires us to consider the difficulties that an infant may have with his or her mother not merely as exclusively between them but within the larger context of familial relationships which in turn are set within communities, societies, cultures, countries, and so forth. This means that contrary to what might be seen as a prevailing neoliberal discourse (Layton, 2009), wherein individualism is celebrated and rewarded, it is instead vital that we all perceive our responsibility toward each new generation and that the legitimization of dismissive attitudes toward the most vulnerable members of our communities are rendered intolerable.

MIRANDA

I haven't seen Miranda for weeks, perhaps even months, but she greets me like an old friend. I realize that after almost five years I probably remain her only consistent worker. In response to my question about how she is, Miranda tells me that she has been with this project for three months after losing her last tenancy. I suspect that the temporary nature of this "emergency" accommodation reduces some of the anxiety she might otherwise feel about the likelihood of getting ejected from it.

As usual her intelligence and insight impress me and yet these characteristics are so fundamentally undermined by her vulnerability and the unrelenting sense of her own worthlessness. Miranda speaks of the reduction she has managed in smoking hash which at one level she knows is not good for her, yet at another it seems something impossible to dispense with. The discussion moves to a recent visit to her mother and brother; she had made a special effort and looked forward to the games she planned to play with her young brother. Barely had she arrived, she told me, than her mother's criticisms of her began and the visit she had so eagerly anticipated became more and more difficult until finally, feeling unable to defend herself she left, vowing never to return—until the next time.

I am aware of the endless cycles of attempted separation and eventual rapprochement between this girl and her mother. Aware too of all the efforts that have over the years, gone in to trying to bring them together in a room, efforts that Miranda's mother would always refuse. Her refusal would be that the difficulty was located in her daughter and had nothing to do with her. I am aware too of Miranda's mother's post-natal depression and the way that her child was moved constantly following her father's death. I see clearly that Miranda has been imbued with an ever present expectation that she will be rejected and abandoned because she is unlovable.

I point out to Miranda my observation that in each new accommodation she begins by behaving so impeccably that those who have heard reports of her problematic behavior can scarcely believe them. Quickly she is welcomed and subsequently held up as a model resident and assigned others to look after. Miranda is greatly amused to hear this and laughingly agrees. She agrees also when I say that I imagine that it might be difficult to maintain this and that the maintenance might generate some resentment. In essence this process reproduces her family situation. I am aware that though less extreme and polarized attitudes seem involved there are concerns about the welfare of Miranda's half-brother. It has been noted that her mother struggles at times to cope with her younger child too, though to a lesser degree. I have heard of the frequent expectation placed on Miranda that she must look after her brother whilst there appears to be no one willing to look after Miranda herself.

Miranda explains that she finds it impossible to say no to demands placed upon her but equally having agreed to things unwillingly she feels incapable of discharging the responsibility she has taken on.

"So who benefits from this process?" I ask her and she laughs ruefully.

"I don't think I can answer," she replies.

We wonder together about this, might it be possible to attempt the impossible and say "No!" and see what follows?

Severe attachment deprivation does not lead to children who simply make different choices in terms of their behavior; rather it causes depletion in the capacity of their frontal cortex and the regular involvement of more primitive rear brain functioning in determining behavior. This more primitive functioning is prompted by the habituated need developed in the individual for a more automatic response to the constant engendered stress they experience. This stress may be actual or simply perceived as their brain becomes so used to the need for a stress response such as fight, flight, or freeze that this happens instinctively when even a potential threat appears to present.

The ways that we are likely to meet with the patterns of interaction manifested by young people who were attachment disordered children have been usefully elaborated by Bateman and Fonagy using the concept of "mentalization" (2006). The authors acknowledge that this is a new word for an old idea. That old idea is one that describes an individual's capacity to recognize their mental states as arising out of their thoughts, feelings, ideas, and motivations and to do the same with regard to the mental state of others (Bateman & Fonagy, 2006, p. 1.)

Arising from attachment theory, Bateman and Fonagy describe the need for appropriate levels of attunement between mother and child. As with other psychodynamic theories they emphasize the importance of the caregiver's capacity to contain and modify the experiences of affect demonstrated by their infants. Critically however, they also draw attention to the necessity for the caregiver not only to be able to 'resonate' with the child's expression of emotion, but also to then 'mirror' this in what they describe as a 'marked' or exaggerated way.

It is this "markedness" of the caregiver's mimicking response that both signals to the child that her expression has been understood and also crucially distinguishes the reflection of the child's emotion from the caregiver's own. The combination of the playful exaggeration of the "marked" response with the contrary expression of a different emotion involved in the response to it, allows the child to witness not only that his or her emotion has been understood but also that the caregiver can contain it. This capacity for containment further distinguishes the mother's emotional state from that of her child. This enables the child to reabsorb a "metabolized" version of their original emotion and then over time to begin to name it, having learned from their caregiver's accurate identification.

Bateman and Fonagy warn that when marked mirroring does not occur there are very detrimental effects on the child's developing personality. This is because if, for example, a child is exposed to a reaction to their emotion that is either frightening or frightened, not only does this provide no comfort for them but also, when it is "reabsorbed," is so at odds with what they have attempted to express that it is experienced as "alien." An accumulation of such alien experiences over time, rather than reassuring the child that her emotions can be borne, understood, and transformed into something manageable and legitimate, instead impact on the child's capacity to express any feelings at all.

Over time when marked mirroring works well, a child acquires the positive experience of their capacity to effect something in their environment, which Bateman and Fonagy describe as a sense of their own agency or "agentive self." In contrast, poorly attached children may come to associate their attempts at achieving the desperately needed proximity with their caregiver and securing attunement with them as generating instead an extremely aversive response from them.

Additionally, when this process goes well the child's model of the world is of a generally benign and supportive place in which his or her needs will be understood and attended to on a "good enough" basis and this will allow him or her to develop a corresponding model of self as worthy of attention. They will carry this expectation with them into the interactions that they encounter as they venture out into the wider world. The internal world that the child needs to undertake these excursions will feel supported by a confidence built in the safe space created with the caregiver that they can retreat to for comfort and support when they encounter difficulties.

When they are successful these "mirroring" interactions by the mother or other caregiver are likely to be constituted in the familiar repetitious "singsong" pattern that some writers have described as "motherese." Optimally alongside the responsive, containing interactions involving marked mirroring the caregiver will also be playing with her child generating processes that synchronize the child's brain waves with her own and thereby contribute further to the stimulation of the child's brain development. Fonagy advises that "The parent of the secure child engages in behaviors such as pretend play, which almost obliges the child to contemplate the existence of mental states" (Fonagy, 2001, p. 67). As the child develops and moves outside the home in the education process too, there is the opportunity for further growth, if playfulness could come to be seen as an essential component of learning rather than a distraction from it.

From an attachment perspective, when marked mirroring fails an *avoidant* child will attempt to avoid considering the mental states of their caregiver and the *resistant* child will be too taken up with his/her own distressed mental state to be involved with another. The *disorganized* child is likely to be hypervigilant in relation to the caregiver's behavior and state of mind but unable to gauge the impact of this on their own mental state which continues to be "disregulated and incoherent" (Fonagy, 2001).

John Bowlby described the way that the pattern and quality of a child's interactions with caregivers come to form a template for their future social interactions based on the model that they form of both themselves and others. Stern (1985) argues that the child's internal working model comes about as a child begins to abstract the features that it encounters repeatedly with a particular person across a range of different social situations. Alan Sroufe (1990) has also suggested that the earliest patterns of interactions with caregivers translate into styles of regulating emotion which in turn determine patterns of interaction they take with them to future encounters in the outside world. The circular self-reinforcing nature of this process for good or ill is what forms the basis of his view of how the world is and the role that he or she has within it along with the extent that it is possible for them to be the agent of any possible change.

For children with poor attachments it is evident that this process does not happen successfully or sufficiently. The interactions that they have instead engender levels of stress that have been described as "toxic" by the Harvard Center on the Developing Child and it is these toxic levels of stress that are then seen to affect brain development by contributing to the evolving structure of the brain in the way that was described earlier.

In working with the troubled young people who are likely to have experienced the most seriously detrimental attachments, those who might have met the criteria for the *disorganized/disoriented* category, I have observed a number of features. Among the most notable of these is the extent to which the young person, despite their chronological age, frequently appears to operate in ways that would be associated with a much younger child. Examples of this would be in their holding of a strong sense of frustrated entitlement and their making of constant and sometimes impossible demands upon caregivers. They frequently have temper tantrums in which they become so lost that they are unable to hold onto any control of their subsequent behavior.

Their greater chronological age however, sees them resorting to dramatic even life-threatening enactments of emotion in order to secure attention and demonstrate desperation.

It is also frequently evident that despite what can be relatively sophisticated insights into their difficulties on occasion, these young people largely experience themselves as incapable of alternative resolutions to their profound despair. It is as if the insight into the causes and consequences of their behaviors are detached from any possible strategies other than the dysfunctional ones they have accumulated to deal with the repeated situations in which they find themselves

JOHNNY

The team tells me that Johnny has been remanded in custody following the latest aggressive incident in which he became embroiled. I have already heard from another project where he was temporarily accommodated, that Johnny on this occasion was drawn into the violence rather than instigating it, but his reputation has gone ahead of him with the police and his participation has been taken seriously.

Johnny's imprisonment has created a breathing space for the team who discuss their experiences of working with him. Frustration is high on their collective list of responses.

"You can have a really good support with him, "Anna tells me "You can really feel that he has opened up and talked about very difficult things from his childhood. . . . You think that you've made an important connection."

The other workers laugh with a mixture of sympathy and irony.

"Yeah," Duncan agrees, "but then half an hour later he is back again banging on the door . . ."

". . . and wanting to go through it all again with someone else," Brian finishes for him.

The pull to join the young person in a repeating dynamic is very strong and has been usefully described by Ryle and Kerr (2003) as a model of "reciprocal roles." In more traditional psychoanalytic theory it might be conceptualized as "projective identification." Projective identification is a process in which one individual projects onto another an aspect of their own psyche which cannot be tolerated and subsequently 'identifies' that projection in the other. As the projected process is one that cannot be tolerated by the projector, their response to the apparent manifestation of it in any other with whom they are dealing, is likely to provoke a powerfully negative reaction.

When we meet with a young person we enter into a dynamic that combines not only the acquired patterns of interaction they have developed but our own patterns too. There will be times when these combinations are relatively straightforward and fruitful and others where they may be more strained and difficult. However, it will always be useful to have a model both for understanding what may be occurring and for maximizing the potential for a successful outcome. For if we can manage not to be drawn into repetitious dynamics and instead can find a way to reflect in the moment about these difficult encounters with young people, there is more hopefulness that we might participate in new patterns of interaction which hopefully, over time, might support them.

Bateman and Fonagy recognize these features and they are incorporated within their discussions about Mentalization. Whilst acknowledging that for everyone the capacity to mentalize will fluctuate, Bateman and Fonagy (2006) have identified three mental states that they consider to "predate" the development of the capacity to mentalize; these are teleological mode, psychic equivalence mode, and pretend mode. In the general population a propensity to regress to one of these states will inevitably be the case under conditions of acute stress. However, for some, seriously inadequate attachments and the prevailing and "toxic" stress that these attachments engender is likely to have left them with a more general and pervasive likelihood of inhabiting one of these states that is characteristic of emotionally unstable or borderline personality disorder.

In *teleological* mode (Bateman & Fonagy, 2006) an individual will require some physical, tangible evidence of concern from those with whom they interact in order to have any confidence that they are genuinely concerned. In the young people we work with that may take the form of repeated attempts to get money from services or letters to support them in gaining accommodation. This mode too may account for self-harming behaviors such as cutting, where only the sight of blood can either confirm to the individual that they are alive or that they are "hurting." In an interaction with an individual operating from within this mode we might experience an urgent pressure to 'do something' on their behalf. It is likely to inspire in us too a considerable anxiety.

Psychic Equivalence mode (Bateman & Fonagy, 2006) may be discernible when an individual is unable to distinguish between their inner world and the outside world. This means that they will be very fixed and concrete in their perceptions and unable to consider any perspective other than their own. Any challenge by another to this inner world from the outside is likely to be experienced as overwhelmingly threatening or simply denied. In interaction with them we may feel frustrated, bewildered, and also increasingly angry as our own viewpoint is completely denied.

Individuals in *pretend* mode (Bateman & Fonagy, 2006) may talk incessantly about their situation and their feelings but will do so in a way that fails to be connected with their emotions, resulting in a kind of fruitless rumination. Any interaction involving someone in this mode is likely to generate in us a similar sense of disconnection, perhaps most usually experienced as boredom or sleepiness.

These modes are not discrete and interactions with those with emotionally unstable personality disorder are likely to involve constant movement between them. One of the main features of working with young people troubled in this way is the capacity to attempt to identify these modes within our interactions and correspondingly the level of emotion associated with them. This can be helpful in judging whether the emotional state is flat and in need of an enlivening response or whether it is 'high' and may need a calming reduction. Alongside this assessment goes a constant emphasis on curiosity about the minds involved in the process rather than the content of any interaction. This means both the mind of the young person and the mind of the therapist with the latter working hard to keep as much transparency as possible in their own process so that those they work with may find their assumptions challenged and this can more accurately align their perceptions of the therapist's demeanor with their own mental state.

In the United Kingdom, an individual must be at least eighteen years old before a personality disorder "diagnosis" is made. Given that the teenage years are turbulent ones for most young people it is seen as important not to make such a diagnosis precipitously since the behaviors frequently associated with this disorder may be manifested by many young people who overcome them as they successfully negotiate the processes of individuation and separation that delineate their maturity. However, this delay means that it may be problematic to legitimize intervention in the chaotic lives of those young people who are highly unlikely to "grow out" of their difficulties. In my experience the disturbance within the presentation of the latter category of young person is significantly different in intensity and pervasiveness from that of the average rebellious teenager. When challenging behaviors are seen in the context of a history of problematic attachment I believe it is possible and necessary to differentiate between the two. I believe that the potential benefits of early intervention are likely to outweigh those of premature identification when the cost of the lack of intervention is so high.

Diagnostic reluctance is exacerbated by the paucity of treatment for borderline personality disorder within the medicalized models that dominate approaches to mental health in the United Kingdom. This sees young people with this difficulty, essentially arising from attachment difficulties set within the context of social conditions, presenting medical services with a dilemma as the evidence for the effectiveness of either medication or hospital admission is minimal. This creates significant tensions when, as happens for many of the young people with whom I work, they act in ways explicitly aimed at achieving a hospital admission or even custodial sentences because these forms of incarceration at least create for them temporarily some small sense of the security they so desperately crave.

Sadly, in hospitals in particular, a vicious circle of interaction frequently occurs where the sense of overwhelming frustration and helplessness in the face of inexplicable and sometimes extremely challenging and aggressive behavior from young people can lead to a strong desire to eject them. This process of expulsion then replicates the feelings of abandonment and rejection that are such a powerful source of distress for the person with borderline personality disorder.

A full mentalization approach involves a tight, structured program even at outpatient treatment level, with concurrent individual and group therapies (Bateman & Fonagy, 2006). In the United Kingdom there are as yet few centers offering this degree of consistent input and fewer still where this is focused on young people. If the current economic climate prevails it may become increasingly difficult to develop programs like this which require intensive and therefore apparently expensive input. Given a current focus on brief manualized interventions that are perceived to save money, longer term approaches that involve spending more to save money later seem increasingly excluded.

Our service offers to those young people who wish to participate, a mentalization informed approach to our attempts to engage with them. Essential components of this are support and empathy and constant curiosity. We aim to demonstrate our curiosity in particular about the way that their mind works and how their thoughts, feelings, beliefs, and motivations underpin their behaviors. For it may be for most of these young people that their behaviors remain the only way that they can convey to the outside world something of the determinants of their inside world. This can be slow work that cannot and should not be rushed. I reflect on how long it can take to build up even the most tenuous trust with young people like Miranda, who in despair told me recently that she had been abused physically, emotionally, and sexually and she concluded, "I'm tired with fighting and trying to keep going."

In attempting to form a therapeutic alliance we have noticed that even one positive figure featuring in a child's past history can make a considerable difference to their ability and willingness to enter into a therapeutic relationship with us. Grandparents, neighbors, or family friends figure significantly in this respect. Occasionally too, a young person will recall a particular teacher who took an interest in them; listened to them, or perhaps even noticed their distress. In some cases a sympathetic teacher would be the person that a child turned to in order to make a disclosure the first time and to ask for help.

I believe that there are a number of ways in which a difference might be made. A teacher who has the capacity to retain an open mind about a troubled young person and to attempt to continue to think with them even when under pressure may be helpful to them. It is especially important not to retaliate when tested by their actions. If that teacher has the capacity not to experience behaviors as personal attacks even though they may have been designed by the child to feel very personal, this may also be significant. A young person will benefit if, however personal the behaviors feel, the person interacting with them is able to see them as very limited and primitive ways of expressing feelings that cannot be recognized and certainly not put into words. Additionally, it is vital that a teacher can hold on to their capacity to maintain and model curiosity with the child when an interaction becomes difficult and challenging and to attempt to explore with them why this may be happening. If, in the moment the child is overwhelmed by feelings, the teacher might revisit what happened at a later date, when the child becomes calm once more.

Perhaps most significantly of all is the need for the teacher to notice the behaviors of the children and young people that they work with and to have a good awareness of the appropriate sources of referral and intervention when one of them presents with behavior that symbolizes acute distress.

By the time my team meets them, in one city in one small country in the international community, considerable damage has taken place to the attachment systems of many of our young people and consequently to the way that their minds are structured and can process interactions. The more that time passes, the greater the loss in brain capacity and elasticity. As a former teacher and present psychotherapist, my experience tells me that when carried out effectively, these roles share characteristics. Among these, empathy, curiosity, and a desire to facilitate growth and learning are paramount. My lost young people, despite their intelligence and their lively minds, have almost invariably found themselves outside of the education process and I wonder sometimes how much, if any, effort went into attempting to secure them a place within it.

REFERENCES

Ainsworth, M. D. S., Blehar, M. C., Waters, E., & Wall, S. (1978). *Patterns of attachment: A psychological study of the strange situation.* Hillsdale, NJ: Erlbaum.

Bateman, A., & Fonagy, P. (2005). *Psychotherapy for borderline personality disorder mentalization-based treatment.* Oxford: Oxford University Press.

Bateman, A., & Fonagy, P. (2006). *Mentalization-based treatment for borderline personality disorder: A practical guide.* Oxford: Oxford University Press.

Bowlby, J. (1980a). *Attachment and loss, Vol. 3: Sadness and depression.* London: Hogarth Press and the Institute of Psycho-Analysis Center on the Developing Child: Harvard University.

Elias, N. (1991). *The society of individuals.* Oxford: Blackwell.

Elias, N. (1978). *What is sociology?* New York: Columbia University Press.

Fonagy, P. (2001). *Attachment theory and psychoanalysis.* New York: Other Press.

Ishiguro, K. (2006). *Never let me go.* London. Faber and Faber.

Layton, L. (2009). "Who's responsible?" Our mutual implication in each other's suffering. *Psychoanalytic Dialogues, 19*, 105–20.

Main, M., & Hesse, E. (1990). Parents' unresolved traumatic experiences are related to infant disorganised attachment status: Is frightened and/or frightening parental behaviour the linking mechanism? In M. Greenberg, D. Cicchetti, and E. M. Cummings (Eds.), *Attachment in the Pre School Years: Theory, Research and Intervention* (pp. 161–82). Chicago: University of Chicago Press.

Ryle, A., & Kerr, I. B. (2003). *Introducing cognitive analytic therapy.* Chichester, UK: John Wiley & Sons.

Schore, A. N. (2003). *Affect dysregulation and disorders of the self.* New York: W. W. Norton.

Sroufe, L. A. (1990). An organizational perspective on the self. In D. Cicchetti and M. Beegly, (Eds.), *The Self in Transition : Infancy to Childhood* (pp. 281–507). Chicago: University of Chicago Press.

Stern. D. N. (1985). *The interpersonal world of the infant: A view from psychoanalysis and developmental psychology.* New York: Basic Books.

Chapter Ten

Bullying and Social Exclusion

Links to Severe Psychological Distress

Marilyn Charles

There is much data that shows a link between trauma, social exclusion, and psychosis, thereby emphasizing the importance of building and reinforcing social links for vulnerable individuals (Charles, 2009). We are also seeing some of the dire consequences of peer victimization in our schools. Perhaps less well understood, however, are the ways in which bullying and peer victimization have been linked to severe psychopathology, most particularly to psychotic spectrum disorders (Schreier et al., 2009). Data from developmental studies and attachment research shows not only the importance of early relationships in building resilience in young people, but also that *early deficits can be moderated* with sufficient attention to the quality of later relationships (Mayes, Fonagy, & Target, 2007; Schwandt et al., 2010). This information is crucial to educators, who are in a unique position to help vulnerable young people to find resources if they are sufficiently aware of risk factors and potential resources. In this chapter, I will try to highlight those vulnerabilities and resources in ways that might be of use to educators.

1. David presents in his early thirties with a stimulant-induced psychotic disorder. He hopes that avoiding stimulants will keep him from undergoing the terrible waking nightmares he has suffered, in which he feels as though he is being hunted by predators intent on destroying him. Increasingly, however, as these episodes continue to occur without any further stimulant use, he is faced with the possibility that he will be struggling with a psychotic disorder in an ongoing way. Predominant in this young man's history is severe bullying in childhood, which resulted in his retreat from the social world to the extent that it

has been difficult for him to develop meaningful relationships or even to maintain employment, in spite of his strong intellectual gifts.

2. Leah presents in her mid-twenties, hoping for assistance in getting back on track with her life. Her career aspirations have been waylaid by the psychotic disorder that occurred in the context of overuse of prescribed stimulants. The voices she hears persist in the absence of drug abuse, even when she takes the antipsychotic medications that also dull her mind and numb her feelings. Leah describes recurring difficulties in childhood with bullying and social exclusion that left her increasingly isolated and alienated from her peers. The various means she adopted for coping, such as severe anorexia, left her increasingly depleted and unable to cope with the cognitive demands of independent living.

3. James presents with symptoms of paranoia, which he attempts to relieve through the compulsive rituals that are invited by his obsessive cognitive style. Although his increasing cannabis use seemed to exacerbate his symptoms, he recurrently turned to the drug as a way of managing his sense of isolation and despair. James tells a story of feeling excluded and demeaned as the 'little brother' who can never seem to catch up, and feels excluded from the tantalizing social world of his older brother. He feels at the fringes, and his life has become a nightmare from which he cannot escape. He is desperate and terrified.

4. Joan experienced a psychotic break in her mid-teens in the context of feeling increasingly alienated from a world in which her religion depicted her as alien and an outcast. The lack of kindness she experienced from others became her most difficult obstacle to recovery.

In the stories of many individuals who struggle with psychosis,[1] there is a history of severe bullying and/or social exclusion in childhood. This anecdotal evidence does not tell us much about cause and effect. We cannot say, in retrospect, to what extent the child became alienated or excluded because of bullying or to what extent the exclusion was in relation to psychotic symptoms or liabilities already in evidence. We do know, however, that psychotic symptoms mark strain that is not being sufficiently attended to. Such strain is often apparent in the classroom, where academic and social pressures may exacerbate other vulnerability factors. In this way, the attentive teacher may be an important resource for the vulnerable child, particularly as teachers' attitudes and behavior are important factors in determining the extent to which bullying will manifest in the classroom (Olweus, 1994).

Although psychosis is often seen as evidence of a degenerative disease process already in place, epidemiological studies provide evidence that psychosis is best viewed as a continuum such that initial psychotic symptoms can be seen as a risk factor for later disorder rather than as a sign of disease per se (Johns & van Os, 2001). This evidence encourages a view of symptoms as warning signals and highlights the importance of early recognition and intervention at the first sign of psychotic symptoms. Early intervention may be crucially important in children during the critical years of emotional and social development, particularly given studies showing that psychotic symptoms may affect interpersonal relationships in negative ways, thereby increasing the likelihood of peer rejection and hostility (Campbell & Morrison, 2007).

Early intervention approaches have shown that swift and intensive attention to the first break of psychosis can result in a marked decrease in the incidence of chronic illness (Seikkula et al., 2006). Notably, early intervention that focuses on strengthening the social bonds and helping the individual and his or her support system to better understand and work with difficulties that are arising have been extremely effective in reducing chronicity. These facts suggest that educators may play a crucial role in recognizing disturbance when it first appears and helping the child to maintain his or her place in the social structure of the classroom while other resources are brought to bear.

Research shows the importance of such social bonds and also affirms the strong link between bullying and social exclusion in childhood and severe psychological distress in later life. Although educators have been aware of this link, it has been difficult to ameliorate the problem. In this chapter, I will first discuss ways in which early childhood experiences affects resilience. I will then discuss the evidence that links bullying and social exclusion to later psychopathology, with a particular emphasis on the link to psychosis. I will then describe possible mechanisms implicated that may help educators better understand this link. Finally, I will note intervention methods that have been created to try to address the problem of bullying within the school setting.

RESILIENCE AND AFFECT REGULATION

Many people experience psychotic symptoms that do not persist or exacerbate over time (Hanssen et al., 2005). One crucial factor distinguishing such psychotic experiences from more chronic, persistent disorder is the extent to which the person is upset by the experience. The sensitive child who is anxious and submissive is more likely to be bullied than his or her more aggressive counterparts. Boys are more likely to be the victims of direct aggression, whereas for girls, the bullying is often more subtle and indirect, taking the form of rumor and social exclusion (Olweus, 1994; Schwartz, Dodge, & Cole, 1993).

Such children are at heightened risk for later problems because distress that is not sufficiently moderated or ameliorated leads to greater reactivity to stress, a mechanism that is conceptually consistent with "behavioral sensitization" (van Winkel, Stefanis, & Myin-Germeys, 2008). This heightened sensitivity, in turn, is linked to a greater vulnerability to severe psychopathology, including psychosis (Myin-Germeys & van Os, 2007). These findings highlight the importance of the availability of empathic others who might recognize signs of excessive strain in children and help to moderate the distress and allay anxiety. For some children, an empathic teacher can be an important moderating factor, helping to provide support and resources through which the vulnerable child might build greater resilience and adaptive capacity.

Perhaps the most crucial factor in individual resilience is the capacity to manage and regulate affect. The literature on early attachment processes between parent and child shows the ways in which stress is initially ameliorated and moderated through the interventions of caretakers. Attuned and attentive parents first meet the child's distress, providing an experienced sense of recognition and understanding. From that point of meeting, the parent is then in a better position to moderate the child's distress through soothing tone, gesture, or touch. Over time, this soothing is actively practiced by the child and then becomes internalized through the implicit memory structures by which we learn to perform essential functions without necessarily recognizing consciously what we are doing or why. We can watch this internalization process at work as in, for example, the young child who soothes a doll, peer, or parent in much the same manner as he or she has been soothed.

We know that some children are more difficult to soothe than others, and we also know that trauma can interfere with the development of self-regulatory capacities. Repetti, Taylor, and Seeman (2002) note the protective factors associated with relatively healthy early environments, through which children learn that they can rely on others to provide for their safety and well-being. Parents who are attentive to the needs and feelings of the child provide opportunities for learning while also providing appropriate boundaries that keep the child safe from external danger and excessive internal dysregulation. In this way, the parent provides safety while also providing opportunities through which the child can acquire the emotional maturity and critical social experiences to be able to manage effectively in the social world. Appropriate protectiveness helps build resilience. The parent who allows the child to explore and learn from his own experience builds frustration tolerance as long as the child is not allowed to suffer excessively.

Overprotectiveness and inattention each leaves the child more vulnerable to experiences of overwhelming affect, which is itself experienced as traumatic by the child (Krystal, 1985). Threat alters both cognition and physiology, at the extreme interfering with the development of the neural structures that underlie plasticity and resilience (Perry et al., 1995). Once sensitized, a particular pattern is more likely to occur. As a result, what would appear to be relatively minor stressors can elicit major responses such as hyperarousal and dissociation. Sex differences have been found in these patterns, with dissociation more likely in females and hyperarousal more likely in males.

The effects of excessive strain are particularly insidious in the developing brain. Whereas trauma may alter the mature brain, during the critical periods of early childhood, it can actually organize the brain systems, profoundly affecting all later development and function (Perry et al., 1995). Such reorganization of the neural systems results in traits/behavior styles that are persistent and relatively resistant to change. The same types of biological abnormalities found in relation to childhood trauma have also been found in individuals diagnosed with schizophrenia, suggesting that childhood trauma may be implicated in the diathesis of psychotic disorders (Read et al., 2001). These factors make early intervention critically important, to decrease the likelihood that the child will develop a persistent pattern of hyperarousal or dissociation and thereby, perhaps, decrease the risk of later severe psychopathology.

The educator should be aware of familial factors that may mark heightened risk for students in her classroom. Both trauma and neglect are associated with negative outcomes in childhood. Repetti, Taylor, and Seeman (2002) warn of the heightened risk associated with family environments in which conflict and aggression are prevalent and relationships are cold and unsupportive. Together, these characteristics disrupt the development of affective regulatory processes and social competence so crucial to adaptive psychosocial functioning, increasing risk for later psychological and physiological disturbance and distress. Even when parents have good intentions, parenting styles characterized by a lack of warmth, support, and engagement can prove deleterious to the developing child. Longitudinal data shows the strong correlation between maladaptive parental behaviors and later distress and disorder. Disregulating parental behaviors include not only harsh treatment and inconsistency but also neglect, in terms of time and the quality of attention offered to the child (Johnson et al., 2001).

The literature linking depressed parents with negative outcomes in children shows the deleterious impact of failures in responsiveness on the developing child (Schmid et al., 2011). Not only does the responsive parent allow opportunities for growth while moderating distress, but this responsiveness also communicates more directly something about one's value as a human being. We learn that we matter, that our needs and feelings are important, through the many ways in which we register in the parent's mind and eyes. The glimmer of delight in the parent's eye registers for us our absolute value in the social world. Without such recognition, it is difficult to build the type of healthy self-regard so crucial to the development of effective coping skills and social competence.

Children's needs for positive mirroring are less likely to be filled by a depressed parent, which makes parental depression a particular risk factor not only for later distress but also for bullying, in particular. The child who does not feel valued at home communicates this lack of valuing in many nonverbal ways. Such a child can be an easy target for bullies, who tend to single out children who are anxious, insecure, cautious, sensitive, and quiet (Olweus, 1994). Further complicating these issues, the depressed parent is also less likely to mirror positive and adaptive coping strategies for the developing child.

Findings show that children of depressed mothers also experience greater exposure to stressful events, in part because of greater interpersonal conflict (Adrian & Hammen, 1993). Whereas effective actions build a sense of mastery and confidence in one's ability to manage the inevitable challenges that life brings, difficulties in coping can lead to feelings of inefficacy and hopelessness, a cycle that can become self-perpetuating. Notably, research shows that situations that are uncontrollable and also involve social-evaluative judgments are the most stressful and most difficult to recover from (Dickerson & Kemeny, 2004). Experiences of social exclusion and marginalization, in particular, lead to social humiliation and shame, a virulent and self-perpetuating emotion (Birchwood et al., 2000).

Bullying is particularly insidious because it leads to the types of negative assumptions about oneself and one's interpersonal world that make traumatic experiences more likely to enhance the vulnerability to shame (Platt & Freyd, 2011). Research has found that shame and loneliness are the most problematic sequelae reported by adults who had been victims of bullying in childhood (Carlisle & Rofes, 2007). Unlike guilt, shame does not easily lend itself to repair but rather breaks the interpersonal bond, inviting withdrawal and avoidance of the very interpersonal engagement that might prove reparative. Shame is a particularly toxic affective experience in part because it designates the person as inferior and alienated from the larger social surround. Vulnerability to shame has been linked not only to interpersonal difficulties but also to the types of cognitive and affective difficulties associated with psychopathology more generally (Tangney, Wagner, & Gramzow, 1992).

Because of its inhibiting effects, shame not only impedes social interactions, it also makes it more difficult for the individual to take the types of risks required for new learning and the mastery of important developmental tasks. Experiences of mastery invite further exploration, helping to build not only positive self-regard but also metacognitive capacities. Metacognition involves the ability to reflect on one's own thoughts and feelings in relation to the thoughts and feelings of others. Under the overarching rubric of metacognitive capacities, Lysaker and his colleagues include mastery, defined in terms of the ability to make use of one's knowledge about others' mental states in pragmatic ways to cope adaptively with life's challenges (Lysaker et al., 2010). Psychosis, and schizophrenia in particular, has been linked to deficits in metacognitive capacities (Lysaker et al., 2011), deficits that, in turn, have been linked to difficulties with executive function, such as mental flexibility and inhibition (Lysaker et al., 2008). In turn, these deficits in metacognitive capacities are linked to difficulties in coping (Lysaker et al., 2011). Gumley (2011) suggests that unsuccessful coping is the key mediator between trauma and impaired metacognition. He notes that whereas avoidant coping styles can serve as a protection against painful thoughts, memories, and experiences, a high price is exacted in terms of decrements in affect regulation and cognitive capacities.

For the educator, bullying poses particular difficulties not only in terms of group dynamics in the classroom, but also in terms of the danger it can cause to the child at risk. Attempts to prevent bullying and to address it quickly and effectively when it first appears may be important interventions in reducing psychological distress in vulnerable children and also reducing the risk of developing a severe mental disorder in later years. These interventions also provide opportunities for respected adults to make a strong statement to the children in their care regarding what it means to be a good citizen and how to recognize and respectfully manage differences between individuals. For children who are being bullied, the classroom, schoolyard, and cafeteria may be areas of high stress in which psychotic symptoms or their precursors begin to manifest. These symptoms may present as agitation or heightened anxiety, a somewhat vacant inattention, unusual verbalizations or speech patterns, or in terms of an apparent absorption that seems odd in that particular context, as can occur when a person is having hallucinatory experiences. Social isolation or exclusion should also be seen as significant warning signs. Whereas at the extreme, bullying increases the risk for developing psychotic disorders, educators should also be aware that bullying increases the likelihood of later depressive and anxiety disorders and suicidality not only for victims, but also for the bullies, themselves. This heightened risk continues during the school years (Klome et al., 2007; Pranjić & Bajraktarević, 2010), and also into adulthood (Meltzer et al., 2011).

BULLYING, SOCIAL EXCLUSION, AND PSYCHOPATHOLOGY

Although psychosis—and schizophrenia, in particular—is often thought of as a genetic disorder, increasing evidence points to the link between early trauma and the later incidence of psychotic disorders (Read et al., 2005). Bullying has been linked with a higher incidence of psychotic-like experiences, which in turn is linked with higher risk for psychotic illness in later life (Kelleher & Cannon, 2011). Characterized by repeated aggressive actions in which there is a marked power imbalance (Olweus, 1994), bullying positions the child as alien to and isolated from his peers and the social environment, and also designates him as inferior to those peers.

Animal studies show the profound devastation that occurs when a member is excluded from the group (Schwandt et al., 2010; Stevens et al., 2009). We are social beings and our well-being depends on our ability to find a valued place in the social structure. The pursuit of such a position, and the sense of mastery that its attainment provides, are crucial developmental challenges for the child in the grade school years. Bullying signals the failure to accomplish these goals, leading to a sense of shame and alienation from oneself and also to a sense of paranoia and alienation from others.

The child who cannot trust in his own resources nor rely on effective assistance from others fails to develop the basic trust that Erikson (1950) recognized as fundamental to the acquisition of later social milestones. Such failure results in the type of anxiety that Freeman and Fowler (2009) suggest may account for the link between trauma and persecutory thinking. Isolation decreases opportunities for moderating or attenuating paranoid ideas as they arise and also increases the sense of "feeling like an alien" that many psychotic people describe (Charles, 2012). Shyness is a risk factor implicated in the higher risk for schizophrenia in individuals who have been bullied in childhood (Parker and Asher, 1987). More generally, children who are socially anxious and socially isolated are more likely to develop schizophrenia as adults than children without these risk factors (Jones et al., 1994).

More specifically, findings link maltreatment, bullying, and other trauma *characterized by the intention to cause harm*, to children's emerging psychotic symptoms (Arsenault et al., 2011). These studies underscore the findings of Perry and his colleagues (1995) regarding the effects of trauma on the child's developing neural structures. In this way, the experience of trauma creates psychological vulnerabilities that can result in the development of psychotic symptoms (Bentall et al., 2001; Garety et al., 2001; Spauwen et al., 2006). The intention to cause harm is particularly insidious because it marks the recipient of those behaviors as not only vulnerable but also as not worthy of the care or consideration of others. This unworthiness then becomes internalized, leading to low self-esteem, internalized shame, and a sense of being not only alienated but also essentially alien (see Charles, 2012).

COGNITIVE BIASES

One hallmark of psychotic disorders is difficulties with cognition. Seven domains of cognitive difficulties have been linked with schizophrenia, in particular: attention/vigilance, working memory, verbal learning and memory, visual learning and memory, processing speed, reasoning and problem solving, and social cognition (Featherstone, Kapur, & Fletcher, 2007). These difficulties have also been linked with amphetamine and cannabis abuse (Featherstone et al., 2007; Solowij, & Michie, 2007). Further complicating this picture is evidence that early trauma is also implicated in the etiology of such difficulties.

Research findings suggest that exposure to early trauma, such as bullying, may increase the risk of later psychosis in part because of biases in cognition that lead to a perception of a lack of control and a tendency to make hasty decisions, a response style that further exacerbates the paranoid thinking that can accompany social isolation (Corcoran et al., 2008; Ehlers & Clark, 2000). These cognitive biases can be linked to the sequelae of severe trauma, experiences that can lead the individual to be fearful regarding interactions with others. Links have been found between post-traumatic stress disorder (PTSD) and psychosis, in terms of a self-blaming attributional style (Morrison, Frame, & Larkin (2003). The persistence of PTSD has been linked with cognitive processing that maintains a sense of current serious threat through overly negative appraisals of traumatic events, along with an autobiographical memory style characterized by relatively poor elaboration and strong perceptual priming (Ehlers & Clark, 2000). This type of style lends itself to the relative strengthening of affectively driven primary process material without the type of contextualization afforded by the more rational constraints of secondary process elaboration. The attentive educator can help the vulnerable child to think through an event, re-introducing some of the contextual factors that may help the child to better make sense of difficult experiences and perhaps find ways of more effectively managing them. Such attention to detail helps to break into the affective intensity that drives the paranoid overlay, and invites the child to recognize and make better use of his or her cognitive capacities.

Once again, it is difficult to ascertain cause and effect from retrospective studies. Some prospective studies show an increased vulnerability to later psychotic disorder in children who had experienced at least one delusional or hallucinatory experience by age eleven (Poulton et al., 2000). There seem to be both specific and nonspecific vulnerabilities in individuals who eventually suffer from psychotic disorders that are not present in those who do not. For example, deficits in "theory of mind" have been linked to peer rejection in childhood (Caputi et al., 2012). Theory of mind refers to the ability to recognize that mental states exist, and to predict and explain social behavior in relation to those mental states. There are suggestions that there may be a theory of mind deficit in individuals who are vulnerable to psychotic disorders that makes it difficult for them to effectively manage difficulties that arise in social interactions. Reciprocally, social understanding is constructed within the context of ongoing social interactions, and is facilitated when the emotions attendant to these interactions are positive (Hughes & Leekam, 2004).

In a review of the relevant literature, Garety and Freeman (1999) found evidence of deficits in the ability to understand the mental states of others in individuals with symptoms of schizophrenia, particularly in those with so-called 'negative' symptoms, such as constrictions in thought, affect, speech, and actions. These findings are consistent with the findings of Lysaker and his colleagues (2010) regarding the centrality of theory of mind deficits in schizophrenia. Notably, Lysaker, Buck, and colleagues (2011) have found that these deficits can be relieved with the type of active modeling that can occur in psychotherapy. This type of active modeling can also occur in the classroom and schoolyard. Lysaker's findings underscore the importance of ongoing contact with engaged, thoughtful, and reflective individuals for those who have difficulties with social interactions.

Along with the constrictions described previously, there are also the 'positive' symptoms associated with schizophrenia, which include distortions of thought, perception, language, and communication. Negative self-appraisals have been linked to positive psychotic symptoms such as hallucinations (Kilcommons & Morrison, 2005). In light of genetic research that highlights differences in etiology and course between specific types of psychotic symptoms and diagnoses, linking specific symptoms with specific cognitive biases and deficits may be important if we are to understand the particular difficulties of a given individual (Garety et al., 2007). For educators, the ability to link particular types of symptoms with their etiological, cognitive, and relational correlates may be beneficial in more effectively assisting the young people in their classrooms as challenges arise.

Bentall and Fernyhough (2008), for example, link hallucinations and delusions with particular cognitive styles. Hallucinations are linked with source-monitoring biases, whereas delusions are linked with the more depressive tendency to jump to conclusions regarding the likelihood of negative interpersonal interactions. With persecutory delusions, specifically, there is a tendency to personalize fault when things go wrong, to attribute blame to a person rather than to a situation (Garety & Freeman, 1999). This tendency is exacerbated with highly emotional or self-referential material. Knowledge of these links may be instructive for the educator, in thinking about how to approach a child who is having these types of difficulties. Whereas the child who hallucinates may need help in grounding their perceptions, the child who jumps to conclusions may need assistance in slowing down and tracking an interaction in the context of a supportive teacher/child relationship.

Research investigating the ways in which trauma increases the risk for later psychotic experiences showed that individuals who had been exposed to early trauma were more likely to experience severe distress in relation to psychotic experiences. They also reported less perceived control over those experiences (Bak et al., 2005). These findings may be due, in part, to the types of physiological changes noted by Perry and his colleagues (1995) in relation to early trauma and abuse that heighten subsequent vulnerability to stress. For example, specific changes have been noted by Anda and his colleagues (2006) that link early trauma and abuse to memory difficulties and to deficits in brain structures important to mood regulation.

Although the brain is resilient, trauma does have enduring effects that are then complicated by the ways in which the trauma is managed. While environmental adversity increases the risk for developing severe psychological problems, including psychosis, those risk factors are moderated by how we think about them (Bentall & Fernyhough, 2008). Recognizing that cognitive biases and deficits may play an important factor determining the extent to which adverse circumstances lead to harm should guide our interventions with children who are facing such difficulties. Attention to the type of cognitive difficulty at play can increase the effectiveness of our interventions.

ADDITIONAL RISK FACTORS

Further complicating this picture, there are indications that individuals at high risk for developing psychotic disorders may be more susceptible to the problematic effects of some illicit drugs, such as cannabis and stimulants, and therefore are at increased risk of developing a persistent psychotic disorder if they indulge in such drug usage. Because each risk factor can increase the likelihood of the occurrence of other risk factors, early intervention at multiple levels is important. For example, the types of cognitive difficulties noted in the previous section have been found to be risk factors associated with both psychotic disorders and illicit substance use (Malone, Hill, & Rubino, 2010; Solowij & Michie, 2007).

These types of cognitive difficulties lead to ineffective coping, often resulting in avoidant defenses such as social withdrawal and substance abuse. In considering the diverse sequelae of bullying behavior on victims, Arsenault, Bowes, and Shakoor (2010) highlight the importance of considering the wide range of difficulties that are experienced by young people who are bullied, including social, emotional, cognitive, and behavioral problems. Such a multifaceted approach to understanding these difficulties is particularly important in light of evidence that dysregulation itself—whether from physiological or social assaults—increases the likelihood of developing severe problems such as psychosis (Stilo & Murray, 2010).

Childhood trauma has been linked to both substance misuse and to increased risk of psychosis. Both cannabis and stimulant use, in particular, have been implicated in the etiology of psychotic disorders (Mathias, Lubman, & Hides, 2008). Although cause and effect are difficult to discriminate, recent findings suggest that cannabis use interacts with childhood trauma to increase the risk of the occurrence of psychotic symptoms in adolescence

(Harley et al., 2010). This risk is heightened by early usage, frequency of use, and higher potency of the drug (Semple, McIntosh, & Lawrie, 2005). Although some substance-induced psychosis relieves over time, there are also cases in which the psychosis persists and becomes a more chronic disorder. The line between schizophrenia and substance-induced psychosis is not clear (Mathias, Lubman, & Hides, 2008), rather the evidence points to alterations in the brain *and* associated cognitive deficits that are found in schizophrenia and also in acute amphetamine exposure, in particular (Featherstone, Kapur, & Fletcher, 2007; Wang et al., 2010).

Although it is difficult to entirely separate cause from effect, it should be noted that the potential toxic effects of bullying are wide-reaching, with implication for both the victim and the bully. Longitudinal evidence shows a link between bullying in elementary school and later impulsivity, substance use, and violence and criminal behavior (the latter linked particularly to the bully) in early adolescence (Tharp-Taylor, Haviland, & D'Amico, 2009) and in young adulthood (Kim et al., 2011). Notably, bullies are more likely to become involved in illicit drug use than those who have been their victims (Niemelä et al., 2011), but some empirical studies do show a significant relationship between victimization in childhood and subsequent illicit drug use (Luk, Wang, & Simons-Morton, 2010).

INTERVENTIONS

It is important for educators to have in mind a multi-layered approach toward intervention, so that bullying can be addressed at the system level while the particular difficulties of vulnerable children are also addressed. Although some studies have found that bullying intervention programs have a greater impact on attitudes and perceptions than on actual behaviors (Merrell et al., 2008), a systematic review of school-based programs showed that these programs are often effective, decreasing bullying on average by 20 to 23 percent, and decreasing victimization on average by 17 to 20 percent (Ttofi & Farrington, 2011). There is also evidence that persistence pays off. For example, in Oslo, repeated interventions over five years showed yearly decreases in bullying behaviors (Olweus & Limber, 2010). School intervention programs tend to be most successful when intervention occurs in elementary grades, but evidence from programs in Norway and the United States show that reductions in bullying also occur when interventions take place in middle and high school grades (Olweus & Limber, 2010).

School-based intervention programs have been most effective when they are intensive and multimodal and include a strict no-tolerance policy (O'Malley, 2009). Systematic monitoring of intervention programs has also been linked with greater effectiveness (Smith et al., 2004). Effective programs offer individual attention to children's needs and feelings (Elledge et al., 2010), parental involvement (Ttofi & Farrington, 2011), and supervision and monitoring of children's behavior (Farrington, 1993). Important, too, are proactive efforts aimed at preventing future bullying behavior, such as attempts to improve social skills, empathic capacity, and relationships between children (Farrington, 1993).

Teachers are in an important position to protect victimized students while also making efforts to reduce the power of those who bully (Craig & Pepler, 2003). They are also well situated to recognize the particular difficulties a child may manifest in the classroom, so that interventions can address the difficulties associated with those particular symptoms (Rudnick, 2001). The larger dilemma, however, is the issue of social exclusion and isolation. Given that many of the deficits associated with psychosis are cognitive and social, it may be particularly important for schools to provide systems whereby adults can endorse a more prosocial way of dealing with difference, and students can learn to become competent participants in such a model.

In Canada, for example, bullying is seen as such an important social problem that a government supported network (PREVNet: Promoting Relationships and Eliminating Violence) has been created to address the problem at the levels of understanding, developing assessment and intervention tools and strategies, advocacy, and policy (Craig & Pepler, 2007). From this perspective, bullying is seen as a destructive relationship problem in which one child is able to aggressively wield power over another child over time. If this pattern is not disrupted, the bully becomes increasingly powerful while the victim's stress and powerlessness increases. Notably, PREVNet takes the stance that interventions for bullying problems must have in mind bullying as a relational problem, and need to focus on systemic change that takes into account the social dynamics involved in the bullying process. Given that bullying is exacerbated because peers are afraid to step in and perhaps become the targets of bullying themselves, victims of bullying become increasingly isolated. This enforced isolation deprives the child of the normal social interactions so crucial to healthy development. Because bullying emerges in a relational context, it needs to be addressed through interventions that actively promote positive relationships and that take the position that eliminating relational violence is a shared responsibility.

Not only are victims hurt by the victim/bullying cycle, the bully suffers as well, in terms of impaired social relationships and a heightened risk of later problem behaviors including substance abuse and criminal convictions (Olweus, 1994). In addition, peers find themselves drawn into secondary roles. Whether they become active participants or onlookers who tacitly promote the aggression, such participation leads to an increased acceptance of bullying and victimization as acceptable behaviors (Craig, Pepler, & Atlas, 2000; Smith, Cousins, & Stewart, 2005). Olweus's intervention program not only succeeded in reducing the current levels of victim/bullying problems, but also in reducing subsequent rates of bullying and also of antisocial behavior more generally.

Olweus's program was based on an attempt to restructure the social environment to make it more positive, while also setting in place firm limits regarding acceptable and unacceptable behaviors. Particularly important was a stance of warm and positive interest and engagement on the part of the adults. Rules against bullying and classroom meetings, along with better supervision in unstructured times were instituted as preventive measures. Consistent nonaggressive and nonphysical sanctions such as serious conversations with offenders and their parents were applied in instances of violations of the rules. Including parents is particularly important because of the tendency for the transmission of bullying behaviors from one generation to the next (Farrington, 1993).

In spite of evidence that bullying has a high cost in terms of individual well-being and social distress, anti-bullying efforts have tended to be ineffective to the extent that too little attention is paid to the importance of intervening at multiple levels. Olweus and Limber (2010) suggest that crucial to a successful intervention strategy are the following: "(a) adequate *knowledge* about the phenomenon, its short- and long-term consequences, and effective prevention and intervention practices; (b) sufficient *motivation* to implement comprehensive school-based efforts; and (c) the *resources* to do so" (p. 132; italics in original). For any school-based intervention to succeed, it is important for teachers to have a strong sense of what is at stake, both for the individual children in their care and also for the social structures in which those children are embedded. To fail to take up this issue in earnest is to become a complicit bystander in the devastation that accompanies this type of peer abuse. Although systemic attention to the need for such programs often occurs in the wake of tragedy (O'Moore, 2000), there is now sufficient evidence of the ongoing need for systematic interventions that target bullying at all grade levels in our schools to alert us to the need to be more consistently proactive in fighting bullying in our schools and in dealing with the sequelae of bullying when it does occur.

CONCLUSION

Returning now to the young people mentioned at the beginning of this chapter, we are perhaps in a better position to consider their dilemmas. Each of these young people was, at least to some extent, "driven mad" by bullying and/or social exclusion. Each was clearly psychotic at various points. None is currently suffering from psychotic symptoms. From a psychoanalytic perspective, psychosis emerges because the person cannot emerge as a separate, autonomous being with his or her own articulated desires (Charles, 2012; Vanheule, 2011). Bullying de-subjectifies the emerging person, objectifying and humiliating them. If one cannot emerge as a respected subject within the social surround, one's identity is foreclosed.

In each of the cases mentioned, the young person developed a pseudo-identity that was based on the desire to be good enough to be included. From the debased position, the antidote was to be so special that one could no longer be vulnerable to such ridicule and humiliation. Given the social difficulties encountered, however, the resources at hand were limited and so they were invented. In Leah's case, for example, her beloved deceased grandmother became the person who offered advice and consolation. For Joan, a new religion offered rescue from the religion that had condemned her. David eschewed people entirely, turning to films to provide companionship, while he spun elaborate grandiose fantasies and, at times, hid away from the ways in which those fantasies turned on and haunted him. James became obsessed with compulsive rituals through which he hoped to make himself safe from a danger that had already intruded, massively impeding his ability to use his mind constructively or effectively. All of these young people were fortunate in having families who were able to continue to provide resources through which each was able, over time, to come to grips with the pain and humiliation they had experienced such that they were able to begin to rebuild their lives.

The hallucination or delusion is a pseudo solution to an impossible problem. It also is a way of marking the problem eluding solution. Although psychosis is often seen as a sign of aberrant brain function—and may, as we have seen, mark such difficulties—it can also be seen as an attempt at solution. Pivotal in such cases, are empathic individuals who can recognize that there is a problem that the young person is trying to solve, and who can view those problems within their developmental context. Anna Freud (1965) was famous for saying that the psychoanalyst's job is to try to help get a child back on track developmentally. For all of us who work with children, this should be the primary goal: to recognize the developmental failures and attempt to address them. For the child who is being excluded, exclusion is a major problem, whatever else may be going on. The teacher, as the primary authority in the classroom, is in a privileged position to model for the students a way of encountering difference and difficulty that is empathic and that recognizes that we are, indeed, more alike than otherwise, and that the well-being of one depends on the well-being of all.

If we see psychosis as a way of communicating with oneself in the absence of relationships in which one can be recognized and understood, then we can perhaps recognize the importance of getting to know the child who stands outside and apart for whatever reason, and who has trouble finding his or her way into the social structure of the classroom. Childhood is a time of identity development, and identity is created within a social structure, through which one learns who one is in relation to others. Interest in difference—rather than fear or disparagement—and inclusiveness are values that can and should be taught in our schools and in our homes. Educators are in a pivotal position to take such stands and, when they take such stands together, the effects are more pervasive. In such a context, individuals can learn to recognize their strengths and vulnerabilities sufficiently to make better use of their own unique capacities.

NOTE

1. I am defining psychosis in terms of a loss of contact with reality, which usually includes difficulties distinguishing between internal and external experience.

REFERENCES

Adrian, C., & Hammen, C. (1993). Stress exposure and stress generation in children of depressed mothers. *Journal of Consulting and Clinical Psychology, 61*, 354–59.
Anda, R. F., Felitti, V. J., Bremner, D., Walker, J. D., Whitfield, C., Perry, B. D., Dube, S. R., & Giles, W. H. (2006). The enduring effects of abuse and related adverse experiences in childhood: A convergence of evidence from neurobiology and epidemiology. *European Archives of Psychiatry and Clinical Neuroscience, 256*, 174–86.
Arseneault, L., Bowes, L., & Shakoor, S. (2010). Bullying victimization in youths and mental health problems: "Much ado about nothing"? *Psychological Medicine, 40*, 717–29.
Arseneault, L., Cannon, M., Fisher, H. L., Polanczyk, G., Moffitt, T. E., & Caspi, A. (2011). Childhood trauma and children's emerging psychotic symptoms: A genetically sensitive longitudinal cohort study. *American Journal of Psychiatry, 168*, 65–72.
Bak, M., Krabbendam, L., Janssen, I., de Graaf, R., Vollebergh, W., & van Os, J. (2005). Early trauma may increase the risk for psychotic experiences by impacting on emotional response and perception of control. *Acta Psychiatrica Scandinavica, 112*, 360–66.
Bentall, R. P., Corcoran, R., Howard, R., Blackwood, N., & Kinderman, P. (2001). Persecutory delusions: A review and theoretical integration. *Clinical Psychology Review, 21*, 1143–92.
Bentall, R. P., & Fernyhough, C. (2008). Social predictors of psychotic experiences: Specificity and psychological mechanisms. *Schizophrenia Bulletin, 34*, 1012–20.
Birchwood, M., Meaden, A., Trower, P., Gilbert, P., & Plaistow, J. (2000). The power and omnipotence of voices: Subordination and entrapment by voices and significant others. *Psychological Medicine, 30*, 337–44.
Campbell, M. L. C., & Morrison, A. P. (2007). The relationship between bullying, psychotic-like experiences and appraisals in 14- to 16-year-olds behavior. *Research and Therapy, 45*, 1579–91.
Caputi, M., Lecce, S., Pagnin, A., & Banerjee, R. (2012). Longitudinal effects of theory of mind on later peer relations: The role of prosocial behavior. *Developmental Psychology, 48*, 257–70.
Carlisle, N., & Rofes, E. (2007). School bullying: Do adult survivors perceive long-term effects? *Traumatology, 13*, 16–26.
Charles, M. (2009). Psychosis and the social link: Fighting chronicity through human connections. *Bulletin of the Michigan Psychoanalytic Council, 5*, 33–44.
Charles, M. (2012). *Working with trauma: Lessons from Bion and Lacan.* New York: Jason Aronson.

Corcoran, R., Rowse, G., Moore, R., Blackwood, N., Kinderman, P., Howard, R., Cummins, S., & Bentall, R. P. (2008). A transdiagnostic investigation of "theory of mind" and "jumping to conclusions" in patients with persecutory delusions. *Psychological Medicine, 38,* 1577–83.

Craig, W. M., & Pepler, D. J. (2003). Identifying and targeting risk for involvement in bullying and victimization. *Canadian Journal of Psychology, 48,* 577–82.

Craig, W. M., & Pepler, D. J. (2007). Understanding bullying: From research to practice. *Canadian Psychology, 48,* 86–93.

Craig, W. M., Pepler, D. J., & Atlas, R. (2000). Observations of bullying in the playground and in the classroom. *School Psychology International, 21,* 22–36.

Dickerson, S. S., & Kemeny, M. E. (2004). Acute stressors and cortisol responses: A theoretical integration and synthesis of laboratory research. *Psychological Bulletin, 130,* 355–91.

Ehlers, A., & Clark, D. M. (2000). A cognitive model of posttraumatic stress disorder. *Research and Therapy, 38,* 319–45.

Elledge, L. C., Cavell, T. A., Ogle, N. T., & Newgent, R. A. (2010). School-based mentoring as selective prevention for bullied children: A preliminary test. *Journal of Primary Prevention, 31,* 171–87.

Erikson, E. H. (1950). *Childhood and society.* New York: Norton.

Farrington, D. P. (1993). Understanding and preventing bullying. *Crime and Justice, 17,* 381–458.

Featherstone, R. E., Kapur, S., & Fletcher, P. J. (2007). The amphetamine-induced sensitized state as a model of schizophrenia. *Progress in Neuro-Psychopharmacology & Biological Psychiatry, 31,* 1556–71.

Freeman, D., & Fowler, D. (2009). Routes to psychotic symptoms: Trauma, anxiety and psychosis-like experiences. *Psychiatry Research, 169,* 107–12.

Freud, A. (1965). *Normality and pathology in childhood: Assessments of development.* New York: International Universities Press.

Garety, P. A., Bebbington, P., Fowler, D., Freeman, D., & Kuipers, E. (2007). Implications for neurobiological research of cognitive models of psychosis: A theoretical paper. *Psychological Medicine, 37,* 1377–91.

Garety, P. A., & Freeman, D. (1999). Cognitive approaches to delusions: A critical review of theories and evidence. *British Journal of Clinical Psychology, 38,* 113–54.

Garety, P. A., Kuipers, E., Fowler, D., Freeman, D., & Bebbington, P. E. (2001). A cognitive model of the positive symptoms of psychosis. *Psychological Medicine, 31,* 189–95.

Gumley, A. (2011). Metacognition, affect regulation and symptom expression: A transdiagnostic perspective. *Psychiatry Research, 190,* 72–78.

Hanssen, M., Bak, M., Bijl, R., Vollebergh, W., & van Os, J. (2005). The incidence and outcome of subclinical psychotic experiences in the general population. *British Journal of Clinical Psychology, 44,* 81–191.

Harley, M., Kelisher, I., Clarke, M., Lynch, F., Arsenault, L., Connor, D., Fitzpatrick, C., & Cannon, M. (2010). Cannabis use and childhood trauma interact additively to increase the risk of psychotic symptoms in adolescence. *Psychological Medicine, 40,* 1627–34.

Hughes, C., & Leekam, S. (2004). What are the links between theory of mind and social relations? Review, reflections and new directions for studies of typical and atypical developments. *Social Development, 13,* 590–619.

Johns, L. C., & van Os, J. (2001). The continuity of psychotic experiences in the general population. *Clinical Psychology Review, 21,* 1125–41.

Johnson, J. G., Cohen, P., Kasen, S., Smailes, E., & Brook, J. S. (2001). Association of maladaptive parental behavior with psychiatric disorder among parents and their offspring. *Archives of General Psychiatry, 58,* 453–60.

Jones, P., Rodgers, B., Murray, R., & Marmot, M. (1994). Child developmental risk factors for adult schizophrenia in the British 1946 birth cohort. *Lancet, 344,* 1398–1402.

Kelleher, I., & Cannon, M. (2011). Psychotic-like experiences in the general population: characterizing a high-risk group for psychosis. *Psychological Medicine, 41,* 1–6.

Kilcommons, A. M., & Morrison, A. P. (2005). Relationships between trauma and psychosis: An exploration of cognitive and dissociative factors. *Acta Psychiatrica Scandinavica, 112,* 351–59.

Kim, M. J., Catalano, R. F., Haggerty, K. P., & Abbott, R. D. (2011). Bullying at elementary
    school and problem behavior in young adulthood: A study in bullying, violence, and sub-
    stance use from age 11 to 21. *Criminal Behavior and Mental Health, 21*, 136–44.

Klomek, A. B., Marrocco, F., Kleinman, M., Schonfeld, I. S., & Gould, M. S. (2007). Bullying,
    depression, and suicidality in adolescents. *Journal of the American Academy of Child and
    Adolescent Psychiatry, 46*, 40–49.

Krystal, H. (1985). *Integration and self-healing: Affect, trauma, alexythymia.* Hillsdale, NJ:
    Analytic Press.

Luk, J. W., Wang, J., & Simons-Morton, B. G. (2010). Bullying, victimization and substance
    use among U.S. adolescents: Mediation by depression. *Prevention Science, 11*, 355–59.

Lysaker, P. H., Buck, K. D., Carcione, A., Procacci, M., Salvatore, G., Nicolò, G., & Dimag-
    gio, G. (2011). Addressing metacognitive capacity for self reflection in the psychotherapy
    for schizophrenia: A conceptual model of the key tasks and processes. *Psychology and
    Psychotherapy: Theory, Research and Practice, 84*, 58–69.

Lysaker, P. H., Erickson, M., Buck, K. D., Procacci, M., Nicolò, G., & Dimaggio, G. (2010).
    Metacognition in schizophrenia spectrum disorders: Methods of assessment and associations
    with neurocognition and function. *European Journal of Psychiatry, 24*, 220–26.

Lysaker, P. H., Erickson, M., Ringer, J., Buck, K. D., Semerari, A., Carcione, A., & Dimaggio,
    G. (2011). Metacognition in schizophrenia: The relationship of mastery to coping, insight,
    self-esteem, social anxiety, and various facets of neurocognition. *British Journal of Clinical
    Psychology, 50*, 412–24.

Lysaker, P. H., Olesek, K. L., Warman, D. M., Martin, J. M., Salzman, A. K., Nicolò, G.,
    Salvatore, G., & Dimaggio, G. (2011). Metacognition in schizophrenia: Correlates and
    stability of deficits in theory of mind and self-reflectivity. *Psychiatry Research, 190*, 18–22.

Lysaker, P. H., Warman, D. M., Dimaggio, G., Procacci, M., LaRocco, V. A., Clark, L. K.,
    Dike, C. A., & Nicolò, G. (2008). Metacognition in schizophrenia: Associations with multi-
    ple assessments of executive function. *Journal of Nervous and Mental Disease, 196*,
    384–89.

Malone, D. T., Hill, M. N., & Rubino, T. (2010). Adolescent cannabis use and psychosis:
    Epidemiology and neurodevelopmental models. *British Journal of Pharmacology, 160*,
    511–22.

Mathias, S., Lubman, D. I., & Hides, L. (2008). Substance-induced psychosis: A diagnostic
    conundrum. *Journal of Clinical Psychiatry, 69*, 358–67.

Mayes, L., Fonagy, P., & Target, M. (2007). *Developmental science and psychoanalysis:
    Integration and innovation. Developments in psychoanalysis.* London: Karnac.

Meltzer, H., Vostanis, P., Ford, T., Bebbington, P., & Dennis, M. S. (2011). Victims of bullying
    in childhood and suicide attempts in adulthood. *European Psychiatry, 26*, 498–503.

Merrell, K. W., Gueldner, B. A., Ross, S. W., & Isava, D. M. (2008). How effective are school
    bullying intervention programs? A meta-analysis of intervention research. *School Psycholo-
    gy Quarterly, 23*, 26–42.

Morrison, A. P., Frame, L., & Larkin, W. (2003). Relationships between trauma and psychosis:
    A review and integration. *British Journal of Clinical Psychology, 42*, 331–53.

Myin-Germeys, I., & van Os, J. (2007). Stress-reactivity in psychosis: Evidence for an affective
    pathway to psychosis. *Clinical Psychology Review, 27*, 409–24.

Niemelä. S., Brunstein-Klomek, A., Sillanmäki, L., Helenius, H., Piha, J., Kumpulainen, K.,
    Moilanen, I., Tamminen, T., Almqvist, F., & Sourander, A. (2011). Childhood bullying
    behaviors at age eight and substance use at age 18 among males: A nationwide prospective
    study. *Addictive Behaviors, 36*, 256–60.

Olweus, D. (1994). Annotation: Bullying at school: Basic facts and effects of a school based
    intervention program. *Journal of Child Psychology and Psychiatry, 35*, 1171–90.

Olweus, D., & Limber, S. P. (2010). Bullying in school: Evaluation and dissemination of the
    Olweus Bullying Prevention Program. *American Journal of Orthopsychiatry, 80*, 124–34.

O'Malley, M. D. (2009). Prevailing intervention to address peer victimization at school: A
    study of California school psychologists. *California School Psychologist, 14*, 47–57.

O'Moore, M. (2000). Critical issues for teacher training to counter bullying and victimization
    in Ireland. *Aggressive Behavior, 26*, 99–111.

Parker, J. O., & Asher, S. R. (1987). Peer relations and later personal adjustment: Are low-accepted children at risk? *Psychological Bulletin, 102,* 357–89.

Perry, B. D., Pollard, R. A., Blakley, T. L., Baker, W. L., & Vigilante, D. (1995). Childhood trauma, the neurobiology of adaptation, and "use-dependent" development of the brain: How "states" become "traits." *Infant Mental Health Journal, 16,* 271–91.

Platt, M., & Freyd, J. (2011). Trauma and negative underlying assumptions in feelings of shame: An exploratory study. *Psychological trauma: Theory, research, practice, and policy,* Advance online publication. Doi: 10.1037/a0024253.

Poulton, R., Caspi, A., Moffit, T. E., Cannon, M., Murray, R., & Harrington, H. (2000). Children's self-reported psychotic symptoms and adult schizophreniform disorder: A 15-year longitudinal study. *Archives of General Psychiatry, 57,* 1053–58.

Pranjić, N., & Bajraktarević, A. (2010). Depression and suicide ideation among secondary school adolescents involved in school bullying. *Primary Health Care Research and Development, 11,* 349–62.

Read, J., Perry, B. D., Moskowitz, A., & Connolly, J. (2001). The contribution of early traumatic events to schizophrenia in some patients: A traumagenic neurodevelopmental model. *Psychiatry, 64,* 319–45.

Read, J., van Os, J., Morrison, A. P., & Ross, C. A. (2005). Childhood trauma, psychosis and schizophrenia: A literature review with theoretical and clinical implications. *Acta Psychiatrica Scandinavica, 112,* 330–50.

Repetti, R. L., Taylor, S. E., & Seeman, T. E. (2002). Risky families, family social environments and the mental and physical health of offspring. *Psychological Bulletin, 128,* 330–66.

Rudnick, A. (2001). The impact of coping on the relation between symptoms and quality of life in schizophrenia. *Psychiatry, 64,* 304–8.

Schmid, B., Blomeyer, D., Buchmann, A. F., Trautmann-Villalba, P., Zimmerman, U. S., Schmidt, M. H., Esser, G., Banaschewski, T., & Laucht, M. (2011). Quality of early mother-child interaction associated with depressive psychopathology in the offspring: A prospective study from infancy to adulthood. *Journal of Psychiatric Research, 45,* 1387–94.

Schreier, A. et al. (2009). Prospective study of peer victimization in childhood and psychotic symptoms in a nonclinical population at age 12 years. *Archives of General Psychiatry, 66,* 527–36.

Schwandt, M. L., Lindell, S. G., Sjöberg, R. L., Chisholm, K. L., Higley, J. D., Suomi, S. J., Heilig, M., & Barr, C. S. (2010). Gene-environment interactions and response to social intrusion in male and female rhesus macaques. *Biological Psychiatry, 67,* 323–30.

Schwartz, D., Dodge, K. A., & Cole, J. D. (1993). The emergence of chronic peer victimization in boys' play groups. *Child Development, 64,* 1755–72.

Seikkula, J., Aaltonen, J., Alakare, B., Haarakangas, K., & Keränen, J. (2006). Five-year experience of first-episode nonaffective psychosis in open-dialogue approach: Treatment principles, follow-up outcomes, and two case studies. *Psychotherapy Research, 16,* 214–28.

Semple, D. M., McIntosh, A. M., & Lawrie, S. M. (2005). Cannabis as a risk factor for psychosis: A systematic review. *Journal of Psychopharmacology, 19,* 187–94.

Smith, J. D., Cousins, J. B., & Stewart, R. (2005). Antibullying interventions in schools: Ingredients of effective programs. *Canadian Journal of Education, 28,* 739–62.

Smith, J. D., Schneider, B. H., Smith, P. K., & Ananiadou, K. (2004). The effectiveness of whole-school antibullying programs: A synthesis of evaluation research. *School Psychology Review, 33,* 47–560.

Solowij, N. & Michie, P. T. (2007). Cannabis and cognitive dysfunction: Parallels with endophenotypes of schizophrenia? *Journal of Psychiatry and Neuroscience, 32,* 30–52.

Spauwen, J., Krabbendam, L., Lieb, R., Wittchen, H,-U., & van Os, J. (2006). Impact of psychological trauma on the development of psychotic symptoms: Relationship with psychosis. *British Journal of Psychiatry, 188,* 527–33.

Stevens, H. E., Leckman, J. F., Coplan, J. D., & Suomi, S. J. (2009). Risk and resilience: Early manipulation of macaque social experience and persistent behavioral and neurophysiological outcomes. *Journal of the American Academy of Child and Adolescent Psychiatry, 48,* 114–27.

Stilo, S. A., & Murray, R. M. (2010). The epidemiology of schizophrenia: Replacing dogma with knowledge. *Dialogues in Clinical Neuroscience, 12*, 305–15.

Tangney, J. P., Wagner, P., & Gramzow, R. (1992). Proneness to shame, proneness to guilt, and psychopathology. *Journal of Abnormal Psychology, 101*, 460–78.

Tharp-Taylor, S., Haviland, A., & D'Amico, E. J. (2009). Victimization from mental and physical bullying and substance use in early adolescence. *Addictive Behavior, 34*, 561–67.

Ttofi, M. M., & Farrington, D. P. (2011). Effectiveness of school-based programs to reduce bullying: A systematic and meta-analytic review. *Journal of Experimental Criminology, 7*, 27–56.

Vanheule, S. (2011). *The subject of psychosis: A Lacanian perspective.* London: Palgrave.

Van Winkel, R., Stefanis, N. C., & Myin-Germeys, I. (2008). Psychosocial stress and psychosis: A review of the neurobiological mechanisms and the evidence for gene-stress interaction. *Schizophrenia Bulletin, 34*, 1095–1105.

Wang, M., Pei, L., Fletcher, P. J., Kapur, S., Seeman, P., & Liu, F. (2010). Schizophrenia, amphetamine-induced sensitized state and acute amphetamine exposure all show a common alteration: Increased dopamine D2 receptor dimerization. *Molecular Brain 3*, 25. http://www.molecularbrain.com/content/3/1/25.

Chapter Eleven

Shame on You, Child

*On Shaming, Educational Psychology, and
Teacher Education*

John Samuel Tieman

in front of the class
she hides her face in her hands
the teacher asks her
if she's ashamed—she chokes
I am I am I yes am
jst

EVERYONE HAS A STORY

There is much talk these days about data-based research. I have for several years studied shaming in the classroom. My studies evince a simple bit of data. Of the hundreds of folks to whom I have spoken, everyone has experienced shaming in the classroom. Everyone. I find no exceptions. It follows that, as every student has experienced shaming, so too have virtually all teachers, and all administrators, used shaming. And everyone has a story.

Forty-six years after the event, an old pal remembers vividly how, after he was caught talking in his ninth grade English class, he was made to stand in the back of the classroom. There he wrote nursery rhymes every day for a week.

Another friend tells how he admitted cheating on a test. He was made to sit and do nothing, while the rest of the class was forced to retake the test.

I have probably had a dozen people tell me of having had their work read to their class as an example of, frankly, stupidity.

227

As students are shamed, so do we teachers and administrators shame them. I recall a student being shamed at length over a school's public address system. An acquaintance, who just got his principal's certification, tells me how he was lectured on the "strategic uses of shaming," something he reports he now feels prepared to do. On a more personal note, I must acknowledge my use, a tactic really, of shaming and humiliation in my classroom. It used to be one of my most common disciplinary tools.

A seventh grader cursed me. "Child, are you out of your mind? There's something wrong with the way you were raised. Stand up. Face the wall, now! You wait right there. We'll call your mother during lunch." I felt uneasy doing this. But there was nothing in my background, certainly nothing in my teacher education, that prepared me to question myself. "Why am I shaming this student? What did this pupil bring out in me? Why this vocabulary—'face the wall,' 'out of your mind,' 'child,' 'the way you were raised,' 'mother'?" Most confusing was the fact that this pupil submitted today, only to act out tomorrow.

This is a chapter by a teacher, and for other teachers and administrators. My hope for this chapter is that it will inform administrators and teachers about shaming in the context of child, adolescent, and adult development. Note that I say child, adolescent, *and adult* development, because I address the child's development as well as that of the teacher and administrator. Shaming is done in the context of a dyad, the student and the adult, a two-person interchange.

Administrators and teachers tend to think of shaming a student as a problem solving tool. Some, who do see it as a problem, might rationalize it as a difficulty in their professional development. But when teachers and principals use shame, they are tapping into their personality formation, a template that is formed long before their professional formation. In other words, the act of shaming comes within the context of relationship. The child acts in a way that the educator deems punishable by humiliation, but, in making the choice to humiliate, the educator looks to his or her own experience with humiliation. From a psychodynamic viewpoint, to borrow the famous metaphor of Selma Fraiberg, there is a ghost in the schoolroom. As we were humiliated, so do we humiliate.

For most teachers and administrators, the only psychology to which they are exposed is exclusively cognitive/behavioral. This exposure is usually fairly limited, often no more than a course or two. As a product of such education, I would argue that this cognitive/behavioral approach tends, in application, to be even narrower than, say, the theories of Skinner (1976). We educators tend to think of educational psychology as utilitarian, instrumental, a tool, the means to elicit submissive behavior. The student does this, then you do that. Problem solved. Thus it is that, on the apparent level, students are humiliated because, for the moment, it seems to work. The student is shamed; the student submits. For the moment.

This chapter first explores transference, countertransference, personality development, and the origins of shaming. Secondly, I discuss a few of the predictable results of shaming. Lastly, I suggest reforms in teacher education that can lead to a healthier environment in the school.

I refer throughout this chapter specifically to shaming. But there is a specific goal, and a larger hope. The specific goal is that teachers and administrators stop shaming their students. Simple as that. But the larger hope is a vision, a vision that we educators will come to see ourselves and our charges in a context, a context in which we envision a web of relationships that are dynamic. Not a static set of behaviors, but a network of fluid relationships. This vision implies an approach to the profession in general, and teacher education in particular, that frankly challenges our current practices.

Put simply, there is also much more in my chapter than a simple call to stop shaming. There is also the way someone stops. That is the challenge.

TRANSFERENCE, COUNTERTRANSFERENCE, DEVELOPMENT, AND THE GENESIS OF SHAMING

My purpose here is to offer administrators and teachers a theoretical framework for understanding the psychodynamics of shame. The literature about shaming, especially in psychoanalytic publications, is extensive. My review is selective. My desire is to give an overview that is concentrated, condensed, and helpful rather than comprehensive. I refer at length in this discussion to Sigmund Freud and Erik Erikson, largely because student teachers are often given, in their training, a passing acquaintance with these psychoanalysts.

The cognitive/behavioral models most familiar to educators tend to view the student as an isolated set of behaviors. There is nothing inherently wrong with charting behavior. But the psychodynamic model, the model employed here, views the teacher/student dyad as dynamic. It is a matter of emphasis. When I discipline, I do not ask, "How do I stop that child from cursing me?" I ask, "What is going on *between us*, such that this child chooses this communication?" To borrow from Martin Buber (1960), I am not concerned with the behavior of the It. I am concerned with the we-*ness* of the I-Thou. The psychodynamic view is of two minds interacting. Hence, I refer throughout to the development of the educator as well as the student.

Before speaking directly about Freud, Erikson, and the developmental process, it is well to pause for two considerations. First, I will speak of discipline, then I will consider transference and countertransference.

Recently, a political and educational theorist, Dr. William Galston (2010) of the Brookings Institute, asked me in an e-mail, "But what does one do—

what do *you* do—when customary methods of discipline fail?" This chapter does not address methods of bringing order to a classroom, which is, I believe, what most people mean by discipline. Discipline, as I see it, it not simply about methods for bringing order. One must, of course, have order in a classroom. But I can walk into a class of strangers, and bring order. And I have. Discipline is about relationship. Indeed, discipline is a relationship.

Much of my classroom experience, the first twenty-plus years of it, was in private schools. A decade or so ago, I accepted the generous offer of an urban public school district. I first taught in a neighborhood middle school. The student population was 100 percent African American. This middle school suffered all the sorrows of being poor and black in America—gangs, drugs, violence, mental illness, parentless children, poverty, homelessness, and so forth. A sixth grader had a miscarriage in the hallway. Today, I teach in an urban high school, a magnet school, a far better environment. A third of my high school students are immigrants. Many of my immigrants are war refugees, who bring another set of problems. Almost all of the rest are African American. My point is that, in these schools, the teacher needs to realize that discipline is a relationship. Students need direction and guidance. The class needs order. A teacher needs to be forceful, even domineering, while still maintaining with the student a dialogue that is open and compassionate, tender and loving.

I do not perceive myself, nor do my colleagues regard me, as radically different from any other teacher. I am a somewhat strict disciplinarian. Which is to say that, on the apparent level, my disciplinary methods do not look different. My students see me as formal but approachable, even avuncular. "Yea, he's cool," I overheard a student say, "'cept for that once when he suspended me on some bogus charges."

Around the middle of last September, Tomyko[1] refused to call me "Sir." It was not so much what he said, as much as the insolent attitude he took before the whole class. So I gave him three days in-house suspension. But I worried about our relationship. As I wrote him up in the hallway, away from the gaze of the other students, I quietly explained my feelings—not my actions, my feelings. Knowing he knows the expression, I used the cliché, "hate the sin but love the sinner." Although I did not say it, I distinguished for him the difference between guilt and shame, the guilt, in a very few words, being about the deed, whereas shame is about the person (Piers & Singer, 1953). Just before he went to the office, I added, "We're still cool, right?" He gave me "a bump," a kind of handshake. To insure the continuance of our dialogue, I visited him in "in-house." I left him a book, the one we were reading in class. My hope was that the book acted as an object that signified our relationship, even though I was not present.

Tomyko became an A student. Perhaps more importantly, on several occasions he chose to confide in me several significant personal problems.

Had I shamed him, our relationship undoubtedly would not have continued on any level except the most pro forma. What makes shaming so damaging is that the central message is not about a fault. Shaming is about how the person is elementally constituted. It is the difference between "You failed the math test because you didn't study," and "You're stupid and will never amount to anything." Of vital importance here is the fact that shame is not just about an aspect of the self: it is about the whole of the self (Lewis, 1971). It is not about being bad at math. The whole of the self is stupid.

It is well also to pause here, and consider the concepts of transference and countertransference. These are important concepts that barely rate a mention in most teacher education. For example, two psychology textbooks, commonly used in teacher education, mention transference in one or two paragraphs (Lefton & Valvatine, 1988, p. 594; Crooks & Stein, 1991, pp. 607–8). Countertransference is given a parenthetical note (Crooks & Stein, 1991, p. 608).

Moore and Fine (1990) define transference as the "displacement of patterns of feelings, thoughts, and behavior, originally experienced during childhood, onto a person involved in a current interpersonal relationship" (p. 196). In *The Language of Psychoanalysis*, Laplanche and Pontalis (1973) note that "[i]n the transference, infantile prototypes re-emerge and are experienced with a strong sensation of immediacy" (p. 455). Consider the student who transfers her feelings about her mother on to her female teacher.

The reaction of the teacher is the countertransference (cf. Laplanche & Pontalis, 1973, p. 92; Moore & Fine, 1990, p. 47). The teacher will have feelings, quite often unconscious, about the student's transference. The teacher's reactions are perhaps most easily observed at, although by no means exclusive to, those moments when a pupil's transference is manifested as, for example, antagonism, dependence, suspicion, or the erotic. I recall a very young teacher, a woman of perhaps twenty-two or twenty-three years, who was quite attractive. A young student, an attractive male, seventeen or eighteen, went out of his way to have her tutor him. She accommodated him, although she would often comment about how she found him "irritating." Her reaction to his sexual attraction, found both in her reciprocal attraction, and her need to distance herself through an expression of anger, was the teacher's countertransference. I have little doubt that all this was unconscious.

Such interaction may well bring tension to the relationship. The key to any successful classroom interaction is the ability to endure the tension without abandoning the relationship. It is easy to shame a student who has sexual feelings for a teacher. That relieves the educator's tension. It might also lead the student to avoid the teacher, even when the child desperately needs help.

Sigmund Freud's thinking on the subject of shame evolved considerably throughout his life (Morrison, 2009, pp. 22–28). Indeed, it has been said that

"Freud's views are neither consistent nor clearly defined" (Morrison, 2009, p. 28). Freud (1989) first mentions shame in "Draft K" of an 1895 letter to Dr. Wilhelm Fliess, a dear friend and much valued colleague. Dr. Freud proposed that "self-reproach" is caused by the repression of sexual experiences, a defense, in effect a reaction formation (pp. 89–96). By 1905, in his *Three Essays on The Theory of Sexuality*, Freud thinks of shame as a form of resistance against drives. "[T]he sexual instinct has to struggle against certain mental forces which act as resistances, and of which shame and disgust are the most prominent" (p. 254).

Freud implies, although he does not explicitly state, that narcissism, particularly narcissistic mortification, is interwoven with the functioning of shame. In his pioneering 1914 essay, "On Narcissism: An Introduction," Freud's thoughts on shame begin to form when he writes about narcissism and the ego-ideal. The ego-ideal is a form of fantasy, the fantasy of the self that is approved of, acceptable, worthy of respect, recognition, and, in a word, love.

Freud never specifically addresses the generation of shame. As Andrew Morrison said, when commenting upon a paper I wrote, "in relation to narcissism Freud first speaks of the ego ideal, and also, I would add, of self-regard—each a major factor in the generation of shame. All the pieces were in place for Freud to develop a metapsychology of shame, but he did not explicitly do so in his 1914 paper. It remained for his successors to specify the relationship of narcissism, and of the ego ideal, to shame" (Morrison, 2009, p. 3).

Franz Alexander (1938) posits that feelings of inferiority are grounded in "a self-accusation based on a comparison, on the simple fact that one feels weaker than another person" (p. 44). While he distinguishes between inferiority and guilt, Alexander goes on to conclude that these are two versions of shame. In 1953, Piers and Singer published their monumental *Shame and Guilt: A Psychoanalytic and a Cultural Study*, wherein they specify the relationship between shame, narcissism, and the ego-ideal. They argue that shame is, in essence, experienced as a tension between the ego and the ego-ideal. In a similar manner, Sandler et al. (1963) postulate that shame could arise from a failure "to live up to ideal standards" (p. 157). In 1991, Otto Kernberg, commenting upon *On Narcissism*, says that Sigmund Freud "postulates that another agency, 'conscience,' evaluates the relation between the demands of the ego-ideal and the actual achievements of the ego, regulating in the process the individual's self-esteem. . . . The demands for perfection, related to idealization processes in the ego-ideal, are implicitly linked to self-attack and self-criticism derived from the prohibitive aspects of the super-ego" (p. 139).

Taken in summary then, the genesis of shame may be stated as follows. If our appraisal of ourselves is at a distance from that vision of the self which is worthy, then shame follows. Put simply, when the ego-ideal is inspecting, and the person being inspected is found wanting, then shame can be one result of this narcissistic challenge.

With this brief historical overview in mind, let us turn now to a theory of psychosocial development. One of Sigmund Freud's best known protégés began his career as an art teacher. Erik Erikson (1959) is best known for his eight stages of psychosocial development, and within that framework, his work with identity. He may well be best known for his book, *Young Man Luther* (1962). For brevity's sake, I concentrate on those developmental stages that occur during the preschool, grade school, middle, and high school years.

For our purposes, these stages are important for two reasons. They provide avenues from which we regress into these earliest shame-based templates. These stages also provide platforms, in and of themselves, for shame.

In Erik Erikson's first stage of development, he sees the child's first major crisis as "Trust Versus Mistrust." Sigmund Freud refers to this stage as the oral stage of development. In Erikson's formulation, the essential task of the child at this stage of development, the first twelve to eighteen months, is to develop a sense of trust in the mother. This is accomplished largely through the constancy of the mother, or primary caregiver. Put simply, the mother acts as a mirror. If the child is comforted, fed when hungry, cuddled, talked to, if the child's loving gazes are returned with love, then the infant is likely to develop trust, and a coherent sense of self. At this earliest stage, shame can result when the child seeks an expected response from the caregiver, and that caregiver fails to respond as expected. These rebuffs can generate an insecure and ill-formed sense of self. Heinz Kohut (1971) refers to this pattern as self-object failure. And thus the experience of shame.

The stage associated by name with shame, the second stage, Erikson terms "autonomy versus shame and doubt." This stage occurs from roughly eighteen months to three or so years of age. It is most closely associated with what Freud calls the anal stage, with muscle development, with potty training, with emotional conflicts associated with holding on and letting go. The child struggles for autonomy. Autonomy is expressed in the sense of bodily control that comes from successful potty training, the sense of separation from the dyadic mother/child bond, the beginnings of the triadic mother/father/child matrix. Children develop trust in themselves as well as trust in the world.

As Erikson (1959) sees it, the child pursues a sense of self-esteem that results from a sense of self-control (p. 70). When the child is thwarted in this pursuit, shame follows. "Shaming exploits an increasing sense of being small, which paradoxically develops as the child stands up and as his awareness permits him to note the relative measures of size and power" (p. 71).

The next stage, which Erikson terms "initiative versus guilt," what Freud refers to as the Oedipal and phallic phase, begins at about age three, roughly during the preschool experience. In this developmental stage, our attention is drawn to the development of the super-ego, which is to say the conscience, the civilizing influences.

From roughly ages six to eleven or so, the child enters Freud's latency period, Erikson's "industry versus inferiority." In this period, the child's tasks revolve around competence, imagination, work, and fun. The child learns to be a good worker in school, but also a good friend and family member. The child begins to develop male and female styles of interaction. This stage is associated approximately with the grade school and middle school years.

Between ages eleven to eighteen, years approximately associated with the middle and high school years, Freud speaks of the genital stage and Erikson refers to "identity versus role confusion." For the purposes of this discussion, the student's major task is to develop a stable sense of identity, a clear sense of "who I am," and "what am I to do." The youth begins to explore forms of identity, including bodily identity, sexual orientation, politics, work, philosophy, and religion.

The next step, Erikson's "intimacy versus isolation," is associated in texts with early adulthood. From my own personal observations, the onset of this stage occurs for some in late adolescence. According to Erikson, having achieved a stable sense of identity, the young person is prepared to develop profound and intimate relationships with sexual partners, friends, and significant others. Failure to do so results in isolation, which can result in shame.

With this brief overview in mind, it's worth noting the most frequent subjects for humiliation in school—morals, work, play, identity, sex. One child is a little thief. One child is a lazy bum. Another child doesn't know how to play with others. That girl is a little hussy. This boy can't keep his hands off that girl. Hence, they are to be shamed. Why? Not because the child's actions are bad—but because the person, the whole person, is judged unworthy.

While this is not an exhaustive list, there is herein a developmental pattern for both teacher and student. One of two things tends to happen in order to generate shame. One possibility is that the processes of shaming, and the feelings associated with being shamed, tend to initiate a regression from the current stage of development to an earlier stage of growth. The other possibility is that the developmental stage per se provides a platform for shame. A child of ten, for example, internalizes feelings of inferiority, feelings that may haunt this person at the time and throughout life.

It should be noted that these stages of development, while sequential, are not strictly linear. There is much overlap, as will be suggested in a story at the end of this chapter. They are, however, useful in that they outline a sequence regarded as traditional among psychoanalytically informed theorists.

It is worth repeating that these stages of development provide avenues from which we regress into this earliest shame-based template, as well as platforms, in and of themselves, for shame. When teachers and principals shame, they draw upon their personality formation, a template that is formed long before they began their careers. This then becomes the platform for today's shaming of the student. Let me restate it this way. The child acts in a way that the educator deems punishable by humiliation. The educator unconsciously senses his or her own experience with humiliation. The educator's experience with humiliation becomes then the platform for shaming the student. It also is worth repeating that the process of shaming is facilitated by transference and countertransference. Transference is the unconscious redirection of feelings from one set of relationships to another. Transference is characterized by the taking of one set of emotions from childhood and redirecting them toward a new object. Thus it is an everyday occurrence for children to transfer feelings from parents to instructors.

Indeed, students will have all manner of feelings toward the teacher. Likewise, the teacher will have all manner of countertransference. A student, for instance, may have sexual feelings toward a teacher. These sexual feelings may be born of an earlier incestuous feeling toward the parent. This transference will evoke feelings from the teacher, which we refer to as the countertransference. The question becomes, for the purposes of this chapter, what does the teacher do? How does the teacher grow in self-awareness? What does the teacher do with that self-awareness? As Karl Menninger once said, "What's done to children, they will do to society" (quoted in Wallerstein et al., 2000, p. 294).

SOME PREDICTABLE RESULTS OF SHAMING

My interest in writing about shaming began with my exploration of my own exercise of shaming in the classroom. And the absolute failure I experienced when using shaming as a disciplinary tactic. Simply put, I began my research with self-examination.

In the years before I began in the public schools, I observed shaming, but I cannot recall using it. Having spent my first twenty-plus years generally teaching in private schools, discipline was not a major concern. Academics were primary. Discipline problems were referred to the front office.

Then I taught in the public schools. Nothing in my experience prepared me for this.

My classes were on the verge of chaos. I became desperate. When I observed other teachers and administrators, shame was what they used. It seemed to work. I used shaming for the same reason that teachers used to whip children. I just could not figure out what else to do. This was my tactic of last resort. Shaming resonated with me in a manner that, at the time, was not self-apparent. I remembered the times that, as a boy, I had been shamed and how I had complied.

Samantha was belligerent. I called her father one day, and asked if we could discuss her behavior. He came up to my middle school, and we met in the hallway right outside my classroom, Room 208. In order to rectify his daughter's misconduct, the father offered to "beat her ass"—and here his gestures indicated literally whipping her behind with his belt—in front of my entire class. Samantha just hung her head. Her humiliation was as obvious as it was overwhelming. I was shocked. I no longer remember what I said beyond the fact that I politely declined. What I do remember is that, shortly thereafter, when Samantha wanted something from me, she became extremely seductive. And it was at this point that I realized how much like Samantha's father I had become. The fact that I was more restrained, and more verbal, did not mean that my use of shaming was any less painful.

Sexual acting out. Humor. Withdrawal. Overcompensation. Shame paralysis. Rage. Shaming can bring all manner of reaction. What follows is a simple list of some, and by no means all, of the typical reactions to shaming, reactions that manifest themselves in the classroom. Some of these reactions may be easily observed; others are far more subtle. My hope is to bring relational awareness to the educator.

Shame is one of the first emotions recorded in writing. Just after Adam and Eve were exiled from Eden, they experienced shame. All manner of situations may trigger a sexual reaction in a student. The student is aware consciously that he is sexually attracted to the teacher, but is unconsciously aware that this repeats the forbidden oedipal desires. The student feels shame. Whatever the trigger, some children can find themselves in a cycle of shame, wherein they feel shame because of sexuality and try to work out this by sexualized behavior which, in turn, brings on more shame.

Another common reaction to shaming is the use of humor. I once taught in an urban public middle school, in which I was one of only two white people, both of us being teachers.

A student once asked me, "Hey, cous', what page we on?"

I run a rather formal classroom. So I turned to him and said, "Mr. Knight, I'm white and you're black. Do I look like any cousin of yours?"

"Honest, Dr. Tieman, it depends on what side of the family we're talking about"

Mr. Knight showed me that he had organized his understanding of self to such a degree that a single reprimand did not threaten the whole of his sense of self-worth. Not every child achieves this. My guess is that every teacher has a student who would much rather be the class clown than admit to failure.

And a large part of the problem for that child is an inability to separate, say, failure in math from failure as a person. "All the other kids in the class can do this problem, Tommy. So what's the matter with you?"

I cannot begin to count the number of students I have known who have used withdrawal as a means of dealing with shame. Frequently, what the child does is to hide, for example, in a daydream. For the teacher, this is perhaps the most difficult to observe, because it does not look like anything. But the substance of such daydreams can be revelatory. I also cannot count the number of children who daydream of being Harry Potter, the nerd who is forced by his step-parents to live beneath the stairs, the dork who finally realizes his true powers.

I remember a young woman, who asked me to read some of her private writings. Since I am an English teacher, this is pretty common. It's uncommon, however, for a student to hand me a three-hundred page draft of her first novel. Students frequently overcompensated for shame by losing themselves in their studies. This can be quite adaptive. We rarely question the motives of the student who gets the best grades, who plays from memory the Mozart clarinet concerto. But the same motives that lead on to, let's say, addiction may also lead a student to other forms of overcompensation that are highly adaptive. The clarinetist, despite the A in music, may yet feel an unbridgeable distance from the ego-ideal.

Every few years, I will get a student in class who has made it all the way to 9th grade, and does not know how to read. Two Septembers ago, I asked Abbey to read. She lifted her book. Then she froze, mouth open, book suspended before her, like some live-action photograph in the newspaper.

Shame paralysis may look like the paralysis illustrated here. But it also "may manifest itself as stagnation and lack of content. Shame can also manifest itself in clumsy sentences, grammatical errors, mixing words in a manner that resembles a reading or writing disorder" (Ikonen & Rechardt, p. 116).

Shaming can bring about all manner of reaction. One result, however, is absolutely predictable. Shaming will result in rage. Erikson (1950) points out, "Shame is early expressed in an impulse to bury one's face, or to sink, right then and there, into the ground. But this, I think, is essentially rage turned against the self. He who is ashamed would like to force the world not to look at him, not to notice his exposure. He would like to destroy the eyes of the world" (p. 252).

Years ago, I taught in an all female Catholic high school. One year, a student died in an automobile accident. A small scholarship fund was set up in her honor. A plaque was erected, along with a description of the scholarship and a 3 x 5 photograph of the deceased. Within a day or two, the picture was stolen.

Following this petty theft, every day at least twice a day, there was an announcement about the return of this photo. These announcements were unequivocal in saying that this thief should be ashamed of herself. After about a week, the photo was anonymously returned. But it was scrunched up in a ball.

I have no idea why this young lady wanted the picture. Perhaps she wanted a photo because she had none of her own. Be that as it may, the result of this public humiliation—albeit anonymous—was clearly rage, one of the most predictable outcomes of humiliation. That said, the school got what it wanted, and what it wanted was submission.

Rage is not always that spectacular. Indeed, it sometimes can be difficult for the educator to observe. About a year after the incident with the photograph, one day Christopher just would not shut up. I kept him from going to recess with his 7th grade buddies. "Okay, young man, you want to play around in my class, and blow-off your English lesson. Fine. Drop out of school. But before you go, I have one last English lesson for you, all the English you'll need for the rest of your sorry life. Repeat after me. Would you like fries with that order?" Before he could respond, I had to go to the door, and talk to another teacher. As we chatted, out of the corner of my eye I noticed Christopher pounding his desk with his fist. But he shut up, which, for the moment, was good enough for me.

As Lansky (1994) quite bluntly puts it, "The rage and attack come from shame . . ." (p. 438). But if this is such a predictable outcome, why do educators resort to shaming as a solution to a discipline problem? The answer is simple. In the immediate, it seems to work. The problem, of course, is in the long term. If one merely looks at shaming as a tool for quieting a student, a tool to solve this or that problem, then if gives the appearance of an immediate solution. In *Identity and the Life Cycle*, Erikson says, "People all over the world seem convinced that to make the right (meaning *their*) kind of human being, one must consistently introduce the senses of shame, doubt, guilt, and fear into the child's life" (1959, p. 74).

The Challenge

Psychoanalytic theory provides depth of understanding. When it comes to the use of shaming in the classroom, there is much to be said for simply knowing that you do it. In some cases, that can be sufficient in order to stop the shaming. The symptom, however, is not the malady. To simply know the behavior, to do no more than to stop the behavior, is to have knowledge without understanding. Knowledge of a behavior does not provide understanding of the behavior. For that understanding, we need to look deeper.

Selma Fraiberg and colleagues (1980) famously spoke of the "ghosts in the nursery," meaning that, when mothers and fathers inevitably bring their conflicts and anxieties into their child rearing, "the ghosts of the paternal past have taken up residence in the nursery" (p. 196). In the school, the educator also carries the sum of his or her experiences. In this chapter, much attention thus far has been paid to the student. However, as the nursery sees the repetition of childhood conflicts in the adult, so too does the school witness a similar recapitulation by teacher and administrators. Like the parent, when the educator addresses his or her own conflicts and anxieties, "the ghosts depart," and the adult becomes "the protector of their children against the repetition of their own conflicted past" (p. 196).

To put it a different way, consider the stages of development just listed above. The burden of my list, as presented, generally emphasizes the student. However, the direction of the list can be reversed. There is just as much, if not more, transference and countertransference in a classroom as in a therapist's office. For example, students are sexually attracted to teachers, yes, but teachers are also sexually attracted to students. This frequently results in the educator feeling, most likely, an unconscious taboo. The educator may then shame the student over, say, a sloppy homework assignment or something seemingly unrelated. The student becomes despised, whereas, in reality, the educator is shamed by the forbidden desire. My point is that my list is not singular but relational. A duet. The we-ness of the moment in the classroom. Hence the need, on the educator's part, is for a working knowledge of how the personality develops, the personality of the child as well as the personality of the educator. The starting point is this knowledge, knowledge of Freud, knowledge of Erikson, knowledge of transference, countertransference, and so forth. That knowledge of psychoanalytic theory leads, hopefully, to an understanding of the self in relationship. Hopefully, indeed, such knowledge leads the educator to understand more than they simply know, a wisdom facilitated by psychoanalytic theory.

It would be easy at this point to say that, if you use shaming in your school, then you ought to stop. But as I have said, a change in outward behavior does little to address the source of the behavior. The analogy to Fraiberg's "ghosts in the nursery" (1980) is appropriate here, insofar as ". . . it is the parent, who cannot remember his childhood feelings of pain and anxiety, who will feel the need to inflict his pain upon his child" (p. 182). In a similar manner, the educator, who cannot remember the source of his/her feelings of shame, may well choose to visit their own woundedness upon the student.

And there is very little in traditional teacher education that prepares us to think psychodynamically about ourselves and our charges.

I am the product of a rather typical education for teachers. I got my bachelor's degree, and my MA, from Southern Methodist University, where I double majored in history and English and minored in education. I did graduate work at Washington University, and graduate research at Oxford, where, in both cases, I read a great deal about the intellectual history of education. I was certified to teach middle school and high school. As an undergraduate, I took an introductory course in psychology during the early 1970s. In order to be certified in Missouri, in the 1980s I took "The Psychology of the Exceptional Child" at Harris-Stowe State College, an historically black college in St. Louis. During my PhD studies, I took an educational psychology course at St. Louis University in the 1990s. I also have taught undergraduate and graduate students in education, and supervised student teachers.

For all my education, I had very little formal training in psychology—just three courses. I read Skinner. I read about Pavlov and all those slobbering dogs. I familiarized myself with the cognitive/behavioral school. But from none of this did I develop a vision of the mind. Least of all did I have a vision of the mind that applied to my job. In sharp contrast to this traditional teacher training, for two years I studied child development at the St. Louis Psychoanalytic Institute, where I studied folks like John Bowlby, Heinz Kohut, Melanie Klien, and read books like Sigmund Freud's *Civilization and Its Discontents* and Anna Freud's *Psycho-Analysis for Teachers and Parents*.

The almost exclusive orientation of educational psychology, and indeed teacher education, toward the cognitive/behavioral is, at the very least, limiting, especially when one considers the narrow exposure to psychology that most student teachers receive. At the very worst, it damns the educator to an image of the student which may actually be harmful because of its limitations.

There are obvious behavioral ramifications. Shaming results in rage, and rage can disrupt the classroom. Therefore, do not shame a child. Behavior may be managed for today, and perhaps for this semester, at which point this student has become some other instructor's nightmare.

But such an approach fails to see the full range of the problem. What is needed is a psychodynamic vision of the mind, a developmental context in which the teacher can frame his or her experience.

And there is more, for this context is one in which the teacher sees him- or herself in a deeply dialogical relationship with the student. Conventional wisdom says that the child is in the student. What we often forget is that the child is also in the educator. Look at it this way. On the professional level, the most apparent level, we respond to students according to our training. More importantly—and certainly more fundamentally—we respond according to how we developed. For most of us, unfortunately, our training teaches us to be always and everywhere cheery and uplifting. But that just encourages a kind of professionally false self. I cannot recall a single methods class in which the instructor said it's okay to be angry with a student who "flips you the finger." Yet any lengthy relationship is going to have a full range of emotions, anger among them. The truly constructive element begins with being simultaneously true to yourself and true to the child.

Let me be perfectly clear. The problem is not the measuring of behavior, which can be quite useful. The problem is the all pervasive singularity of the cognitive/behavioral approach. Indeed, it is possible to argue that, in schools of education, it is not simply an approach. It is an ethos. It is as if no one has a mind anymore—all we have is behavior.

We educators are encouraged to be compassionate, to love. But there is little in our training that helps us look into ourselves, to truly open ourselves, to open ourselves to the full range of emotions, to ask about our own motivations, to accept ourselves and all that has made us. In three words, to love ourselves.

In the end, I refer throughout this chapter to more than simply how we think about shaming, or how we consider our profession. I refer here to how we think about ourselves in relationship. In this case, the setting is work, the other is the student, and shaming the specific event.

When quoting Tolstoy in *The Year of Living Dangerously* (McElroy & Weir, 1982), Billy Kwan asks, "What, then, must we do?" Let me finish this chapter with a little story.

About fifteen or so years ago, I was teaching in an all female, Catholic high school. A few weeks before graduation, two female students were caught kissing in the bathroom. One student, Marla, was a current student of mine. The other, Diane, I had taught a few years before. Both were very good, serious students, and had never been in any trouble that I know of. Diane was the introvert, and Marla the extrovert.

Since the bathroom was just down from my room, the teacher who caught them, and the principal, brought them to my room. I had the period free. The discomfort of the other teacher and the principal, both nuns, was almost tangible. As was their hostility. They alternated between bursts of anger, threats of humiliation, and awkward silences punctuated by glares at the students. Marla and Diane were stoic, silent, and outwardly impassive.

I too remained a silent observer. But I knew this could not go on like this. I felt like we were made of brittle crystal and one more high C would shatter us.

I finally asked them,"Would you like me to handle this?" I asked this because another question silently occurred to me—Why did the adults choose my room? Indeed, why me? The principal's office was at the end of the hall, and the other teacher's room was catty-corner from me. In any case, everyone seemed relieved that I asked. From this moment on, the other two adults never involved themselves in the matter. Indeed, they never even asked about it. They just left.

Then I said three things to my students before our conversation, a conversation that, in truth, would continue for the rest of the year. First, I assured them that, "No matter what you tell me, I will accept it." Secondly, I assured them that, no matter what, "I will continue to be your teacher."

It is worth noting also that I ever so briefly explained to them that, while I am not bound by confidentiality, "you know, like your priest in confession," I will "let personal stuff stay personal stuff."

I remember Marla's blue eyes flashing, then darting between me and Diane as she asked, "You mean like you'd get me help if I said I ate some pills, but you'd pretty much just listen if I said I like French kissing?"

"Yea, that's pretty much it."

Marla and Diane gazed at me intently. I am absolutely sure that they were judging whether or not it was safe to let me into their world. There was a pause, then an audible exhale. The relief was felt by all three of us. I also feel sure that their trust rested upon the fact that our relationship was healthy in that, among other things, I had never shamed them.

Following this, I actually said very little. That I would accept them, that I would not get angry, that I would not shame them, that I would continue my relationship with them, this seemed to be all they really needed to know. Over the years, I have become accustomed to the fact that students often do not want advice; they just want someone to listen. I tell my student teachers, "Sometimes the kids just want to leave something on your desk. They really don't want you to pick it up and grade it." This was such a case.

That first day they confided how they were more worried about the reaction of the teachers than the students. Apparently the students already knew of their affair. They told me of their dreams of getting married, having kids, owning a house.

Over the next few weeks, there were a number of similar conversations. My only interjections were to occasionally focus on the here-and-now. Once, for example, they spoke of moving to another state in order to get married. "Today. Right after school." I reminded them that senior finals were in just a couple of weeks. I also reminded them that "The Big Plan," their term, was to finish high school, go to the state university together (they had been accepted to the same university), live together, then get married.

But most of the time I just listened. Often, they showed great insight. Once Diane said, "We're teenagers. We're supposed to be experimenting with sex! It's like our job. Why is everyone so shocked?" Other times, their dreams were the dreams of young people everywhere. I felt at this point that possibly, just possibly, Marla and Diane were beginning to explore a stable sense of their sexual identity, this as opposed to being shamed into role confusion. I also felt that they were developing the skills of intimacy, and that this hopefully would spare them the pain of isolation so often felt by homosexuals and bisexuals.

They graduated from high school. They went off to the university. Their romance did not last very long. But they remain close friends to this day. And they learned that love is possible. I do not want to portray myself as a saint. But I like to think that I, their teacher, helped a little with all of that.

NOTE

1. All children's names have been changed and identifying details disguised to protect the children's privacy.

REFERENCES

Alexander, F. (1938). Remarks about the relation of inferiority feelings to guilt feelings. *International Journal of Psycho-Analysis, 19,* 41–49.

Buber, M. (1960). *I and thou.* (W. Kaufman, Trans.). New York: Scribner's.

Crooks, R., & J. Stein. (1991). *Psychology: Science, behavior, and life.* Chicago: Holt, Rinehart and Winston.

Erikson, E. (1950). *Childhood and society.* New York: Norton.

Erikson, E. (1959). *Identity and the life cycle.* New York: Norton.

Erikson, E. (1962). *Young man Luther.* (2nd ed.). New York: Norton.

Fraiberg, S., Adelson, E., & Shapiro, V. (1980). Ghosts in the nursery: A psychoanalytic approach to the problems of impaired mother-infant relationships. In S. H. Fraiberg (Ed.), *Clinical studies in infant mental health: The first year of life* (pp. 164–96). London: Tavistock.

Freud, A. (1979 [1935]). *Psycho-analysis for teachers and parents.* (Barbara Low, Trans.). New York: Norton.

Freud, S. (1961 [1930]). *Civilization and its discontents.* (J. Strachey, Trans.). New York: Norton.

Freud, S. (1989 [1885]). Draft K. In Peter Gay (ed.), *The Freud reader* (pp. 89–96). (J. Strachey, Trans.). New York: Norton.

Freud, S. (1968 [1914]). On narcissism: An introduction, *The standard edition of the complete psychological works of Sigmund Freud, 14,* 73–102. (J. Strachey, Trans.). London: Hogarth.

Freud, S. (1989 [1905]). Three essays on the theory of sexuality. In Peter Gay (Ed.), *The Freud reader* (pp. 239–93). (J. Strachey, Trans.). New York: Norton.

Galston, W. E-mail message to the author. 2 June 2010.

Ikonen, P., & Rechardt, E. (1993). The origin of shame and its vicissitudes. *Scandinavian Psychoanalytic Review, 16,* 100–24.

Kernberg, O. (1991). A contemporary reading of "on narcissism." In J. Sandler, E. Person, & P. Fonagy (Eds.), *Freud's "On narcissism: An introduction"* (pp. 131–48). New Haven, CT: Yale University Press.

Kohut, H. (1971). *The analysis of the self.* New York: International Universities Press.

Lansky, M. R. (1994). Shame: Contemporary psychoanalytic perspectives. *Journal of the American Academy of Psychoanalysis, 22,* 435–36.

Laplanche, J., & Pontalis, J.-B. (1973). *The language of psychoanalysis.* (D. Nicholson-Smith, Trans.). New York: Norton.

Lefton, L., & Valvatine, L. (1988). *Mastering psychology.* Boston: Allyn and Bacon.

Lewis, H. B. (1971). *Shame and guilt in neurosis.* New York: International Universities Press.

McElroy, J. (Producer), & Weir, P. (Director). (1982). *The year of living dangerously.* United States: MGM.

Moore, B. E., & Fine, B. D., (Eds.). (1990). *Psychoanalytic terms and concepts.* New Haven, CT: Yale University Press.

Morrison, A. (1989). *Shame: The underside of narcissism.* New York: Routledge.

Morrison, A. (2009). Comments upon "*The ghost in the schoolroom,*" by John Samuel Tieman, PhD, e-mailed to the author.

Piers, G., & Singer, M. (1953). *Shame and guilt: A psychoanalytic and a cultural study.* New York: Norton.

Sandler, J., Holder, A., & Meers, D. (1963). The ego ideal and the ideal self. *Psychoanalytic Study of the Child, 18,* 139–58.

Skinner, B. F. (1976). *Walden two.* New York: Macmillan.

Tieman, J. (2007). The ghost in the classroom: A primer in the lessons of shame. *Schools: Studies in Education, 4, 2*, 39–55.

Wallerstein, J., Lewis, J., & Blakeslee, S. (2000). *The unexpected legacy of divorce: A 25 year landmark study.* New York: Hyperion.

Chapter Twelve

Moments of Meeting

Learning to Play with Reading Resistance

Gail Boldt and Billie A. Pivnick

Despite the fact that the reading development of any child involves multiple and variable social, cognitive, and emotional factors, many children learn to read fairly easily over time. Nevertheless, in the contemporary era of high-stakes education accountability, learning to read is treated as an on-going potential crisis, putting children under great pressure to learn to read within a prescribed time frame and in specific, demonstrable ways. Children who do not test as proficient, independent readers by third grade are viewed as having reading difficulties that represent a very real threat to teachers and schools. Under the Adequate Yearly Progress provision of *No Child Left Behind* in which every student in the United States must test as proficient in reading by 2014, children designated as "failing" will guarantee that the school will be classified as "failing." Such a designation can bring major consequences to a school, including the eventual firing of teachers and administrators, turning management of the school over to a private company, or closing the school.

Faced with the requirement that all children demonstrate reading proficiency by the age of eight or nine, anxious administrators searching for solutions press preschool and primary grades teachers for early identification and intervention into any signs of difference in reading development. These efforts communicate a sense of crisis, exacerbating the considerable anxiety of parents and teachers, and contribute to a mounting sense of fear and humiliation often felt by the children. Increasingly, children as young as four to seven years old experience themselves as failing at one of the most fundamental tasks in school. As the early school years pass and problems persist, many of these children—identified as "struggling readers" and overwhelmed

245

by feelings of anxiety and shame—become resistant to reading and often to school itself. Even when teachers attempting to help these children have a solid understanding of good reading practices, teachers rarely receive any training to understand and work with children's emotional responses. Teachers may feel and enact their own negativity—anger, uncertainty, resentment, shame, or fear—in response to the affective enactments of an angry or withdrawn child's resistance.

In this chapter, we take a psychoanalytically informed stance to argue for more productive and sympathetic understandings of reading resistance that address intra- and inter-psychic dimensions of reading for students who are struggling. We draw case material from a young boy, Nick, who was identified in the first grade as at-risk in reading development and who had developed resistance to reading. We propose understanding Nick's resistance as a defense against affective misattunement and loss. Reading and learning to read are important intersubjective events and reading failure threatens loss of support in relationships between the children and important adults and peers, as well as loss of an important relationship to texts themselves.

Just as a child can have difficulty coping with certain forms of frightening and/or contradictory behaviors in a caregiving figure, leading to a collapse or absence of attentional and behavioral strategies for coping with stress, a child can become fearful of text that yields pleasurable mastery only unpredictably while also stimulating punishing anxiety. The expectation that a text cannot be mastered can create disorganized behavioral responses indicative of "fright without solution" (Hesse & Main, 2000). To experience fear without recourse to an effective response can result in the activation of contradictory biological propensities both to approach and to take flight. We characterize this as analogous to disorganized attachment. Disorganized attachment leads to disoriented, controlling, and/or role-reversing behavior on the part of the child (Hesse & Main, 2000) and has been associated with heightened adrenocortisol levels (Spangler & Grossman, 1993)

Children typically feel security in relationships with caregivers that balance the need to explore and master the world with the need to find emotional safety and protection. The child faced with unpredictable or frightening caregivers learns that neither avoidant fleeing nor assertive fighting is a reliable strategy for managing their negative emotions. Instead, they may try to activate both stratagems in combination—leading to freezing and disorientation—or in alternation, leading to disorganized behavior. This fear response repeated over time becomes an internal destabilizing force when it is generalized to, or recruited in, other relationships (Fonagy, 2001; Lyons-Ruth, 1999; Lyons-Ruth et al., 2003). Although the term "disorganized attachment" is usually applied to a certain pattern of relationship between a child and caregiver, we are using it here more metaphorically, to refer to the relationship between a child and a text. We propose that Nick's experiences of humiliation and fear led to a form of disorganized attachment to text.

Because texts and teachers can become objects that induce a flood of fear, shame, and disorganized behavior, children's ability to work with texts and teachers in ways that allow their reading to improve can became severely constricted. Faced with the daily school requirement of engaging with the very thing they wish to avoid, these children's anxiety escalates and their capacity for the kinds of abstraction needed for effective reading can falter. For this reason, what has to be attended to is the child's expectation about whether relationships with people or materials are going to be gratifying or punishing. What has to be reshaped is not their explicit factual knowledge, but their implicit (procedural) understanding of relational and textual experiences, represented non-symbolically as how to be with others. Such "implicit relational knowing" often remains out of awareness but integrates cognition with emotions and interactive behaviors. These more unconsciously understood procedures often form a foundation for what comes to be represented symbolically in language.

Although Nick was in serious distress in first grade, following Nick across time, we are able to describe significant positive changes that occurred for him when, as a second grader, he worked with a reading tutor—Nita—who showed great sensitivity to the emotional and physical manifestations of Nick's struggles. We analyze Nita's work with Nick in two ways. First, we examine how Nita created a "field of play" or, as Winnicott (1971a) would call it, a "potential space," that bypassed Nick's less effective learning pathways. Second, we analyze the work Nita did with Nick through the Boston Process Change Study Group's (2010) idea of "moments of meeting," to argue that before Nick could begin to overcome the many problems he had developed as a resistant reader, he needed to bring together, in himself and with another person, an experience of himself as someone who could comply with reading conventions while still feeling creatively authentic.

A BRIEF PORTRAIT OF NICK AS A YOUNG READER

The only child of two educators both holding advanced degrees, Nick was read to regularly from infancy.[1] As his language skills developed in early childhood, Nick regularly engaged in talk about the books that were read to him, and he frequently played with books and produced language from books in his play and daily speech. When he began to play with writing at age four, his mother noticed an unexpected pattern in his literacy development. Nick was able to identify phonemes, for example, saying things like "dog, dog, da, da—that's a d!" However, this statement was almost inevitably followed by the question, "How do you make that?" In other words, although he could discriminate among sounds and name the corresponding letters, Nick could not remember how to write the letters nor could he recall the name or sound of letters he saw in print. In fact, Nick was nine years old before he could consistently look at certain graphically similar letters (e.g., u, v, w, y) or single digit numbers (e.g., 8 and 9) and name them—a task that is usually mastered by four- to six-year-olds.

Nick went to a play-based preschool where the children were read to daily and where the children had access to books for their own purposes. Nick and his friends frequently chose to play in the book room, being read to, engaging in playful early reading-like behaviors (Doake, 1985), and enacting book-related play themes. During this time, Nick exhibited no anxiety about reading at preschool or at home. In kindergarten, Nick started to complain that reading was hard. Nick's teacher was careful to keep any concerns she might have had from Nick and responded with consistent affirmation toward his efforts. Nick, however, was increasingly aware that his peers were able to do things with reading that evaded him.

In first grade, Nick was confronted with a teacher who had spent the previous thirty years teaching upper grades and had no discernible training in early literacy development. She immediately identified him as having "a reading problem" and initiated a number of interventions whose primary effect was to increase his anxiety massively. He experienced her as punitive and was so frightened of her that he became hyper-vigilant and cried frequently in school, eventually developing a strong school phobia. Once at school, he spent long hours crying in the counselor's office, demanding to go home. He suffered from serious sleep disturbances and developed a chronic stomachache. Nick usually refused to work on reading at home with his parents, although he continued to love being read to at bedtime.

A video of Nick reading at age four (preschool) shows a playful approach to reading. The video shows him sitting comfortably in his father's lap while engaging in what Doake (1985) described as "fluent early reading-like behavior." As is usual in this form of emergent reading, Nick had no idea what the words printed on the page were, and therefore ignored them. Although Nick had heard the book read to him only three times before, he could "read" the book (P. D. Eastman's 1966 illustrated classic, *Go Dog, Go!*) by remembering the patterns, rhythms, and meanings of the text with the help of ample cues provided by the illustrations. He produced a reading that communicated the play of the dogs, complete with voices and sound effects, that was sometimes quite close to the actual text and at other times demonstrated his understanding that the language of the book drew from sizes and colors of dogs and spatial relationships but that was not closely matched to the actual text on the page. Nick was joyful throughout his play with the text, but particularly exuberant whenever he came to pages that repeated a dialogue pattern between two dogs. After completing the book, he leaned forward excitedly toward the camera and exclaimed, "I wanna read another book!"

A video of Nick reading the same book in first grade showed him in a much more sober mood. Nick clearly knew, as he did not at age four, that each chunk of letters not only represented a word, but dictated a specific word that he would either read correctly or incorrectly. Under the influence of his first-grade teacher who treated reading primarily as phonetic decoding, Nick largely abandoned his previous willingness to hypothesize the text based on the illustrations, language patterns, and story context. Rather, he pointed to and attempted to pronounce each word, but given his difficulties with matching printed letters to sounds, his "sound it out" strategy was often ineffective. As he plodded painfully through the pages, he held his head up with one hand, arm propped on the table where he sat, and frequently sighed. After reading only a few pages, he asked in a plaintive tone, "Can we stop now?" Although his anxiety about getting it right and the fact that he found the task largely unpleasant were apparent, Nick nevertheless stopped reading to comment on happenings in the story, and when asked which parts were his favorite, he recalled the same repeated dialogue passage he had relished as a four-year-old, and then spent several minutes actively searching for each instance that pattern appeared in the book. He was intensely concentrated during those minutes he pursued his own agenda, and seemed to experience more pleasure while doing so.

PSYCHOANALYTIC PERSPECTIVES ON INTERSUBJECTIVITY AND PLAY IN LEARNING

We know that early on, Nick had a highly pleasurable and playful relationship to reading, mediated through relationships to adults, peers, and the texts and their stories. Just a few years later, Nick's experience of reading changed dramatically, as a result of his difficulty matching sounds to their symbols at the expected age. With a focus on the early development of reading fluency, his neuropsychological processing difference created difficulties with the expected pathway of reading development. His attempts to adapt to a conflict between his wish to please his teacher and his urge to flee experiences of shame and fear led to resistant behavior. This in turn caused disturbed interpersonal relationships with his teachers, parents, peers, curriculum, and ideas. Although we do not have space to explore all dimensions of this, much psychoanalytic research exists that can help elucidate several intersubjective aspects of learning to read that can help us to understand Nick's experiences of reading and suggest pedagogic consideration for Nick and other struggling readers. We will consider here two dimensions: working with resistance and working with implicit aspects of relationships.

In traditional psychoanalytic theories, resistance is considered to be a response to the pressure to eliminate the symptoms created by a conflict between a patient's wishes and the environment's demands for compliance to social conventions (cf., Reich, 1990). A child psychotherapist typically works to make the child patient more aware of the symptoms and underlying conflicts that produce a defensive, resistant stance to using more effective self-regulatory strategies in the face of experiences of intense emotional vulnerability (Chethik, 2000). In more contemporary psychoanalytic theories—based on the idea that symptoms arise in the context of intersubjective relationships with others—it is the child's relationship to others and its implicit assumptions that are the focus of therapeutic efforts to understand and alter resistances to change. Because failures to read early and in highly specified ways can be so fear-ridden and shame-inducing, an approach that is critical of the child's resistance will only exacerbate the child's stubborn reluctance. For that reason, an intersubjective approach can be more effective even while seeming more indirect.

Intersubjectivity involves the ability to read one's own and other people's motivations and to distinguish between one's own wishes and those of the other person. This creates a mental representation system, or "theory of mind," that allows the child to interpret what is happening in an interpersonal relationship (Fonagy & Target, 1996). One of the primary ways children develop this understanding is through play. Play tends to take place in the presence of another. Piaget (1959) famously described the experience of a child at play as being "enveloped with the feelings of a presence, so that to speak to himself or to speak to his mother appears to him to be the same thing" (p. 243). This is the prototypical play space—a "potential space," in Winnicott's (1971b) terms—in which a child and another co-create meanings. It is largely through play with others in the early years that the sense of personal authenticity and agency develops (Pivnick, 1998, 2010). Meares (1993) argues that the self, which we imagine as private, develops through public interactions. At the same time, the inner world is created from experiences with external physical things, such as toys and bodies. When a child engages in play, an illusory sense of self, destined to become the inner world, feels creative and full of the possibility of intersubjectivity. However, at the same time, the child has that other more public sense of self, the social self. In that mode, the child feels oriented to the real, the mundane, the adaptive tasks of the social world, and his or her mind is more alert and vigilant to the outer world's demands. If the internally oriented and the socially oriented modes are well integrated, the child learns she can have her own perceptions, experiences, and ideas, and share them with someone who will be interested in her point of view. The child will have to capacity to be interested in the perspectives of others.

Later, children begin to engage in more complex play in which familiar experiences are represented as *events* like going to the store, putting the baby to bed, or having a sword fight. An event representation like this includes the "who," "what," "where," "when," and "how" of a story, but played out with actions that have unfolding purpose. These playful scenarios, often done with others, help guide the child's understandings in similar contexts, shaping their interpretations of others' behavior. This play also enacts events that become the foundation for language representation (Nelson, 1996; Tomasello, 2003). In other words, language is based in social interactions and on the developing understanding of procedures and events, rather than on objects as Piaget (1959) argued (Pivnick, 1998).

Another kind of play that is important in language understanding is mimetic or imitative play, that is, socially shared, physically enacted gestures and games relevant to actions in the real world (Donald, 1991; Nelson, 1996). These mimetic games and songs, with repeated gestures—"The Wheels on the Bus" and "Hide and Seek," for instance—reorganize the child's experiences of events in ways that are more culturally sanctioned. They also help children develop an embodied understanding of concepts that are hard to understand abstractly, such as round, fast, slow, up, and down. These somatic experiences are the bases for linguistic categories (Lakoff & Johnson, 1999).

In psychoanalytic child therapy, the child utilizes all these modes of play in service of creating a sense of personal agency, improved self-regulation, diminished anxiety, and the ability to relate creatively to themselves and others they are close to. They come to be able to do these things both in self-expression and private thought. Central to this endeavor is the assumption that even the strangest symptoms have meaning and that all actions have an emotional underpinning, often one that has grown out of a particular set of relational parameters as internalized by the child (O'Loughlin & Merchant, 2012). For this reason, it is important that the therapeutic environment create emotional safety and the opportunity for imaginative self expression, whether through gesture or language.

D. W. Winnicott (1971a), a British child psychoanalyst, developed a game that would allow the child to express his or her needs or wishes without the impingement of an adult's more socialized understanding or demands on the child. It was called "The Squiggle Game," and involved the child and analyst, as equals, each drawing a scribble, followed by the other making the nonsense shape into something more meaningful, but without any expectation or pressure that they "get it right." A deep conversation without words was allowed to develop over the time of playing this game.

French psychoanalyst Andre Green likened psychoanalytic psychotherapy to The Squiggle Game:

> The spontaneous movement of a hand, which allows itself to be guided by the drive, a hand that does not act, but rather expresses itself, traces a more or less insignificant or formless line, submitting it to the scrutiny of the other, who deliberately transforms it into a meaningful shape. What else do we do in the analysis of difficult cases? Meaning is not discovered, it is created. It is a potential meaning. . . . To actualize it means to call it into existence . . . out of the meaning of two discourses . . . and by way of . . . the analyst . . . in order to construct [a symbolic construction that is co-created in the potential space between patient and analyst]. (Green, 1993, p. 219)

Language acquisition happens in much the same way (Tomasello, 2003). Even in reading, we associate to both the cocreative and the physical experiences words represent. For most children, the implicit, symbolic-play-derived, and event-basis for understanding words is handled unconsciously. However, when working with a certain class of struggling readers, these unconscious modes can be deliberately engaged. As we will describe in what follows, a playful approach relies on this latter strategy.

PLAYING IN READING

Britton (1970) observed that children initially engage reading and writing as forms of play that combine socially adaptive, creative, and expressive modes. In Nick's preschool years, he saw texts as a source of emotional connection and comfort with family members, adult friends, and preschool caregivers. With his friends, texts became a "ticket to play" (Dyson, 2003), a source for both word play and for adventurous storylines that could be played out later (Boldt, 2009).

Between preschool and first grade, Nick's relationship to text transformed from playing with text to feeling pressured to comply with demands for conformity to the rules and conventions of decoding. The transition to learning to read in ways valued in elementary school meant the loss of both personal intimacy and playfulness. Increasingly, his primary reading interactions took the form of decoding on demand and answering questions that required demonstration of tightly bounded (not dreamy, not idiosyncratic) interpretations of the text. The responsibility of becoming literate meant that treasured ways of being with adults, peers, toys, and texts were regularly and relentlessly moved aside. Especially in first grade, his ability to relate to adults and peers through texts and to relate to texts as full of meaning and opportunity were constantly impinged upon on by the demands of a hurried curriculum interpreted by a teacher who had no use for the ways playfulness is essential to the creation of meaning.

In her belief that only a phonetic approach would enable him to read, Nick's teacher ignored the important role of creative play in reading. In contrast, Shaywitz (2003) has shown that language-processing difficulties can be bypassed if the child can recruit visual-spatial pathways that are more stimulated by novelty than routine (Goldberg & Costa, 1981; Kandel, 2012). This is done by giving preference to insight and pleasure-based ways of processing information rather than linguistic pathways based on a precon-structed hierarchy of rules, such as is found in phonics-based approaches to reading. Many children can make effective use of an approach to learning that depends upon the imposition of rules that allow routines to become automatic. However, a more playful approach to learning creates increased arousal which activates unconscious, pleasure-based pathways and helps the child bypass the routine-based pathways that can create such problems for children like Nick (Kandel, 2012).

Nick was one of many children whose neurological processing did not allow him to make effective use of decontextualized strategies for reading such as parsing phonetics. This is particularly problematic in an environment that demands early reading. These children need time to develop enough experience with the world and with language use to be able to interpret the intentions and patterns of the text's language. This allows them to make highly effective use of word prediction in the context of that text. These children have the potential to become effective and efficient readers, if they are given enough time in an environment that does not quash their ability to tolerate the delay in reading development. For such children, it is critical to engage reading approaches that draw heavily on the evocation of contextual cues and event-based associations. The increased arousal of playing makes this more likely to succeed.

Vygotsky (1978) reminds us that all higher psychological functions origi-nate in social interaction. In learning to read, the child is forming a relation-ship first to parents and teachers, who in turn mediate the texts they encoun-ter together—in the process, sharing feelings, affects, ideas, and attributed meanings. While working to decode texts, the child experiences relationships to others and to texts that evoke mental and emotional expectations of both pleasure and pain and a sense of success and failure. These new experiences meet the child's existing implicit and explicit understandings of self and other and the child continuously creates and recreates an emergent self—a reading-self or a text-playing-self—that may confirm, modify, or dramatical-ly challenge his or her already existing sense of selfhood.

Nick's early image of himself as a reading self was deeply grounded in pleasurable relationships with his family, friends, and preschool and kinder-garten teacher. By age six, Nick's expectation of pleasure in reading was disappointed by his interactions with his teacher. Reading itself began to signal that an unpleasant experience was unfolding. Nick and his teacher were co-constructing an expectation that the procedure of interacting with a text was going to evoke a sense of failure and that the teacher would disapprove of him. What he was now learning was that he could not exert control over actions that would allow him to achieve an outcome he wanted. In psychoanalytic language, we could argue that Nick's internal play space was broken up—his creative and socially adaptive uses of reading could no longer mesh (Fonagy & Target, 1996; Meares, 1993). Lacking internal consistency, his behavior appeared alternately too stubborn, too flighty, or too disorganized, and was considered by his teacher to be "resistance to reading." But viewed from the perspective of his conditioned expectations, his responses could be considered a disorganized attachment to a fear-inducing text and teacher, and be seen as efforts to adapt to and cope with a genuine problem.

It is critical in working with children who have developed a resistance to reading that we not simply repeat the same kinds of interactions and procedures that caused the child to feel like a failure in the first place. Rather, what is required is a perspective that honors the child's integrity as a person able to make his or her own demands to be recognized and respected, already in possession of many strengths and resources, and capable of choosing to learn, grow, and change for his or her own purposes. Nick needed a reparative relationship to help him reintegrate the creative and supportive, intersubjective approach to reading that had worked for him prior to first grade. It was critical that this relationship would involve pivotal encounters with an instructor that would reshape his experience of reading in the presence of another to more closely resemble the original, playful context that allowed him to succeed and that would also allow him to tolerate the more task-oriented demands of reading skill development. These kinds of relational encounters are precisely the sort of social events that generate the procedural knowledge of how to be with another person, which the Boston Change Process Study Group (2010) calls intersubjective "moments of meeting." Nick had the opportunity for such restructuring moments of meeting when Nick's mother brought in a tutor, Nita, a PhD student in literacy education with a strong background in early reading development, to work with Nick at home. In what follows, we will describe how Nita created a field of play that mediated Nick's experiences of humiliation and failure and altered his sense of himself and reading sufficiently that he was able once again to re-engage both the play and the hard work of learning to read.

CREATING A FIELD OF PLAY

Nick began his tutoring with Nita at the beginning of second grade (age seven). In the first tutoring sessions, Nita spent time talking with Nick about his interests, looking at the toys and the books in his room, asking him about popular culture, and watching him interact with his family and pet. She asked him what he would like to read or learn and based on her understanding of his interests, she brought fiction and non-fiction books, magazines, poems, and materials from the Internet as possible material for their reading together. Through the next several sessions, she allowed him to browse through the materials. Nita offered no comment when Nick began and quickly abandoned a number of texts. She read to him during each session and did not force him to read to her when he proved resistant. By offering him choices based on his interests, in a low-pressure environment, Nita hoped to achieve the goal of engaging his willingness to work with her on reading.

Even with her careful approach, Nick's initial tolerance and/or willingness for the work was very slight. He made resistance into an art-form. He squirmed and scratched and played with small objects. He went to the bathroom several times each hour, went for water and snacks that he subsequently spilled and had to clean up. He dropped pencils, books, and toys, blew his nose, and frequently asked what time it was and when tutoring would be over. He noticed things outside the window and leapt to answer the ringing telephone or remembered a note in his backpack that demanded his mother's attention. He hummed and sang and got up to demonstrate impromptu dance moves. He bounced a ball that careened off the table, chased his dog when she retrieved the ball and then discovered that the dog needed to be fed. In a particularly memorable moment, he got a Koosh toy stuck in his dental retainer, and extracting it without damaging the retainer took up a good portion of the session. When pushed to work, Nick splayed out on the floor or across the table, yawning, groaning, and sighing loudly. He complained constantly. "I can't. I'm tired. I don't feel good."

While Nick's resistances to working on reading were usually expressed indirectly, he also offered more direct expressions of anger about being forced to confront reading in Nita's twice-weekly presence. He often complained vociferously to his mother before his sessions. He used jokes to test Nita's willingness to tolerate his anger. At one point he began calling her his "toot-er." "Toot-er? Do you get it? That means you fart!" he explained to her gleefully. On another occasion, he took up her invitation to write about his love of skateboarding by drawing a picture of her splayed on the ground, blood spurting, as he stood on top of her with his skateboard.

Nita saw Nick's resistance not as a sign that he would not work, but rather as a sign that he was trying to find a way that would allow him to cooperate without being overwhelmed once again by humiliation. Nita responded to all forms of Nick's resistance and anger with a stance of active and deliberate patience, refusing to become punitive and taking the position that her job was to learn from him how best to work with him. She spoke empathetically with him about how angry she felt on his behalf about how hard reading was for him. She accepted his skateboard drawing, saying that she imagined that sometimes he must feel that way about having to read with her. Importantly, many of the things that Nita might have interpreted as resistance she instead understood as an effort on Nick's part to take what she was offering and make it usable. When, in response to a book they were reading about shapes, Nick spontaneously lay on the floor to match his body to the illustrations, she praised him for his involvement and initiative, later suggesting that Nick was modifying her ideas for how they might read together in order to make the work his own.

Over the course of six months, Nita offered dozens of possibilities for ways that Nick might engage literacy. When she realized that Nick's anxiety about reading meant that he was having difficulty calming down long enough to delve into the work, she made movement a part of reading. When Nita suggested they incorporate singing, movement, and readers' theater, he became excited about the idea of using the tape recorder or video camera to prepare and record performances. He wandered around the neighborhood with her camera, photographing things he might like to write about.

Nita made it clear to him that she was following his lead as he identified the books, topics, and activities that he wanted to pursue. She interacted with him playfully, laughing at his jokes and complimenting his expertise with "burp speech." She brought books that involved puzzles, codes, riddles, and games. When he mastered some joke or solved some mystery, she sat back while he raced around the house showing his work to anyone who might be around. She observed his responses in order to understand which modes of working together were acceptable to him. She gave him space to muck around, asserting her unshakable confidence that Nick could find a way to use literacy for his own purposes, but not being overly anxious about what that path would be.

Nita allowed Nick to abandon pathways, to hide in the facade of detachment, and she let him identify the things for which he wanted public acknowledgement. As Nita calmly affirmed her acceptance of his anger, resistance, and playfulness, reassuring him repeatedly that he was in safe territory, Nick's ability to tolerate reading increased. He was better able to concentrate and needed fewer breaks. He accepted Nita's guidance more easily; he was less anxious and slower to experience frustration and negativity. His somatic complaints largely disappeared. He overcame his automatic aversion to books. He began to look forward to his tutoring session and to speak of his love for Nita. Eventually, Nick began to reidentify with the pleasures and playfulness of reading. Perhaps this was most obvious when he started to take a copy of Calvin and Hobbes (Watterson, 1988) and a flashlight to bed with him for nights when he had trouble sleeping. The source of torment had become the source of comfort.

MOMENTS OF MEETING

Although psychoanalytic literature on "what heals" in the clinical setting provides many ways of thinking about how Nita's work with Nick effected a strong and positive change in his relation to reading, we have chosen to analyze it both through her use of play and pleasure, and through the Boston Change Process Study Group's (2010) concept, "moments of meeting." In a psychoanalytic clinical relationship, "moments of meeting" are events in the session that rearrange knowledge of usually implicit or procedural aspects of being in a relationship for patient and analyst alike. In other words, these moments grow out of an unfolding understanding of each participant's intentions, so that how to be with one another shifts, and in turn, alters the patient's experience of his or her emotional state and of the relational context. Considering Nita's work with Nick through the lens of "moments of meeting" suggests several insights into how a teacher, tutor, parent, or therapist might recreate with the child a field of playing with texts in which both the modes of social adaptation and creative fantasy described by Winnicott (1971b), Meares (1993), and Fonagy and Target (1996), can coexist and eventually unite to scaffold the child's growing competence in the world of reading.

One important moment of meeting occurred as Nita's stance of patient acceptance brought out what was for Nick a more authentic set of behaviors in relation to reading. Nick had experienced misattunement through his first grade teacher's expectation that reading was to be accomplished only in the ways that she already recognized and sanctioned. She did not understand her job as requiring her to learn from Nick how to support him as he actively constructed a set of practices and understandings that would allow him to be a reader. Rather, she believed that if Nick would just do what she instructed, he would learn what he needed. For her, his failure to learn became evidence that he had a bad attitude, that he was willful or uncooperative. For example, while his teacher believed that reading was to be accomplished seated passively in a chair, Nick's response to reading involved almost constant motion, which she couldn't tolerate. Nick complained that she would not allow him to stand by the side of his desk as he read or to whisper or talk out loud to himself as he worked through a text, a set of restrictions that Nick said made it impossible for him to read. She had no sense that Nick brought any implicit self-knowledge of his own ways of learning to the engagement with reading.

Nick's experience with Nita in tutoring stood in stark contrast to this. For Nita, who took the time to observe Nick carefully, the dominance of Nick's motion created a change in her understanding. She saw Nick's need to move and she incorporated this in an approach that actively encouraged him to move. As the sequence of emergent knowledge of, and ability to predict, each other's intentions in their partnered endeavor unfolded, Nick slowly became more excited by the possibilities of discovery—thus altering his expectation of what reading could entail other than phoneme detection. This allowed Nick to recruit formerly useful strategies for meaning making, specifically imitation, which is the earliest form of symbolization. He lay on the floor and made bodily shapes that matched the illustrations. As their confidence in one another's ability to dance together grew, Nita continued to give Nick the lead, and increasingly refined her strategies based on his input about what worked for him.

Another important moment of meeting was facilitated by Nita but occurred between Nick and the texts themselves. Initially in the tutoring, Nick displayed signs of physical distress even at the request that he open a book. It appeared that he was in the grip of shame and anger, which Tompkins (1991) described as a painful disruption in the relationship with a person, thing, or even idea toward whom/which we had at one time felt love or enthusiasm and hoped for the same in return. The rebuffed love produces, according to Tompkins, feelings of intense shame that we experience physically—the break in eye contact, dropped head, burning cheeks, constricted chest, and pit in the stomach—that often then translate into anger and rejection of anything that reminds us of the humiliation. This is a form of object loss, in which Nick experienced the loss of texts as sources of companionship and fun. Nick would comply with the request that he choose a book. He would then glance at the first page of the book, say that he could not read it, and almost immediately push the book away. When confronted with a demand that he read, emotional flooding occurred which interfered with Nick's cognitive functioning. He drew himself in, defending against the reactivated feelings of loss and humiliation. His affect, his physical movement, his speech and his cognitive capacities were all immediately constricted; he could not, in fact, read in those moments.

However, using texts as part of his play with Nita, Nick came to experience text increasingly as something with which he could have a positive relationship. This matched his earlier experiences of text as a source of pleasure, for instance, pleasure felt during his nightly bedtime reading with his parents. It wasn't simply the emotional warmth, comfort, and nurturing he shared with his parents in the low-stress experience of being tucked in and read to. He and his parents shared a love of fantasy and adventure books and they shared a sense of excitement over what was happening in the stories, wondering what would happen next to Bilbo Baggins or what Nick would do if he went through a wardrobe to Narnia or had to fight a dragon or pirate. As Nick came to be able to tolerate and overcome the shame of reading in Nita's presence, he was increasingly able to work with her on developing the skills that gave him greater independence with text, and thus he could begin once again—as he had in preschool—to derive pleasures and comforts from texts themselves, this time with the added ability to enjoy not just the illustrations and remembered cadences of the text, but also able to read the text on his own. The internalization of this pattern of more gratifying "moments of meeting" with texts, mediated through Nita and his parents, could be seen in his choice to use independent reading of *Calvin and Hobbes* (Watterson, 1988) comics collections as a way to soothe himself to sleep. In fact, this pattern of using texts as a form of self-soothing has continued to the present day, as Nick acquired an IPod and began the habit of listening to a handful of beloved books to lull himself to sleep nightly. This pleasure in listening to the same familiar books over and over enhanced his fluency as an independent reader, as the books he listened to became books that he was able to read and that he enjoyed reading.

A final example of a moment of meeting occurred when Nita's experience of reading as pleasurable was modified by Nick's sense of humiliation and rage toward reading. Breaking away from the common literacy education perspective that learning to read is natural and fun, Nita began to experience that for Nick, reading was an intrusive demand that caused him frustration and fear. She began to voice this for Nick, creating a "holding environment" (Winnicott, 1960) in which she gave expression and meaning to Nick's difficult and frightening feelings. Her calm acceptance of these difficult emotions prompted the reshaping of Nick's crucial understandings about the nature of this important reading relationship. He was able to recover the experiences he had had in preschool, in which reading happened in relationships that were warm, loving, and supportive. This in turn allowed for the reorganization of other mental actions and behaviors, reflected in Nick's growing ability to regulate his emotional and physical responses to reading, to remain alert, focused and responsive, and to manage and repair disruptions.

During the six months that Nita worked with Nick, she created an environment that could contain Nick's humiliated rage toward the demand that he learn to read and that he read in prescribed ways. As a result of their mutual improvisation, the socially adaptive lessons in reading became suffused with the creativity of intersubjectivity, and a more integrated self emerged—a self that combined adaptation to reading conventions with meaningful play and fantasy. Nick's relationship with some texts and some people who presented him with opportunities and demands for reading were no longer persecutory but sought after. Nick developed a sense of his own efficacy as a reader and often fought to control how reading functioned in his life. When in fifth grade he had a teacher who refused his assertion that his then-favorite texts—English translations of Japanese graphic novels (*manga*)—were appropriate for school reading, Nick not only smuggled the books into school for his own moments of secret reading, but he also spread his love of *manga* and established his peer identity as a reader by starting an underground lending library with his classmates. Nick persisted in his insistence that manga was worthwhile reading and he eventually convinced his teacher to relent in her position. He had become a powerful player in the fields of both intersubjectivity and texuality.

CONCLUSION

American teachers are burdened with the impossible task of producing children who are all able to reliably give, on-demand, a narrow and rigidly defined demonstration of reading capacity. Teachers are expected to achieve this in an anxious educational era in which play has all but disappeared from early learning environments, replaced by a uniform curriculum in which children are understood as passive recipients of someone else's meanings. Learning to read has become a serious business indeed.

Many teachers and children find ways to accommodate and play with these demands (Dyson, 2003; Kontovourki & Siegel, 2009) and most children learn to read in the time and ways demanded. For those who do not, it is critical that teachers are provided opportunities to understand and enact learning to read as something that is not exclusively a matter of the child's individual capabilities, volition, or even neuropsychological make-up. Learning to read is an intersubjective act. Teachers, parents, communities, texts, and political and social expectations and expediencies all make up the field in which a child has to negotiate the demand that she or he learn to read. When reading does not come easily, when the demands of adults or school are experienced as moments of frightening or humiliating misattunement, many children do the only thing they can do—they defend themselves against reading. Unfortunately, with little support for engaging resistances in constructive and empathetic ways, teachers' efforts to help these children through the introduction of ever more rigid and arid reading interventions often make matters worse.

The work of teachers and of psychoanalysts is not the same, and yet there are points of important overlap. Psychoanalysts and psychologists are interested in the ways that arousal functions in learning, self-regulation, and intersubjective relationships. Educators have known at least since the time of Dewey (1938/1997) that what excites us enough to be retained is experience. It would be an injustice to many teachers to imagine that they do not believe in the importance of loving and empathic relationships with children and of playful, experience-based curricula. Teachers nationwide are demonized by politicians who cynically use education as a wedge to appeal to ideologically driven voters and by those who embrace the neo-liberal drive to privatize education (Salvio & Boldt, 2009; Boldt & Ayers, 2012). Many teachers despair at the loss of professional control that means that they are often unable to interact with children and teach in ways that they know are humane and stimulating of children's self-efficacy and creativity (Salvio, 2004). As long as teachers are driven by the demands of a hurried and politicized curriculum to see their relationships with students as mainly implicit and embedded in the interplay of classroom culture, they are forced to ignore the ways that children's experiences of the teacher, classmates, and curriculum are mediated through physically and emotionally embodied experiences of success, love, approval, and recognition or of failure, rejection, reprisal, and misrecognition. When required to measure only the individual student's developing competence with texts in narrowly defined ways, teachers lose the possibilities for those important moments of meeting that come along with utilizing more socially mediated interactions for fostering experience-based excitement in learning.

Recognizing these limitations, we present this account of learning to read as a complex undertaking that unfolds in idiosyncratic ways in intersubjective relationships. We hope that this work will contribute to the knowledge and determination of teachers who are working to achieve attunement with their struggling students. We hope that it will give psychoanalysts and other clinicians a clearer picture of some of the issues and needs of children who are struggling under the weight of politicized educational systems in which literacy carries an exaggerated level of burden and blame for social inequities (Smith, 1989). Finally, we hope we have demonstrated our support for those teachers who are fighting to maintain classroom space as a field of play among teachers, students, and texts—a field rich with feelings, affects, ideas, and attributed meanings—in which those vital "moments of meeting" can develop.

NOTE

1. Nick is Gail's son. For a discussion of the ethical, professional, and personal issues this raises, see Boldt, 2006.

REFERENCES

Boldt, G. (2006). Resistance, loss, and love in learning to read: A psychoanalytic inquiry. *Research in the Teaching of English, 40*, 3, 272–309.

Boldt, G. (2009). Kyle and the basilisk: Understanding children's writing as play. *Language Arts, 87*, 1, 9–17.

Boldt, G., & Ayers, W. (Eds.). (2012). Challenging the politics of teacher accountability: Toward a more hopeful educational future. *Bank Street Occasional Papers, 27*. New York: Bank Street College.

Boston Change Process Study Group. (2010). *Change in psychotherapy: A unifying paradigm* New York: W. W. Norton.

Britton, J. 1970. *Language and learning.* Miami, FL: University of Miami Press.

Chethik, M. (2000). *Techniques of child therapy: Psychodynamic strategies.* New York: Guilford Press.

Dewey, J. (1997 [1938]). *Experience and education* (1st Touchstone ed.). New York: Simon & Schuster.

Doake, D. (1985). Early reading-like behavior: Its role in learning to read. In A. Jaggar (Ed.), *Observing the Language Learner*. Newark, DE: International Reading Association.

Donald, M. (1991). *Origins of the modern mind: Three stages in the evolution of culture and cognition*. Cambridge, MA: Harvard University Press.

Dyson, A. H. (2003). *The brothers and sisters learn to write: Popular literacies in childhood and school cultures*. New York: Teachers College Press.

Eastman, P. D. (1966). *Go, Dog, Go!* New York: Random House Books for Young Readers.

Fonagy, P. (2001). *Attachment theory and psychoanalysis*. New York: Other Press.

Fonagy, P., & Target, M. (1996). Playing with reality: I. Theory of mind and the normal development of psychic reality. *International Journal of Psycho-Analysis, 77*, 217–33.

Goldberg, E., & Costa, L. D. (1981). Hemisphere differences in the acquisition and use of descriptive systems. *Brain and Language, 14*, 144–73.

Green, A. (1993). Analytic play and its relationship to the object. In D. Goldman (Ed.). *In one's bones: The clinical genius of Winnicott*. Northvale, NJ: Jason Aronson.

Hesse, E., & Main, M. (2000). Disorganized infant, child, and adult attachment: Collapse in behavioral and attentional strategies. *Journal of the American Psychoanalytic Association, 48*, 1097–1127.

Kandel, E. (2012). *The age of insight: The quest to understand the unconscious in art, mind, and brain*. New York: Random House.

Kontovourki, S., & Siegel, M. (2009). Discipline and play with/in a mandated literacy curriculum. *Language Arts, 87*, 1, 30–38.

Lakoff, G., & Johnson, M. (1999). *Philosophy in the flesh: The embodied mind and its challenge to Western thought*. New York: Basic Books.

Lyons-Ruth, K. (1999). The two-person unconscious: Intersubjective dialogue, enactive relational representation, and the emergence of new forms of relational organization. *Psychoanalytic Inquiry, 19*, 4, 576–617.

Lyons-Ruth, K., Melnick, S., Bronfman, E., Sherry, S., & Llanas, L. (2003). Hostile-helpless relational models and disorganized attachment patterns between parents and their young children: Review of research and implications for clinical work. In L. Atkinson & K. Zucker (Eds). Attachment issues in psychopathology and intervention (pp. 65–94). Mahwah, NJ: Lawrence.

Meares, R. (1993). *The metaphor of play: Disruption and restoration in the borderline experience*. Lanham, MD: Jason Aronson.

Nelson, K. (1996). *Language in cognitive development: The emergence of the mediated mind*. New York: Cambridge University Press.

O'Loughlin, M., & Merchant, A. (2012). Working obliquely with children. *Journal of Infant, Child, and Adolescent Psychotherapy, 11*, 149–59.

Piaget, J. (1959). *The language and thought of the child*. London: Routledge & Kegan Paul.

Pivnick, B. A. (1998). Wriggles, squiggles, and words: From expression to meaning in early childhood and psychotherapy. In A. Robbins (Ed.), *Therapeutic presence: Bridging expression and form* (pp. 39–83). London: Jessica Kingsley.

Pivnick, B. A. (2010). Left without a word: Learning rhythms, rhymes and reasons in adoption. *Psychoanalytic Inquiry, 30*, 1, 3–24.

Reich, W. (1990 [1972]). *Character analysis* (3rd edition). New York: Noonday Press.

Salvio, P. (2004). A dangerous lucid hour: Compliance, alienation and the restructuring of the New York City schools. In W. Ross and K. Kesson (Eds.), *Defending public schools* (pp. 242–55). Santa Barbara: Praeger Press.

Salvio, P., & Boldt, G. (2009). "A democracy tempered by the rate of exchange": Audit culture and the sell-out of the progressive writing curriculum. *English in Education, 43*, 2, 113–28.

Shaywitz, S. (2003). *Overcoming dyslexia*. New York: Knopf.

Smith, F. (1989). Overselling literacy. *Phi Delta Kappan, 70*, 353–59.

Solomon, J., George, C., & DeJong, A. (1995). Children classified as controlling at age six: Evidence of disorganized representational strategies and aggression at home and at school. *Development and Psychopathology, 7*, 447–63.

Spangler, G., & Grossman, K. (1993). Biobehavioral organization in securely and insecurely attached infants. *Child Development, 64,* 1439–50.

Tomasello, M. (2003). *Constructing a language: A usage-based theory of language acquisition.* Cambridge, MA: Harvard University Press.

Tompkins, S. (1991). *Affect, imagery, consciousness (Vol. 3): The negative affects: Anger and Fear.* New York: Springer.

Vygotsky, L. (1978). *Mind in society: The development of higher psychological processes.* Cambridge, MA: Harvard University Press.

Watterson, B. (1988). *The essential Calvin and Hobbes.* Kansas City, MO: Andrews McNeel Publishing.

Winnicott, D. W. (1960). The theory of the parent-child relationship. *International Journal of Psychoanalysis, 41,* 585–95.

Winnicott, D. W. (1971a). *Therapeutic consultations in child psychiatry.* New York: Basic Books.

Winnicott, D. W. (1971b). *Playing and reality.* New York: Basic Books.

Chapter Thirteen

"Why Do They Hate Learning French?"

Thoughts on Shifting Subjectivities and Psychical Resistances in the Language Classroom

Colette A. Granger

A lot goes on in today's language classroom. In addition to traditional vocabulary quizzes, memorization exercises, dictations, reading and recitation, there may be video and film, skits, collaborative projects, role-plays, and music. Usually there is plenty of talk. But along with that talk there may also be silence; achievement can be accompanied by disappointment; activity and enthusiasm sometimes turn into resistance. Things do not always go smoothly in any classroom, but disruptions in the language learning context seem at times to have particular qualities about which a psychoanalytic perspective might have something useful to say. In this chapter I use several textual "snapshots" from language classrooms, and several key concepts from psychoanalytic theory, as "objects-to-think-with" (Turkle, 2004, p. 24) about some of the moments in language learning settings when what is supposed to be happening isn't happening, when what is being learned is not what the curriculum demands, and when the "work" being done is not what the teacher has assigned. Here is the first snapshot.

> In an elementary school in a small city not far from Toronto, Canada, a veteran French teacher enters the staffroom following her first meeting with a new Grade 7 "core"[1] French class, and announces to her colleagues: "It's exactly the same every year. The first questions they ask me are, 'How do you say *seal* in French?' And 'How do you say *push*?' If I tell them they can't stop laughing. And whether I tell them or not, they keep asking. They don't care about anything they've learned other than those two words. Why do they hate learning French?"

It seems that the words *phoque* (pronounced /fɔk/) and *pousser* (/puse/) sound enough like the English profanities "fuck" and "pussy" that merely hearing a teacher say them incites twelve-year-olds to uproarious laughter— never mind the opportunities for repetition! This oft-repeated question and the students' reaction to its answer, along with the staffroom complaint of their teacher, mark the moment where my psychoanalytic thinking begins. But first, here is a brief summary of some of the numerous potentially useful explanations offered by applied linguistics and sociolinguistics for moments when students' goals do not seem to coincide with those of their teacher or of the curriculum.

WHY? FACTORS AFFECTING LANGUAGE LEARNING

In applied linguistics the critical period hypothesis refers to a developmental window outside which the second-language (L2) learner "is no longer capable of attaining to native-like levels of proficiency; needs to expend more conscious effort than in earlier L2 acquisition; and/or makes use of different mechanisms from those deployed in L2 acquisition during childhood" (Singleton & Muñoz, 2011, p. 409). Consensus is not universal regarding when this period ends, but it does seem that learning a language becomes more difficult with age: while some linguists take the view that a later start can produce highly fluent speakers (Bongaerts, Mennen, & Van der Slik, 2000; Singleton & Lésniewska, 2009), others argue that puberty may mark the end of the capacity to acquire perfect native-level proficiency (Hyltenstam & Abrahamsson, 2003; Long, 2007). Both views connect successful learning among older individuals, whatever the eventual level of competency, with substantial deliberate effort.

The observation that learning becomes increasingly deliberate with age applies not just to the L2 classroom but to all cognitive domains (see, for example, Feldman, 2009). Nevertheless, a shift in the ease of learning could account for at least some degree of lost or diminished interest. Age is not the only factor, however, in an individual's relationship with language learning. It is one piece in a complex puzzle that includes both external and internal influences, ranging from culture, gender, and socioeconomic status to learning styles and strategies, memory and brain hemisphere specialization, extroversion, self-esteem, anxiety, and the ability to tolerate ambiguity (Brown, 1994; Ellis, 1996; García, 2009; Granger, 2004; Larsen-Freeman & Long, 1991; Tannen & Saville-Troike, 1985). All of the elements that contribute to a learner's makeup are bound to affect that learner's motivation and attitude toward language (and indeed any) learning. Moreover, these factors may shift for particular learners over time and in different contexts. For example, a primary teacher contrasts her reluctance to speak aloud in her second language as a university student—"I intentionally skipped my first-year oral French exam and voluntarily surrendered 15 percent of my final grade"— with her delight at doing so as a teacher: "One of the things I enjoy most about teaching is that I can do all the things in front of children that my judgmental self will not do in front of adults, such as sing, dance, and speak French."

Attitude and motivation, and of course success, can also be affected by the type and structure of the program and the pedagogical and instructional methods used. For example, significant rates of attrition in immersion programs (Quiring, 2008) can give rise to concerns about whether full proficiency can be achieved by all learners in either the target language[2] or other subject areas. More generally, Duff (2007, p. 149) observes that in Canada "the implementation and outcomes of . . . government policies [around bilingualism and multiculturalism] nationally are less impressive than the rhetoric would suggest." And from the teaching side of things, some researchers have noted that questions persist regarding "how immersion and content can be seamlessly integrated in both the larger curriculum and in daily lessons" (Song & Cheng, 2011, p. 99). Even in core programs, where the target language is itself the focus, a curriculum imposed from above and delivered via prepackaged materials can be practical from an institutional point of view but may not hold the attention of all students equally. In the preservice teacher education program in which I work, adult students recalling their experiences learning a second language frequently comment that it simply grew boring after a time. Remarks one, "I'll never forget how to order a pizza in French—we learned that three years in a row. So dull."

WHY NOW? RESISTING LEARNING IN ADOLESCENCE

If learners are bored, teaching becomes difficult. And certainly there are some aspects of learning language in a classroom that, while necessary, are less than exciting. So perhaps we should not be surprised that students sometimes resist language learning. But in trying to understand this particular moment of resistance, in which students insist on "making" the teacher pronounce obscene sounding words, psychoanalysis may have something to offer.

Crucial here are two reminders: first, that using psychoanalytic theory as a hermeneutic aims not for "the *application* of psychoanalysis to pedagogy" but toward "the *implication* of psychoanalysis in pedagogy and of pedagogy in psychoanalysis" (Felman, 1982, pp. 26–27; italics in original); second, that the psychoanalytic project looks at what is going on *inside* the individual psyche, and at goings-on between individual psyches in relation with other psyches, as well as with the entire social realm *outside* the self. These questions persist even when all is well, but are especially insistent when it is not. It is in this spirit that I use psychoanalytic concepts as tools for meaning-making or objects to think with: first, about the apparent devotion of the grade 7 pupils to particular words in translation. I have told this story at numerous meetings with language educators and in teacher education courses on communication, pedagogy, and adolescent development. Whenever French teachers—or former students of French—are present, it resonates with familiarity. In the inevitable sea of nodding heads and the chorus of "Yes, it was grade 7!" and "I remember that" and "So true!" (and notwithstanding the equally inevitable protestation: "Not everyone hates French"), I read a reaffirmation of the multi-pronged clue the story offers—the age of the students; the focus on *seal* and *push* and the profane/sexual connotations of their translations; and finally, the word *hate* in the teacher's question. Let us leave this last element for later, and consider first what psychoanalytic theory suggests about the form and the timing of this act of resistance to the teacher's official lesson.

Grade 7 students typically range in age between eleven and thirteen, when puberty and adolescence are imminent or underway; the observation that native-like fluency becomes difficult during roughly this same period (Hyltenstam & Abrahamsson, 2003) seems more than coincidental. Psychoanalysis posits two fundamental tasks of adolescence, both crucial for healthy identity[3] development: sexual maturation, and separation from the family. In explicitly psychoanalytic terms, the goal, facilitated by the revival of previously latent libidinal and oedipal dynamics, is "to keep childhood love objects—parental and sibling love objects—at a distance or to break ties with them" so as to avoid the psychical threats posed by "reawakened pregenital urges, or—worse still—the newly acquired genital ones" (Young-Bruehl, 1996, p. 306). One path toward this goal lies in forming or joining groups, another in the frequent, sudden changes in attitude, interests, routines, emotions, modes of dress, and interaction that are so familiar to adults who work with adolescents, or who remember their own adolescence. Both are grounded, asserts Young-Bruehl, in a renewed upswing of formerly repressed urges and fantasies. Such urges trouble the psyche, especially the superego, which works to transform them from childhood's polymorphous eroticism to the adult's genitally focused and regulated sexuality. One defense mechanism used to mitigate against these troubles is projection: an "operation whereby qualities, feelings, wishes . . . which the subject refuses to recognize or rejects in himself, are . . . located in another person or thing" (Laplanche & Pontalis, 1973, p. 349). Young-Bruehl's discussion centers on prejudices as one specific form projections can take, but I suggest that the curse-words-in-translation of our young friends in French class might also provide an outlet for impulses the superego deems inappropriate.

In the classroom these words are conjured up as an "innocent" question qua joke—can we not imagine the student's wide eyes and half-smile? Freud connects sexual jokes with "the desire to see what is sexual exposed" (1905, p. 98) and with the substitution of touching with looking, or speaking. Such jokes compel "the person who is assailed to imagine the part of the body or the procedure in question and show her that the assailant is himself imagining it" (p. 98), requiring, alongside the joke-maker, another person who is "the object of the hostile or sexual aggressiveness, and a third in whom the joke's aim of producing pleasure is fulfilled" (p. 100). Here the teacher and the language are the joke's objects. The claim to innocence of the words' translations is a ruse. Everyone knows this. Everyone also knows that the teacher is both authorized and obliged to provide the translations. Questions about *seal* and *push*, through which a student "makes" the teacher say "bad words," form a linguistic feint that projects onto that teacher—and onto her language—the young adolescent's renewed but unauthorized preoccupation with, and curiosity about, acts and body parts that remain off limits, both in the classroom and for the superego. Simply put, by putting words in the teacher's mouth the learner ostensibly keeps them out of his own.[4] And doing so disrupts both the lesson and the language.

Accompanying the adolescent's second task—a move away from identification with family and toward adult autonomy that makes "getting away *with* something" a purposeful (albeit unconscious) part of getting away *from* something—is the demand to determine his own values. This may require the partial or complete rejection, at least temporarily, of those he has learned through culture, family, or teachers. The importance of education generally may be one among these values; the importance of competence in more than one language may be another. What better way to turn on those values than by resisting education? And in the language learning context, what better tactic to turn on[5] the teacher, who represents those values, than by using "bad" language or making her use it? Here the insistence on translating words into their obscene-sounding French counterparts functions as a delaying tactic, a resistance to whatever the teacher is actually trying to teach.

Similar things do, of course, happen outside French class. My own recollection of searching the atlas with a geography classmate for places such as Brest, Bangkok, Intercourse (Pennsylvania), Come-by-Chance (Newfoundland), and, naturally, all peninsulas supports the view that sexually suggestive language is especially interesting to young adolescents. But my clandestine missions involved neither a second language nor any response from the teacher. The French students' question involves both, suggesting something about the language education setting as a useful domain for working through some of the tasks of adolescence. This is not the whole picture, however; resistance to language learning can happen in many ways and at multiple ages.

WHY HERE? RESISTING LEARNING IN LANGUAGE CLASS

Sometimes there are pragmatic reasons for resisting language learning. Perhaps students "don't see the point" and wonder, "Why bother?" A student in my adolescent development course, whose siblings' language education has had very mixed results, remarks: "If students do not see a reason for pursuing a second language then they will not have the passion or the drive to do so." This possibility is particularly germane vis-à-vis French language-learning in anglophone Canada. English is the dominant language within the nation overall and worldwide, and understandings of French as cultural capital (Bourdieu, 1991), or as the language of trade and diplomacy that opens professional doors, have lost much of their conviction as Mandarin and Spanish rise to global prominence. Perhaps as adolescents make decisions about secondary education and beyond, concern about achievement in other subjects may outweigh that related to language learning—for students, parents, or both. Too, some anglophone Canadian parents in particular may retain some of the resistance to French that followed the 1969 *Official Languages Act*, as demonstrated by this note from a father at that time:

> TO MISS KING FRENCH TEACHER. JACK DOES NOT WISH TO LEARN TO SPEAK FRENCH, AND I DONT [sic] WANT HIM TO HAVE DETENTION OR ANY KIND OF PUNISHMENT, FRENCH IS ONLY BEING TAUGHT TO PLEASE QUEBEC, IF THEY HAD MADE THEM SPEAK ENGLISH IN THE FIRST PLACE WE WOULD NOT HAVE A DEVIDED [sic] COUNTRY NOW, SO NO FRENCH FOR MY SON AND I MEAN IT. D. GOODMAN: FATHER[6]

Such sentiments are not limited to Canada nor to French. Here is a second snapshot, this one from a primary English immersion classroom in Madrid, Spain:

> The Spanish-English bilingual teaching assistant is instructed to speak only English, the rationale being that learners will develop English proficiency more rapidly that way. But after several months during which this ruse is successful, a seven-year-old overhears the assistant speaking Spanish to the regular teacher. His protest is taken up by a number of his classmates, who march around the classroom chanting: "*¡Injusticia! ¡Manifestación! ¡Queremos que nos habléis en español!*"—which roughly translates into English as: "It's unjust! We protest! We want you to speak Spanish to us!"

These indignant messages, separated by an ocean and several decades and articulated by individuals a generation apart, speak to an intersection between the political and the profoundly personal. For if the demand to learn a second language to "please" someone else is understood as a threat to cultural/political identity—a self divided as well as a nation—or if being denied the right to speak (or listen) in one's native language while others maintain that right is viewed as an injustice, even by seven-year-olds, perhaps more is going on in the language classroom than meets the eye. If, as Bruner points out, the making of a self—and thereby a life—"begins very early and is a strikingly systematic process that is deeply enmeshed with the mastery of language itself—not just its syntax and lexicon, but its rhetoric and its rules for constructing narrative" (1991, p. 73), might such demands sometimes be perceived as threats to that self and that life?

Making a self through language is not a straightforward process, not for psychoanalysis anyway. To consider its beginnings we must journey backward past the adolescent language classroom, past the first second-language lesson, all the way back to the world of the infant for whom, in Freud's conceptualization, birth "is not experienced subjectively as a separation from the mother, since the foetus . . . is totally unaware of her [mother's, or her own] existence as an object" (Freud, 1949, p. 95). Birth marks the beginning of a shift from imagined "omnipotence," in which the objects that meet the infant's needs are perceived as part of itself, to an object-relation in which the child is aware of something outside itself. Then comes the first judgment:

> Expressed in the language of the oldest—the oral—instinctual impulses, the judgement is: "I should like to eat this," or "I should like to spit it out"; and, put more generally: "I should like to take this into myself and to keep that out." That is to say: "It shall be inside me" or "It shall be outside me" . . . (Freud, 1925, p. 237)

This moment of recognizing that inside and outside are separate is key both for the developing child and for psychoanalytic thinking as always in some measure a conversation about the inside, the outside, and the relations between them. That this is an *oral* judgment, however, connects it especially usefully with considerations of language acquisition. In physical terms the infant's mouth is an important source of nourishment and pleasure. It is not easy to accept that these are vulnerable to external factors: the absence of breast or caregiver; the intrusion of loud noises or chilly breezes. We might additionally understand language, which comes initially from outside the self, as comprising a disruption to that self. Phillips (1999) speaks of such disruptions as losses that paradoxically, even painfully, accompany the gains of maturation generally, and language acquisition in particular:

> At the time when [the child's] curiosity is becomingly increasingly sophisticated, . . . she has to give up what she can never in fact relinquish, her inarticulate self, the self before language. . . . The child at nursery school is at that age when he or she is making for the first, but not the last, time that fateful transition—that can never be complete, that can never be whole-hearted because the renunciation, the loss of the unspoken self is too great—to joining

the language group. . . . [W]hat exactly must be given up in order to speak? (pp. 42–43)

The Freudian baby, in separating from the mother, gains independence but loses omnipotence; Phillips's language learner accesses the world of speech but loses that earlier omnipotent state in which speaking was unnecessary. In a psychoanalytic framing these moments are connected. Difficult or traumatic experiences are never completely forgotten but rather remain in the unconscious in repressed and attenuated form, like marks on a "mystic writing pad" (Freud, 1924).[7] Losses inhering in the transition from "omnipotent" infant to individuated self may likewise persist as a kind of ghostly echo, or "memory-trace" (Freud, 1914), in the subsequent transition from pre-language to speaking self. And beyond: my claim is that second-language learning, with its demands for a kind of "translation" not just of a lexicon but of one's self, might reawaken those loss-echoes yet again. This is slightly complicated, because in the translation from a first-language to a second-language self the individual does not lose the first-language self in quite the same way that the pre-language self was lost in the earlier move into language as such. But, I maintain, subsequent translations might still recall and demand that the psyche re-experience something of the subjective experience of those earlier iterations, if not their precise qualities.

Further, since so much of who we are, and of how we communicate ourselves to the world (and the world to ourselves), is constructed, reconstructed, and performed through language (Bruner, 1991), at stake in language learning (first, second, or beyond) are our relationships with language, other people, and ourselves. Thus the second-language learner struggles not only with the echoes of his pre- or first-language self but also with his inability to represent himself fully in the new language, either to the world or to himself. This may be the biggest challenge for those acquiring a new language who cannot even recognize, much less articulate, the un-representable aspects of either the language acquisition process or the versions of the self that preceded and resulted from that process. As Ehrman and Dörnyei note, resistance to learning may come about partly because learning "requires rejection of one's own deficiency" (1998, p. 185). Specifically, accompanying the understanding that one needs not just language, but *another* language, is the inference that the old language (or the pre-language state) and the corresponding earlier version of the self are now insufficient. Might this learning echo that earlier realization of the self's separateness from its environment, and a related conclusion about the inadequacy of that self? And to return to the personal-political connection mentioned earlier, might a threat to social identity be experienced as flowing over into personal identity, such that the threat perceived as political is also personal or, more specifically, intra-personal?

While psychoanalysis offers hints about what might be going on in some individuals resisting language learning, it also recognizes the uniqueness of individuals and experiences. My own approach to thinking about the curious dynamics of resistance in these and other contexts (Granger, 2004, 2010, 2011) is equally tentative. Some of us acquire new languages easily; some work hard and eventually succeed. Others are unsuccessful despite all efforts; still others never try. Since for psychoanalysis the "unspeaking" self, by its nature, cannot be articulated, we cannot know for certain what the subjective experience of language acquisition (first or subsequent) is like for anyone, much less for everyone. Indeed, we do not have to look very far to find settings in which language learning appears to be experienced quite differently than the snapshots already presented suggest. I turn now to consider two such contexts.

WHO ELSE? ALLOPHONE AND MULTILINGUAL LEARNERS

In second-language learning settings in Canada, one challenge to the suggestion that language learning involves echoes of previous psychical losses comes via a category of students whose arrival at school constitutes a de facto immersion in the dominant language. These students are allophones; their first language is neither English nor French. They may be recent arrivals to Canada, either with their families or through international adoptions, or they may be children of new Canadians who are not fluent in either official language. Whatever their origins, their home language is not that of the school system. Significantly, the percentage of allophone students enrolled in French immersion is high relative to those of the population as a whole (CPF, 2010). It is important to recognize that these children effectively undergo a double immersion: they speak one language at home, experience mass media and community life in a second, and are schooled in a third. Significant numbers also attend "heritage language" classes on weekends.

Here are two additional snapshots. The first is from a French immersion class in a small city in Ontario. The class is made up of five- and six-year-olds, almost all allophones. The classroom functions with little friction, pupils succeed in all subject areas, and the teacher sees no resistance to the target language. Moreover, she tells me, the children are fascinated by one another's home languages. She recalls one afternoon when those at the "math centre" had finished their assigned tasks and began asking one another for translations, in those other languages, for the names of classroom objects:

> They were looking around, asking each other, "How do you say . . . light switch?" "What's the word for, um, computer?"—and they turned over their math papers and started showing each other how to write those words down! I told them, "If you've finished your math, you could get a book." They looked

so disappointed that I said, "Or, you could just keep on with what you're doing." At the end of the class I let them keep the papers they'd been writing on—they usually hand them in—and they were thrilled!

The next vignette is from a "core" French class in Zurich, Switzerland, where German is the native language of virtually all the students. The story is told by a Canadian student-teacher who is visiting the school to observe second-language classes because, she writes, "I have spent two full months teaching grade 9–12 French [in a Canadian teaching placement], trying to understand why after four years of instruction, 95 percent of those grade 9 students are unable to speak/understand a word of French."

> Yesterday was my first day observing in "secondary school." I sat through a French as a second-language lesson and was extremely impressed. This is the same course I was teaching back in Canada, except that these kids were engaged and motivated. No one was sleeping at their desk, or fiddling around with something non-related, or doodling, or talking to their friends, or on their cell phone. The teacher was speaking entirely in French. The kids were responding fully in French. From time to time, some German would be spoken to explain something. After the class, I told the teacher her grade 10s were very impressive, that my grade 10s back home could never follow a conversation like that in French. She looked at me, confused, and said, "These children are in grade 7." If you'd been there, you would have understood the shock I was in. "Secondary school" in Switzerland is grades 7–9, as I later learned. I asked the teacher how long they have been studying French in school. She replied . . . two years. (They start in grade 5, whereas in Canada students start in grade 4.) Later, I observed an English as a second-language class. The same thing. I left that day in awe of the students' ability to pick up languages. Why is it that in two countries where exposure to the French language is equal, Canadian students can't converse the way the Swiss kids can?

Clearly, the moments described in this chapter are just that, and grand claims would be inappropriate. Still, the dynamics in these last two vignettes, seemingly so different from those in the Toronto core French class notwithstanding their commonalities (geographical setting and target language in the Canadian primary class; student age and one of two target languages in the Swiss setting), invite questions. Are these two apparently keen groups of students the exception or the rule? What might make Swiss students, or Canadian allophones, more attentive language learners than Canadian anglophones? What other factors might contribute to their attitudes, behaviors, and progress? And, given the foregoing discussion, how might psychoanalysis explain these differences? For if, as the psychoanalytic story goes, our early experiences remain with us always, albeit as psychical echoes of their earlier iterations, how can we account for a category of learner for whom acquiring a(nother) new language does not seem to be difficult at all—or for whom difficulty appears not to be an issue? What are the differences between the learners who seem eager not only to learn the language on offer but also to become acquainted with one another's *other* languages?

We might begin to respond to these questions by recalling the explanations offered by socio- and applied linguistics in regard to motivation and socioeconomic factors; the Swiss German speakers arguably possess greater instrumental (utilitarian) motivation (Larsen-Freeman & Long, 1991) to learn English than the Canadian anglophones have to learn French. But that alone does not account for either the equally high enthusiasm and engagement of the Zurich French class, or the curiosity of the young Canadian allophones about their peers' home languages, though there integrative motivation—the wish "to identify with another linguistic group" (p. 173) might certainly contribute. An extensive sociolinguistic investigation of these and other factors such as curricula, language pedagogy, and institutional structures would offer other explanations. But that is not my mandate here. Rather, I turn again to the psychoanalytic notion of the pleasure-ego mentioned earlier in relation to the infant's developing awareness of itself as separate from the environment.

The story of loss and separation, inaugurated in early life in the form of a shift from an imagined omnipotent self, and perhaps re-experienced with the acquisition of language, is, for Freud, a story of wishes and their sublimation; of primal urges informing early unconscious mental processes that in turn "strive toward gaining pleasure . . . [and draw] back from any event which might arouse unpleasure" (Freud, 1911, p. 36). Eventually the reality principle and reality ego take over, and the ego's desire for what is useful in the longer term causes the id's urge for immediate pleasure to be given up "in order to gain along the new path an assured pleasure at a later time" (pp. 40–41).

In comparing the grade 7 core French students in Toronto, first with their English- and French-learning counterparts in Zurich, and second with the primary French-immersion class in Ontario, two features stand out. One is the normalization and naturalization of bi- and/or multilingualism per se in the larger social setting. On one hand Switzerland, located within a multilingual Europe, has itself four official languages, with English an unofficial fifth; on the other hand the largely allophone immersion class in Ontario is already developing in at least two other languages. Both groups contrast with the core French students, who are mostly monolingual anglophones and all of whom live in communities where French is used rarely, if ever. The second factor, partly overlapping the first, is the power, perceived or real, of the target language. As anglophones (or at least English-speaking bilinguals), the core French students are already in possession of a locally and globally dominant language, while the Swiss students of English are gaining it.

Here, then, is a set of moments that helps illustrate psychoanalytic theory's usefulness in understanding relations between the individual psyche and the social realm (the "inside" and the "outside") in connection with learning. Could it be that growing up in more than one language, or where multilingualism is normalized and even expected, or where the target language is seen as more socially and economically advantageous than the mother tongue, might somehow facilitate the psychical move away from the pleasure urge, expedite the reality principle's arrival, and solidify its influence despite those repressed memory-traces of early difficult separation experiences? We might understand this as an expedited fading of memory-traces over time. Yes, these ghostly echoes of early separations and psychical losses reawaken with each new demand to "translate" the self into a new language, but their influence diminishes so that we "get used to" these self-translations as the reality principle brings to the fore factors that are less worrisome and more reality-focused: success in learning a language, positive experiences to which that learned language has been put, and the cultural and social approval and even privilege attaching to possession of and facility with that language. Such a dynamic might be summed up, in reference to both the Swiss setting and the Canadian French immersion classroom—where bi- and multilingualism may be a stronger thread in the social fabric than in the core French classroom—as a result of the growing influence of the reality *principle*, perhaps enhanced by a stronger pro-multilingualism *reality* that is external to the learners yet internalized by them. Taken to its logical extreme this argument would imply that the older one gets the easier it ought to be to learn languages; that this is seldom if ever the case further reinforces the view that psychical, social, cognitive, and other factors must be considered together.

One of Freud's reasons for naming psychoanalysis an "impossible profession" (1937, p. 248) is its interminability. The foregoing discussion offers a reading of some of the dynamics that might be at play for some language learners in moments of resistance. But for psychoanalytic thinking—which for better or worse is bound more by word limits than by interpretive possibilities—that cannot be the end of it, in part because the learner is not the only party to the pedagogical relation. Let us turn now to consider the other one.

WHO ELSE (AGAIN)? THE TEACHER

Early on I promised to return to the question in the textual snapshot with which I began: "Why do they hate learning French?" As teachers themselves often say, *hate* is a strong word; its use is therefore worthy of note, even (or especially) when the emotion to which it refers is attributed to someone else. I would be remiss, therefore, not to examine it here, since however correct the teacher's assumption of her students' emotions may be, in the moment of speaking the word *hate* belongs to her. It is she who utters it in her complaint about the students' apparent lack of concern for her official lesson, raising the possibility that, something like the adolescent learner projecting his sexual curiosity onto the teacher and into her language, she might be projecting something of her affect onto her students. After all, there are other ways to interpret the translation request: we could surely understand the students' enjoyment of the words *phoque* and *pousser* as a play with language that in a sense is the very opposite of hate. So why does the teacher perceive it as she does?

While I do not assume that the teacher who uses the word necessarily hates her students, psychoanalysis might read the question as representing a complex set of moves in which the teacher's interpretation of the learner's question as hateful suggests that in that moment she herself may be experiencing something other than love—perhaps *from*, but also *for*, her students. Put differently, if someone's self-concept is threatened it may not only be that of the learner. Similarly, if there is hate involved, it may not be just the learner who hates, and it may not be just the language per se that is hated. The dynamic is a complex one, though, involving several twists and turns. If hate is being projected onto the learner, what is its true source, and what its true target? Who is hating whom—or what? And why?

Again I raise the caveat that my work here is not to "psychoanalyze" teachers either individually or as a group, but rather to consider the theory's implications for teaching, by using this question about hate as a jumping-off point for thinking about some aspects of educational interactions. Nevertheless, from a psychoanalytic standpoint the teacher in our little scenario might well be correct. Hate can be "a symptom of not being able to approach one's own vulnerability in relation to new objects, whether those objects are people, ideas or even old conflicts" (Matthews, 2007, p. 189). Or, I would add, new languages, along with the various threats to the learner's self that they might embody. So might a learner come to hate language as a learning-object that threatens his sense of himself, how he expresses that self to the world through language, and how he interprets the world to himself. Moreover, keeping in mind the age of the students demanding translation of the swear words, if adolescence is a time for giving up familial (or quasi-familial) love-objects and finding new ones, it might be that the teacher, a former parental stand-in who also represents education and adulthood, takes on new roles for learners moving into and through adolescence.

If, as Young-Bruehl suggests, adolescents are "on constant high alert to temptations issuing from their own desires and from their environments" (1996, p. 305), might a teacher function simultaneously as a useful collecting basket for the acknowledgment (subtle or otherwise) of those temptations and desires, an outlet for their expression (here in the resistance to language inhering, paradoxically, in a focus on taboo-sounding words), and a target for the displacement of familial and quasi-familial love-objects—including the teacher herself? Simply put, if adolescents are acquiring new love-objects, are they also acquiring new objects of hate? And might the language teacher somehow perceive her subject, and by extension herself as the teacher of that subject, as one such object?

Framed this way, the question behind "Why do they hate learning French?" might be, "Why do they hate the French I offer them?" or even, "Why do they hate me?" Hate and love are not necessarily opposites. But teachers speak of love far more often than hate in relation to their students. This is unsurprising if we recognize the common perception of the teacher as a quasi-maternal figure who protectively "watches over 'her' children in order to bring out their latent talents" (Miller, 1996, p. 100).[8] Given these perceptions of teachers and teaching, and recalling the adolescent's task of moving away from the familial dynamic and toward adult autonomy, we begin to sense a kind of double counter-resistance on the teacher's part: first to the learner's apparent insistence on changing the terms (metaphorically and literally) of the learning, second to challenges to her vision of herself as one who loves, but who never, ever hates. For that is simply not how things are supposed to go.

Yet if teaching-subjects (meant two ways: the subjects teachers teach, and the teachers themselves) can be hate-objects for students, the opposite is also possible. Drawing on Winnicott (1992), Matthews suggests some reasons why teachers might well hate students: among them, the student does not recognize the teacher's sacrifice, fails to value the teacher's knowledge (or values it differently), presents a danger to the teacher's authority, or becomes disillusioned (Matthews, 2007, p. 188). These reasons point to a second twist, this one a behind-the-question admission: "Sometimes I hate them." The admission cannot be uttered even silently, however, as that would cause an unhappy collision with the prevailing discourses of schooling, deeply internalized by the teacher, which tell us that it is "love which will win the day, and . . . the benevolent gaze of the teacher which will secure freedom" for the learner (Walkerdine, 1990, p. 19). In this conceptualization hate cannot be acknowledged, lest it threaten the teacher's vision of what teaching is or ought to be, and what she as a teacher is, or ought to be.

It is a commonplace to say that if we imagine that our work as teachers is precise or transparent or unchanging, a perfect translation of the life we (think we) remember having as a pupil, or of the life (we imagine) some once-beloved teacher had, we are sure to be disappointed. Taubman reckons that student-teachers' (and teachers') fantasies of teaching centered around "loving and sacrificing for the students" serve to defend against "very power-ful aggressive impulses" that we must take into account in order to mitigate against the psychical shock of finding out that sometimes, in fact, we hate our students (2006, p. 30). The teacher who is presumed never to hate may at times have a nagging unconscious suspicion that at least some of the hate in the pedagogical relation originates with her. She deflects these unwanted feelings by projecting them onto her students. In so doing she lightens some of the pressure of knowing, however unaware she might be of that knowing, that she is not what she has imagined herself to be, but something rather more human. In the present context, the process moving in reverse goes from "Sometimes I hate them" to "Why do they hate me?" to "Why do they hate French?"

Before leaving this discussion I look briefly at one more angle. In still another manifestation of the inside-outside dynamic mentioned earlier, which forms an important part of how psychoanalytic thinking can be used to understand how the social world meets the internal, psychical one, I am drawn to hints provided by two of the teachers I contacted while preparing this chapter. These hints gesture at the ways in which French teaching, and some French teachers, may themselves be marginalized within larger educational contexts, in ways that affect their own relationships with the language they are teaching and, in turn, the attitudes of their students. The first hint is in the story of the French immersion teacher whose class is discussed above. Born in Québec and fluent in French, she encounters resistance not in students but in colleagues, who tell her repeatedly that certain Québécois-French words and phrases are "wrong" and to substitute for these with continental French equivalents.[9] The other hint was passed on to me by one of my current teacher education students. She recalls that in her own elementary school experience French was typically understood as an "extra," such that if a class had to be missed for a team practice or some other event French was the usual choice. In general, "French was something so separate from whatever else was happening . . . [that] no one took it seriously," including the French teachers themselves: "You had them saying to the kids, 'Don't worry, after grade 9 you can drop it,' and you better believe I did [even though] I was runner up for the French award." This disconnect arises, she believes, "because the elementary schools do not support the French teachers as colleagues." This lack of support apparently persists to the present day; referring to a core-French-teacher colleague whose class the student-teacher is observing, her practicum supervisor remarks contemptuously, "Watch her. She loses total control of the grade 8's"—a comment, notes my student, that seems to reveal a lack of understanding around precisely how difficult it might be to develop "control" with students who lack fluency in the language.

A teacher's "loss of control" of students this age speaks to the foregoing discussions about language learning as potentially disruptive to identity, and about the adolescent's work of moving away from the control of family (and other similar settings). But in addition, we might imagine that a teacher who

perceives her *teaching subject* or her knowledge of that subject as marginalized or isolated even to the point where she can be seen herself to be trivializ-
ing it ("after grade 9 you can drop it") is ripe for understanding herself, a
teacher *of* that subject, as also isolated, marginalized, viewed with contempt,
even despised, implicitly and at times explicitly—as in the case of the resistant colleagues. This thought returns us once more to the intricate relations
between, first, *language* as a means to represent the self to the world and the
world to the self, as well as a social, political, and economic tool of greater or
lesser currency; second, *language learning* as a potentially disruptive process; and third, *language teaching* as, arguably, a gauge of some hierarchy of
professionalism.

WHAT TO DO? FINAL THOUGHTS

How shall we think about the multiple factors at play here? From a psychoanalytic perspective there are early psychical disappointments, adolescent
resistance, ghostly unconscious memories, love and hate in teaching; there
arc also personal and cultural notions of the value of multilingualism and the
work of teaching, the relative economic and social power of specific languages, individual learner differences, and pedagogical approaches. Together
all these factors form a complicated nexus of relations, at the core of which, I
have argued, lie questions of identity and self-concept, both the learner's and
the teacher's.

One pedagogical response to these multiple elements in all their combinations might simply be a kind of patient waiting that allows the language
learner to work through the challenges to self that a new language might
inaugurate (Granger, 2004, p. 123). It is tricky, though, to advocate for such
approaches in an educational climate of demands for production, results, and
assessment. Still, increasingly in use are pedagogies that recognize the usefulness of a first language in learning a second: for instance, the primary
French immersion teacher, whose pupils take pleasure in translating their
classmates' home languages, encourages them to use their home languages
as needed and to make connections between those languages and French.
Similarly, in the French class in Zurich, when clarification is required German is used without disapproval or stigma. Such approaches, in which new
languages and those already acquired are used in conjunction, may not only
improve understanding of the target language but reinforce first language
capabilities, facilitate content knowledge acquisition in all subject areas (especially in immersion programs), maintain respect for non-dominant first
languages, and, crucially in relation to the concerns discussed here, permit
more self-determination in regard to the "translation" of the self into a new
language. At the same time it might be worth attending to moments when a

learner's wishes take the form of a resistance—be it a loud demand, a quiet whisper, or utter silence—that can be met in ways no instruction manual can ever anticipate. Can we imagine, for instance, what a core French language classroom would look like in which teacher and students together made lists of "surprising words" in both that language and English?

My aim here has been to put forward the view that while we can never supplant the traditional linguistic and social considerations of motivation, learning style, and linguistic environment, in trying to figure out what makes language learners advance or withdraw, we do them a disservice if we do not attempt to get a little behind what appears to be going on: to think about *what else* a learner might be resisting or otherwise responding to; to explore how language underpins self in ways that might, for some individuals, constitute the demand to translate the self into a new language as a threat to that self; and to consider other intrapersonal dynamics that might, at various ages and for various learners, have an impact either on language learning or on attitudes toward it. And so, while the variety of available language education approaches is wide, and growing (see Duff, 2007; García, 2009; Hinkel, 2011), and while it is crucial to match, as best we can, the pedagogy to the learner and the learning setting, we must acknowledge this as a difficult task, as no two language learners are identical.

We must also remember that no two language teachers are alike. And in this vein it may be useful to consider some of the odd and often contradictory inter- and intrapersonal dynamics that circulate in the language-teaching setting alongside sometimes problematic pedagogies, curricular demands, and social, economic, or institutional expectations. Simon is not writing about language teaching per se when he talks of teaching as a gift rooted in a "desire to arouse and instruct the desire of others" that demands, in return, "the student's acknowledgement of the act of giving and value of the gift" (1995, p. 96). But I think his words are instructive. For if as teachers we fail to recognize that the "gift" of our teaching may at times be received, consciously or unconsciously, by various learners and for various reasons, as more an order than an invitation, or a weapon that wounds rather than a tool that edifies, we may confuse our students' desires and needs with our own in ways that make impossible the meeting of either. If, on the other hand, we attend to these matters, perhaps by engaging in *conscious* resistance to moments when our own desires get in the way of our relations with the learners in our charge, we might become more able to help those learners work through their own *unconscious* resistances. Ultimately, we might eventually be less surprised by, and therefore more accepting of, those moments of resistance: moments when the "inside" refuses the demands of elements outside itself, including parents, teachers, the goals of education, even the social world as a whole, to remake itself in a new language.

ACKNOWLEDGMENTS

I am grateful to Matea Mišić, Ellen Murphy-Dunn, Emma Quarter, Kathleen Saint-Onge, and Desirée Tomanelli, as well as to students in the 2011–2012 Consecutive Teacher Education program at York University, for their stories of language teaching and learning, and for conversations and comments during the writing process. Your thinking has furthered mine.

NOTES

1. In Ontario "core" second-language programs are those in which some class time each day is dedicated to the target language. Other forms of language education include "immersion" programs in which the target language is used for all subjects, and "heritage language" programs which teach languages other than English and French; these latter programs are offered by school boards but customarily take place on weekends and lie outside provincially mandated curricula. In this chapter I consider moments in various types of settings, but my focus is primarily on the intrapersonal dynamics of individual learners in relation with teachers, curricula and so on rather than on the structures of programs as such.

2. Hinkel uses the term "partner language" (2011, p. 5), but I will stay with "target language" throughout to refer to the language on which the teaching is focused.

3. Of late the word *identity* has become troubling; it seems to imply a stasis that troubles postmodernist conceptions of the self as always in flux. I recognize this conceptualization of self as labile—indeed the idea lies at the heart of my thinking—but for ease of reading I align my use of the terms *identity*, *self*, and *self-concept* with those of the theorists to whom I am referring.

4. Again for readability, teachers are referred to throughout as female; learners as male.

5. As with "getting away with something" the double meaning in "turn on the teacher" alludes, if understood psychoanalytically, to a doubling, however unconscious, of his purpose (or at least of my reading—and writing—of that purpose).

6. All names have been changed to protect identity.

7. The toy (today usually called a "magic slate"), made of a wax slab overlaid with celluloid and a sheet of waxed paper, functions almost like a paper pad, except that since the stylus leaves no deposit the marks disappear when the top layer is lifted. They can, however, be seen on the wax below, and traces remain even after repeated overwriting. For this reason Freud likened this toy to the unconscious.

8. Bolstering this cultural view of the teacher as quasi-maternal are the frequent slips made by learners themselves: rare is the elementary teacher who has never been called "mommy" by a distracted pupil.

9. For example, she has been advised not to use *les vidanges* or *un bicycle* ["garbage" and "bicycle" in Québec French] but rather *les ordures* and *une bicyclette*.

REFERENCES

Bongaerts, T., Mennen, S., & Van der Slik, F. (2000). Authenticity of pronunciation in naturalistic second language acquisition: The case of very advanced late learners of Dutch as a second language. *Studia Linguistica, 54,* 2, 298–308.

Bourdieu, P. (1991). *Language and symbolic power.* Cambridge, MA: Harvard University Press.

Brown, H. (1994). *Principles of language learning and teaching* (3rd ed.). Englewood Cliffs, NJ: Prentice-Hall.

Bruner, J. (1991). Self-making and world-making. *Journal of Aesthetic Education, 25*, 1, 67–78.

Canadian Parents for French (CPF) (2010). Voices of new Canadians: Fact sheet for educators. In *State of French-second-language education in Canada 2010*. Ottawa: Canadian Parents for French. Online at www.cpf.ca/eng/pdf/Fact%20Sheet%20for%20Educators.pdf.

Duff, P. A. (2007). Multilingualism in Canadian schools: Myths, realities and possibilities. *Canadian Journal of Applied Linguistics, 10*, 2, 149–63.

Ehrman, M., & Dörnyei, Z. (1998). *Interpersonal dynamics in second language education: The visible and invisible classroom*. Thousand Oaks, CA: Sage.

Ellis, R. (1996). *The study of second language acquisition*. Hong Kong: Oxford University Press.

Feldman, R. S. (2009). *Development across the lifespan* (5th ed.). Upper Saddle River, NJ: Prentice Hall.

Felman, S. (1982). Psychoanalysis and education: Teaching terminable and interminable. *Yale French Studies, 63*, 21–44.

Freud, S. (1905). Jokes and their relation to the unconscious. In J. Strachey (Ed. and Trans.), *The standard edition of the complete psychological works of Sigmund Freud (volume VIII)*. London: Hogarth Press and The Institute for Psychoanalysis.

Freud, S. (1911). Formulations on the two principles of mental functioning. In J. Strachey (Ed. and Trans.), *The Penguin Freud library (volume 11): On metapsychology: The theory of psychoanalysis* (pp. 35–57). London: Penguin.

Freud, S. (1914). On the psychology of the grammar-school boy (S. Whiteside, Trans.). In A. Phillips (Ed.) (2006), *The Penguin Freud reader* (pp. 354–57). London: Penguin.

Freud, S. (1924). A note upon the "mystic writing-pad." In J. Strachey (Ed. and Trans.), *The Penguin Freud library (volume 11): On metapsychology: The theory of psychoanalysis* (pp. 429–34). London: Penguin.

Freud, S. (1925). Negation. In J. Strachey (Ed. and trans.), *The standard edition of the complete psychological works of Sigmund Freud (volume XIX)* (pp. 233–39). London: Hogarth Press and The Institute for Psychoanalysis.

Freud, S. (1937). Analysis terminable and interminable. In J. Strachey (Ed. and trans.), *The standard edition of the complete psychological works of Sigmund Freud (volume XXIII)* (pp. 209–53). London: Hogarth Press and The Institute for Psychoanalysis.

Freud, S. (1949). *Inhibitions, symptoms and anxiety*. London: Hogarth Press.

García, O. (2009). *Bilingual education in the 21st century: A global perspective*. Chichester, UK: John Wiley & Sons.

Granger, C. A. (2004). *Silence in second language learning: A psychoanalytic reading*. Clevedon, UK: Multilingual Matters.

Granger, C. A. (2010). The split-off narrator: Coming to symptoms in stories of learning and teaching. *Teachers and Teaching: Theory and Practice, 16*, 2, 219–32.

Granger, C. A. (2011). *Silent moments in education: An autoethnography of learning, teaching, and learning to teach*. Toronto: University of Toronto Press.

Hinkel, E. (Ed.). (2011). *Handbook of research in second language teaching and learning, volume 2*. New York: Routledge.

Hyltenstam, K., & Abrahamsson, N. (2003). Maturational constraints in SLA. In C. J. Doughty & M. H. Long (Eds.), *The handbook of second language acquisition* (pp. 539–88). Oxford: Blackwell.

Laplanche, J., & Pontalis, J.-B. (1973). *The language of psycho-analysis*. (D. Nicholson-Smith, Trans.). New York: W. W. Norton.

Larsen-Freeman, D., & Long, M. H. (1991). *An introduction to second language acquisition research*. London: Longman.

Long, M. H. (2007). *Problems in SLA*. Mahwah, NJ: Erlbaum.

Matthews, S. (2007). Some notes on hate in teaching. *Psychoanalysis, Culture and Society, 12*, 185–92.

Miller, J. (1996). *School for women*. London: Virago.

Phillips, A. (1999). *The beast in the nursery: On curiosity and other appetites*. New York: Vintage.

Quiring, S. (2008). *Challenging the French immersion orthodoxy: Student stories and counter-stories*. Unpublished doctoral dissertation: University of Saskatchewan.

Simon, R. (1995). Face to face with alterity: Postmodern Jewish identity and the eros of pedagogy. In J. Gallop (Ed.), *Pedagogy: The question of impersonation* (pp. 90–105). Bloomington: Indiana University Press.

Singleton, D., & Lésniewska, J. (2009). Age and SLA: Research highways and byeways. In M. Pawlak (Ed.), *New perspectives on individual differences in language learning and teaching* (pp. 109–24). Poznań-Kalisz: Adam Mickiewicz University Press.

Singleton, D. & Muñoz, C. (2011). Around and beyond the critical period hypothesis. In E. Hinkel (Ed.), *Handbook of research in second language teaching and learning, volume 2* (pp. 407–25). New York: Routledge.

Song, X., & Cheng, L. (2011). Investigating primary English immersion teachers in China: Background, instructional contexts, professional development, and perceptions. *Asia-Pacific Journal of Teacher Education, 39*, 2, 97–112.

Tannen, D. & Saville-Troike, M. (1985). *Perspectives on silence*. Norwood, NJ: Ablex.

Taubman, P. M. (2006). I love them to death. In G. M. Boldt and P. M. Salvio (Eds.), *Love's return: Psychoanalytic essays on childhood, teaching, and learning* (pp. 19–32). New York, London: Routledge.

Turkle, S. (2004). Whither psychoanalysis in computer culture? *Psychoanalytic Psychology, 21*, 1, 16–30.

Walkerdine, V. (1990). *Schoolgirl fictions*. London: Verso.

Winnicott, D. W. (1992). *Through pediatrics to psychoanalysis: Collected papers*. New York: Mazer Books.

Young-Bruehl, E. (1996). Adolescence and the aims of hatreds. In *The anatomy of prejudices* (pp. 299–339). Cambridge, MA: Harvard University Press.

Chapter Fourteen

Love and Fear in the Classroom

*How "Validating Affect" Might Help Us Understand
Young Students and Improve Their Experiences
of School Life and Learning*

Alex Moore

EMOTIONALITY AND THE CLASSROOM

In her book *An Introduction to Psycho-analysis for Teachers*, Anna Freud
ascribes to the early education of children the characteristics of a war:

> We know that the child acts throughout the whole period of development [up
> to the age of five] as if there were nothing more important than the gratifying
> of his [*sic*] own pleasures and the fulfilling of his powerful instincts, whereas
> education proceeds as if the prevention of these objects was its most important
> task. In consequence there arises a kind of "guerrilla war" between educator
> and child. Education wants to substitute for love of dirt a disgust of dirt, for
> shamelessness a feeling of shame, for cruelty sympathy, and in place of a rage
> for destructiveness a desire to cherish things. Curiosity and the desire to handle
> one's own body must be eliminated by prohibitions, lack of consideration for
> others by consideration, egotism by altruism. Step by step, education aims at
> the exact opposite of the child's instinctive desires. (Freud, A., 1931, pp.
> 55–56)

More recently, Megan Böler has observed:

> Emotions are a feature always present in educational environments, yet rarely
> do we find educational histories that systematically explore, or even mention,
> the significant role of emotions as a feature of the daily lives of teachers and
> students. . . . [W]ithin educational practices, emotion is most often visible as

something to be "controlled." The control of emotion in education occurs through two primary ideological forces: explicit rules of morality, strongly influenced by Protestant values; and explicit values of utility and skills measured through the "neutral" gaze of social sciences which frame the virtuous student in terms of efficiency and mental health. (Böler, 1999, p. xxii)

Both Freud and Böler draw our attention to the ways in which emotionality is routinely pathologized and effectively ostracized when it comes both to understanding classroom interactions (including the behaviors of our students), and to assessing—and being assessed in relation to—our own practices as teachers. Neither suggests that formal education is (so to speak) fundamentally undesirable, or that the more destructive characteristics of the socially and biologically developing child should be promoted as the child grows into adult life; nor do they advocate teachers regularly and routinely exposing themselves psychically to their students. (Society is inevitably more demanding of the ego and the superego than of the id!) What they do suggest is that we should endeavor to recognize the existence and significance of emotionality in sites of formal teaching and learning (most notably, "the classroom") and to understand it better, in order to become better at how we, as adults, work with our young charges as—with our complicity—they evolve as learners and as people.

This chapter is about the play of emotions—of "affect"—in classroom interactions, both among young learners and between young learners and their teachers, who very often carry into the classroom with them the affective after-effects of their own home-school upbringings (Britzman & Pitt, 1996; Moore, 2004, 2006, 2011b). It is about how emotionality (or at least, certain manifestations of it) is routinely demonized or at best ignored by teachers, as the bearers of rationalist, rationalizing educational policies and discourses, in relation to the learning experiences of their students—despite its obvious and continual impact on learning itself and on the ability to express learning. It is about how young learners can be simultaneously aware and unaware of the impact of emotionality on their learning; and about how the "authorization" of affect—that is to say, its public acceptance and de-pathologization, at least in what Bernstein (2000) calls the "pedagogic recontextualizing field" of teacher practice, though more importantly perhaps in the "official recontextualizing field" of public policy—can assist both teachers and students in the development of more productive, rewarding, and collegial classroom experiences.

In exploring these issues, the chapter draws on a two-and-a-half year study, funded by the UK's Economic and Social Research Council and carried out by the author and colleagues at the Institute of Education University of London, into the ways in which young learners at a culturally diverse, inner-city state elementary school perceived themselves as learners and experienced their learning (Bibby et al., 2005–2007). Adopting an ethnographic, case-study approach, the research team of four academics shadowed one class from Year 4 (ages eight to nine) to Year 6 (ages ten to eleven), covering the period July 2005 to December 2006. The research involved interviews with children and teachers, as well as observations in and around the school and during lessons, with the principal researcher regularly spending the whole day in class and, from the students' perspective, becoming an accepted member of the group. In line with the project's concern, reflected in some other studies of classroom experience (e.g., Laerke, 1998; Pollard & Triggs, 2000), not just to privilege children's own agendas and contributions but to challenge some traditional understandings of formal education that cast the child in a primarily passive role, we were concerned from the outset to focus on "the processes whereby *both* adults *and* children continuously position and identify each other and their selves" (Laerke, 1998, p. 3). Consequently, children also participated in the project by joining one of three separate research groups facilitated by the adult research team. After some initial research training, each of these groups of young researchers developed and used interviews, questionnaires, and observations to explore a question or issue that they had identified as particularly interesting and relevant to their learning. The three topics selected were: *What do children mean when they say something is "fun" or "boring"? What are teachers really like?* and *Why do we feel different when we do tests and challenges?* While there is no room in this paper to explore the possible significance of these choices in any depth, it is hoped that their relevance to the paper will become evident in the discussion that follows.

THE TEACHERS' VIEW: A CARING SCHOOL

An interesting feature of our research data was the school's teaching staff's insistent references in interview to the importance of inclusion and empathy in their practice. The picture they painted was of a caring staff, aware of the importance of recognizing, understanding and responding to their students as individual human beings, anxious to make learning an enjoyable experience, and, by and large, able to do so. (This was despite the pressures imposed on both teachers and students by SATs [graded national Standard Assessment Tests in the case of the United Kingdom], taken by all students at ages ten to eleven just prior to leaving elementary school in order to attend high school—which were the cause of a great deal of anxiety both to the children and to their teachers.) In one of a pair of two hour-long interviews with a member of the research team, the principal repeatedly referred to his school as having an ethos that prioritized children as learners, that promoted student "voice," that fostered collaborative learning, and that foregrounded debates about what is meant by "teaching"—including the concepts of facilitation, support, meta-learning, and teachers-as-learners. Working with a diverse student population in a multi-ethnic area of the inner city, many of whom experienced on a regular basis considerable personal difficulties outside the classroom, a policy of inclusion at the school was overtly underpinned by a recognition that different children learn differently and that consequently learning must be "personalized" for each child.

The principal was also very keen to illustrate the school's caring approach in relation to his students' *feelings* through reference to specific cases—such as a child's loss of a close family member or a case of chronic bullying—which he felt he and his colleagues had dealt with sympathetically and supportively, resulting in teachers adopting what he called a temporary "softly softly" orientation that "made allowances" on the student's behalf and recognized that for a while their behavior and learning might unavoidably be "untypical." While this view was broadly endorsed in interviews with teachers, it became increasingly evident that this "softly softly" approach was not always as generously adopted as the principal had implied, embedded as it was within an often overwhelming sense of urgency on the teachers' part as the SATs approached and as time became ever shorter. In answer to a general question to the class teachers as to the extent to which they were aware of the impact of children's emotions on their learning and behavior and whether they, as teachers, had the time and space to respond appropriately, one teacher's response offered an important clue as to how the school's articulated policy of care underwent a subtle but significant change as it was recontextualized (Bernstein, 2000) into actual classroom practice and the exigencies of the school curriculum:

> Any good primary teacher is going to be aware, sometimes, that children walk into the class and are not very happy, for some reason or another. It might be that they have had an argument with their mum on the way in to school, it could be for all sorts of reasons, but it is very likely to happen, and most people would pick that up occasionally. I think most people would pick that up sometimes. . . . And I do think you should be interested in the children, and have some concern over their well-being and their background and what goes on for them out of school, but basically our job is to teach them when they are here. And if something is impeding that teaching, be it that they are turning up late every day, you can make an effort to deal with that, but really you just have to manage to teach them despite that. If you can change it then that is great. ("Lisa," Year 6 teacher.)

In this teacher's part-recognition of the impact of emotionality on children's capacity to concentrate and work, there is buried the seed of a difficulty which became increasingly obvious as our research progressed and which became one of the chief foci of our attention and analysis. For one thing, the teacher's insistence on teaching "despite" the absence or presence of well-being in the child seemed to position teaching as something external to the child, which *can* occur without the child's engagement or desire to learn, preferable though such conditions might be. This concurs with the teacher's understanding of emotional impact as occurring essentially and principally as a result of factors *outside the classroom*, or at least outside what is official and sanctioned *within* the classroom (such as problems with parents or home life, or teasing and bullying by peers)—rather than as a result of any *internal dynamics* that structure the children's relationship with their teachers and with one another: an understanding iterated elsewhere in the data, when the principal elaborated at length the efforts made by the school to counsel a child whose father had died, or by a teacher who talked of the need to understand the "external" pressures on the children brought about by the SATs: "I saw children that were so stressed in those exams that they just stopped, and didn't even achieve a fraction of the potential, the weight of the exams was just too much."

THE CHILDREN'S VIEW: LOOKING FOR LOVE, FEARING REJECTION

What made the teachers' superficially unremarkable comments concerning the emotional impact of "outside" events on their students' learning and behavior remarkable was the extent to which they were contradicted by the testimonies of many of the children, which revealed that the larger part of their expressed classroom emotions came from perceptions of favoritism, and that these were largely experienced *within* the classroom, including in relation to their teachers. It is true that the principal and class teachers were not, in the initial interviews, specifically invited to talk about the role of emotionality in the teaching and learning context. However, neither were the children. What is interesting is that the children *introduced* the topic in interview, and that they discussed it in very specific ways—revealing feelings that were quite unlike the simple recognition of anxiety identified by their class teachers. The children were keenly aware, for example, that one's emotional state can be somewhat unstable; that it can change quickly and without warning; that it can be affected by a range of sources (many of them, unlike the pressure of exams, outside the knowledge and experience of the teacher); and that it is not always obvious to someone else exactly what the impact of emotional stress is on learning and behavior. An additional perception, which also conflicted very noticeably with that of their teachers, was that whereas the teachers self-perceived as caring, loving practitioners who had their students' best interests at heart, the children's view of their teachers tended to be of a group of adults who did *not* understand their differences or their needs, who did *not* care for or about them, and who did little to make learning the enjoyable experience it was supposed to be. Not unrelatedly, while the teachers tended to view their students' learner identities as relatively "fixed" ("good at this," "interested in that," "talkative," "head-down," and so forth—an understanding embedded even in the principal's inclusive, "personalized" strategy in which students had "preferred learning styles" and whose "natural abilities" required "cutting your cloth according to what you've got"), the children's testimonies bore evidence of identities that were both far more complex and far more fragile.

In talking to the children and their teachers and trying to make sense of these divergent and contradictory readings, we were reminded of Bendelow's (1998) critique of the artificial duality typically set up by adults between the "rational" and the "emotional," and of Laerke's parallel concerns about much cognitive anthropological theory wherein "[c]hildren's actions would appear bounded by a 'cognitive function' through which all experience and expression are processed" (Laerke, 1998: 2). Though rather less relevant to our theoretical approach than these commentators, the observation of Harris (1989) regarding the ways in which children's developing emotional literacy is centrally involved in the development of their communication skills also rang true—particularly once we had started to talk to the children about their learning experiences. Harris's accounts (1989, pp. 160–65) of children's developing understandings of how emotional states can take up occupancy of our consciousness, making it difficult to concentrate on anything else, certainly seemed to be borne out in our discussions with the children. This left us to wonder when and how that understanding weakens or disappears—or, at least, appears to disappear—during the course of the child's journey into adulthood, and how this impacts on changing (love-and-power) relations between students and their teachers.[1]

NICE PICTURE, NASTY PICTURE: THE PRESENCE LOVE, THE FEAR OF NON-LOVE

It is to this specific tension between the adults' perceptions of what is going on and the students' articulated experiences that I now want to turn. Of particular interest here is the contrast between the teachers' view that they made efforts to understand their students as individual human beings (in terms of "learning style," "potential," and so on), constructing pedagogies on those understandings that were aimed at bringing about effective learning (what Edwards & Mercer [1987] have described as "principled knowledge," carried away by the students for future, independent use), and the children's view that the teachers did not understand them at all—and, worse, that they generally made no real efforts even to *try* to understand them (as we shall see, a view that promoted "ritualistic knowledge" [Edwards & Mercer, 1987], which was more concerned with teacher-pleasing than with learning itself).

The following extract—the start of a group interview with three children which used as its starting-point some drawings they had been asked to make to illustrate how they saw themselves as learners—provides a graphic example of this gulf between the children's perceptions and preoccupations and those of their teachers. The children had each been invited to draw two pictures to illustrate "nice" and "nasty" experiences of classroom life. In the extract, a particular child begins by talking about her "nasty picture," illustrating the downside of her experiences as a learner; then, she talks about her "nice picture," illustrating the positive aspects.

Nasty Picture

R: Is anyone going to start and tell me what they have drawn on their picture?

H: Me.

R: OK.

H: OK. I'll do my horrible one first.

R: Do you want to put it down so we can all see it?

H: Okay. . . . The reason why I hate this one, that I hate school, is when [Miss X] is angry, because it makes my day horrible as well and I'm not a very good drawer, so there's no point looking at mine.

R: Well, let's look at what you've written here.

H: I wrote here: "Miss, they're being horrible to me, saying horrible things," and [Miss X] says "Stop being horrible to [H]," and then there's the little boy saying "It was him!" and then he's saying "It was him!"

R: Okay. . . . So when [Miss X] gets angry, that makes you have a bad day?

H: Yeah. [And] you can't concentrate, because there's something in your head and it stays there. [. . .] It's a bit like when my dad died and I came back to school. It was really difficult . . . I kept on thinking what my mum was doing, because I stayed with my mum for a week at home.

Nice Picture

> H: In my nice picture—not a nice drawing, but—at school, it's all my teachers; and on [the picture of the Researcher] it says "I think you should give her five [reward slips] and that is so sweet" [. . .] and Miss X is saying "That's so sweet of you, H: two [reward slips]." And I say "I love you, [Miss X, classroom assistant] and [researcher], you're the best teachers in the world."

> R: Right. . . . Well, that's lovely. And what's happening with your learning there?

> H: I can concentrate better because I'm happy, and when I'm happy I can understand a lot more.

> R: And why do you think that is?

> H: Well, when I'm happy and I get a question right, then I get lots of questions right, then I'm working harder.

> R: Right. . . . Okay. So you're happy when you get the questions right because you learn better, and when you get the questions right you get even happier.

> H: Yeah. Then I'm on fire!

> [Laughter all around]

There is so much to be said about this testimony that it is hard to know where to begin. Of immediate interest is not simply the child's focus on the way in which her emotions affect her learning (rather, for example, than the tasks she is given, the teaching materials to which she has access, her notion of her own "intelligence," "ability" or even "identity," her own or her teacher's strategies), but the fact that she chooses, quite deliberately, to talk about the negative experiences first and the positives second. What is quickly apparent from the testimony itself is that there are interrelated affective factors that impact positively or negatively on the child's learning—and that these are both recognized and articulated by the child, though they do not seem to form part of the discussions of learning and meta-learning between teacher and student that was suggested in the school principal's and teachers' interviews with us. It is particularly noticeable that the child's capacity to learn is affected:

- By emotional states brought about by factors "external" to the immediate teacher-student relationship (e.g., the death of a close relative; other children "being horrible")
- By the teacher's response to these (in the "nasty picture," the teacher is somewhat perfunctory in dealing with the latter kind of problem);
- By the teacher's own emotional behavior (e.g., displays of anger);
- By the way in which the teacher (as well as the other *students*) displays affection and (in H's words) "love" to the student—demonstrable both through words and through a reward system.

What is very evident from H's testimony is that when she feels happy, valued and loved she learns well and enjoys her learning, feeling a strong sense of motivation, self-belief, and joy in the learning activity ("I'm on fire!"), and that when she feels unhappy and not valued or loved, learning is very difficult for her. This is perhaps not very surprising. What is more surprising, perhaps, is just how much her teacher's feelings about her *matter* to the child, and how ready she is to find both love and not-love in the adults with whom she shares the classroom—most of whom are adept at spotting "fallings in" and "fallings out" of friendship *between* students, but far less adept at spotting or addressing the negative impact of their *own* words and behaviors on their students. Certainly, H appears, at times, to be occupying a different classroom from her teacher: one primarily experienced and understood— often in a markedly developed and quite sophisticated way—not so much in terms of cognitive development as in terms of desire. To quote from a little later on in H's testimony:

> I think that sometimes [Miss X] can like me [but] she only likes me when there's somebody else that she really hates, OK. So, say there are two people that you hate, but there's one better than the other, well you're going to pick that person, aren't you? So that's what she did, erm. . . . But when it's maths or literacy you have to take your time to think, just in case you get the wrong answer. She doesn't do that; then you get the wrong answer.

It is hard to imagine the adults at this school having this kind of debate— even "in-the-head." It is a perspective that is routinely omitted from their discussions of teaching and learning, almost appearing to have taboo status. Certainly, it struggles to gain a foothold within pedagogy as practiced, and nowhere is this more evident than in a sharp division, hinted at in H's testimony, between the teachers' professed understandings of learning (articulated in turn to their students) and those of the children themselves. While the teachers, as part of their professed student-centered, inclusive pedagogies, declare an allegiance to more "open," "exploratory" approaches to learning, in which children are to be encouraged to "find things out for themselves," appreciate the "intrinsic rewards of learning," understand that there may sometimes be more than one answer to a question, and know that in any event the process of getting there is often more important than the answer itself, the students "know" that there are always "right answers" and "wrong answers" to any question, and that it is through identifying and articulating right answers that *validation* and *affection* are to be achieved *in addition to* (and perhaps more importantly than) academic success.

The children's quest and respect for right answers is, furthermore, inextricably interwoven with the teacher's perceived conduct: in particular, the teacher's choice of whom to ask, and the teacher's response to the answer given. In H's understanding, Miss X will only ask *her* if she "hates" somebody else (and presumably, part of asking H is to send a message out to that currently hated person!): *that is to say, Miss X's very choice of whom to ask is itself conceived not as a fair, rational, pedagogical decision, but as an emotional one, loaded with desire and used by the teacher to communicate affection or lack of affection, validation, or lack of validation, to her students.* Sometimes, as H observes, a snappy answer is required by the teacher. But H wants time to think: the emotional impact of getting an answer wrong, both in terms of what the teacher will think of her—how the teacher will *value* her—and what her classmates will think of her is too great to risk. Herein lies the problem for H: a quick answer will receive validation and respect *only if it is right and acknowledged by the teacher as right*; however, to get a right answer you sometimes need to take time to think, and thinking-time is not always available. An inevitable slowness to respond results in the teacher moving on from H to another child, or going for someone who *has* been bold enough to take the risk and raise an arm, itself resulting in validation for some other child. For H, this is a lose-lose situation; either way, she is likely to miss out on the validation and affection she desires and needs.

The theme of wanting to be loved—and, indeed, wanting *to love* and to feel one's own love rewarded, coupled with the fear of not being loved, of not having one's love recognized and rewarded—both by other students and by the teacher ("in *loco parentis*," perhaps, in more ways than commonly understood by the term), resurfaced too often in discussions with the children for it to be dismissed or attributed only to a handful of students, and was nearly always introduced by them rather than by the researcher. Here, for example, is another student, "N," complaining about the (same) teacher ignoring her:

N: [Miss X] sometimes ignores me and stuff, and I don't really like it. [. . .] If I want to show my work, then everyone quickly comes, yeah, and she goes with them.

[. . .]

R: How does that make you feel when that happens?

N: It hurts my feelings. [. . .] And I like open my book and see that I get all the questions wrong, wrong, wrong, wrong. [. . .] And it's not my fault that I got everything wrong; it's [Miss X']s fault that I got everything wrong.

R: So what happens when you get it wrong?

N: I feel guilty.

R: You feel guilty?

N: Yeah.

R: Because?

N: [Miss X] ignored me. [. . .] It's still quite my fault because I got the answers wrong a bit, but it's normally Miss X's fault.

The children's obsession with right and wrong answers becomes very understandable once we begin to explore their experiences in this way, and they form an interesting counterpoint to Miss X's own observations, in interview, in which she talks very warmly about the sympathy she feels toward children who come up with wrong answers (in, for example, mathematics). What is particularly striking about N's comments, as with H's testimony, is the way in which the whole business of learning is wrapped up in issues of desire and, in particular, in the desire to be validated and loved—as a learner, as a human being, as a child. For N, there is a mix of emotions involved in this business: anger and blame on the one hand (it's Miss X's fault that I got something wrong because she doesn't understand me), guilt and poor self-image on the other (it must be my fault that I got something wrong, my fault that Miss X is not pleased with me). Such complexities bring to mind Zizek's account (1989), after Lacan (1977, 1979), of the way in which our "identities" as social, emotional beings are constructed through a kind of interplay between "ideal" and "imaginary" *identification.* Imaginary identification here relates to "identification with the *image* in which we appear likeable to ourselves": the image, that is of "what we would like to be" (Zizek 1989, p.105). Symbolic identification, on the other hand, concerns the way in which we perceive ourselves within and in relation to the "symbolic order" of language, ritual, custom, and representation—of society, indeed—within which we operate and within which we perceive and understand all "experience." As such, it is more concerned with (to quote a rather older student cited in Moore, 2004) the way in which *we see other people seeing us.* In Zizek's words, symbolic identification is effectively an identification with the "place" (within the symbolic order) from which we are being observed, "from where we look at ourselves so that we appear likeable, worthy of love" (p. 105). It is not stretching a point too far, I think, to suggest that the young learners in our study struggled simultaneously with a desire for popularity (with teachers but of course with certain peers also) that had little to do with academic success ("imaginary identification"), *and* a desire to be a "good student" ("symbolic identification") that had everything to do with it—but that from the viewpoint of their relationships with their teachers, both desires coincided: in other words, to gain the love, the affection, the acknowledgment of my teacher, I must conform to their image, which in turn must be my image, of the good (enthusiastic, academically able) student, by whatever means I can.

EMOTIONALITY, LEARNING, AND COMPETITION

The children's need for mutual recognition, validation, and love was closely associated with their wholehearted embrace of two of the central characteristics of the UK education system embedded within and supported by national, individual-oriented test and examination regimes, not to mention the wider neoliberal politics and market economies within which they are in turn embedded: those of competition and competitiveness—once again revealing a significant mismatch between the professed approaches of the teaching staff and the lived experiences and understandings of the children. For the school principal, each child was different and, within the framework and constraints of a common curriculum, needed to be encouraged to work to their "maximum potential" and to be allowed, again as far as was permissible and practicable, to get there using their own preferred learning styles (or at least adaptations of or extensions to these). This approach was intended to promote "deep," lasting learning that would be—and could be seen by the learner as—of immediate and future personal use, and to encourage children to concentrate on their own learning rather than, as the principal put it, "worrying about what their peers are or are not doing." It is clear from our data, however, that for the children, it was not just getting the "right answer" (or in some instances *any* answer)—preferably ahead of their peers—that was important: it was to get it as the quickest route to teacher approval (cf. Edwards & Mercer, 1987). It was easily grasped by the children, too, that right answers can be achieved at times with only minimal understanding of associated concepts: an understanding which, as we shall see, contributed to a not always healthy and frequently unethical battle for attention within the classroom, in which learning itself was often the victim. To elaborate a little further, there appeared to be a tension between the teachers' (understandable) cognitive imperative (to promote their students' academic development lead-ing to improved performance as measured through national test scores) and the children's more pressing socio-affective concerns of securing affection. To an extent, this tension was resolved—though in the manner of compro-mise—by the teachers through citing both the demands of SATs and the "evidence" of SATs scores in justification of their approach (we only want the best for those we truly love—or as one teacher said: "the important thing in our busy lives is to get the grades; we can't spend too much time sorting out classroom tiffs"), and by the children through prioritizing the winning of praise and validation for what might loosely be termed academic activity.

The following extract, from one of the field researchers' observation notes, neatly illustrates this tension. The researcher had accompanied the class on a field trip to the Local Authority's Learning Centre to do some collaborative science-related work using computer technology. At the start of the session, the children had been introduced to the idea of data logging:

> The [presenter] tells the [children] they are going to do an experiment. He uses Google Earth to zoom in on New Orleans and describes how the city was under water. Assuming that the children are rescuers, they must do an experi-ment to measure which colour paper is the most reflective (so that the rescuers or victims can be seen). He has a censor device hooked up to the computer that is able to measure light, sound and temperature. The children are wowed by the direct translation of light reflection on to a solid graph on the screen and urge [the presenter] to measure the lamp directly.

A little later in the day, the children were asked to carry out experiments of their own, first along the lines of the "New Orleans experiment," then about heat insulation: specifically, to insulate a cup with different materials and then test whether these materials keep hot water warmer for longer than a non-insulated cup and, if so, which material was the most effective insulator. It became evident that once this small-group work had begun the children's initial sense of wonder at the technology, and their enthusiasm for learning, was quickly replaced by a sense (sometimes quite cruelly expressed) of com-petitiveness, and an enthusiasm for *completion*. One group, for example, began bickering among themselves when their first experiment did not go as planned, swiftly engaging in blaming activity, while during the course of the second (insulation) experiment other groups resorted to cheating—artificially keeping their water hot by placing it under a lamp—in order to be first over the finish line and thereby be declared the "winners." The researcher's field notes recount the story:

> [The presenter] asks them about the control variable and K is first to come up with the idea of using [a] non-insulated cup to measure difference. [The chil-dren] can choose two materials from bubble wrap, newspaper, cardboard and

tin foil. I watch N's group again, who decide to use bubble wrap and tin foil. [. . .] Once JK pours the water in their cups they can start logging on the computer. A line graph immediately appears and as time elapses the graph compresses to fit the line. One line for each cup runs along the page and the girls remark "that's quite cool." We try to figure out which cup is which line and I ask whether the lines are the same. N notices that "they are parallel, but now they're splitting." D comes over to the group and brags that his group's temperature is 47 and theirs is 43, despite the fact that D's group received their water last so the other groups have had more time to cool down. "I don't care," answers N. Then she decides that this is "boring" and asks me why they are doing this and what they are learning. N says that everyone has used the same materials anyway, so there's no point [in doing the experiment]. I guess that they haven't, and she goes around to check. Meanwhile N and T get upset that the other groups are "cheating." Some have put their lamps over their cups so that (presumably) the water will stay warmer. I have a hard time understanding this as surely it just invalidates their experiments altogether, so why does it matter. But then I realise that the children seem to view the whole thing as a contest over who has made the best insulator, despite discrepancies in starting times and water temperatures. So keeping your water warmer to them means that they have "won." "It's not fair," says N. I try to point out that they have different materials so it's not a contest but N comes back and tells me they've all used tinfoil and bubble wrap except one group who couldn't because it had run out. I attempt to reason it out to our group (that it's the differences between the lines that matters) but feel in the end that in fact N is right and the other groups have cheated.

The researcher's account of the children's day out offers an interesting and important counterpoint to observations made by the principal and class teachers about the importance of collaboration and talk in children's learning. On the one hand, there is clearly some evidence in the data that some "principled" learning (Edwards & Mercer, 1987), involving genuine concept development, might have been taking place and that the collaborative experimentation might have helped this. (N, for example, as the field researcher went on to point out, applies a mathematical concept—"parallel"—to a science experiment in the form of a graph, and immediately recognizes its practical application.) However, the entire exercise appears to have become dominated by the quest not just for right answers but for *quick* answers: so much so that this (social/affective imperative) becomes more important than the cognitive learning itself, and indeed masks, at least for some children, the very purpose of the exercise or indeed of the day as a whole.

AUTHORIZING AFFECT

It is evident from the children's testimonies, and from their interactions with one another, that they were far more in touch than their teachers with the extent to which emotions can impact on our capacity to learn and to "perform." They were also more aware that their emotional states could fluctuate quite dramatically and frequently, rendering their learner identities far more fragile than was allowed for in the adults' conceptualizations and related pedagogic strategies. Of particular interest in our own study was the extent to which the children were often very quick to be convinced that their teachers did not like them, and habitually convinced of and disturbed by their teachers' apparent aloofness to their feelings and their effects. In their desire, sometimes bordering on desperation, to break down this aloofness, one obvious strategy involved "getting there first"—by whatever means they could, and regardless of whether or not any academic learning had taken place. In this way, the children's social/affective imperative took clear precedence over the cognitive/goals-based one prioritized in the accounts of the school principal and the classroom teachers. Some of the children—perhaps all of them—clearly spent much of their time in school thinking about personal relationships and sometimes troubling events in their lives—in some cases having developed, away from the formal curriculum, a quite sophisticated set of views and understandings about emotionality and human relationships. Such views appeared sometimes (as in H's case) to be predicated on a lack of self-confidence, even a lack of self-worth, whose impact surfaced regularly in conversation in connection with descriptions of their own work and achievement. When introducing her "nasty picture," for example, H felt obliged to distance herself from it as a work of art by adding "I'm not a very good drawer, so there's no point looking at mine," and repeating the aside when introducing her "nice picture" by the insertion "not a nice drawing." Although H reported elsewhere in the interview that Miss X had told her that she was "clever" (and that this was why she ignored H!), H's perception of herself, and her suspicion of her teacher, were such that she believed neither the sincerity of the view nor its reality: "[S]he says 'I only ignore you because you're so clever.' But that's not true [. . .] I think it's just she doesn't like me . . . I don't think she likes me . . ."

The teachers, meanwhile, appeared to remain (as the children suspected) oblivious to the underworld of emotional highs and lows playing out in front of them on a daily basis—or, beyond a quite superficial level, to the effects of such turbulences. Given what was, to the research team, the obviousness of such effects, we need to ask the question "why?" Was it, for example, because, in their judgment, it simply wasn't important (not worthy of "notice")? Or was it because, for whatever reason or reasons, they were simply unwilling or unable to engage with it?

There are no easy answers to these questions, whose causes are, no doubt, over-determined. They give rise, however, to two related clusters of questions whose consideration might offer a set of useful entry-points into exploring them further. These are:

1. (Why) is an acknowledgment and understanding of the effects of emotionality in the classroom so important? Should the emotionality of
   young learners matter to us in any case? (Is it not, as might be implied
   in the quotation with which this chapter opened, just a phase they are
   inevitably going through? An aspect of their pre-pubescence that we
   would do well to leave alone?)
2. If such an awareness is desirable, why might teachers themselves be
   so resistant to addressing their own and their students' emotionality in
   teaching and learning situations—let alone doing anything constructive about it?

What is to be gained by de-pathologizing emotionality and referencing it in
our pedagogy? Is it not the teacher's job simply to "teach"? And in any event,
what qualifies the teacher to make secure judgments about their own and
their students' emotional states and their impact on teaching and learning?
These are valid and reasonable questions; however, an answer to all of them
may be found in the testimonies of the young learners in our study. Allowing
emotionality not just into teaching and learning as they are practiced and
experienced, but into our understandings and analyses of classroom interactions—"validating affect," that is, as opposed to acting as if affect was an
educational and social irrelevance—is important precisely because of the
potential negative impact of emotionality on children's learning and self-
esteem: an impact that (Moore, 2004, 2011a, 2011b) can have very long-term
effects, impacting on the ways in which we learn, socialize, and *experience*
learning and socialisation, into adulthood (including, for some of us, an
adulthood that draws us back into the classroom as teachers). Our study
suggested that affect can impact on children's learning in at least two key
areas: first, in reducing the child's capacity and willingness to learn *at all* (to
quote "H": "[Y]ou can't concentrate, because there's something in your head
and it stays there."); second, by impelling children into shallow or pseudo-
learning activities in which the principal object is to win immediate, short-
term teacher approval rather than to enjoy learning for its own sake or to
internalize it for future use.

These might be lesser problems, of course (though problems still), if we
understood and approached teaching and learning as a mere matter of "transmission" and "reception" or as about simply keeping our students busy and
"on task." As Anna Freud has argued, however, the incorporation of understandings of the role of affect into our teaching can only benefit our practice
and our students' learning, given that it extends "the teacher's knowledge of
human beings . . . and his [*sic*] understanding of the *complicated relations*
between the child and the educator" (1931, p. 104, emphasis added). That the
relations between "child and educator" *are* "complicated" has not always, of

course, been broadly accepted, and Anna Freud and others are to be thanked for reminding us that this is indeed the case.[2]

If we adopt the much subtler understanding of classroom learning and teaching proposed by Anna Freud, it becomes necessary not just to attempt to understand our students as individual, idiosyncratic subjects and learners with unique backgrounds and experiences—students who might require other kinds of reward, such as acknowledgment, love, and a sense of self-worth—but to adopt a more reflexively critical approach to our own practice and its development, including more helpful and nuanced understandings of our own idiosyncratic experiences of classroom life. (Why, for example, does Miss X become "angry" with an apparent impunity that is denied her students?—And how might this kind of public display of "negative emotion," which has a clear and detrimental impact on some of her learners' capacity to learn, be explored by Miss X and perhaps eliminated from future encounters?)

If the "authorization of affect"—that is to say, including it as a legitimate and important element in our practice, our reflection on practice, and our understandings of our students' and our own experiences and behaviors—is so clearly important, why should it be so difficult to do so? There are, no doubt, many contributory factors to be taken into account in attempting to answer this question—some intra-psychical, embedded in the very resistance that renders such considerations hidden and difficult to access in the first place; some related to fears of a more obvious and immediate material nature, such as the fear of losing control, of not being seen to "cover the curriculum," even, ultimately, of losing one's job. Others are related to the fact that school-teaching in general tends to be embedded in discourses and public policies which themselves discourage such perspectives and approaches, tending to consign emotionality to the "cutting-room floor" (cf. Pinar, 2004) in favor of increasingly narrow conceptualizations of "professionalism." Within such discourses, almost without thinking, emotionality (other than that which is considered "benign," such as the joy of "success," the gratitude for help or for a job well done) is effectively "cut out" of any discussions of student learning or teacher practice, or at best domesticated, rationalized, and academized through such notions as "emotional intelligence" and "emotional literacy." It is precisely for this reason that we need to be very careful and clear about what we might be asking teachers to accomplish in this area—recognizing that whatever else it is, it won't be easy.

In their account of the way in which teachers often struggle, without much help, approval, gratitude, or advice, to make sense of their students' behavior through the invisible lens of their own unauthorized emotionality, Britzman and Pitt draw on Sigmund Freud's conceptualizations of repression and "new editions of old conflicts" (Freud, 1968: 454) to paint a picture that, though we might not always choose to acknowledge it, will be very familiar to many of us who have experienced life in public school classrooms and glimpsed ourselves reverting to childlike behavior or to the intransigent scolding of a disapproving parent:

> The classroom invites transferential relations because, for teachers, it is such a familiar place, one that seems to welcome re-enactments of childhood memories. Indeed, recent writing about pedagogy suggests that transference shapes how teachers respond and listen to students, and how students respond and listen to teachers. . . . [T]eachers' encounters with students may return them involuntarily and still unconsciously to scenes from their individual biographies. (Britzman & Pitt, 1996, pp. 117–18)

Referencing Anna Freud's position, they continue:

> Such an exploration requires that teachers consider how they understand students through their own subjective conflicts. . . . The heart of the matter, for Anna Freud, is the ethical obligation teachers have to learn about their own conflicts and to control the re-enactment of old conflicts that appear in the guise of new pedagogical encounters. (Britzman & Pitt, 1996, p. 118)

This is heavy stuff! It is not simply *useful* or *optional* for teachers to bring affect into their considerations of teaching and learning and their ongoing professional development; it is an "ethical obligation," a professional requirement—something that, if they do not do it, renders them seriously culpable.

Unfortunately teachers can only go as far as they are allowed to go. In some circumstances—in some schools, in some local and national education systems—this might be quite far; in others, not very far at all—and there is bound to be considerable variability in the ways in which Anna Freud's "ethical obligation," if accepted, is translated into practice. It might, however, be possible to agree to a "bottom line" on the matter —which is simply to recognize the importance of our own and our students' emotionality in and out of the classroom situation, to take some account of it in our judgments, our understandings, and our responses, and, as far as we are able, to work with the grain of affect rather than symbolically (and sometimes physically) dismissing it. If we feel, as teachers, that we have a duty of care that embraces both the promotion of learning and the development of our students as happy, socially secure subjects able to make the most effective use of that learning, and if we work according to theories of learning and human development that understand learning as fundamentally social and interactive in nature, Anna Freud's ethical imperative may appear immediately less unreasonable and out of reach than on our initial encounter with it—even in circumstances in which teachers, like their students, are continually pushed by public policy into the quick fix and the immediacy and tyranny of "the right answer."

This is not about telling children not to be competitive or not to worry about how others perceive them: such messages were repeatedly transmitted to the children in our own study, only to be dismissed by them in light of ample evidence to the contrary. It is more about understanding our young students better and, substantially, about understanding the impact our own words and behaviors can have on them, however "irrational" or "foolish" or "over-reactive" this might appear to us—and modifying our practice accordingly. It is also about non-complicity—and about acknowledging the difference between complicity and compliance. We all have, to a certain degree to be compliant; however, that does not mean we have to agree to or internalize the principles upon which that to which we must comply are based. Although received wisdom, as reflected in public policy, may continue to mark affect as an inappropriate consideration for teachers and—more often than not—a pathology in children, there remains an important argument to be made and to be won if children are to be what governments always tell us they want them to be: that is to say, happy, positive, socially comfortable, enthusiastic, and independent young learners. If our non-complicity achieves nothing else, it keeps opposition to "anti-emotionalism" alive and, if we do it right, makes the often difficult, emotionally turbulent lives of our young students a small but significant bit better.

NOTES

1. In an interesting hypothesis of the way in which young learners' fascination with their teachers can move, through the passage of time, from demanding love and validation, and from experiencing the miseries of teacher rejection, to recognizing their teachers' *own* need for love and validation, and seeking to *produce* misery *through* rejection, Keck [2012] talks of "[t]he [pubescent] students' own 'hidden curriculum' and sinister delight, [which] is to break through the teacher's identity discourse to reveal its soft underbelly."

2. Those "others" include developmental psychologists such as Piaget, Bruner, and Vygotsky, whose work has achieved a great deal in moving understandings of teaching and learning away from simplistic behaviorist models based on "transmissive" teachers and "receptive" learners, governed almost exclusively by the donation and receipt of tangible "material" rewards, toward understandings and practices that recognize the fundamentally social nature of the learner-teacher relationship (Vygotsky, 1962, 1978), emphasize the active, meaning-making, "constructivist" nature of learning itself (Piaget, 1926), and, in Bruner's case, acknowledge the impact on children's learning—including their willingness and capacity to learn—of the social and economic circumstances of their wider lives (see, e.g., Bruner 1972, 1996).

REFERENCES

Bendelow, G. A. (1998). *Emotions in social life: Critical themes and contemporary issues* London: Routledge.

304 *Alex Moore*

Bernstein, B. (2000). *Pedagogy, symbolic control and identity* (revised edution). Lanham, MD: Rowman & Littlefield.

Bibby, T., Moore, A., Clarke, S., & Haddon, A. (2005–2007). "Children's learner-identities in mathematics at Key Stage 2." ESRC-funded research study, Institute of Education, University of London.

Böler, M. (1999). *Feeling power: Emotions and education*. New York: Routledge.

Britzman, D., & Pitt, A. (1996). Pedagogy and Transference: casting the past of learning into the presence of teaching. *Theory into Practice 35, 2, 118–23.*

Bruner J. (1996). *The culture of education*. Cambridge MA. Harvard University Press.

Bruner J. (1972). Poverty and childhood. In *The Relevance of Education*. Cambridge MA: Belknap Press, 132–61.

Edwards, D., & Mercer, N. (1987). *Common Knowledge: The development of understanding in the classroom*. London: Routledge.

Freud, A. (1931). *Introduction to psycho-analysis for teachers: Four lectures*. Trans. B. Lowe. London: George Allen and Unwin Ltd.

Freud, S. (1968). Introductory lectures on psycho-analysis, part three. In *Standard Edition, vol. 17* (J. Strachey, Trans.). London: Hogarth Press.

Harris, P. L. (1989). *Children and emotion: The development of psychological understanding*. London: Blackwell.

Keck, C. (2012). Radical Reflexivity? Assessing the value of psycho-spiritual practices as an ethical and pedagogical "training" for teachers. Unpublished PhD thesis, Institute of Education, University of London.

Lacan, J. (1977). *Ecrits*. London: Tavistock.

Lacan, J. (1979). *The four fundamental concepts of psycho-analysis* London: Penguin.

Laerke, A. (1998). By means of re-membering: notes on a fieldwork with English children. *Anthropology Today 14, 1, 3–7.*

Moore, A. (2004). *The good teacher*. London: Routledge.

Moore, A. (2006). Recognising desire: a psychosocial approach to understanding education policy implementation and effect. *Oxford Review of Education, 32*(4), 487–503.

Moore, A. (2011a). Love and fear in the classroom: the role of affect in the adoption and implementation of resisted policies in public school settings. Paper presented at the Annual Conference of the Association for the Psychoanalysis of Culture and Society, *Pathos, Politics and Passion*, Rutgers University, New Brunswick, NJ. 4–6 November 2011.

Moore, A. (2011b). The authorization of affect: identification, repetition and the reflexive turn. Paper presented at the Annual Conference of the Association for the Psychoanalysis of Culture and Society, *Pathos, Politics and Passion*. Rutgers University, New Brunswick, NJ. 4–6 November 2011.

Piaget J. (1926). *The language and thought of the child*. London: Routledge.

Pinar W. (2004). *What is curriculum theory?* Mahwah, NJ: Erlbaum.

Pollard, A., & Triggs, P. (2000). *What pupils say: Changing policy and practice in primary education*. London: Continuum.

Vygotsky, L. S. (1962). *Thought and language*. Cambridge: M.I.T. Press.

Vygotsky, L. S. (1978). *Mind in society*. Cambridge: Harvard University Press.

Zizek, S. (1989). *The sublime object of ideology*. London, Verso.

Chapter Fifteen

Encountering Autism

Learning to Listen to the Fear

Eileen E. Brennan

Psychologists, social workers, and educators have learned through Daniel Goleman's work in *Emotional Intelligence* (1995) that as long as a child is afraid no real learning happens. The Yale researcher posits that fear interferes with decision-making, individual success, control of one's impulses, self-motivation, empathy, and social competence in interpersonal relationships. A child with autism lives with intense anxiety that develops at a very early age, during a stage of development that is pre-verbal. Therefore, the cognitive and verbal development of autistic children challenges the appropriate integration and expression of thought and feeling in word. Psychoanalytic theory helps us to listen to and understand the significant amount of non-verbal and verbal communication that scaffolds autistic communication. Object relations theory and drive theory can help us understand how to listen to and understand autistic children and reverse the severe impact on cognition and capacity for relatedness.

In using psychoanalytic theory to address autistic disorder spectrum I limit my discussion in this chapter to the classical theory of Freud, the object relational theory of Tustin, and the drive theory of Spotnitz. My aim of examining developmental communication, within these three psychoanalytic theories, is to both expand our knowledge of autism and to generate new child-centered questions. Questioning enriches each of our encounters with autism and drives us to learn to listen to the communication of each individual child diagnosed on the autistic spectrum.

The *Diagnostic and Statistical Manual of Mental Disorders* (*DSM*, American Psychiatric Association, 1994) identifies autism as a disorder that is developmental and originating early in life. The psychoanalytic theories of

Tustin and Spotnitz combine to specify typical and atypical growth and inhibition observed in early development. Further, each psychoanalytic theory describes specific substages within early development. Each substage is defined by the ego task to be mastered, a common fear that inhibits appropriate mastery, and a coping strategy most frequently chosen by a child with autism.

The origins of autism can reach back to the earliest days of infancy. Detailed knowledge of autistic-related inhibitions and autistic-style coping strategies developed during infancy encourage us as practitioners to reconsider diagnostic criteria and reflect on the following question: Are the dynamics of autism as presented by the child a disorder or a difference? Or, has this child chosen a coping strategy that is not only different, but also inappropriate and inefficient? That is, informed by the diagnostic criteria set forth in the *DSM*, and informed by the modern psychoanalytic theories of Spotnitz and Tustin, can we discover what drives this child's responses to life's challenges?

Established criteria focuses our attention on a rigid repetition, dominated by the aggressive drive and often observed in destructive *repetitive use of language, lack of variety, and restricted repetitive and stereotypic patterns*. Repetition placed in the service of development is generally spontaneous and frequently incorporated within a child's play. When Freud (1920) presents his observation of his grandson at play he considers the exact same dynamic behaviors and discovers the creative energies facilitated by repetition and rigid interactions with hard objects.

Freud (1920) watched as his grandson, sitting in his pram and crib, staged and restaged the disappearance and reappearance of a small toy. The child played alone and manipulated, in soothing rhythm, a small wooden toy attached to a string. The toy was thrown away and retrieved as he said/sang aloud the words *fort-da* (here-there). Freud theorized that the child used these auto-sensuous play strategies to learn how to tolerate the anxiety provoked when the object disappeared. Repetition of the *fort-da* (here-there) game, brought comfort and developed an ability to transfer the concept of come-go/ go-come to master his fear of separating from his mother. Freud's observations of the game inform our understanding of autistic communication. It suggests the initial question with which to begin our assessment of the child: Does the child demonstrate an ability to play? Any indication of such ability identifies the child in an autistic state as an appropriate candidate for psychoanalysis (Tustin, 1997).

The psychoanalyst and the educator study play to observe the child's typical and atypical development across the domains. Freud's *fort-da* game demonstrates typical development that incorporates appropriate, repetitive, early learning experience. Age-appropriate growth across the three domains—cognitive, affective, and psychomotor—is clearly observed and maturation is easily assessed. In Freud's study, the toy consisted of both the hard wooden object and attached soft string. As the child watched the toy appear, disappear, and then reappear, the young lad developed awareness of a separation process. Autism blocks this level of comfort and creative thought and the child continues to perceive separation as a terror-filled experience. The child's repetitive use of the toys demonstrates the use of compulsive repetition that blocks creative thought and awareness of the fear of separation.

Cognitively, the child is demonstrating purpose-filled sound reproductions and the early enunciation of distinct words. Understanding of the meaning of each word is demonstrated as the word aligns, correctly, with the direction of the moving toy. The infant's brain integrates touch and sight, aligns rhythmic sensuous sound with pleasure-filled sensuous sight, and creates the integrated sensing-viewing-thinking of a specific pattern: appear-disappear-reappear. The child thus experiences a degree of control over the environment.

Maturation within the affective domain is observed in the tone and rhythm of the child's vocalizations, in the child's willingness to be alone, and in the ability to self-entertain. Further, the game becomes a rehearsal, a set of repetitions preparing to tolerate a new level of anxiety provoked by mother's leaving. Through the repetitive tangible, concrete, experiences of an object, and integration of two senses, the ego develops.

Play-filled repetitions develop an open, unblocked system of language and thought, and integrate, with tolerable levels of anxiety, images provoked by the input of four senses. Repeated tactile experiences with the soft flexible string and the hard wooden toy are pleasurable and introduce thinking skills supportive of differentiation. Coordination of the five senses involves at least two patterns, and two levels of integration. One pattern connects the simultaneous seeing, feeling, and *speaking* of the object. The second pattern involves the seeing and the speaking of the disappearance, the *not there*. Through the comfort of rhythmic repetition the sensation of the empty gap provokes a tolerable level of anxiety. The image of the *not there* can be kept in awareness and can drive early stages of ego development in support of separation and individuation. Further, detailed observation of the *fort-da* game demonstrates the meaning-filled integration of the very early integration of the senses. Through repetition the infant increasingly integrates sight and sound, thought and emotion. Communication begins to flow as an open, authentic system of self-expression. The child's singing/humming fort-da is soothing and auto-sensuous. It facilitates self-experiencing. The coupling that links the two distinct sounds is an internal self-produced vibration and an *external echo*. The verbal production, authentic early language, contains two one-syllable words. Each word contains a single syllable. Taken together, the two syllables suggest the safe, securing experience of one complete whole, with a beginning and an end. Separation does not then become a shattering blow to the self. The ongoing/repetitive, pleasure-filled, rhythmical sensation of the two sounds coordinates with a specific visual experience that reinforces the meaning of each word. However, the meaning of each word, reinforced by the sight, provokes opposite emotions.

Maturation does not come from the mere integration of the three senses. What becomes the essential developmental experience of the game is not the isolated tactile element, not the speaking, and not only the viewing sensation, but, in fact, an integration of all three. The child continues to advance successfully through the early stage of separation-individuation because the ego develops. Certain instincts become cognitive habits. Expressive communication seeks visual-facial affirmation. The speaker searches the face of the other for assurance that s/he is seen and understood. The combined senses of seeing and holding the toy brings pleasure. The physical and visual gap/void/separation increases anxiety. The repetitive reappearance makes awareness of the disappearance tolerable.

Through play, driven by creative repetition, the self-controlled *hold-throw-pull* and manipulating of a concrete object provokes an abstract self-soothing image. Freud's description of his young grandson's playing captures self-mastery across the domains. Developing motor skills of coordination and body rhythms were evident in the grandson. Self-produced musical sounds serve to contain the child's anxiety. Visual and audio sensations strengthen positive emotions. The data flowing from at least three of the five senses is integrated. Physical and emotional strengths invested in play transition and develop into the real experience of separating from the mother.

Through his shared observations of his infant grandson, Freud demonstrated that this integration of the senses is critical to development through the mastery of separation and individuation. Freud showed that the multiple repetitions, flexible and rigid, were supported by the integration of vision, language, and play. The contrast between the flow of Freud's scenario and the rigidity noted within autistic communication suggests that our informed initial response to the repetition presented by a child may be to reflect, self-observe, and clarify its texture: Do I experience this child's repetition as rigid and isolating or flexible and mastering? Reversal of autistic self-expression is supported by listening that envisions a nurturing blend of rigid and flexible repetitions

MODERN PSYCHOANALYTIC PERSPECTIVES ON AUTISM: SPOTNITZ AND TUSTIN

Hyman Spotnitz and Frances Tustin, two twentieth-century psychoanalysts, were trained in Freud's classical theory of psychoanalysis and read his case studies to build their psychoanalytic knowledge of child development. While maintaining a personal and professional commitment to Freudian theory, Tustin (1916–1994) shifted away from classical theory toward modern psychotherapy driven by object relations theory, and Spotnitz (1908–2008), a dual drive theorist, conceived of what has come to be known as modern psychoanalysis. The psychoanalytic theories and techniques of Tustin and Spotnitz, combined, best support our ability to listen to the communications of a child with autism. While each analyst affirms a contrasting psychoanalytic theory, both are rooted in classic Freudian psychology, and understand autism as an infantile strategy chosen to defend against intolerable levels of anxiety provoked by experiences of explosive aggression. Beginning in the early 1950s Frances Tustin's clinical work at London's Tavistock Clinic exposed her to the object relations theory of Melanie Klein and to the developmental needs of a very specific group of children referred to as autistic. In her major text, *Autistic States in Children* (1997), Tustin combined her extensive clinical and private practice experiences to detail the psychodynamics and treatment of children with autism. Around the same time, but on the other side of the Atlantic in New York City, Hyman Spotnitz treated children with schizophrenia at the office of the Jewish Board of Guardians. In his frequently referenced text, *Psychotherapy of Preoedipal Conditions* (1987) Spotnitz detailed his theory of modern psychoanalysis and described a personal set of techniques to work with preoedipal conditions with autistic characteristics. Both Tustin and Spotnitz stressed that the apparent narcissistic self-love presented by a child with autism is, in reality, self-hatred.

In 1949 Spotnitz addressed the American Psychiatric Association and described his methods for resolving defenses originating early in life. At the core of his technique is Freud's (1920) concept of an *innate* destructive drive. That is, the roots of a severe pathology like autism can begin at birth with a general inability to process impulses. Spotnitz's techniques, capable of reversing many autistic conditions, both observe the expansive role of Thanatos (i.e., Freud's death instinct) in the emotional blockages defining autism, and develop an ability to hear and see body communications about conflicts. Spotnitz placed the responsibility for resolving autism on the efforts of the psychoanalyst to see and to listen to the autistic communications, verbal and non-verbal, of the child with autism.

Tustin and Spotnitz, grounded in the classical psychoanalysis of Freud, understood autism to be a defense against intense anxiety developed early in life. However, the two psychoanalysts held contrasting perspectives on the earliest stage of infant life. While each analyst stressed the dominant role of aggression in autism, each identified a different point in development at which aggressive instincts emerge. This developmental difference scaffolds a contrasting developmental perspective on the emergence of anxiety, on the nature of infantile communication, and on the skills of listening to pre-verbal communications. Tustin indicated that at birth the infant experiences a single libidinal drive along with an ability to sense the presence of an object. She suggested that after a short defining period of time the infant's aggressive impulses develop. This concept of a brief developmental space structured first by only one, and then by two, sets of impulses, shaped Tustin's understanding of infant communication, the core of early, autistic language. For Tustin, it was possible for the infant, and therefore the child with autism, to present some self-expressions free of destructive pressures and to have these directed toward an object. This understanding of every early stage of communication defined by a single libidinal drive flowing toward a container-type object encouraged Tustin to include interpretation as a very early response to the verbal and nonverbal stressed-filled communications of the child with autism.

Spotnitz focused uniquely on Freud's dual drive theory (1920) and hypothesized that life is defined by two sets of drives that are present at birth. That is, beginning at the moment of birth, humans, in an attempt to manage levels of stimulation, struggle with one set of drives to live/create and one set of drives to die/destroy. Spotnitz expanded Freud's hypothesis that the death drive is innate and rendered possible the treatment of emotional conditions like autism previously hidden behind a 'stone wall of narcissism.' Thus, while Tustin and Spotnitz disagreed about the content of the infant's earliest expressions, the two analysts agreed that at a critical developmental point in the early months of infancy healthy narcissism becomes pathological. Both analysts recognized that it is the child's withdrawal that defines autism as dominated by significant self-hatred and an infant life dominated by destructive aggression.

Spotnitz and Tustin posited that autism is dominated by a gross inability to invest early aggressive impulses in personally and socially appropriate activity. Both psychoanalysts agreed that the infant, initially, experiences an intolerable level of frustration and then chooses autism as a defensive strategy to avoid intense levels of stress and anxiety. To begin to describe the infantile auto-sensuous characteristics of this defense Tustin generally employed the metaphor of hard shell while Spotnitz described layers of protective insulation. Tustin most frequently referenced the autistic defense as an encapsulation. In *Autistic States in Children* Tustin detailed the physical and sensual attributes of hard encrustation that frequently shape the textures of early autistic language and detailed a series of early ego tasks that frequently provoke a greater desire for a protective shell. Physically, she described how the infant's body becomes rigid like a shell, resisting the hold of the caretaker. She further described the infant's internal early autistic sensation of hardness: if the young child sits in a chair its body senses the qualities of the surface of the chair as characteristics of its own body. The infant with autism senses hardness of chair as hardness within its self. Tustin linked the body rigidity often assumed by the infant with autism to the concept of a defensive hard protective shell, then to the blurred cognitive integration of a sensuous experience of *hard* and further extended the critical role of the concept *hard* to the autistic child's intense external manipulation of hard objects.

Spotnitz, like Tustin, envisioned withdrawal, critical to the autistic defense, as a strategy to feel protected from intolerable levels of stress. Both analysts related the pressure to withdraw to the child's experience of explosive impulses. Spotnitz understood withdrawal as increasing and decreasing layers of insulation driven by the theory of dual drives and economics (1987). A healthy shield of insulation, driven by the fused drives, was like skin, flexible and with few layers. Pathological insulation was dominated by both aggressive drives and the intensity of the explosive impulse. Like Freud (1926), Spotnitz posited that the intensity of stress and anxiety experienced by the child as *intolerable* was an *economic* factor, defined by significant amounts of energy seeking discharge. Both Tustin and Spotnitz frequently referred to this concept of discharge as intolerable levels of explosive anxiety. For Spotnitz the amount of discharge to be defended against drove the numbers of layers of insulation to be created by the child with autism. Spotnitz posited that pressure to discharge, and the instinct to hate are innate, present at birth. The impulse to undo and destroy proceeds from birth as an integral component of development. Resistance to, and a wish to escape from, the internal pressure for discharge of destructive drives defines typical and atypical development. To Spotnitz autism is a pre-oedipal condition, driven by destructive aggression, aiming to become detached and isolated from the fear of the consequences of acting on one's own aggressive impulses. Increasing levels of fear provoke increasing levels of anxiety characteristic of autism, and drive the infant's ever increasing sense of need for insulation. Spotnitz posited that the pathological use of projection drives the severe withdrawal characteristic of autism.

Both Tustin and Spotnitz detailed that when autism is established as the defense of choice, the infant's defensive use of emerging cognitive skills provokes a cycle of ever increasing intense need. Both psychoanalysts identified the infant's three dominant developmental coping skills as projective identification, introjection, and splitting. The extreme overuse of these skills provokes a pathological sequence that begins with the infant's experience of overwhelming frustration that next provokes aggressive impulses and then the need to defend against the release of destructive energy resulting in the inability to assimilate supportive and nurturing narcissistic supplies from an object perceived to be totally bad. The distressed infant survives through the repeated use of projection and introjection. First, the infant projects all of his or her dangerous, explosive destructive impulses into the object. Then the infant introjects an image of the object. As this cycle is repeated the reintrojected image now contains its originally perceived otherness plus the destructive components originally expelled. The infant's fear increases and stronger protection is sought to defend against ever-increasing levels of anxiety. At a sensual and emotional level, the suffering infant increasingly repeats the project-introject cycle, blocking critical awareness of the image of the feared object. The infant chooses eventually not to perceive the anxiety-provoking object. The image is no longer seen or trusted by the infant who is now driven by destructive aggression and dominated by the pathological defense of autism.

Spotnitz and Tustin studied the intense anxiety that defines autism and recognized this intolerable level of stress to be a signal of danger. Each analyst described, again, a contrasting developmental point at which the over-sensuous pressure originates. Spotnitz, like Freud (1926), places anxiety within the dynamics of the dual drive theory and innate destructive aggression. He indicated that prior to sensing any internal or external image of *other*, the infant is overwhelmed by its own destructive impulses. Spotnitz concluded the anxiety presented by a child with autism might be confined to an autosenuous experience with no awareness of the analyst's presence. Spotnitz (1976) posited that the infant or child whose autistic pathology is dominated by destructive aggression, will defend against anxiety by fragmenting the ego and creating a narcissistic defense. Freud described narcissism, metaphorically, as a stone wall which brings the psychoanalytic process, and the reversal of autism, to a complete halt. Spotnitz guarded against providing any response that would intensify this level of pathological narcissism.

Tustin's observations of autistic states expanded our developmental understanding of anxiety. Perhaps one of the most significant contributions that this British psychoanalyst made to the study of autistic states was to link a specific type of anxiety to a particular defense chosen at different stages during infancy. Like Klein (1975), Tustin believed that during the first year of life mental structures were organized around two positions, Paranoid-Schizoid, and Depressive. Each was assumed to last about six months and to develop specific characteristics or mechanisms. Tustin suggested that during the paranoid-schizoid stage the infant uses incorporation, splitting, projection, and projective identification as primary methods of organizing the world. She found that during these first six months the infant's anxiety stems from a perceived threat of disintegration of self and fears of explosiveness. In the paranoid-schizoid position, anxieties of a primitive nature threaten the immature ego and lead to the mobilization of primitive defenses. The infant with autism, at this stage of development shows a characteristic lack of insight and resistance to change. Tustin states that in the depressive position, during the second six months, the infant's defenses are more highly organized and held together by narcissistic relationships in which pathological satisfactions are sought.

Tustin's understanding of specific developmental anxieties, each with specific developmental defenses, along with Spotnitz's critical positioning of the narcissistic defense, enable us to listen to the developmentally fixated, defensive specific, non-verbal, anxiety-filled expressions of an infant with autism. The language-free communications of school age children on the autistic spectrum express affect disconnected from thought and word. Our professional task is to discover ways to make, for this child, the fear-filled unthinkable safely thinkable.

Spotnitz and Tustin understood that an on-going struggle with the developmental task of separation and individuation provoked this early intense anxiety. Each posited that the critical developmental task of separation, when stimulated too early provokes, in the infant, overwhelming fear and anxiety. In an effort to avoid awareness of separation and to avoid the resulting anxiety, the child with autism will seek to remain merged with the omnipotence and superiority of the caregiver. In an effort to avoid emerging experiences of differentiation, and awareness of the resulting anxiety, the infant and young child depend on the strategy of splitting. Drives are split with the domination of destructive aggression sustaining the isolation characteristic of autism. Objects are divided and experienced as totally good or totally bad with no one or no thing capable of being both liked and, at times, disliked. As a result autistic communication becomes fragmented and drives fail to be fused. An understanding of "I" and "you" is obliterated; images and perceptions of objects remain either totally good or totally bad. The bad images, provoking high levels of anxiety, are defensively and pathologically removed from awareness and drive the production of autistic communication.

Spotnitz and Tustin demonstrated through their clinical experiences and private psychoanalytic practices that the *talking cure* is able to reverse, to a degree, the pathology of autism for some children. They understood that the process of reversal is developmental, and they focused on the verbal and nonverbal communications of the child with autism. Both prioritized the attentive, reflective responses of the psychoanalyst but they held distinctly contrasting opinions on the embedding of interpretation within the psychoanalytic process. Both psychoanalysts aimed to reconnect thought with feeling and words, and they attended to the holistic nature of the analytic experience to discover the authentic content of the communication. Tustin judged that a young child demonstrating an ability to play is able to reverse, to a degree, the pathology of autism. From the earliest encounters Tustin observed the young child's non-verbal and verbal expressions of fear and almost immediately interpreted them to the child with autism. Spotnitz seldom interpreted any communication until the ending months of the psychoanalytic relationship. He depended upon the child's level of contact to guide his response. When a high level of withdrawal was present, Spotnitz sat quietly and mirrored the child's low level of recognition of the analyst's presence. Through these initial silent responses the analyst demonstrated to the fear-filled child a depth of self-control, creating a sense of safety within the analytic process. As the child initiated some contact Spotnitz responded in kind. As the child's talking skills developed and as Spotnitz's ability to listen to the non-verbal and verbal language of the child increased, the process of reversing autistic communication advanced slowly. Spotnitz posited that a psychoanalyst's use of contact functioning lessened the child's pathological defensive use of autistic strategies and frequently contra-indicated the analyst's intrusion that would come from offering interpretations.

Spotnitz depended on the technique of *contact function* to respond to the child with preoedipal conditions. He prioritized creating a safe environment for the child filled with intolerable, explosive, aggressive impulses. To create the lowest level of tension Spotnitz began by mirroring the level of contact the child made with the analyst. Only when the child demonstrated significant maturation did Spotnitz interpret the autistic non-verbal and verbal communications. Maturation was evidenced in efforts to begin to practice ways to fuse the drives. Spotnitz, ever vigilant of the pathological domination of the aggressive drive, posited that the child's dynamic emerging self-awareness of hatred and self-hatred linked to the possibility of speaking a threatening, but developmental, thought: I hate myself so I don't have to hate you. Eventually a maturational-related thought may emerge: I hate you but you listen to me. Reversal of autistic communication begins with this possible early infantile risk to connect love and hate, to a minimal degree, in one object. The modern psychoanalytic experience, as understood by Spotnitz becomes a developmental process in which the over-stimulation and intolerable levels of anxiety and fear that drive the early choice of autism as a pathological coping strategy diminishes and the thought "this unwanted feeling will pass" emerges.

LEARNING FROM A SINGLE LONGITUDINAL CASE STUDY

Ten years ago Gabe,[1] aged nine years, bounced into my office. His mother and I had been meeting for about a half-hour discussing her concerns about her son's social and emotional difficulties. Together we decided that she would invite her son into the office and that she would then leave.

The transition went smoothly. Without hesitation, or invite, Gabe sat in a chair opposite mine. He arranged himself "Indian-style" and placed my box of tissues in his lap. He said "Hello," told me his grade, what he was reading, that he had a sister, and that his father was at work. He talked non-stop. For each new thought he presented he plucked a tissue from the box, crunched it up, and threw it on the floor. Our shared time went quickly and I felt entertained by his one-person show. He created an impressive monologue and incorporated interesting gestures. However the flood of words seemed to build a barrier between us. Gabe asked me no questions but told me that he would be very happy to return the following week. Gabe returned the following week and continues to return, without resistance, each week since then.

During our third session I suggested that he might lie on the couch, explaining, "That is often where we do some really good talking." Without hesitation, Gabe bounded onto the couch and started to tell a story. "We went to visit my grandma. . . . We went for a walk on the beach. Grandma had a grandma, and she had a grandma . . . and she had . . ." As his talking transitioned into a singsong it felt as if he were traveling through space, alone, in a capsule that provided me little protection.

In our sessions Gabe's breathing was relaxed and without congestion. Between sessions his mother reported a concern about his breathing that was quickly becoming a problem. She stated that at bedtime, on the evenings that the father left to work a night shift, Gabe would become asthmatic and she would take Gabe into her bed. The mother explained that she reported to the doctor that the asthma was becoming more severe, and that the pediatrician wanted to put Gabe on medication. She said she wanted my advice. I asked her to tolerate her son's difficult breathing until the next scheduled visit with the doctor but, each evening, leave Gabe in his own bed. If she felt the need to keep him close, she might just lie on the floor beside Gabe's bed. Within a week of not going into his parent's bed Gabe's breathing eased and no medicine was prescribed.

For several years Gabe filled our sessions with words but he never used them to communicate what he was thinking. He came every week, lay relaxed on the couch, moved very little, and told a story. In the summer between 5th and 6th grade Gabe's routine and presentation changed. He came to therapy dressed in shorts and sandals. Without explanation he sat on the edge of the couch and said he wanted to see me. It felt as if he wanted to take charge and re-arrange our space. Verbally, he remained pleasant. His session remained wall-to-wall empty words. Each week he retold the events of each day since our last session. The words sounded like a grocery list and it felt as if he were piecing together segments of his life. Non-verbally, his body was telling a story of rage and self-hatred. His legs were covered in mosquito bites that he never let heal. When a scab formed he immediately scratched it off and made the bite bleed. He stopped bathing and the body odor, like his many words, defined his presence and filled the space. He developed more than a dozen boils across his back that wept and stuck to his tee shirt. He told me that part of getting ready for bed involved ripping his shirt off and making the boils weep. On occasion he passed gas and by the end of our session my office smelled intensely foul. His skin and orifices communicated the intensity of his self-hatred and anxiety. In his refusal to bathe, to follow the basic rules of hygiene, it seemed as if Gabe were trying painfully to birth himself. In his foul smells I actually felt okay, struggling to survive the unwanted aromas.

When school began Gabe changed back to shoes, but he still refused to bathe. He developed an in-grown toenail, and told no one until the toe became badly infected. At times his swollen, heavily bandaged foot provoked in me feelings of being rejected and powerless. I had the recurring thought that he preferred a hands-on doctor, a doctor that made physical contact. I said, "I feel like holding that foot of yours to make it all better." He said nothing but tears streamed down his face.

Mid-June of 7th grade brought the science-fair. On the night of the event, about a half hour before its close, two things happened. Gabe learned he was winning his class award and his teacher asked him to be in charge of some classmates for five minutes while she went away. The teacher exited and within one minute he burned himself so badly with a glue gun that he had used in his own science project, that he had to be taken to hospital. As Gabe told his story I felt his anger and disappointment. I had a clear sequence of thoughts: His work had won the approval he yearned for; he had won the teacher's attention and she spoke to him and not to his classmates; his work wasn't good enough to keep them connected. As she walked away he felt left behind. His pain was beyond words and burning himself expressed his rage. I said to Gabe, "Gee it wasn't good enough for you to do the best science work in the class, now you had to be the best monitor." He whispered, "You're right" and his eyes filled with tears.

At the end of 8th grade Gabe's parents planned that he would go away to camp for a week. His mother prepared him for the week apart and for the first five days of camp he was appropriate and cooperative. On the sixth day the sun was shining brightly. On his own, Gabe rowed a boat to the middle of the lake and stayed there for over two hours. He took off his shirt and did not use one ounce of the sunscreen his mother had packed. Gabe deliberately received severe sunburn across his entire back. He disregarded all the preparations and warnings that his mother presented prior to his separation from her and home. His mother was powerless as he tried to take charge of his own body. I remained silent and simply listened. My wish was that he would feel his power. About thirty minutes after telling this story he stood to leave. As he placed his hand on the doorknob he said, "I like when you listen."

To date this has been the last story Gabe has told of inflicting significant damage to his body when experiencing deep-filled hurt. At first the non-verbal, the sensational scratching of his legs, seemed like explosive, impulsive action. There were no 'matching' words. The narcissistic transference became clearer during the retelling of that first body burning. I felt a pang of pain and neglect that I perceived mirrored his anger about being left behind and separated from his teacher just when he felt accepted and joined. Recently I was able to recognize the nature of his *un-thought* pain.

During the early years of school Gabe and his family had a morning routine. On her way to work his mother drove him to school. Upon arrival his young sister went into the schoolyard to play and his mother eventually drove off. Gabe hugged the fence. Recently he recalled how angry he felt that she could go live her life, live a whole day, without him. Separation, in any form, remains difficult for Gabe to tolerate.

As Gabe used his skin less frequently to express his struggles with separation and individuation non-verbally, he increasingly, inappropriately, manipulated his eyes. Even though he had significant difficultly maintaining eye contact, Gabe moved one last time from lying on the couch to sitting in a chair directly opposite mine. At the beginning of each session he would use his hair as a drape to cover his eyes. If he answered a question he would immediately wet the tip of his index and middle finger, pull down his lids, and almost gouge his eyes. It was as if he were erasing his words. Through the transference I began to feel he was struggling to see and speak his own words.

Gabe's struggle to see his own words has been life long. By the age of 18 months, at least once a day, he watched *The Nightmare before Christmas* (Selick, 1993). He reports that he memorized the opening dialogue of the movie and used this dialogue to greet each person he met. He was in kindergarten before he simply greeted anyone with "hello." In 6th grade his teacher assigned him to work with a classmate, Matt, to collaborate on language arts projects. For several months Matt and Gabe sat together in class and then, they began sitting together voluntarily during lunch and writing dialogues. Gabe began to make sketches to illustrate the dialogue that was frequently drafted by Matt. Eventually, after school, the two lads made videos using the dialogue and images created in school. Through these successful projects the boys became comfortable with each other. At times he thought of Matt as a friend, "like what other people have." Gabe reported, "Without Matt, I'm nothing. He's my other half; he completes me. He has the words, I see the images."

The summer after graduating 8th grade Gabe returned to designing videos in order to create a communication. Without talking about them he was trying to tolerate change and separations. He anticipated September when he would have to travel, alone, on public transportation to high school. To increase his level of confidence and lower his now intense anticipatory anxiety, his parents and Gabe agreed that Gabe would, independently ride the subway to and from my office. My office is in my home, a century-old Victorian structure complete with front porch and screen doors. That first summer morning Gabe stood alone on my front porch and rang my doorbell. He walked past me carrying under one arm a copy of the *New York Times*, and in one hand he held two small paper bags. Without hesitation he walked into my office, and, turning directly toward me, he extended one bag to me and reported, "I didn't know how you took your coffee so I got yours black."

Gabe sat down, sipped his coffee, and began to discuss the work of Mel Brooks. His posture was erect and different from his usual somewhat relaxed slouch. His words flowed, teaching me all that I presumably did not know about the world-famous artist. With no introductory remark, he reported, "Mel Brooks is a great filmmaker because he writes great dialogue. To imitate his dialogues is a great tribute to his genius." He continued speaking about moviemaking, non-stop, until the end of the session when he stood and remarked, "We will meet next week, same time, same place." To me, my office and the completed session felt like a staging, a series of images being used to tolerate the anxiety provoked by the many changes in his life.

In a recent session Gabe returned to discussing his connection to *The Nightmare before Christmas*. His thoughts demonstrate an emerging strength to master his fear of separation and individuation.

> My mom and dad are different. My dad understands how I played. My mother didn't have a clue. My mother bought the movie and later my parents used coupons off the cereal box to get me the toy figure. I played with the figure and broke the head off. My dad just glued the head back on. My mother said, "Why can't you take care of your toys?" My dad understood me, my mother didn't." See in the movie when Marley danced he took his head off and held it in his own hands. My figure was dancing just like Marley.

Gabe's explanation seemed to be a deliberate effort to communicate with me. I responded with a question, "Do you think you ever tell me a story but keep part of it a secret?" He smiled and for a brief time, made comfortable eye contact. Then he explained, "Sometimes I've told you stuff about my friends but never tell you what was really important."

Gabe's reference to small hard toys has been very common in our sessions. From our earliest sessions he repeatedly described his unending pleasure playing with Legos. He would fill with obvious pride as he explained, "Each time I get a Lego set I first put it together following the directions. Then I put it together in a way no one else has thought of. Then I take a unique piece from one and combine it into another set in a way that I didn't even imagine." Gabe seldom repeats any story. However this Lego sequence of connecting playing, hard toys, and imagination, is repeated frequently. Perhaps, like a dream that cannot be totally remembered because it's meaning is buried at a safe distance from his consciousness, the incomplete understanding of the Lego play can be safely repeated. I frequently feel close to Gabe when he tells a Lego story. His body relaxes and he makes confident direct eye contact. His eyes stop darting around the room and storytelling feels safe. It seems like a fleeting moment when he and I almost make contact.

Gabe's recent references to the Legos provoked a new set of thoughts in me. The feel of the hard toy is a tactile sensation and aligns with Gabe's earlier inappropriate use of his skin and his eyes to communicate negative impulses. As the Legos were used to build new, previously unthought of objects, Gabe's authentic self-expression was developing, and his words were developing content and meaning. They were focused and he knew he was able to focus my attention where he wanted. I yearned to "see" what he was saying. For several sessions I continued to watch his body and listen to his words. In my imagination I stared at a small, configured Lego set and, for a while, no new thought or feeling came. Then I became aware of the most simple of new thoughts. It was as if he finally got my attention, indicated where he wanted me to look, and I was simply focusing on what he wanted me to look at. In that moment I felt confident that he and I were sharing an early infantile exchange. Before this moment I had not connected the very early, auto-sensuous visual component of our communications.

Gabe's detailed description of the sequence of the increasingly complicated Lego pattern seemed to mirror his uninhibited thought. Gabe, indirectly, was letting me know, "I genuinely like this private experience." Talking about repeatedly completing the Lego building process lowered Gabe's anxiety and provided him with a sense of safety when handling a "not-me." Each time he retold this Lego sequence I didn't feel bored. I wanted to see what he was creating. He described building the object and used his words to focus my attention on his creation. It felt as if through the *fort-da* of the Lego building story it was finally safe for Gabe to be aware of my hearing and seeing him.

FRAMING NON-VERBAL AND VERBAL COMMUNICATION WITHIN PSYCHOANALYSIS

Spotnitz and Tustin taught us that autism, and other preoedipal conditions, can sometimes be mitigated using psychoanalytic technique. The autistic child's non-verbal and verbal communications are understood to be products of the destructive drive. Autistic non-verbal communication is best understood as rooted in the early, auto-sensuous stages of maturation, containing intolerable levels of anxiety with developmental-specific defenses. Autistic verbal communication is frequently experienced as impulsive *words-in-action* aiming to relieve explosive feelings and to convey little meaning. Spotnitz, a dual drive theorist, posited that communication, driven by love and hate, commences at birth. He perceived autistic communication as fragmenting the ego and disconnecting thought from feeling and words. He believed that an autistic experience of primary sensation and failed sensory integration, dominated by hate, may be presumed to exist prior to the paranoid-schizoid and depressive positions referenced by Klein and Tustin. Both Tustin and Spotnitz theorized that the child with autism continues to struggle with the earliest infantile developmental tasks of separation and individuation. As we strive to learn to listen to the verbal and non-verbal communications of children with autism it may be appropriate to envision an *autistic-contiguous* or *auto-sensuous* developmental stage with infantile mental structures emerging within the initial stage of the paranoid-schizoid position. This most undifferentiated stage of development, containing the dual drives, is an experience of isolated, auto-sensuousness, and is defined by pre-symbolic body sensations. In these early days of life, frustration may provoke aggression and a resulting anxiety that floods from a perceived threat to the surface of the body. Spotnitz hypothesized that this earliest form of anxiety may be observed in autistic communication that defines the low developmental levels of the autistic spectrum.

In *Autistic States in Children* (1997) Tustin described how the auto-sensuous stage of development serves as a basis for classification of pathological autism. She detailed how attributes of the physical body of a child with autism can embody symptoms of psychic pathology. In chapter 4, "Autogenerated encapsulation" and chapter 5, "Confusional entanglement" Tustin outlined numerous critical characteristics contrasting autistic encapsulation and autistic entanglement. The following chart organizes specific descriptors that are relevant to the case study of Gabe.

Autogenerated Encapsulated	*Confusional Entanglement*
Arrested	Regressed
	Good physical health Poor health with respiratory, digestive, and other physical difficulties
Unresponsive to holding	Molds to holding
Highly intelligent, easily grasps spatial relationships	Some language, but with slurred, indistinct speech
Early withdrawal with tantrums	Confusion between self and other
May be echolalic	
Fascinated with mechanical toys	Clumsy and ill coordinated; Encrusted in a shell; Relations with mother too open Lacking in boundaries (Tustin, 1997, pp. 46–74)

Tustin presented the contrasting concepts of encrusted and entangled characteristics of autism to encompass all the possible physical defenses against the intense fear of separation and individuation. She suggested that these sets of body descriptions exist across each stage of development. Observations of Gabe's body at different stages in his journey with early autism demonstrates the presence of several of the diagnostic characteristics from both the *encapsulated* and *entangled* categories. Gabe can appear encapsulated with his rigid body and his ever-darting alert eyes. He frequently threw tantrums at the start of the school day and he remains fascinated with mechanical toys. At the same time he can appear entangled, suffering from asthma and eating problems, appearing clumsy, and lacking the coordination to ride a bicycle. It is possible that Gabe's flexible movements between the physical-psychic categories are relevant to the stage of development just prior to that of the paranoid-schizoid position, the *auto-contiguous* position. Perhaps because an auto-sensuous pathology, as perceived by Spotnitz, originates in an undifferentiated stage of development, when any effort toward separation and individuation provokes intense levels of anxiety, bodily pathological characteristics remain in a state of flux. When autism is chosen at birth as a strategy for survival, the domination of the aggressive drive, as described by Spotnitz, and the anxiety-specific defense, as outlined by Tustin, combine to suggest that the earliest, pathological auto-sensuous stage of development is an explosive state, defined by a common set of characteristics but not yet organized, shifting between encapsulation and entanglement, grouping and regrouping, seeking defense rather than development. To facilitate the psychological development of the child with autism, our listening must become visibly focused on dynamic sets of multiple auto-sensuous defensive components of the child's nonverbal and verbal communications.

Tustin and Spotnitz taught us that an autistic state is developmental, originating in the early months of life, filled with pathological narcissism, driven by a destructive aggressive drive, strengthened by an overuse of splitting and projecting. These two psychoanalysts posited that autism may be a reversible pathological narcissism provided that the analyst learns to listen to the analysand's overwhelming self-hatred, and recognizes the defensive overuse of splitting and projection. Such psychoanalytic listening to the verbal and nonverbal language of autism involves skillful use of contact functioning and timely interpretation. Contact functioning, prioritized by Spotnitz, creates the internal and external sense of safety that nurtures the early maturational needs of the withdrawn child, and encourages the taking of small, developmentally appropriate risks by the child. Timely interpretation, as encouraged by Tustin and Spotnitz, scaffolds the child's fragmented thoughts and isolated feelings, encourages the fusion of the drives, and may help reverse the narcissistic pathology of autistic communication for some children.

NOTE

1. All material about Gabe (pseudonym) has been disguised to protect his identity. The patient has given permission for this information to be shared.

REFERENCES

American Psychiatric Association (1994). Diagnostic criteria 299.00 Autistic disorder. *Diagnostic and Statistical Manual of Mental Disorders*. Fourth Edition (DSM-IV). www.autreat.com/dsm4-autism.html, accessed June 15, 2012.

Freud, S. (1920). Beyond the pleasure principle. *Standard Edition, 18*, 7–26.

Freud, S. (1926). Inhibitions, symptoms, and anxiety. *Standard Edition, 20*, 77–175.

Goleman, D. (1995). *Emotional intelligence*. New York: Bantam Dell.

Klein, M. (1975). *Envy and gratitude and other works 1946–1963*. New York: Free Press.

Selick, H. (1993). (Director). *The nightmare before christmas*. Touchstone Pictures.

Spotnitz, H. (1987). *The psychotherapy of preoedipal conditions*. Northvale, NJ: Jason Aronson.

Tustin, F. (1997). *Autistic states in children*. [Revised Edition]. London: Tavistock/Routledge.

Chapter Sixteen

The Power of Conscience

Jiminy Cricket's Legacy

Devra B. Adelstein and Judith L. Pitlick

Five-and-a-half-year-old Natalie runs out of her kindergarten classroom screaming, "No! I'm not cleaning up." By the time her teacher, Mrs. Hart reaches her, Natalie is lying on the hallway floor, crying. Mrs. Hart, feeling frustrated and helpless tries to coax her back into the room, restating the rule that children need to clean up. Before returning to the classroom, Mrs. Hart, compassionately offers, "I know you will look inside yourself and find a way to come back and do your job." A few minutes later Natalie peers into the room and sees her friends enjoying snack. She realizes she wants to be part of the group, walks back into the classroom and cleans up. After snack, when her teacher asks what helped her, Natalie says, "I remembered how you helped me think about being nice to myself and not missing fun times."

Mrs. Hart found an opportunity to help Natalie listen to her conscience, or superego. When Natalie initially ran out of the classroom, she was attempting to run away from the harsh, yelling voice inside of her. Mrs. Hart saw Natalie's distress and rather than issue an ultimatum, helped her access her kinder internal voice. Mrs. Hart knew that Natalie's conscience was becoming internalized, meaning she was taking in parental rules and making them her own.

Early in the process of internalization, a child often experiences the voice of conscience as harsh and disapproving. The harshness can interfere with the child's ability to use the conscience as a guide. It can also impact learning, relationships, and overall progressive development. For some children, the process of internalization of conscience almost goes unnoticed. Others struggle a bit but manage to work through the process with minimal assistance. Most challenging are those children who become stuck and need active help from a loving and trusted adult such as Mrs. Hart, to move the process along.

Natalie's struggle over what to do led her to run out of the classroom in distress. She worked to calm down and reenter the classroom, knowing that if she listened to her conscience she could make a good decision. She needed her teacher to support, not punish or coerce her. The best outcome for Natalie is an integrated conscience she can rely on and feel good about. Out of a fear of punishment or a wish to please, many children develop solutions that are less satisfactory. Pleasing one's self while meeting appropriate life expectations is optimal.

In this chapter, we will discuss the path of conscience development from a psychoanalytic perspective. Our discussion will include milestones of conscience development, the establishment of the conscience in latency, and clinical examples based on experiences with real children. We will illustrate how it is possible for teachers and other adults to connect empathically with children, resulting in a nurturing conscience that will be a guide throughout life.

THE DEVELOPMENT OF CONSCIENCE: FINDING A FRIEND FOR LIFE

How does the conscience become a fully functioning part of the personality? Ideally it is kind yet firm, and emerges as an internal compass that guides a person to make good decisions. An understanding of child development is essential to appreciate how one builds a conscience. Mastery at each developmental phase in the earliest years results in an integrated personality, which is necessary for healthy conscience development (Winnicott, 1965; Furman, 1987).

Psychoanalytic thinking teaches that in infancy the quality of the relationship between a baby and his/her parents establishes the foundation of emotional health, essential for a reliable conscience. Babies learn to understand themselves and the world around them through their relationships. When a parent responds in a loving way to the baby's experience of tension or pain, the baby feels secure. When babies experience too much discomfort, their ability to self-regulate and feel good may be compromised, later interfering with the process of conscience development.

By early toddlerhood, children have developed a beginning awareness that they are separate from their parents. They learn what is expected of them through the relationship with their parents. This awareness of parental expectations can be anxiety producing as well as reassuring. In an effort to maintain love and approval, toddlers struggle to meet parental expectations. Toddlers who are too frequently and too harshly admonished or punished may have significant trouble sustaining loving feelings for themselves and their parents. The repeated loss of parental love can be devastating. Parents who provide a consistent loving presence help their toddlers sustain the good feelings essential for further growth and development.

While helping children learn limits, parents can model the appropriate expression of anger and other feelings. Fraiberg (1959) discusses obstacles to healthy conscience development during these early years. She suggests that too lenient an approach, as well as one that is too harsh, can result in a child having difficulty taking responsibility for his/her own actions.

Children move into the preschool years still reliant on their parents' external control to help them manage. They need parental support because the conscience is still not internalized. The essential next step is for children to progress toward integrating the rules, that is, making the rules their own.

Achievement of autonomy and mastery is important in all areas of development, particularly in the area of conscience development. Furman (1991) discusses the idea of gradual progression toward independence and interdependence. She outlines the course of development from dependency to autonomy and mastery, and its application at each new phase. During the preschool years, ages three to five, children advance in their ability to know right from wrong, and to say "no" to themselves. Their capacity to sustain this knowledge falters without the loving support of parents and teachers. By age four, children are more able to maintain inner standards without a caring adult present. To illustrate, Rachel, age four and a half, was able to speak politely when another classmate bumped into her work. After preschool that day, Rachel proudly told her mother that she stayed calm and polite even though she was angry.

Anny Katan (1961) underlines the impact of verbalization on mastery of both impulses and bodily expression of feeling. The process of verbalization allows the child time to think and "judge the situation" (p. 187). When this occurs, the child can channel destructive impulses in a more constructive direction. Mastery of specific tasks at each developmental level is essential for healthy conscience building.

It is during the preschool years that we sometimes see children making decisions in order to please their teachers and parents. Steven, age 4, had separated from his mother for the preschool day, knowing she wanted him to be a big boy. He heard her say that mommies stay at school for just a short time. Steven seemed alright at first, but then would start to cry when his teacher asked him to find something to do. Over the next few weeks, the teacher noticed that Steven was not having fun at school. She concluded that although Steven had complied with the separation plan to please his mother and teacher, Steven's needs and feelings had been overlooked.

Preschool children often compare themselves to peers, sometimes causing anxiety. Experiences and relationships that intensify anxiety about measuring up to others can affect the harshness of the conscience. For example, when five-year-old Andrew compared his drawing to his classmate's, he commented to his teacher, "My picture isn't as nice as Kate's. My picture is no good at all." With this statement, Andrew expressed his feeling that if his picture was "no good," he was "no good." Andrew's teacher helped him understand that although he felt his picture was not his best work, he could still like himself and try again.

The parental voice inside the mind of the child sometimes sounds like the child's own yelling voice. Children can feel trapped when their own harsh internal voice is accompanied by an adult's chastising voice. Mrs. Hart, the teacher in our introduction, knew that to chastise or punish Natalie might interfere with Natalie's ability to listen to her internal voice.

In kindergarten, children begin to enjoy relationships outside the family with peers and other adults. They put aside some anxieties from early childhood, which helps them feel free to pursue a place in the outside world. This step ushers them through the oedipal phase of development into the latency phase, which promotes the internalization of conscience. Internalization means that the rules they have experienced as outside of themselves are now experienced as their own responsibility (Kessler, 1966).

During the latency years when children are away from their families for much of the day, they begin to learn the skills they will need to function effectively in society. During these years the conscience must be established as an integrated and helpful part of the personality. Adults and peers outside the family can help with this important task.

THE ESTABLISHMENT OF A CONSCIENCE: A LATENCY TASK

The conscience is comprised of rules, prohibitions, and experiences of early childhood that occur during the first five years of life. The surprising, forceful intrusion of the conscience at latency makes most children feel uncomfortable. Despite its gradual development up to this point, when the conscience ultimately moves from outside to inside, it may be experienced as a foreign body, unrecognizable to the child as a part of him/herself.

When called upon to describe this experience, children respond in a variety of ways. Some hear it as a loud voice inside their heads. For example, Hannah, age six, told her parents that her conscience sounded like a recording that yelled all the bossy, mean things her parents had ever said to her. Other children describe their new conscience as a feeling. For example five-year-old Ellen said that her conscience made her feel bad all over whenever she did something wrong. Still other children talk about the intrusive nature of their conscience. For example, nine-year-old Zach told his third grade teacher that when he was six years old, it felt like a stealth bomber had zoomed into his mind.

The latency conscience dictates a full set of demands, including: be careful, be polite, be patient, always tell the truth, share with your friends, work hard, and do not make mistakes. Now the child is expected to deal with the outside world with a new sense of responsibility. The demands can no longer be attributed to others and have not as yet been honed or made tolerable to the child.

Children describe the demands of their conscience in various ways. Many children feel distraught, such as Anthony, age six, who told his teacher that there were too many rules in kindergarten. Greg got a stomachache every morning before school, describing first grade as much too hard, and feeling he could never finish his work. These children found the demands of their conscience to be harsh and overpowering. Furman (1980) describes children in this phase of development, stating,

> In observing young children during entry into latency, one is struck with how uneasy they feel with their newly acquired superego [conscience], how little it as yet feels like a part of them, and how hard it is for them to understand its signals and to utilize them effectively in their behavior. (p. 270)

The expression of the struggle to meet the demands of the conscience is what parents and teachers often see as negative behavior. They describe these children as disobedient, argumentative, unable to pay attention and listen to instructions, while sometimes seeming perfectionistic, and hard on themselves. There are contradictions in these children's behaviors; sometimes they disregard school rules, while at other times they punish themselves for the smallest of mistakes.

There are numerous ways children cope with these new internal messages and demands. They need to learn to tolerate and live with their conscience. A typical way of coping during latency is the use of externalization, so named because it is an attempt to attribute the conscience to others outside of one's self. Furman (1980) explains the usefulness of externalization in that it "not only changes an inner battle into an outer one: it also supplants a very harsh inner threat with a usually milder punishment from the outside" (p. 271).

When the child is successful in his/her efforts to externalize a harsh conscience, it can look as if the child has no conscience at all. Instead, the parent or teacher is left holding the uncomfortable feelings that belong to the child. Children who cannot bear their harsh conscience often misbehave in an attempt to provoke harshness or punishment from the outside. When this stimulates greater harshness on the part of the adults, the child feels justified and may continue to misbehave, seeking punishment as temporary relief from his/her own uncomfortable feeling of badness. For example, Tommy, age seven did a messy job on his first grade worksheet and then abandoned the worksheet that needed to be finished before lunch. Tommy felt so bad about his erasure filled paper, that he could not finish it. His teacher insisted that he stay back from lunch and finish his work. Later that afternoon, Tommy sobbed to his mother that his "mean teacher" did not let him go to lunch with his friends. Tommy exclaimed, "I hate her and I'm not going to school tomorrow!" A conversation between mother and teacher helped the teacher understand that Tommy could not continue his work, because he felt so bad about his paper. Tommy's anger at himself was so intolerable that instead he made his teacher angry, and he moved away from her, labeling her the mean one.

Another way children attempt to cope with their new conscience is argumentativeness. When children hear unwanted messages from their conscience, they fight against these messages. Children often argue with others about rules, because an argument with another does not create as much anxiety as an argument within oneself. For example, six-year-old Jenna could not have any fun during recess. Every time she played a game, she felt tempted to cheat so she could win. Jenna struggled not to cheat but instead policed her classmates, insisting that they play fair and follow the rules, often accusing them of cheating.

Yet another way children attempt to cope with their conscience is to deny or avoid its unwanted messages. These children appear to daydream, lack focus, or fail to listen to instructions. Becoming deaf to the conscience is one explanation for such difficulties. While tuning out messages from the conscience, these children often tune out necessary messages from the outside, such as their teacher's instructions. When this happens, children can feel alone without an inside compassionate guide.

One of the more constructive coping mechanisms children employ is learning to make reparation. Children learn that mistakes can be repaired through a genuine apology or a decision to learn from their mistake and do a better job next time. For example, Justin, age six, in the midst of an angry outburst, broke his brother's favorite toy. Following this episode, Justin continued to misbehave and tried to provoke punishment for his misdeed. Justin's mother was able to help him earn money by doing chores at home, so that he could replace the broken toy and regain his self-esteem.

There are some children for whom the aforementioned coping strategies are not sufficient. They experience interferences and disruptions in their lives that may require assistance beyond what parents and teachers can provide. An environment that challenges the child beyond his/her ability to cope, such as one that includes persistent abuse or neglect, serious medical difficulties, experiences of loss, or parental emotional disturbance, can negatively impact conscience and overall personality development. Fraiberg (1980) discusses clinical examples of mothers who project their own serious difficulties to their young children, thereby unconsciously creating emotional disturbances in the children.

Children who are not helped or encouraged to listen to their internal conscience, often remain in the earlier phases of development. These children do not look inside themselves for a sense of right and wrong. They seem to feel bad only if a teacher or parent catches them. All attempts to escape one's conscience leave a child compromised in the ability to feel independent and to enjoy being alone. These children remain overly reliant on others and miss out on one of the most important experiences of feeling good, namely listening to their internal voice.

Sorting out normal developmental problems from more serious difficulties can be challenging. While guilt feelings are essential in helping children make their own decisions, too much guilt can be problematic. Fraiberg (1959) discusses how an overabundance of guilt can significantly interfere with healthy personality development. She highlights the idea that guilt can be useful or destructive, as illustrated by the case of a boy who destroys a toy in an outburst of anger and needs to make reparation versus a child who is afraid to use his full strength in a game or to voice a contrary opinion. The latter child may view every thought or act of aggression as dangerous or destructive. Children who have overbearing guilt and anxiety about their aggression may be unable to use their full strength in learning, relationships, and age appropriate activities. They may even limit the use of essential constructive, aggressive strivings. These children may require psychotherapeutic treatment to help them resume healthy, progressive emotional development.

How the latency phase progresses can affect future development into adolescence, and even adulthood. Without help from important adults, a harsh, adversarial internal voice can become a permanent fixture of the personality. Parents, teachers, and mental health professionals have the unique opportunity to assist latency age children with the development of an integrated conscience that will become an ally throughout the course of their lives.

CLINICAL EXAMPLES: EIGHT VOICES OF CONSCIENCE[1]

Trevor: Making Reparation

Trevor, age five, knew he did the wrong thing and at first he felt justified. Then he felt bad. He might as well just be bad for the rest of the day and take his punishment at school and then at home. He had kicked his friend Max, who was bothering him and would not leave him alone. He knew the kindergarten rule, "hands and feet to yourself," but Max went too far and Trevor felt he deserved it. Now it was Trevor's problem. He was worried about the punishment: no TV, no iPod, forced to say "sorry." Even more, he wanted to get rid of this awful feeling that he did something wrong and was not a good boy. As his kindergarten teacher approached, Trevor geared up for the inevitable consequence.

Children frequently find themselves in a position such as Trevor's, having done something wrong and then feeling a sense of regret. Even adults find themselves making split second choices they wish they could reverse. We all take our seemingly well-deserved punishments from the outside, but it does not quell the discomfort on the inside of having, for the moment, abandoned our conscience. In Trevor's case a harsh consequence from his teacher would not have been helpful. What he needed instead was a way to get back in touch with his conscience and make reparation, so he would not feel stuck. Trevor knew he had to take responsibility for what he had done, and he had to try to do better the next time.

Even though it might seem counterintuitive, Trevor needed his teacher to show compassion, which can be difficult when one child has hurt another child. When the adult is empathic with the aggressive child, that child can borrow empathy to get in touch with his/her own feelings. If Trevor's teacher could model forgiveness for him, he could access his own kind feelings and make reparation. Trevor lost sight of the kinder part of himself when he knew he had done something wrong and felt guilty. Trevor needed his teacher to be empathic with his difficult position, so he would be able to find his way back to his conscience.

According to behavior theory, to forgive the aggressor might well reinforce negative behavior. On the contrary, we believe that making someone feel bad does not teach a useful lesson. What is helpful is the knowledge that people have a place within themselves—their conscience—that they can rely on. Most often, people make better choices when guided by their conscience, rather than by an overbearing feeling of guilt. Trevor treated his classmate badly and then felt that no one would ever forgive him, but his teacher surprised him. She told him that for the moment, he must have lost sight of knowing how to treat others, but that he could get it back because it was still inside him. He would have to find some way to make reparation. After taking some time to think it over, Trevor decided what he would say to Max: "I feel bad that I kicked you and I know you're mad at me. Can I have another chance to be your friend?" Trevor felt grateful to his teacher for her empathy, which allowed him to find his way back to his conscience. Trevor was able to regain his balance as a kindergartener.

Jamie: Struggling to Feel Good

"It's asleep!" snapped nine-year-old Jamie when his dad asked him to use his conscience so he could figure out how to tackle the job of cleaning his room.

"Well," said his dad, "I think you had better wake it up so you can listen to it."

"Oh," countered Jamie, "I forgot, it's in Florida!"

"Then we had better send it a ticket right away, because you can't be without it," said his dad.

Jamie and his dad laughed, but they both knew that Jamie was struggling to listen to his conscience and do the right thing. Jamie's dad reminded him that he was expected to clean his room by the end of the day and that his parents would not struggle with him about it—it was up to him. His dad encouraged Jamie not to end up in a struggle with himself and ruin his day, but to take responsibility for his room. He assured Jamie that he would feel pretty good about it.

Jamie moaned and groaned his way up the stairs to his room and flopped down on his bed. He tried to find the book he had been reading. He thought he had left it on his bed last night when he turned out his light, but his bed was such a tangle of sheets and blankets, that he could not find anything! "Why do I always lose everything? Why can't I find my stupid book?" he complained. Although he tried he could not seem to distract himself from his internal struggle. At one point, he went downstairs and started an argument with his mom about what to eat for a snack. She sent him to his room. Now he was really stuck with his struggle; he wanted to please his parents, but he wanted to make his own decision. Giving in to his parents made him feel little, but refusing to do something he knew he should do, made him feel bad. He stayed in his room thinking about how he could please everyone. After a while he came up with an idea. He went downstairs to find his dad and suggested that they compromise. He would clean up his room early the next morning before breakfast. His dad was a bit skeptical, but understood Jamie's need to feel independent. He went along with Jamie's idea, but on the condition that if Jamie did not follow through, his dad would not be flexible the next time. His dad added that if Jamie needed help getting started in the morning, he would be glad to help. Jamie was pleased and felt understood. Jamie's dad took a chance by being flexible. He understood Jamie's struggle and wanted to help him through it without making Jamie feel powerless. Jamie's dad was trying to avoid struggling with Jamie because the struggle was really Jamie's with himself. When his dad could step back, Jamie had an opportunity to work out a solution. It is easy for adults to jump in and take over a child's conscience so the child will make the choice the parent desires, but that does not offer an opportunity for a child to use independent thinking.

Accessing one's conscience can be challenging. Adults need to allow a child time to grapple with his/her conscience and emerge with a viable solution that is in harmony with the child's wish to do the right thing. This course of action can take varying amounts of time, depending on the situation and age of the child. Despite feelings of frustration and anger, when adults are patient and resist interfering they model the use of one's conscience to feel good. Jamie's dad had to keep himself from getting mad at Jamie or forcing him to clean his room. He had to stay calm and be willing to listen to his own conscience in order to help Jamie listen to *his* conscience.

Lexi: Finding a Kind Voice

The students in Mr. Brent's second grade class were outside playing on the playground. Amanda asked her friend Lexi if she could join the jump rope game that Lexi and a few girls were playing. Lexi said no, remembering that just the other day Amanda had excluded her from a game. Before storming off, Amanda said in a very loud voice that Lexi was mean and they were no longer friends. Mr. Brent heard the interchange and approached a tearful Lexi. After sitting together for a little while Mr. Brent asked Lexi if she was feeling bad that she had been mean to Amanda.

"No," said Lexi, "She's the mean one, not me!"

"Maybe you were both a little mean," offered her teacher.

"Maybe," said Lexi, "but she was meaner!"

"Well," said Mr. Brent, "that doesn't really matter. What does matter is that you look inside yourself and find the kind part of your conscience that helps you figure this out."

"I don't have a kind part,"responded Lexi.

"What?" asked her teacher, "Everyone has a kind part. I guess your conscience just sounds mean most of the time."

Lexi nodded. Her teacher went on to identify the kind things Lexi does without even thinking: cleaning the chalkboard erasers, saying thank you to her teacher and friends, helping other students with math, or making good choices.

"But that's no big deal, everybody does that stuff," Lexi retorted.

"Sure," said Mr. Brent, "but these are still things you can feel really proud about and your conscience helps you do them."

Lexi had only been able to hear the judgmental part of her conscience that chipped away at her self-esteem. It made her feel bad most of the time and sometimes she blamed others. She needed to be able to counter her own harsh voice, by thinking about her kind actions. The idea that she could be nice to herself just by *being* herself was new to her. In the situation with Amanda, she had to figure out which was more important, saving face or keeping a friendship. Even though Lexi felt embarrassed about the interaction with Amanda, she was also quietly relieved that Mr. Brent overheard what happened.

Lexi wondered if her conscience could really help her with this choice. Her mom and her teacher always tried to help, but maybe she could help herself too. She started to listen more to the voice inside her head. It was a tall task, because sometimes the voice did not tell her what she wanted to hear or what was easy. Sometimes this voice even put her in more of a struggle for a while until she figured it out. In the end she felt more confident and more able to help herself.

A few days after the incident with Amanda, Lexi went to school and waited outside the classroom door for her friend. Shyly, she approached Amanda and said, "I'm sorry we were mean to each other, can we try again today? I brought my jump rope." It was crucial that Mr. Brent was alert and available to help. Conflicts between children often arise during unstructured or transition times, requiring adult assistance. Lexi and Amanda would likely not have resolved this conflict as successfully on their own.

Elliott: To the Victor Belong the Spoils

Elliott, a first grader, brought home a note from his teacher each day. The note was addressed to his mother and usually detailed Elliott's lack of focus, inability to sit still, and difficulty keeping his hands to himself. Elliott seemed so wrapped up in his own thoughts that he could not hear the teacher's instructions, needing his teacher to repeat herself while the other children waited and listened for a second time. At her wit's end, Miss O'Brien, who had tried everything, requested the mother's help. Miss O'Brien wondered if Elliott had ADHD and whether he might be helped with medication. In time, Elliott's mother consulted a child therapist to help herself and her child.

An only child, Elliott spent most late afternoons and evenings with his mother, while his father's schedule kept him away from home. The therapist learned that Elliott longed to spend time with his father, but did not feel free to express these wishes because it was explained to him that the father had no choice. He had to work hard so the family could have their beautiful house and possessions. Whenever Elliott complained, his parents would get angry, calling him ungrateful. Elliott was so hurt and angry over the neglect he felt from his father that he began to spend time in his room preoccupied with video games and with angry, violent thoughts that expressed his hurt and rage. To complicate matters, Elliott so enjoyed having time alone with his mother that he felt guilty about having her all to himself.

In a session one afternoon, Elliott shared his favorite video game with his therapist. Each time the evil alien was injured and debilitated in the game, Elliott, the slayer, would have a momentary look of joy, and then invariably he would begin to misbehave. He would tease the therapist, threaten to destroy something in her office, or otherwise try to get her to be harsh and controlling. In time, the therapist suggested that Elliott might be feeling guilty about his victory in the game and might feel he needed to be punished. As they continued to work on this conflict, Elliott slowly became aware of his hurt feelings and his wish to hurt his father. The therapist helped Elliott's parents listen to him express his hurt and anger. As the father understood Elliott's conflict he began to spend more time with him whenever possible.

Elliott's mother learned that when Elliott felt guilty, his conscience made him feel so bad that he preferred to make her angry rather than listen to his own harsh internal voice. The mother helped Miss O'Brien understand how Elliott might seek punishment at school so that he did not need to suffer with his guilt. When Miss O'Brien was able to avoid struggling with Elliott, he was able to practice using his conscience independently.

Khalil: Solving Problems and Fixing Mistakes

The kindergarten class was doing a baking project and it was five-and-a-half-year-old Khalil's job to break three eggs into the bowl. His hand slipped and he dropped all three eggs on the floor, making a mess. At first he was paralyzed, not knowing what to do. He felt terrible and was scared that his teacher, Mr. Gray, would yell at him. Red faced, Khalil ran into the bathroom. His harsh conscience was yelling at him that he was stupid and clumsy. He covered his ears as if the yelling was coming from the outside. At that point, Mr. Gray, who was helping the other children, could not attend to Khalil. Mr. Gray's assistant, Ms. Flowers went to help. She put her arm around Khalil, attempting to comfort him, telling him he was okay, not to worry, everything was fine, and she had cleaned up the mess. To her surprise, this did not satisfy Khalil. He was inconsolable and said that he had done a terrible thing. Feeling helpless, Ms. Flowers returned to the classroom.

After a few minutes, Mr. Gray found Khalil in the bathroom, still crying. He put his hand on Khalil's shoulder, saying that dropping the eggs was not so terrible; it did not hurt anyone or anything. He added that he knew it felt like it was a huge mistake, because it made a big mess and ruined all the eggs. Khalil nodded, knowing his teacher understood. Mr. Gray told Khalil that he could reach way down inside and find the part of himself that knew it was a small mistake and could be fixed. He knew Khalil had this part inside because in the past he had seen him be kind and repair mistakes. Khalil breathed a sigh of relief as he listened to his teacher. Together they walked back into the classroom and joined the group. Mr. Gray asked Khalil if there was something he would like to do to make himself feel better. Khalil thought and thought. He decided he could bring three new eggs the next day to replace the ones he broke. Khalil and Mr. Gray shook on it.

Mr. Gray knew it would be more productive to help Khalil rather than get upset with him. Ms. Flowers tried to help and thought that reassuring Khalil and taking care of the mess would suffice. Unfortunately this is a common misconception on the part of adults. Ms. Flower's solution did not help Khalil, because it robbed him of an opportunity to learn to use his conscience and feel active in making a situation better. Taking part in the solution makes everyone at every age feel better.

It is important to consider the feelings of all the children in the classroom when one child is struggling. The fact that Mr. Gray was kind to one student and helped him find a satisfying solution, reassured every child in the classroom that s/he would also be treated well and fairly. What could be better for healthy conscience building?

Sarah: Too Good to be True

At the autumn second grade parent teacher conference, seven-year-old Sarah's teacher exclaimed, "Sarah is a pleasure to have in class. She is attentive, polite, and I never have to ask her to do anything twice. She is a model student." Sarah's parents were pleased with the teacher's evaluation but simultaneously worried that at home Sarah seemed unhappy. Six months later at the spring parent teacher conference, Sarah's teacher still sang her praises, but now she had become concerned about Sarah's perfectionism. Sarah could not tolerate making mistakes, and if she erased one answer she had to start all over again on a fresh piece of paper. If she made a spelling error it would ruin her whole day. It was at this point that Sarah's parents decided to consult a therapist. The therapist helped them understand Sarah and her excessively high expectations of herself.

It turned out that Sarah felt best when she pleased others, reassuring her for the moment that she was a good girl. At home Sarah felt that pleasing her parents was nearly impossible; they were never happy, nothing was ever good enough for them. Sarah's expectations of herself dovetailed with her parent's high expectations. Her work in psychotherapy helped Sarah understand that she had been overly dutiful in order to keep herself feeling like a good girl. This helped keep her nagging conscience at bay. She was afraid to express her angry feelings, lest she displease her parents and lose their admiration.

Children who are dutiful often suffer. Under the aura of goodness and obedience the child may develop a conscience that is problematic in its severity. When this occurs, the child does not learn to make decisions for him/herself, but rather acts to gain acceptance and admiration through pleasing others. Karen Horney (1950) discusses a concept which she calls "the tyranny of the should" (p. 164), explaining that a person requires him/herself to be an idealized self at all times. She elaborates that such a person feels that s/he "should be able to endure everything, to understand everything, to like everybody, to be always productive" (pp. 64–65).

Many children are not as fortunate as Sarah. Children who are well behaved and high achieving often fool parents and teachers into thinking all is well. When teachers understand that conscientious children may struggle with perfectionism, they are better able to help these children. According to Alice Miller (1997), serious difficulties can develop in some children when the need to please the parents is so pervasive that little room is left for children to know their own needs. She discusses the irony of individuals who, while successful and admirable on the surface, struggle with feelings of emptiness and self-alienation.

Peter: Playing Cricket

The story of Pinocchio is a childhood tale, remembered because it has helped children throughout the ages find a way to listen to the voice of their conscience. Rather than relying on external controls, Pinocchio slowly learns to value honesty and consideration. By the end of the story, the more childish ways of telling right from wrong, such as getting caught, give way to more independence in evaluating how to make decisions. In order to become a "real boy," Pinocchio has to learn to listen to Jiminy Cricket's advice, "let your conscience be your guide."

Peter, age ten, found it hard to play fair. He often felt slighted, and he didn't feel good unless he was the best. In team sports, winning was everything to Peter even if he had to cheat. He always worried about getting caught when he was dishonest, but sometimes he could not help himself. Peter's classmates did not like it when he lied. One day Peter came in from recess with a small super ball he claimed he had found outside. As he played with it, his friend Jake yelled, "Hey Peter, that's my ball and you know it!"

"Prove it." said Peter.

"You saw me playing with it," said Jake, feeling frustrated and mad.

Peter went home from school that day with his new ball, but something still nagged at him and made him feel bad. He was surprised because usually if he didn't get caught he felt fine. Something was different this time. Peter put the ball in the drawer of his night table. He went downstairs and turned on the TV, because it always made him feel better. Peter's dad came in and asked if his homework was finished. "Yeah," Peter lied, "it's done." Peter's younger sister Maria asked what he was watching. "Go away," he snapped. "It's not for babies." At dinner that night, Peter noticed he was not hungry. He had a funny feeling in his stomach and asked if he could be excused from the table. He went up to his room, and took out the ball. He tried bouncing it to see if he could make it touch the ceiling, but it didn't feel fun. "Why isn't this fun anymore?" he wondered. He tried to distract himself with his video games, but it did not work. He thought it might be fun to play with Jake, but he was still too mad. "Am I really mad at Jake?" he thought. He was starting to think he might be mad at himself. "Maybe I should come clean with Jake," he thought. He spent the rest of the evening thinking about how to save face and save his friendship with Jake at the same time. Peter was not sure exactly how he was going to do it, but he fell asleep certain he could figure it out.

Given time, space, and maturity, children are better equipped to struggle with their conscience independently. With the help of parents and teachers they build a foundation upon which they later can begin to develop their own solutions.

Nathan: In His Own Words

Upon completion of his kindergarten year, six-year-old Nathan wrote a story as a gift to his teacher. The story is based on *The Tale of Peter Rabbit* (Potter, 1907), which he read with his mother. He wanted his story to end differently from Potter's. Nathan crafted an ending that created an opportunity for his rabbit to be empathic with the farmer so both could feel pleased with the outcome. Nathan's ending illustrates a step in the internalization of his conscience. Although he wrote the story with his mother's help, the ideas were all his own.

The Rabbit

A story about a rabbit that is trying to get carrots from a farmer.

Chapter 1

Once upon a time there was a hole, not just any hole, it was a rabbit hole! A farmer found it and decided he wanted to make sure the rabbit that lived there did not eat the carrots that he planted. He took his carrots and planted them farther away from the rabbit hole. The rabbit, a young bunny named Kai, saw everything the farmer was doing and began to make his plan.

Kai planned that he would jump into the clothes the scarecrow in the garden was wearing and then he planned that he would get close to the carrots. Then he decided to quickly climb down and snatch the carrots. Then he would run back to his hole. Then he would gobble the carrots up. His plan sounded fantastic to him when he was still cozy inside his burrow. He thought, "There is no way this plan can fail!" Happy, he went to sleep so he could be well-rested for the big day.

Chapter 2: The Next Day . . .
Kai woke up and put his plan into action. First he ran toward the scarecrow. He looked around and jumped right into the scarecrow's clothes. He sat there for a minute, catching his breath. Suddenly, he heard a loud noise! The noise was a truck driving up. The truck was animal control. There were looking for animals on the farm that were lost. The farmer had asked for their help. Kai didn't know what to do—what if they caught him? He quickly put the other part of his plan into action. He quickly hopped toward the carrots. Suddenly, out of the corner of his eye, he spotted the farmer and his wife. "Oh, no!" thought Kai, "What do I do now?" He quickly ran inside the house. There were a bunch of carrots on the table. He snatched them all. He ran back to his hole and jumped in. He gobbled up the carrots and his tummy was full. Too full. All of a sudden, he began to feel bad. He had taken the farmer's food right off the farmer's table. How could he make it right?

He thought of making right by planting some new carrots for the farmer and giving them to him. He did it. He was happy. THE END.

A NOTE FROM THE AUTHORS

The material in this chapter is a compilation of ideas about conscience development derived from our psychoanalytic training and experience in working with children and their parents over the last thirty-five years. All case material has been disguised and all names are pseudonyms. There are many authors who have influenced and guided our thinking. We mention a few of them briefly here, and we have cited some of their works in the reference list for interested readers.

Anna Freud's work on understanding child development and the inner life of the child is the foundation of our development as psychoanalysts. Anna Freud's seminal works serve as a base for assessing, understanding, and treating children and adolescents.

Selma Fraiberg brings early childhood experiences to light from the perspective of the child. She has written for parents and mental health practitioners, deepening their understanding of the inner experiences of children. Fraiberg also published articles and case studies that highlight the interferences with normal infant development.

Anny Katan, who brought child psychoanalysis to Cleveland, Ohio, has influenced our understanding of work with children and adolescents. Her article on the importance of verbalization in early childhood is relevant not only to students of child psychoanalysis, but also to parents, educators, and mental health professionals.

Erna Furman, a child psychoanalyst, has written extensively on all aspects of development and psychoanalytic treatment of children. Her writings are particularly pertinent to our topic, as she clarifies the intricacies of the child/parent relationship.

D. W. Winnicott, pediatrician and psychoanalyst, is an author relied upon by professionals and parents throughout the world. He encourages his readers to embrace an in-depth understanding of the issues central to child development.

Other authors who have written on the topic of conscience development include Robert and Phyllis Tyson, Jack and Kerry Kelly Novick, Alice Miller, Karen Horney, and Louise Kaplan. Jean Piaget has enhanced the understanding of cognition in relation to psychoanalytic thinking. These authors may assist parents and professionals in their quest for further understanding of conscience development. While this is just a short list of contributors to the topic, their writings are compelling.

We would like to extend our appreciation to Gail Boldt, Carola Chase, Scott Dowling, and Michael O'Loughlin for their editorial contributions. And to Nathan, his mother, and his teacher for allowing us to share Nathan's story.

NOTE

1. All children's names have been changed and identifying details disguised to protect the children's privacy.

REFERENCES

Fraiberg, S. (1959). *The magic years: Understanding and handling the problems of early childhood.* New York: Scribner's.

Fraiberg, S. (1980). *Clinical studies in infant mental health: The first year of life.* New York: Basic Books.

Freud, A. (1965). *Normality and pathology in childhood: Assessment of development.* (Vol. 6). In *The Writings of Anna Freud.* New York: International Universities Press.

Freud, A. (1936). *The ego and the mechanisms of defense.* (Vol. 2). In *The Writings of Anna Freud.* New York: International Universities Press.

Furman, E. (1980). Transference and externalization in latency. *The Psychoanalytic Study of the Child, 35,* 267–84.

Furman, E. (1987). *Helping young children grow: "I never knew parents did so much."* Madison, CT.: International Universities Press.

Furman, E. (1991). *Toddlers and their mothers*. Madison, CT.: International Universities Press.

Horney, K. (1950). *Neurosis and human growth*. New York: Norton.

Kaplan, L. (1996). *No voice is ever wholly lost*. New York: Touchstone.

Katan, A. (1961). Some thoughts about the role of verbalization in early childhood. In *The Psychoanalytic Study of the Child, Vol. 16*, New York: International Universities Press.

Kessler, J. (1966). *Psychopathology of childhood*. Englewood Cliffs, NJ: Prentice-Hall.

Miller, A. (1997). *The drama of the gifted child: The search for the true self*. New York: Basic Books.

Novick, J., & Novick, K. (1996). *Fearful symmetry: The development and treatment of sadomasochism*. Northvale, NJ: Jason Aronson.

Piaget, J. (1952). *The origins of intelligence in children*. New York: International Universities Press.

Potter, B. (1907). *The tale of peter rabbit*. Philadelphia: Henry Altemus Co.

Tyson, R., & Tyson, P. (1990). *Psychoanalytic theories of development: An integration*. New Haven: Yale University Press.

Winnicott, D. W. (1965). *The maturational processes and the facilitating environment*. London: Hogarth Press and the Institute of Psycho-Analysis.

Chapter Seventeen

Raising the Curtain

Conversations with Child and Adolescent Analysts

Almas Merchant and Leon Hoffman

CONVERSATIONS WITH ANALYSTS

In this chapter, we hope to delineate the struggles of analysts when working to foster change in children and adolescents, particularly through the formation and maintenance of relationships with their patients and their families. In an effort to better understand the nuances of working with children and the analytic conceptualizations of child and adolescent cases, we interviewed child and adolescent analysts who play and interact with children every day of their professional lives. In order to convey a psychoanalytic sensibility and demystify some analytic notions and to promote discussion among colleagues across different disciplines, it is useful to explore and understand the work of contemporary psychoanalysts, their passions, their struggles, their motivations for working with children, and the guiding principles of their therapeutic practices.

We interviewed twenty individuals[1] who were all trained as child and adolescent psychoanalysts and had been practicing for at least ten years. Prior to their child and adolescent analytic training, these analysts had been trained in adult and child psychiatry, clinical psychology, social work, or education. We developed a semi-structured interview which took between an hour and a half and three hours to administer. It consisted of three sections. The first section inquired into demographic and professional questions concerning the nature of each analyst's practice, their training, and the impact of their psychoanalytic education on their practice. In the second part, participants were asked to describe anecdotes or details of sessions with adult, child, and adolescent patients that they had treated in analysis at any point in their careers. They were also invited to describe their feelings about the sessions. The third part of the interview consisted of questions concerning each analyst's personal life, lifestyle, and social circle. The questions for this interview came out of our belief that we had much to learn about the real world experience of the emotional dialogue between child and analyst. Such an in-depth interview, we believed, would give us multiple lenses through which to view the deeply personal underpinnings of working with children. This chapter focuses on the first section of the interview, that is, the process of training and the ways in which psychoanalytic training impacts their practice.

Key themes that came into focus for us, as we explored the interview, included how these analysts played with children, their work with parents in an effort to help them understand the nature of their children's difficulties, and finally, the nature of the relationship with children and adolescents that these analysts developed and the ways in which it brought about change. We first present some of the responses of the analysts in the interviews. We then review psychoanalytic literature in order to provide readers with a basis for understanding how these analysts worked.

Maura

Maura spoke at length about her education and the ways in which she found it helpful in her understanding of the way children play:

> [My education] focused a lot on . . . trying to understand the meaning of play, how one uses play for interpretation, how one translates the knowledge of play to interpretations in the child's life. And the item that really stands out the most and it is something I quote a lot. . . . It matters less what you do or what you don't do with the child. What's more important is that you try to understand the meaning of the behavior of the play that you did, to try to understand the meaning. That was really a key concept.

For Maura, play and engagement were important in relating with the child. It is interesting that the actual content of the play, for Maura, could be used for interpretation only if the analyst engaged in the play and tried to first digest its meaning for the child. D. W. Winnicott (1964) described the importance of play occurring within a relationship, proposing that relational patterns of play arise out of the mother-infant dyad and have their roots at birth. Winnicott famously noted that "there is no such thing as a baby . . . if you set out to describe a baby, you will find you are describing *a baby and someone*" (p. 88, emphasis added). The engagement of the adult in the child's play promotes the child's ability to work through emotional difficulties within their play.

Maura was keen to describe the ways in which she worked with parents, which, for her, was a key aspect of working with children. As she puts it, "It's very crucial to have the parents' support and cases fall apart when the parents don't support the treatment." In her work with parents, her techniques reflect an engagement with the parents on multiple levels:

> [With] the little kids, I always see the parents before the child; with adolescents, I try to . . . judge what the parents are like over the phone whether I am going to see the adolescent first or not. That decision depends on the nature of the parents' ability . . . to allow their adolescent child to be more autonomous. . . . During my ongoing treatment, I see [parents] for either parent guidance or information or support. I try to be as instructive as I can about what I'm doing with the child. . . . I really don't know what the standard of practice is, but at least with little, little kids, I give the parents a lot of details about what I do with the kid in those first few sessions. I show them the pictures with the answers they give to some of these questions and I really try to . . . stress to parents that . . . [psychoanalysis] allows a re-experiencing within the session with me, the troubles that the child experiences in his/her day to day life. And I say to them things like, "the ideal goal would be for the problems to be happening with me and they would then decrease at school and at home." I empathize with their time issues, money issues, all these things . . . [I explain to them that] the kid is an individual . . . within the family, there are factors of which both parents and children are not conscious of . . . that determine a lot of the behavior. There are obviously a lot of biological factors, physiological factors rather . . . that may or may not be involved and most importantly that past influences the present, that stuff that . . . happens now has determinants from the past . . . one of the things that used to bother me, in fact, during my training is . . . parent blaming . . . people would giggle and laugh at the silly things parents did. I think I am more aware of the normal parenting that happens and that the perception of a parent by one child is often very different from another.

The importance of empathizing with parents who may feel humiliated by taking their child to a mental health professional is clearly reflected in analytic literature (Silverman, 1973) and reflects much of Maura's work with her patients' parents. Maura also recognizes and describes the importance of parents who are able to be present in the child's life despite their own personal difficulties:

> . . . these parents are very nice parents. They have their own problems, they're rigid . . . but they have really fully engaged with me, we e-mail all the time, they come more or less regularly. More recently, they stopped for . . . business reasons, they haven't been coming so much but what's been really important is that . . . they're interested, they respond . . . what's been noticeable is that there are obvious clashes between the two of them. . . . But in terms of the kid's treatment, it's extremely supportive. They're there all the time and they're very involved with the school . . .

Maura speaks with candor and ease describing the failures she experienced when working with children, describing a scenario of an abrupt ending to treatment:

> One kid I was seeing, a little kid, he must have been eight or something. . . . And we would play [games] in the play room . . . he would obviously cheat and it must have really gotten to me, in terms of my countertransference, and at some point I made a comment to him . . . "gee I don't understand, how come every time . . . [I win] it doesn't count or it was a mistake" and he went out screaming to his mother who was waiting outside, "Doctor Maura called me a cheater" and that was the end of the case. And I clearly, did not empathize enough with his vulnerability.

Maura brings to light the ways in which countertransferential difficulties impact treatment and how a failure to work through the countertransference may lead to the swift end of a treatment. As Ghent (1990) has noted, "What other occupation requires of its practitioners that they be the objects of people's excoriations, threats and rejections. . . . What other occupation has built into it the frustration of feeling helpless, stupid and lost as a necessary part of the work?" (p. 133). Maura's brief anecdote, however, provides us with some insight into the ways in which analytic work can be doubly challenging because the work is being carried out within the familial frame of the child. An openness to acknowledge emotional responses to the child may lead us to somewhat uncomfortable, but richer learning opportunities.

Jonathan

Like Maura, our interview with Jonathan brought us to similar descriptions around work with parents:

> If you can't work with parents, you are not going to have a child in treatment. My education focused on the extraordinary importance of forming an alliance with them. And, it takes a certain skill as you have to have empathy for parents. I have to say, being a parent myself, I can understand how difficult a job it is to be a parent. When you have to bring your kid for treatment, it's really painful.

Even as parents recognize that their child requires treatment, they may feel ambivalent about the role of the child or adolescent analyst. Often, bringing a child into treatment may cause parents to feel shame and failure as a result of not having met their child's needs. In many cases, this ambivalence can be justified as children are dependent upon their parents to provide a safe and nurturing environment where they might thrive emotionally. Oftentimes, one can see that a child's difficulties are related to inadequate parenting. However, empathizing with their struggle and normalizing their ambivalence, as

Jonathan explains, can be a key factor in providing the family support in an effort to optimize treatment. Parental support, also, can be useful for the analyst in creating a therapeutic space that meets the child's needs:

> I have a child in treatment right now, and the mother has, unfortunately, a severe psychiatric disorder, but she recognizes her son's anxiety and she really feels that she herself has benefitted from her treatment and she is the one who thought that the child needed to be in treatment and she is the one who calls me up and says well, "this happened" or "that happened" and it's affecting this little boy. [Also], her husband, who I don't think ever had any treatment, is very psychologically aware and also very supportive of the treatment and a very good reporter.

Effective psychoanalytic work with children can thus depend on the ways in which we communicate with parents, and it can often lead to relationships with parents such as the one described above. The analyst, as Jonathan describes, impacts the environment of the child and facilitates the move towards an emotionally enriching experience for her or him:

> You become somewhat of a more real object if you're working well with the parents—you have an effect on the environment. On the other hand, if you're not working well with the parents, you have a real detriment, because they're stuck in their home and they can't get out, whereas an adult is out of that.

Further, while most therapists ascribe to specific theoretical and technical constructs, psychoanalytic work occurs in the meeting of two individuals who coconstruct a unique therapeutic dyad that cannot be replicated (Aron & Zafirides, 2012). For Jonathan, the uniqueness of the co-constructed dyadic relationship is further impacted in his approach to his work with different age ranges; he describes the very basic differences that arise when working with his child patients as compared to his adult patients:

> I think I have the same theory all through; [using] the life cycle, that doesn't change. But of course, technique changes with the age of the patient. You wouldn't expect to be able to make certain interpretations to a young child. The most obvious thing is that when you have a very young child, their superego or conscience hasn't been formed yet so you're not going to be talking in terms of guilt. Also, of course, [you consider] how you would word something. When I have a very young child, we're just going to play. For instance, a patient who usually plays with fire engines and there is always a fire in the house, is reflecting the chaos in his life through play. [Her] parents are divorced and don't get along at all. There's a lot of disruption and fiery tempers and I think that we talk about it in the play. If you have an adult patient, who is in analysis and whose parents are divorced, you can put it into words. [It is] the same kind of feelings, but in words. It's different.

Given the age of the patient, the goals change too. Jonathan describes how the goals of the work with children can often be quite different from that of the adult patient. While the basic tenets of psychoanalysis remain the same, that is, that most of mental activity is unconscious and the past influences the present, Jonathan's technique takes into consideration the impact of development and the cognitive capacities of the child, specifically when it comes to the development of defensive structures or coping mechanisms. Defensive structures, which bolster against excessive anxiety, were identified by Anna Freud (1946) in terms of a hierarchy from primitive to sophisticated. Cramer (1987) further explored the development of defenses based on chronological age and, according to her, infants begin with rudimentary defensive structures that become increasingly more complex. Based on her work, we can better understand how Jonathan sees the importance of working in tandem with development:

> With child analysis, the goal would be different; you try to get the child back on to developmental track. So, if they've slid off the track, or they're a little fixated; let's say they're six years old but they're still anally fixated, you try to move them to where they should be developmentally. The goal is still, for me, to make what is unconscious, conscious and to give them better means of coping, better defenses. So, that's the same thing for adults. You try to work with their defenses and make them more adaptive. The thing about child analysis is that we have development on our side. So, development is always pushing you forward and it's a much greater sense of movement.

Perhaps the most consequential impact of the analyst lies in the ways in which an analyst relates to the child. Earlier, Maura explained how such work can impact the dynamic between patient and analyst and the unfolding of play scenarios. Jonathan describes another aspect of the work, the importance of a safe and consistent space for expression of conflicting feelings, this way:

> One thing, for many children [is] that they have a safe environment in which they can express their feelings. This has a very positive effect on a child and also the fact that you're going be there and you're usually pretty steady. Maybe once in a while you might get sick or something, but you're there. Just the structure and knowing that they have a safe environment and that whatever they say is something that's going to be appreciated has beneficial effects.

The notion of creating a space that is safe for the child or adolescent in order for transformative change to take place has been explored by many psychoanalytic theorists and practitioners. For example, Winnicott noted that

> psychotherapy has to do with two people playing together. The corollary of this is that where playing is not possible then the work done by the therapist is

directed towards bringing the patient from a state of not being able to play into a state of being able to play. (1971, p. 38)

Winnicott introduced the notion of a play space, which shaped early psycho-analytic thinking in a pivotal manner, adding to Freud's idea of a cure— where once the ability to work and love was considered pertinent for success, now the ability to play was added by Winnicott as a necessary ingredient (Luepnitz, 2003). For a child to develop the capacity to play, Winnicott suggested the need for a transitional space where the child could separate from the parent and learn to navigate the internal emotional world while becoming more aware of the (m)other. Analysts who work with children and adolescents may often see children who were not provided this initial safe space within which to express their emotional world without fear of punish-ment or rebuke. Winnicott suggested that the therapist must have the capacity to play in order to move the patient from a state of "playless dread" to a space of playful engagement (Winnicott, 1971).

Emily

Given the significance of a transitional space, psychoanalysts consider safe-guarding a child or adolescent's confidentiality and managing the boundaries of confidentiality explicit as exceptionally important. Managing parental ex-pectations while maintaining rapport can prove to be a complex task. The onus is on the analyst to balance the delicate relationship with a child and their parents; it is the interplay of the emotional lives of the parents, the child, and the analyst that is negotiated within the psychoanalytic relationship by the analyst in an effort to provide a space for the child or adolescent to alleviate suffering. Emily recognizes the importance of meeting with parents with regularity and explores the direct ways in which she addresses these ethical concerns around working with children and their parents.

Essentially, [I was] always taught that children only came with parents and if you felt that you were going to be successful working with a child without first and . . . continuingly maintaining a relationship with parents, you were soon going to realize the error of your ways. And, so a very bedrock part of our training was to begin with parents and to first get a rapport in a relationship with parents. And a way we talk about it is we think about working with that part of the parents' ego that represents their healthy investments in parenting. Even though there may be other parts to their personality, that's the part we want to speak to: that they're willing to come to us and trust their child in our care. They have at least a part of personality that's available to the work, and that's what we would try to build a relationship with. The other thing that we always try to watch for is whether we feel that the parents can identify with the aims of the work. So, that they have to be able to not only want their child to have help but appreciate that this is an assistance that's going to have to be

> given to their child by someone other than themselves. [This allows them to] identify with that process but not feel like they have to be an intimate player in that process; but they're supportive of that process, they understand that there will be times when their child will say "I don't want to go anymore, and it's stupid" and then they might need to say, "well, take that up with Dr. E, talk that through because there must be something that belongs there."

Additionally, Emily is careful to explain the ways in which confidentiality is maintained with adolescents. Specifically because the issues around separation and autonomy can often be a central factor with adolescents, Emily's approach around working with adolescents creates an atmosphere of openness and directness, allowing for a therapeutic relationship to develop.

> With adolescents, especially if they're already adolescents at the point [that] they're coming to me, I might say to them at the outset, during the first meeting, "have you and your father or mother discussed whether you want to meet with me together or privately?" And I will defer to that. What I will then usually explain to an adolescent that might opt for that private meeting is that it will be necessary for me to have a relationship with his or her parents but I explain that our relationship will be a confidential one and my contact with the parents will be organized toward the idea of helping them with their parenting.

Emily's description brings us to one of the most influential aspects of change in psychoanalysis, namely the importance of the therapeutic relationship and the role of transference, a concept first described by Sigmund Freud (1905). As well as managing transference, the analyst also attempts to manage his/her own counter-reactions to patients' attempts to provoke gratification or rejection. Consequently, understanding the nature of the transference allows patient and therapist to address the patient's conflicts in other relationships and in an effort to make unconscious feelings states more conscious. When considering children, however, contemporary analysts, in these interviews, reported that they serve as a developmental object and not just a transferential one. Anna Freud's teachings with regard to the role of the developmental object have been explored by many child and adolescent analysts and is qualitatively distinct from an insight providing, transferential object (Sandler, Kennedy, & Tyson, 1980). Sugarman (2003) provides two distinct functions of a developmental object. First, the child's view of the analyst shifts based on the child's developmental stage. Second, a developmental object serves those developmental needs of the child that are not being met elsewhere in the child's life such as limit setting or affect regulation.

Since much of the analytic work with children is carried out through play and within the dialogue of make-believe, the function of the analyst as developmental object can be seen within this context as well. Freud's (1920) original theory of play focused on the discharge of anxiety and the repetition compulsion, that is, a child played to overcome anxiety around difficult moments with caregivers, and this anxiety was worked through by repeating the scenario until mastery was gained over it. For Klein (1923) too, the presence of primary objects impacted the play of the child, in that the child sought to separate from their primary attachment figures and develop an autonomous understanding of external reality. However, Anna Freud (1965) first expanded upon the concept of the relational component within play. For her, the shift was towards socialization and an increased capacity for autonomy and mastery, rather than a displacement of anxiety. As one of the interviewees, Aaron states:

> I would say that my model is still largely ego psychological and I guess I have a pretty broad definition of ego as all the adaptive functions and think about how do they work with hindrances and what used to be called the automatic or autonomous ego functions but they're malfunctioning in these kids. . . . I think with children I am much less explicit. I don't think children can use as much explanation or interpretation as they do learning from what they are doing, how they are feeling, how we interact. So I think that I'd say relatively less aimed towards the self-conscious or the self-reflection and more just how I respond to what they are doing in the game or how we are being together. I guess, past age fourteen or so, it's more about sitting and talking about it, telling the story of what they are saying. So, it's more interpretive, it's more listening and responding to defenses, whereas with the younger kids, I am thinking about what they are doing and why they are doing it but I am not likely to say as much about it to them and more likely to just shift the way I respond sort of socially the way I play my hand and or part in the game. It's much more sort of improvised drama. With the younger children, it really is in the play. I do think I do less interpreting than a number of my mentors or teachers would have done.

Aaron's ideas also take a theoretical stance that is object relational, ideas which were first explored and expanded upon by Winnicott in 1958. Rather than a space that was the opposite of reality, play was a world unto itself, a space between reality and fantasy. Play allowed a child to relive the world of interactions created in the first explorations between mother and infant. For Winnicott, then, play was "a basic form of living," necessary for all individuals to navigate their interpersonal relationships (1971, p. 50). This idea, regarding mother-infant interactions and its impact on later relationships, is reflected also in Beebe, Lachman, and Jaffe's (1997) research. These researchers make use of Winnicott's theoretical standpoint in their explorations around the dyadic communication between mother and infant. While not explicitly looking at the child's play, their work brings attention to the coconstructed mother-infant dyad and how their interaction is closely monitored from moment-to-moment within a relational paradigm. They state, "What is initially represented is not an object, but an object-relation: self-in-relation-to-object. These presymbolic representations of self and object are simultaneously constructed, and are constructed *in relation to* each other. What is represented is an emergent dyadic phenomenon that cannot be described on the basis of either partner alone" (p. 172). A safe and open play space, particularly with a partner, allows children to explore their complementary, dyadic roles and find parts of themselves of which they may not be completely aware.

Thus, children require an adult who is willing to see, accept, engage, and reflect upon their play in an effort to promote healthy emotional and cognitive development. When parents cannot provide this function, it falls upon other adults, who become developmental objects within the child's life, to ensure the child's development of play. The analyst's role in the life of a child is to provide a safe, transitional space in which the analyst both engages with the child's play, and in which the analyst retains a critical distance that allows for an objective stance to help the child make meaning of internal conflicts. What makes this relationship even more significant for the child is that the child is encouraged to be as open as possible without any fear of punishment, rebuke, or inattention. The analysts we interviewed reported the impact such a relationship had as a curative factor in analysis. For Jonathan, the analyst plays a dual role of developmental and transferential object:

> I think what needs to be appreciated in working with children and adolescents is that they're not finished products. And so, while they might be transferring things on to the relationship with the analyst [as they] inevitably will, they are also using the analyst as what we refer to as a developmental object, someone that they really are trying to identify with [or] observe to learn another way of being a person. And so, it's really not just transference. It's also growth and identification that comes from the modeling about how to manage painful feelings or how to problem solve, how to be observant.

On the other hand, Emily stresses that while a transferential relationship is taking place between child and analyst, the analyst is also entrenched in the 'reality' of the child's life, giving the therapeutic relationship a layer that is often lacking in adult analytic relationships:

> Analysts serve as objects of identification and children are hungry for positive adult figures, and often times I have discovered in my work with young children, that they often become identified with the analytic function in the sense that they become the person that all their friends talk to. And they identify with the analyzing function of the analyst. And it's helpful to them. It's helpful to them to raise their self esteem, and in terms of their sense of who they are, and in terms of their having a tool . . . for subsequent difficulties.

Aaron emphasizes the importance of the merger of multiple theories that inform his technique and impact his understanding of the therapeutic relationship with children:

I do largely think about the individual and the individual reacting with me, but in the individual reacting with me, I have been very influenced by infant dyadic work and attunement. . . . So, I really try to get attuned to my child patients and follow their lead and help them. So, it's like in ego psychology therapy with adults, where you try to let them keep expanding what they are able to say and talk about, it is trying to help kids explore with action and play, without it becoming disorganized or unraveling or over-stimulated. . . . It's trying to stay in the sweet zone where their observing ego and planning ego and creative ego is functioning and they are expressing themselves and they are enjoying the experience of expressing themselves with a shared partner, who is not taking it all in the partner's direction but staying with them. It's very consistent with Greenspan's ideas of Floortime. It's a lot like a more grown up version of Floortime.

The successful navigation of the complexities of the analytic relationship delineated above with a child or adolescent patient is what allows child and adolescent analysts to bring about lasting change. Additionally, working with parents in helping them manage their own anxieties around the relationship an analyst develops with their child, can help with the treatment of the child. While analysts often see the problem the child brings into the consulting room as stemming from the parent, the analysts we interviewed recognized the importance of managing multiple relationships that involve keeping the needs of both parents and children in mind. We come back to Winnicott's (1964) notion of a baby with (an)other, that is, a child does not develop in isolation or in a vacuum. The adults in the child's life allow for a play space to occur, in order to help the child develop his or her capacity to play. When the child cannot, for environmental or organic reasons, develop this capacity, the onus falls upon the individuals who work with children and adolescents to create a transitional space for the child. Child and adolescent analysts shed light for us into such a space, and offer us a unique and creative way to engage a child's narrative in an effort to make meaning from it.

NOTE

1. The identities of all analysts have been disguised to protect the analysts and the children they worked with.

REFERENCES

Aron, L., & Zafirides, P. (2012). When stress causes pain: Dr. Lew Aron interview. *The Healthy Mind Podcast*. www.thehealthymind.com/2012/10/03/when-stress-causes-pain-dr-lew-aron-interview/.

Beebe, B., Lachman, F., & Jaffe, J. (1997). Mother-infant interaction structures and pre-symbolic self and object representations. *Psychoanalytic Dialogues, 7,* 133–82.

Cramer, P. (1987). The development of defense mechanisms. *Journal of Personality, 55,* 4, 597–614.

Elkind, D. (2007). Preschool academics: Learning what comes naturally. *Exchange: The Early Childhood Leaders' Magazine Since 1978, 4*, 178, 6–8.

Freud, A. (1928). *Introduction to the technique of child analysis* (L. P. Clark, Trans.). New York: Nervous and Mental Diseases Publishing Company.

Freud, A. (1946). *The ego and the mechanisms of defense.* New York: International Universities Press.

Freud, A. (1965). *Normality and pathology in childhood: Writings of Anna Freud, Vol. 6.* New York: International Universities Press.

Freud, S. (1905). Fragments of an analysis of a case of hysteria. *Standard Edition 7*, London: Hogarth Press, 1–122.

Freud, S. (1920). Beyond the pleasure principle. *Standard Edition 18*, London: Hogarth Press, 1–64.

Ghent, E. (1990). Masochism, submission, surrender: Masochism as a perversion of surrender. *Contemporary Psychoanalysis, 26*, 108–36.

Klein, M. (1923). The development of a child. *International Journal of Psychoanalysis, 4*, 419–74.

Luepnitz, D. A. (2003). *Schopenhauer's porcupines: Intimacy and its dilemmas.* New York: Basic Books.

Sandler, J., Kennedy, H., & Tyson, R. L. (1980). *The technique of child psychoanalysis: Discussions with Anna Freud.* Cambridge: Harvard University Press.

Silverman, M. (1973). Working with parents at the beginning of treatment. In M. Hossein Etezady (Ed.), *Treatment of neurosis in the young: A psychoanalytic perspective* (pp. 9–18). Northvale, NJ: Jason Aronson.

Sugarman, A. (2003). Dimensions of the child analyst's role as a developmental object. *Psychoanalytic Study of the Child, 58*, 189–213.

Winnicott, D. W. (1958). *Collected Papers: Through paediatrics to psychoanalysis.* London: Tavistock.

Winnicott, D. W. (1964). *The child, the family and the outside world.* New York: Perseus Publishing.

Winnicott, D. W. (1971). *Playing and reality.* London: Tavistock.

Index

Abraham, N., 41n4
Abrams, S. M., 77
accountability-oriented schools, 3
Adrian, C., 212
affect: authorization of, 18; behavior and,
    72, 83; encounters, 84; negative, 78;
    positive, 78; regulation, 86–87, 209,
    212, 348; split-off, 73; states of, 72, 83;
    validation of, 19
affective enactments, 245
Agamben, G., 10, 33
agentive self, 199
aggression: attachment failure and, 155;
    autism and, 309; death drive and, 153;
    destructive, 153, 310–313; as drive,
    153; during sleep, 102; explosive, 308;
    family environments and, 211; healthy,
    153; masculine, 7; natural, 101;
    tolerance, 152–153; toward sons, 102;
    unmodulated, 20; violence and, 10,
    151–154
Ainsworth, M., 73, 194–195
Alexander, F., 232
aliveness: to child, 34; in the analyst, 35
Allen, J., 72
alliance: as baby-watchers, 5, 75;
    therapeutic, 106, 120, 204; working,
    139
allomothers, 48, 55
alloparents, 4, 51
allophones, 273–275

alpha: elements, 11, 178; function, 179;
    transformations, 178; transmissions,
    178
Alvarez, A., 36
analytic: function, 350; space, 23
ancestral: epistemologies, 39; history, 40;
    inheritances, 39; legacies, 4; memory,
    63
ancestry, 4, 40
anger: acceptance of, 256; adult, 58;
    archaic, 130; as signifier, 38; defensive,
    188; explosive, 183; expression of, 77,
    89, 121–122, 153, 231, 255, 325;
    feelings of, 57, 332; grief and, 82;
    humiliation and, 258; hurt and, 139,
    334; management, 138; memories of,
    49; projection of, 60; resistance and, 16,
    255; shame and, 258
annalist, 40–41
annihilation: anxiety, 90; emotional, 32;
    subjective, 3
anorexia, 116, 208
anti-social behavior, 171–184
anti-violence initiative, 10
anxiety: annihilation, 90; anticipatory, 317;
    autism and, 305–321; castration, 98;
    catastrophic, 20; collective, 144;
    corrosive role of, 3; discharge of, 348;
    displacement of, 348; disorders, 113,
    213; explosive, 311; guilt and, 329;
    levels of, 307–314, 319–320; post-

About the Contributors

Devra B. Adelstein, LISW/S is a clinical social worker and child psychoanalyst in private practice in Cleveland Heights, Ohio. She works with children, adolescents, adults, and families, and consults with area schools and psychotherapists. She works with families and teachers at the Hanna Perkins School and is on the faculty of the Hanna Perkins Center where she received her psychoanalytic training and supervises candidates in psychoanalysis. Mrs. Adelstein teaches and supervises in the Psychoanalytic Psychotherapy Course of the Cleveland Psychoanalytic Center. She has published an article in the journal, *Child Analysis,* entitled, "A Young Girl's Return to Treatment" and is currently at work on a book for elementary teachers entitled, *Beyond Teaching: Understanding Children's Developmental Crises, A Psychoanalytic Perspective.* Adelstein is a graduate of New Directions, the writing program through the Washington Center for Psychoanalysis.

Ann E. Alaoglu, MD, is board certified in pediatrics as well as adult psychiatry and child and adolescent psychiatry and completed psychoanalytic training at the Washington Psychoanalytic Institute. She was on the staff of Chestnut Lodge Hospital from 1989 to 2001 and became the head of Child, Adolescent, and Family Services. She has worked at both public and private residential treatment centers in Maryland and currently is in private practice and consults at the Frost Center, a program that houses a group of special education settings, including the Lodge School. She is on the faculty of the Washington Center for Psychoanalysis.

E. James Anthony, MD, FRCPscyh, is a retired researcher and child and adolescent psychiatrist and analyst. He came to the United States as the first endowed chair in the world in child psychiatry, the Ittleson Chair at Washington University. In 1986, he became director of Child and Adolescent Psychotherapy at Chestnut Lodge Hospital, and continued at the Lodge until it closed. He has held many leadership positions, including presidencies of the American Academy of Child and Adolescent Psychiatry, and its international counterpart, the Association for Child Psychoanalysis, and the World Association of Infant Psychiatry. He has published 310 scientific articles and 18 books, many of which have been translated into several languages. His research focuses on resiliency, risk and invulnerability, groups, and many other aspects of childhood.

Gail Boldt, PhD, is an associate professor of education at Penn State University. She teaches courses on children's literacy development in the undergraduate teacher education program. She is the professor in charge of the doctoral program in Language, Culture and Society, and teaches PhD seminars on structural and post-structural theories of culture and identity. Among Boldt's research interests are the emotional and social experiences of children who struggle at school. In 2003–2004, Boldt was a visiting scholar at the Chicago Institute for Psychoanalysis and recently completed the Washington Center's New Directions on Psychoanalytic Thinking Program, where she worked on a series of articles about the influences of psychoanalytic thinking in contemporary elementary school writing pedagogy. Boldt also writes about education politics and co-guest edited Bank Street Occasional Papers' *Challenging the Politics of Teacher Accountability* (http://bankstreet.edu/occasionalpapers/) with Bill Ayers.

Eileen E. Brennan, PhD, a certified, licensed modern psychoanalyst and an assistant professor of early childhood education, strives to recognize the voice of the child. Within her private practice, children on the spectrum communicate, verbally and nonverbally, their earliest experiences of profound fear and their current struggles to avoid thoughts and feeling of "self-as-separate." Her analytic listening patiently strives to hear expressions that emerge beyond the child's comfort and safety of echo and repetition. Her current school-based research expands her search for the "voice of the child" into digital storytelling. Cameras serve as tools of expressive and receptive communication. Young children are provided digital and flip cameras and encouraged to record and video their experience of a school day inside and outside the classroom. Dr. Brennan's clinical and academic work is driven by the psychoanalytic theories of Frances Tustin and Hyman Spotnitz. This analyst-educator strives to hear and see from within the encapsulated world of each child. Dr. Brennan serves on the New York State Council for Exceptional Children Executive Board and is repeatedly invited to present her research on *Digital Identify* at *EIfEL*, European Institute for Electronic Learning.

Andrew C. Carroll earned his PsyD from George Washington University's Center for Professional Psychology, where he is currently assistant clinical professor of clinical psychology. He is program director for Outpatient Mental Health at Suburban Hospital, Johns Hopkins Medicine, and a principal of AMH Healthcare Partners, LLC, both in Bethesda, Maryland. He has a private practice in Washington, DC. In 2000 he trained in psychological assessment at Chesnut Lodge Hospital.

Marilyn Charles is a staff psychologist at the Austen Riggs Center and a psychoanalyst in private practice in Stockbridge and Richmond, MA. She is on the faculty at several psychoanalytic institutes, and a member of the editorial boards of numerous psychoanalytic journals. As the co-chair of the Association for the Psychoanalysis of Culture and Society (APCS) and also co-chair of the APA Division 39 Early Career Committee, she is actively engaged in mentoring and promoting community involvement for those in the helping professions. Research interests include creativity and psychosis. Marilyn has presented her work nationally and internationally, publishing over seventy articles and book chapters and four books: *Patterns: Building Blocks of Experience* (2002), *Constructing Realities: Transformations Through Myth and Metaphor* (2004), *Learning from Experience: a Guidebook for Clinicians* (2004), and *Working with Trauma: Lessons from Bion and Lacan* (2012). She is currently working on a volume of her collected papers on psychoanalysis and literature to be titled *The Stories We Live: Psychoanalysis, Literature, and Life.*

Bertram Cohler, PhD, was the William Rainey Harper Professor of Social Sciences in The College and the departments of Comparative Human Development, Psychology, and Psychiatry at The University of Chicago. A graduate of the Chicago Institute for Psychoanalysis in adult psychoanalysis, Dr. Cohler served on the Institute's faculty, educational council, and Board of Directors. Among his many scholarly, research, and clinical service interests, Dr. Cohler was particularly interested in the relationship between psychoanalysis and education and in the application of psychodynamic perspectives in therapeutic work with disadvantaged children. He was in large part responsible for imagining, creating, and supporting the City Project. Dr. Cohler died in May, 2012 at the age of seventy-three.

Vincent Del Balzo, LCSW-C, is a research social worker in the Clinical Brain Disorders Branch of the National Institute of Mental Health. He has been a family, group, and individual psychotherapist at Chestnut Lodge Hospital and the Lodge School. He has a private practice in Rockville, Maryland.

Nathaniel Donson, MD is affiliated with the Association for Child Psycho-analysis Executive Committee (chair, Liaison Committee), American Acade-my of Child and Adolescent Psychiatry Psychotherapy Committee (with an annual topical panel presentation under the title "Contributions from Child Psychoanalysis"), American Psychoanalytic Association, American Psychi-atric Association, and New Jersey Psychoanalytic Society. He is on the facul-ties of Columbia Psychoanalytic Center for Training and Research (New York City), Institute for Infant and Preschool Mental Health (East Orange, New Jersey): Private practice—Adult, Adolescent, and Child Psychiatry and Psychoanalysis (Englewood, New Jersey). He has a special interest in father hungry families at the above East Orange Institute, and in non-medical clini-cal approaches to "ADHD" diagnosed children. E-mail: MNDonson@aol. com .

Enid Elliot, PhD, has been an early childhood educator for many years now. Over that time she has worked in Turkey, California, New York, and British Columbia in a variety of contexts and settings. She is continually surprised, intrigued, and delighted by the children, families, and early childhood educa-tors with whom she is engaged. Babies and toddlers have been a particular source of interest, inspiration, and joy. Doing doctoral work helped her to develop different perspectives on that inspiration and her dissertation re-sulted in the book, *We're Not Robots: Listening to the Voices of Daycare Providers*. Recently Enid has begun to investigate the influence of outdoor natural settings on children and early childhood educators. Currently she is an adjunct professor at University of Victoria, British Columbia, and on faculty at Camosun College, Victoria, British Columbia.

Richard C. Fritsch, PhD, ABPP, earned a PhD from George Washington University and is a graduate of the Washington Psychoanalytic Institute. He has a private practice of psychoanalysis and psychotherapy in Chevy Chase, Maryland. He currently is associate professor of psychiatry and behavioral sciences at the George Washington School of Medicine and Health Sciences. He is a supervising and training analyst and currently is also director of the Washington Psychoanalytic Institute. He is certified in psychoanalysis by the American Psychoanalytic Association and the American Board of Profes-sional Psychology. He is the author or co-author of over twenty published papers and numerous presentations. He was formerly the director of the Adolescent and Child Division at Chestnut Lodge Hospital and currently is a consultant to the Lodge Program at the Frost Center, which was originally the school associated with Chestnut Lodge Hospital.

Paul M. Gedo earned his PhD in Human Development from the University of Chicago. He worked at Chestnut Lodge Hospital/CPC Health from 1988 until 2001, where he conducted intensive psychotherapy, psychological assessments, and served as clinical administrator of an on-grounds adolescent residential treatment center. He became CPC Health/Chestnut Lodge director of psychology training in 1997 and chief psychologist in 1998. He has worked at the Lodge School from 1988 to 2006 and 2010 to present. Dr. Gedo has been an associate professor of professional psychology at George Washington University since 2005 and maintains a private practice in Rockville, Maryland. He has published papers summarizing psychotherapy research conducted at Chestnut Lodge, and considering the functions and technical challenges of dissociative phenomena, ways adolescents' maladaptive repetitions manifest in schools, and the uses of theory for psychodynamic psychotherapists. He served as editorial assistant (1987–1988) and consulting editor (1988–2001) for *Psychoanalytic Psychology*. Dr. Gedo completed psychoanalytic training at the Washington Psychoanalytic Institute.

Colette A. Granger, PhD, has taught, researched, and written since 1998 in the areas of second-language learning and acquisition, teacher education, academic writing, and technological changes in education. She has published journal articles on topics related to all of these, and is the author of two books: *Silence in Second Language Learning: A Psychoanalytic Reading* and *Silent Moments in Education: A Psychoanalytic Autoethnography of Learning, Teaching, and Learning to Teach*. Currently teaching at York University and the University of Toronto, she is also working on a third book, in which she uses psychoanalytic theory as a hermeneutic for exploring the potential of personal narrative to facilitate the working-through of linguistic, cultural, and disciplinary transitions, and resistances to them, in educational settings. Guiding all her work is a curiosity about moments of collision between social goals, curricular objectives, and the unconscious lives of education's participant's.

Leon Hoffman, MD, chief psychiatrist at West Day School, has been a psychiatrist for four decades and a psychoanalyst for three decades. He is a board certified adult, adolescent, and child psychiatrist as well as certified in adult, adolescent, and child psychoanalysis by the American Psychoanalytic Association. He has extensive experience with children with social and emotional difficulties, their parents, and the educators who work with them. He has been at the West End Day School for nearly two decades and has helped develop an interdisciplinary approach at West End Day School with psychodynamics as an umbrella feature of the educational and socio-emotional approach. He has published widely in a variety of areas both for the professional as well as general public.

Richard Imirowicz, MD, is board certified in child and adolescent psychiatry. A graduate of the Yale Child Study Center, he was director of the Adolescent Inpatient Unit at Chestnut Lodge Hospital from 1997 to 2000. He is currently in practice at the Regional Institute for Children and Adolescents (RICA)-Rockville, Maryland, and is assistant professor of clinical psychiatry at the Georgetown University School of Medicine.

Karol Kullberg, LCSW-C, is the clinical director and program coordinator of the Lodge Program at the Frost Center in Rockville, Maryland. She practiced in New York City before joining the staff at Chestnut Lodge Hospital in 1995, and became the director of the Lodge Day Program, a partial hospital and outpatient program for the treatment of affective disorders. She is in private practice in Rockville, Maryland, and on the faculty and board of the Washington Center for Psychoanalysis.

Hillary Mayers, LCSW, is a graduate of the Columbia School of Social Work and the postgraduate Institute for Child, Adolescent and Family Studies. Along with a private practice in Manhattan, she works with high-risk children, adolescents, babies and their families in the *Chances for Children* Program, which she and her co-director, Elizabeth Buckner, founded in 2000. (Please see website: www.chancesforchildren-ny.org). She has published and presented on the *Chances for Children (CFC)* Teen Parent Infant Project for the past ten years in national and international conferences. Published articles on the program include:

Mayers, H., Hager-Budny, M., & Buckner, E. (2008). Chances for Children Teen Parent- Infant Project: Results of a pilot intervention for teen mothers and their infants in inner-city high schools. *Infant Mental Health Journal, 29*(4), 320–342;

Mayers, H., & Siegler, A. (2004). Finding each other: Using a psychoanalytic- developmental perspective to build understanding and strengthen attachment between teenaged mothers and their babies. *Journal of Infant, Child and Adolescent Psychotherapy, 3*, 444–465.

Mayers, H. (2005) Treatment of a traumatized adolescent and her toddler son. *Clinical Social Work Journal, 33/4*, 419–431.

In addition to direct service, Ms. Mayers trains, supervises and consults on the CFC model, which has been expanded to serve parents of all ages in local community-based sites. In September 2012 the *Chances for Children Institute at RMHA* opened at the Riverdale Mental Health Association, where Ms. Mayers continues to provide training and direct service to families with children from birth to five years of age.

Lauren Mazow, PhD, is a clinical psychologist in Chevy Chase, Maryland. She has worked at Chestnut Lodge Hospital, The Lodge School, and in private practice. Her special interests include psychodynamic psychotherapy and poetry therapy.

Almas Merchant earned her PhD at Adelphi University's Derner Institute of Advanced Psychological Studies. She is currently the field coordinator at State University of New York's College at Old Westbury, New York, where she manages and coordinates the undergraduate field program for the Psychology Department as well as supervising students taking the Field Experience and Research course. She is also the program psychologist for SCO Family of Services' Close to Home Program in New York City. Here she works with a treatment team dedicated to assisting adolescents who have been incarcerated in the juvenile justice system successfully complete their high school education and reconnect with their families while carrying out their sentence in community residences.

Alex Moore is an emeritus professor at the Institute of Education, University of London. He has researched and published widely on issues related to students' and teachers' experiences of learning and classroom life, including his award-winning book *The Good Teacher*. His current interests are in the relationship between psychic and political/economic life, and in particular in the processes through which initially unpopular, often resisted education policies become accepted, internalized and instrumentalized in classroom practice. His most recent work draws heavily on the work of Deleuze and Guattari, as well as on the sociology of education and on the psycho-analytic writings of Freud and Lacan.

Michael O'Loughlin, professor at Adelphi University, New York, is on the faculty of Derner Institute of Advanced Psychological Studies and in the School of Education. He is a clinical and research supervisor in the PhD program in clinical psychology and on the faculty of the Postgraduate Programs in Psychoanalysis and Psychotherapy at Adelphi. He published *The Subject of Childhood* in 2009 and edited *Imagining Children Otherwise: Theoretical and Critical Perspectives on Childhood Subjectivity* with Richard Johnson in 2010. He is co-editor with Cora Smith and Glenys Lobban of *Psychodynamic Psychotherapy in Contemporary South Africa: Theory, Practice, and Policy Perspectives*, to be published by Wits University Press in Johannesburg in 2013. He is editor of the companion volume to this book, *Psychodynamic Perspectives on Working with Children, Families and Schools*, also published by Jason Aronson. His interests include the working through of intergenerational and collective trauma, the social origins of psychosis and schizophrenia, and the emotional lives of children. He is currently co-chair of the Association for the Psychoanalysis of Culture and Society and he is treasurer of the Joint Psychoanalytic Conference. He is a research affiliate at Austen Riggs Center where he conducts research on psychosis in collaboration with Marilyn Charles.

Judith L. Pitlick, MA, LPCC, is a child, adolescent, and adult psychoanalyst and psychotherapist in private practice in Shaker Heights, Ohio, who works with individuals, couples, parents, families, and supervises psychoanalysis and psychotherapy. A graduate in psychoanalysis from the Hanna Perkins Center and the Cleveland Psychoanalytic Center, she is on the faculty of both programs. She is an active member of the psychoanalytic community and is a recipient of the Edith Sabshin Teaching Award from the American Psychoanalytic Association. As a certified teacher in regular and special education, she previously taught in a therapeutic school, in addition to teaching in area colleges and universities. Consultation with directors, teachers, and parents at area schools and day centers has always been a focus. She has had two articles published in the journal, *Child Analysis,* entitled "When There Are No Words From The Patient: Beginning Work With A Child Who Would Not Speak In Analysis " and "A Mother's Misfortune, A Child's Fortune: Work With A Family In Treatment Via The Parent." Miss Pitlick is a graduate of New Directions, the writing program through the Washington Center for Psychoanalysis.

Billie A. Pivnick, PhD, is faculty and supervisor in the Child and Adolescent Psychotherapy Training Program at The William Alanson White Institute and at Columbia University Teachers College. She is also on the faculty of the Institute for Contemporary Psychotherapy, the New Directions Program in Psychoanalytic Writing, and is consulting psychologist to Thinc Design partnered with the National September 11th Memorial Museum. In private practice she specializes in treating patients confronting difficulties with loss and trauma. She is in private practice in New York City. Her 1990 study, *Symbolization and its Discontents: The Impact of Threatened Object Loss on the Discourse and Symptomatology of Hospitalized Psychotic Patients*, won IPTAR's Stanley Berger Award for its contribution to the field of psychoanalysis. Recent articles include: *Wriggles, Squiggles and Words: From Expression to Meaning in Early Childhood and Psychotherapy*; *Left without a Word: Learning Rhythms, Rhymes and Reasons in Adoption*; *Enacting remembrance: Turning to memorializing September 11th; What the living did: September 11th and its Aftermath.*

Arie Plat, BA, education and history; trained in social psychology and group consultation at the Pichon Riviere Social Psychology Institute in Jerusalem. Plat is a psychodramatist, community development, organizational, group, and personal training consultant in non-profit organizations, in mental health, social welfare and education professional team of AGAS, an NGO dedicated to the promotion of coping with hidden and overt violence through organized workshops and study days (including "Why war?" with Tel Aviv University), and organizational and community interventions. Consultant for the

Commission for Equal Rights of Persons with Disabilities–Ministry of Justice, Israel. Consultant, Shatil, the New Israel Fund's Empowerment and Training Center for Social Change Organizations in Israel. He is a member of the Israeli Association of Group Coordination and Psychotherapy; OPUS, UK, for the Promotion of Understanding in Society; and PSYCHOACTIVE, mental health professionals for human rights. In the past, Plat was head of the Supervision In-service Training Program for the staff of the National Association of Community Centers. He was coordinator of psychodramatic and sociodramatic activities, staff trainer, Kfar Shaul Psychiatric Hospital, Jerusalem. He was also a community worker in the Nahlaot, Rehavia, and Shaarei Hesed Community Council, Jerusalem.

Rebecca E. Rieger (1921–2012), PhD, earned her BA from Hunter College, an MA in Speech Pathology from Columbia University, and a PhD in Clinical Psychology from Catholic University. She worked at Chestnut Lodge for forty years, serving as chief psychologist from 1961 to 1991. She conducted psychological assessments and served as supervisor and mentor to generations of psychologists. She was renowned as a generous and thought-provoking teacher and supervisor. She taught psychological evaluation, diagnosis of children and adolescents, and contributions of psychological assessment to the therapeutic process at the Washington School of Psychiatry for decades and also served in administrative roles there. She was a clinical professor in George Washington University's Department of Psychology. She taught assessment seminars at Saint Elizabeth's Hospital for over thirty-five years. Dr. Rieger gave invited lectures in Sweden, focusing on the Rorschach and the Exner Comprehensive System. She was an active member of the Society for Personality Assessment, which elected her a fellow in 1989 and a board member from 1993 to 1996. Rieger conducted research and published papers with Hans Strupp, Reginald Lourie, Richard Fritsch, Wells Goiodrich, and Ida Baron, as well as authoring papers on adoption, adolescent adjustment to the inpatient milieu, bulimia as it manifests on the Rorschach, integrating psychological and neuropsychological evaluations, and integrating Rorschach and modern psychoanalytic perspectives. She also maintained a private practice.

Aileen Schloerb is the City Project director and a therapist at the Center for Child and Adolescent Psychotherapy and the Adult Clinic at the Chicago Institute for Psychoanalysis. She completed a PhD in modern letters at the University of Paris, and additional graduate and post-graduate studies in education, social work, and communication sciences and disorders at the University of Chicago, University of Michigan, Loyola University, and Northwestern University. In addition to work with schools in the United States, she has worked with humanitarian organizations and refugee communities in France and in Northern Iraq. She is interested in the applications of psychoanalytic psychotherapy to work with underserved communities.

Erika Schmidt, MSW, is director of the Center for Child and Adolescent Psychotherapy, a mental health clinic for children and adolescents, at the Chicago Institute for Psychoanalysis. She is also the Institute's director of Clinical Services for Children and in this capacity responsible for the City Project. A graduate of the Chicago Institute in both child and adult psychoanalysis, she practices psychoanalysis and psychotherapy in Chicago and is on the faculties of the Institute's child and adult Psychoanalytic Education Program. Her interests include the effective use of psychoanalytic principles to promote the emotional development of children and adolescents and their families, through therapeutic intervention and through work in the systems of service that support childrens' development; the teaching and training of child psychotherapists; and the history of psychoanalysis.

Burton Norman Seitler, PhD, is a psychoanalyst/clinical psychologist in private practice. He is the Director of Counseling and Psychotherapy Services-R (C.A.P.S.-R), with offices in Ridgewood and Oakland, New Jersey. Dr. Seitler is the former Director of the New Jersey Institute's (NJI) Child and Adolescence Psychotherapy Studies Program. He is a training analyst and faculty member at NJI. His is interested in cases that present unusual challenges, autism, psychosis, ADHD, neurological impairment. His publications include: Is ADHD a real neurological disorder or collection of symptomatic behaviors: Implications for treatment in the case of Randall E. *J. Infant, Child and, Adolescent Psychotherapy* (2011); Intricacies, complexities, and limitations of research on autism treatments: An examination of seven treatment approaches, *Ethical Human Psychology and Psychiatry* (2011); DSM diagnoses for emotional dilemmas: Nothing more than labeling and name-calling. *J. Critical Psychology, Counseling and Psychotherapy* (2011); New information that people in high places do not want us to know about autism, *Ethical Human Psychology and Psychiatry* (2010); Separation-individuation issues and castration anxiety: Their curious influence on the epigenesis of myopia, *American Journal of Psychoanalysis* (2009); Successful child psychotherapy of attention deficit/hyperactive disorder: An agitated depression explanation, *American Journal of Psychoanalysis* (2008); On the implications and consequences of a neurobiochemical etiology of ADHD, *Ethical Human Psychology and Psychiatry* (2006).

Silvia Silberman, MA, is a psychologist, psychotherapist, consultant for organizations, groups, and learning disabilities and lecturer at the Schechter Institute of Jerusalem. In the past she was director of the Psycho-educational Services of the City of Jerusalem and she led initiatives on primary prevention, group work with teachers, crises interventions in schools related to the ongoing conflict and wars, and to all other events perceived by schools as critical, like fatal illness, death, accidents, and so forth. She is now in private practice for psychotherapy with children and adults and for diagnosis and psychotherapy of learning disabilities in children and adults. She is a member of the professional team of AGAS, an NGO dedicated to the promotion of coping with hidden and overt violence through workshops, study days (including "Why war?" with Tel Aviv University), organizational and community interventions. She is also a staff member in different Tavistock style Working Conferences in Israel and abroad including OPUS UK, for the Promotion of Understanding in Society, OFEK, Israel for the Study of Group and Organizational Processes, HEPI, Israel Association of Psychologists, and PSYCHOACTIVE, mental health professionals for human rights.

John Samuel Tieman, PhD, has been a certified teacher for almost forty years. He is a member of the Schools Committee of the American Psychoanalytic Association, for which he chairs the sub-committee for the annual Educational Achievement Award. Dr. Tieman is a widely published essayist and poet, whose work has appeared locally, nationally and internationally in translation. *A Concise Biography of Original Sin,* a chapbook of his poetry, is published by BkMk Press of the University Of Missouri At Kansas City. He teaches in the St. Louis Public Schools.

Sue Wallace is a group analyst and senior adult psychotherapist working with a specialist personality disorder and homelessness team in Glasgow, Scotland. With a background in teaching at secondary and University levels, she has a particular interest in working with young people who have frequently exhausted the patience and resources of mainstream services. Sue also has a particular interest in the impact of psychodynamics on organizational effectiveness and worked as a lecturer in management education for several years.

Nigel Williams, MSc, has been a psychotherapist for thirty years. He is an activist in promoting accessible and low cost services in the community for mental health. He has worked in the third (charitable) sector and the NHS in the United Kingdom in this context. He is concerned about the abiding connections between poverty and mental illness. He has been involved in counseling and psychotherapy training and more recently in academic work around Psycho-Social research and intervention. He is also an organizational consultant and clinical supervisor. His current research is in the role and importance of inter and transgenerational memory in individual and social life. He is a senior lecturer in psycho-social studies at the Centre for Psycho-Social Studies at the University of the West of England, United Kingdom.